Wine, Terroir and Utopia

T0293731

Wine, Terroir and Utopia critically explores these three concepts from multi-disciplinary and intersecting perspectives, focusing on the ways in which they collide to make new worlds, new wines, new places and new peoples.

Wine, terroir and utopia are all rooted in natural, spatial and temporal realities, yet all are unable to exist without purposeful human intervention. This edited volume highlights the theoretical and analytical lens of diverse scholars, who critically discuss a dazzling array of intersecting realities and imaginaries – economic, political, cultural, social and geological – and in doing this, challenge many of our deeply-held responses to utopia. Drawing on an impressive range of international examples from South Africa to Bordeaux to New Zealand, the chapters adopt a range of theoretical and methodological approaches.

This volume will be of great interest to upper level students, researchers and academics in the fields of Sociology, Geography, Tourism, Hospitality, Wine Studies and Cultural Studies. It will also greatly appeal to practitioners and enthusiasts in the worlds of wine production, consumption and marketing.

Jacqueline Dutton is Associate Professor in French Studies at the University of Melbourne where she also lectures in wine courses. She has published widely on contemporary French and comparative literature and culture, including a monograph in French on 2008 Nobel Laureate JMG Le Clézio: *Le Chercheur d'or et d'ailleurs: L'Utopie de JMG Le Clézio* (2003). Utopianism is a key thread in her research on world literature, food writing and travel writing. Her recent work on wine includes articles on identity and authenticity for European winemakers in Myanmar (2016), and on visual codes on French wine labelling for cross-cultural marketing in China and Australia (2019) (http://academyofwinebusiness.com/). She is currently working on a cultural history of wine in Bordeaux, Burgundy and Champagne.

Peter J. Howland is a former tabloid journalist by mistake, an anthropologist by training, currently a sociologist by occupation (Massey University, Aotearoa New Zealand), and a neo-Marxist by moral and analytical compulsion. He has long-standing research interests in wine production, consumption and tourism and their role in the evolving constructions of middle-class identity, distinction, leisure, elective sociality, notions of rurality and urbanity, and reflexive individuality. He is the editor of *Social, Cultural and Economic Impacts of Wine* (2014) and author of *Lotto, Long-drops & Lolly Scrambles: an anthropology of middle New Zealand* (2004).

Routledge Studies of Gastronomy, Food and Drink

This groundbreaking series focuses on cutting edge research on key topics and contemporary issues in the area of gastronomy, food and drink to reflect the growing interest in these as academic disciplines as well as food movements as part of economic and social development. The books in the series are inter-disciplinary and international in scope, considering not only culture and history but also contemporary issues facing the food industry, such as security of supply chains. By doing so the series will appeal to researchers, academics and practitioners in the fields of gastronomy and food studies, as well as related disciplines such as tourism, hospitality, leisure, hotel management, cultural studies, anthropology, geography and marketing.

Series Editor: C. Michael Hall, University of Canterbury, New Zealand

Wine and Identity
Edited by Matt Harvey, Warwick Frost and Leanne White

Social, Cultural and Economic Impacts of Wine in New Zealand
Peter J. Howland

The Consuming Geographies of Food
Hillary Shaw

Heritage Cuisines: Traditions, Identities and Tourism
Dallen J. Timothy

Food Tourism and Regional Development
Edited by C. Michael Hall and Stephan Gössling

Food, Wine and China
A Tourism Perspective
Edited by Christof Pforr and Ian Phau

The Shape of Wine
Its Packaging Evolution
Henry H. Work

Wine, Terroir and Utopia
Making New Worlds
Edited by Jacqueline Dutton and Peter J. Howland

For more information about this series, please visit: www.routledge.com/series/RSGFD

Wine, Terroir and Utopia
Making New Worlds

Edited by
Jacqueline Dutton and Peter J. Howland

Routledge
Taylor & Francis Group

LONDON AND NEW YORK

First published 2020 by Routledge

2 Park Square, Milton Park, Abingdon, Oxon OX14 4RN

605 Third Avenue, New York, NY 10017

Routledge is an imprint of the Taylor & Francis Group, an informa business

First issued in paperback 2022

British Library Cataloguing in Publication Data
A catalogue record for this book is available from the British Library

Library of Congress Cataloging-in-Publication Data
Names: Dutton, Jacqueline, author. | Howland, Peter, 1961- author.
Title: Wine, terroir and utopia / Jacqueline Dutton and Peter Howland.
Description: Abingdon, Oxon ; New York, NY : Routledge, 2019. |
Series: Routledge studies of gastronomy, food and drink |
Includes bibliographical references and index.
Identifiers: LCCN 2019009497 (print) | LCCN 2019017294 (ebook) |
ISBN 9780429492471 (eBook) | ISBN 9781138588141
(hardback : alk. paper)
Subjects: LCSH: Wine and wine making--Social aspects. |
Terroir. | Utopias. | Wine tourism.
Classification: LCC TP548 (ebook) | LCC TP548 .D88 2019 (print) |
DDC 641.2/2--dc23
LC record available at https://lccn.loc.gov/2019009497

ISBN: 978-1-138-58814-1 (hbk)
ISBN: 978-1-03-233830-9 (pbk)
DOI: 10.4324/9780429492471

Typeset in Times New Roman
by Taylor & Francis Books

Contents

Illustrations

Figures

Boxes

Contributors

Steve Charters MW, MA (Oxon), PhD (ECU) is Professor of Wine Marketing and a researcher at Burgundy School of Business in Dijon, responsible for developing teaching and research programmes focusing on all aspects of the culture, history and business of wine. He formerly worked at Reims Management School and Edith Cowan University in Perth. His research focuses on consumer behaviour, and wine and place (including terroir, wine tourism, and territorial wine management). He gained his PhD from Edith Cowan University in 2004 and is one of 350 members of the Institute of Masters of Wine. He has written and edited a number of books about the business and culture of wine and has published in the *Journal of Business Research, Tourism Management,* the *Annals of Tourism Research,* the *European Journal of Marketing, Consumption Markets* and *Culture and Marketing Theory.*

Moya Costello is a writer, and Adjunct/Casual Lecturer in Writing at the Schools of Arts and Social Sciences and Business and Tourism, Southern Cross University. Her research interests include food and wine, experimental Australian literature, and ecopoetics. Her scholarly and creative publications on wine include those in *Gastronomica, The Conversation, China-Australia Entrepreneurs, Environmentally Sustainable Viticulture, Griffith Review, Locale, M/C Journal Media Drive, Sample* and *TEXT.* She has four books: short creative prose (*Kites in Jakarta* and *Small Ecstasies*) and novellas (*The Office as a Boat* and *Harriet Chandler*). She writes a wine column for The Village Journal, Clunes Clues and two Blogspot blogs.

Marion Demossier holds a Chair in Anthropology in the Department of Modern Languages and Linguistics at the University of Southampton. She has previously taught French and European politics and society at the University of Bath. She holds a PhD in Social Anthropology from the EHESS (École des Hautes Études en Sciences Sociales) in Paris. She has published more than twenty scholarly articles in leading academic journals in Britain, France and the United-States, including the *Journal of the Royal Anthropological Institute, Cultural Analysis,* the *Anthropological Journal of*

European Cultures and *Modern and Contemporary France*. She has recently completed her third monograph on the anthropology of wine and terroir: *Burgundy: a Global Anthropology of Place and Taste* (Berghahn 2018). She has also written widely for a student audience, contributing chapters to prestigious series such as *A Companion to the Anthropology of Europe* and *Culinary Taste*.

Rumina Dhalla is an Associate Professor of Organisational Studies and Sustainable Commerce in the Department of Management, College of Business and Economics (CBE) at the University of Guelph, Canada. She is also the CSR Coordinator for CBE and the MBA Graduate Coordinator. She is an international member of the University of Newcastle's Wine Studies Research Network. Her main research interests are in organisational identity and reputation and their implications for organizational strategies, sustainability and CSR. Most of her work explores identity at firm and industry levels. Her recent research projects include sustainability in the Australian wine industry and social enterprise in emerging economies.

Jacqueline Dutton is Associate Professor in French Studies at the University of Melbourne where she also lectures in wine courses. She has published widely on contemporary French and comparative literature and culture, including a monograph in French on 2008 Nobel Laureate JMG Le Clézio: *Le Chercheur d'or et d'ailleurs: L'Utopie de JMG Le Clézio* (2003). Utopianism is a key thread in her research on world literature, food writing and travel writing. Her recent work on wine includes articles on identity and authenticity for European winemakers in Myanmar (2016), and on visual codes on French wine labelling for cross-cultural marketing in China and Australia (2019) (http://academyofwinebusiness.com). She is currently working on a cultural history of wine in Bordeaux, Burgundy and Champagne, and is co-editor (with Peter J. Howland) of *Wine, Terroir and Utopia: Making New Worlds* (Routledge 2020).

Vincent Fournier is Associate Professor at the Département de communication sociale et publique at the Université du Québec à Montréal, Canada. His research interests are the ethnohistorical study of wine production and commercialisation in Calabria (Italy), the study of socialisation practices on the Internet around wine consumption and the study of place promotion. His current research project consists of an anthropological study of the wine industry in British Columbia (Canada).

John Germov is Provost and Deputy Vice-Chancellor (Academic) at Charles Sturt University, Australia. John has an international reputation in the social determinants of health and his research spans food consumption and production, public health nutrition policy, workplace change, youth and health behaviour, alcohol consumption and harm minimisation, wine studies, and the history of sociology. He has published 24 books, including:

Public Sociology: An Introduction to Australian Society (4th edn 2019), *Second Opinion: An Introduction to Health Sociology* (6th edn 2019), *Hunter Wine: A History* (2018), and *A Sociology of Food and Nutrition: The Social Appetite* (4th edn 2017).

Graham Harding returned to the study of history after a career spent building the UK's largest independent specialist marketing and branding agency. He is currently an independent researcher attached to St Cross College, Oxford. He has written several books including *Bluff your way in marketing* (1987) and *The Wine Miscellany* (2005). More recent publications on wine include an article on the dominant nineteenth-century wine and spirit distributors, W. & A. Gilbey, published in the *Journal of Retailing and Consumption* (2016), and a chapter on 'Champagne in Britain, 1860–1914' in *Devouring: Food, Drink and the Written Word, 1800–1945* (Routledge, 2017). A chapter on wine connoisseurship in nineteenth-century Britain will be published in 2019 in *Connoisseurship,* edited by Christina Anderson and Peter Stewart. His 2018 DPhil thesis, *The Establishment of Champagne in France and Britain, 1800–1914,* focused on the links between England and France in the long nineteenth century and how French producers and English merchants and agents created the oenological and marketing template for champagne as we know it today.

Peter J. Howland is a former tabloid journalist by mistake, an anthropologist by training, currently a sociologist by occupation (Massey University, Aotearoa New Zealand), and a neo-Marxist by moral and analytical compulsion. He has long-standing research interests in wine production, consumption and tourism and their role in the evolving constructions of middle-class identity, distinction, leisure, elective sociality, notions of rurality and urbanity, and reflexive individuality. He is the editor of *Social, Cultural and Economic Impacts of Wine* (2014); author of *Lotto, Long-drops & Lolly Scrambles: an anthropology of middle New Zealand* (2004); and co-editor (with Jacqueline Dutton) of *Wine, Terroir and Utopia: Making New Worlds* (Routledge 2020).

Kelle Howson has recently completed a PhD in Development Studies at Victoria University of Wellington. Her research focuses on ethical certification in global production networks for agro-food commodities.

John S. Hull is an Associate Professor in the Tourism Management Department at Thompson Rivers University, Canada. He is also a Visiting Professor at the Harz University of Applied Science, Germany, a member of the Sonnino Working Group in food and wine tourism, Italy, a member of the ICNT international tourism education network, and a member of the New Zealand Tourism Research Institute (NZTRI). His research interests are focused on food and wine tourism, wellness tourism, mountain tourism, tourism futures, tourism planning, and community-based tourism in peripheral regions.

Christopher Kaplonski is Director of Research at Anthroenology (anthro-enology.org), which focuses on wine, sustainability and the senses. He is a social anthropologist who has taught at a number of universities across three continents. Chris was one of the first Euro-American anthropologists to carry out fieldwork in post-socialist Mongolia in the early 1990s. He specialised in collective memory, political violence, identity, and coming to terms with the past before turning his academic taste buds to wine. He also holds a Distinction in the WSET Level 3 Advanced wine certification.

Julie McIntyre is a Senior Lecturer in History at the University of Newcastle (UON), Australia. She is the 2018 State Library of New South Wales Merewether Fellow and a 2019 Fulbright Senior Scholar. She will conduct her Fulbright research on American-Australian collaboration in wine science at the Shields Library, University of California (Davis). Her many publications on the role of wine production, distribution and consumption in Australia's past include *Hunter Wine: A History* (with John Germov, 2018). She is an Associate Editor of the *Journal of Wine Research* (UK) and leads the multidisciplinary Wine Studies Research Network at UON.

Barbara J. McNicol is a social environmental geographer conducting research at the interface between sustainable tourism planning and management and environmental and natural resource management while emphasizing parks, tourism, recreation, and community land use. Barbara is in the Department of Earth and Environmental Sciences and is Assistant Director for the Institute of Environmental Sustainability at Mount Royal University in Calgary, Alberta, Canada.

Warwick Murray is Professor of Human Geography and Development Studies at Victoria University of Wellington, New Zealand. He has held university positions in the UK and Fiji and has been a visiting professor at universities in Europe and South America. He is President of the Association of Iberian and Latin American Studies of Australasia. He has served as editor on a number of journals including *Asia Pacific Viewpoint* and *Journal of Rural Studies*.

John Overton is Professor of Development Studies and Human Geography at Victoria University of Wellington, New Zealand. He has held university positions at four other institutions including the Australian National University. He is past President of the New Zealand Geographical Society and former Director of the Commonwealth Geographical Bureau. He has served as an editor for a range of journals including *Asia Pacific Viewpoint*.

Mikaël Pierre holds a Masters in History from Université Bordeaux-Montaigne (UBM), France, and is a dual award PhD candidate with the University of

Newcastle, Australia, and UBM. He is investigating the significance of French influence on the emergence of the Australian wine industry from the late eighteenth to the late nineteenth century, and the negligible converse influence of Australian winegrowing in France in this period. His thesis is focused on the substantial transfer of vine stocks, ideas and practices about viticulture and winemaking from France to Australia, and the less common movement of people between the two countries.

Donna M. Senese is Associate Professor of Geography at the University of British Columbia, Canada. She is a member of UBC's Centre for Environmental Impact Assessment, Kwantlan Polytechnical University's Okanagan Bioregion Food Systems Project, and Founding Director of the Sonnino Working Group, an international trans-disciplinary research and writing collective centred in Tuscany, Italy, where Donna continues her research in rural resilience and landscape change and instructs experiential field courses in rural sustainability, tourism, food and wine.

William Skinner holds a PhD in Anthropology from the University of Adelaide, where he works as an academic instructor in the School of Social Science. He has conducted ethnographic research in the South Australian wine region of McLaren Vale since 2012, exploring the ways local producers and consumers experience, understand and represent place, landscape, heritage and terroir.

Robert Swinburn received his PhD in anthropology from the University of Melbourne. His dissertation explored the motivations of urban professionals who became winegrowers in the rural periphery of Geelong, and argued for a more nuanced understanding of the French notion of terroir to explain the connection that winegrowers feel towards their environment. His publications include a chapter in *Wine and Culture: Vineyard to Glass* (Black, R.E. and Ulin, R.C., eds, 2013), which explores the French notion of terroir in an Australian context. He is also a wine grape grower, winemaker, and consultant based in the Bellarine Peninsula.

Acknowledgements

Several of the contributors to this volume presented and debated their ideas on wine, terroir and utopia at the 21st Symposium of Australian Gastronomy entitled 'Utopian Appetites' organised by Jacqueline Dutton and Kelly Donati and held in Melbourne, 2–5 December, 2016.[1] The Wine Studies Research Network, University of Newcastle, Australia, led by Julie McIntyre and John Germov, also brought many of these wine scholars into contact for the first time at the 'The Worlds in a Wine Glass' hosted by the Menzies Centre for Australian Studies, Kings College, London, 9–10 May, 2016; as did the Wine & Culinary Futures Conference, University of British Colombia, held in Kelowna, 17–20 October, 2017 and organised by Donna Senese, John Hull and a band of very hospitable collaborators. The co-editors are grateful for the opportunity to work with such a diverse and interdisciplinary range of writers whose commitment to the project and conviviality around the process have been, quite frankly, utopian, understood in its most positive sense. We acknowledge how fortunate we have been to work with the polite, positive, patient and professional Emma Travis and Lydia Kessell at Routledge. Our sincere thanks to all those who have contributed to bringing this volume to fruition – especially to each other. Our idea for co-editing this book, developed over a glass of wine in Melbourne in 2016, has been realized, accompanied by a few more glasses along the journey. Indeed, one of the most civilized things in the world.

Note

1 www.gastronomers.net/symposium-archive/the-21st-symposium-of-australian-gastro nomy/the-21st-symposium-of-australian-gastronomy-call-for-papers-2/ (accessed 24.02.19).

Making new worlds

The utopian potentials of wine and terroir

Peter J. Howland and Jacqueline Dutton

Introduction

Wine, terroir, utopia: all three concepts take on different connotations according to historical traditions, cultural and class capitals, disciplinary biases, and widely varied socio-political agendas, rendering them particularly rich terrain for intellectual enquiry within, and adjunct to, the increasingly globalized world of wine. All three are redolent with ambiguity, defy definition, and are constantly evolving in dynamic intersectionalities of practice, meaning, value and consequence. Moreover, all three are currently trending as topical foci of both popular and academic discourses, and are pertinent to a wide range of economic, political, provenance and origin issues, cultural identity, and 'new world' imaginaries and aspirations that are being generated in what are increasingly challenging times.

Wine, terroir and utopia are engaging topics for conversation and study – anyone can express an opinion, although deeper questioning often proves challenging. This edited volume aspires to explore critically wine, terroir and utopia from multiple disciplinary and intersecting perspectives, focusing on ways in which these concepts and practices collide to make new worlds, new wines, new places and new peoples. The chapters feature research by scholars from anthropology, business and marketing, cultural studies, geography, history, tourism studies and sociology, offering both textual and practical studies, to expose the varied traditions and intrigues that ferment in the intersecting worlds of wine, terroir and utopia.

Wine

Unlike food, wine is not a universal product required to sustain our corporeal needs, but it does figure in most Judeo-Christian cultural histories and has now spread to every corner of the world. Its journey from a healthful, caloric and safe drink to a hedonic product to be consumed in moderation has passed through many socially important phases, including religious consecration and rejection, class, gender and age distinctions, and many other representational differences. Wine is never neutral. It is laden with values, charged with political meaning, contestatory in its very essence. Nor is wine 'natural' in the literal sense of the term, despite its roots in the fruit of the grape vine; it is a human invention, honed and delivered for individual pleasure and commercial benefit. Wine makes worlds anew and new worlds make wine. Understanding how and why this happens is an inherent objective of our work in this volume.

Terroir

Inspiring for some, terrifying for others, terroir is a French term used to emphasise the relevance of particular natural and cultural elements influencing the production of wine (and other items), including land, climate, tradition, method and people. Its nebulous status outside Europe tends to strengthen the divide between Old World/New World winemaking. Yet the recognition of quality related to space is now practised throughout the wine world, resulting in geographical indications and other clearly demarcated denominations of origin. This leads us to question whether terroir's work is already done as soon as a space is conceived as producing quality. Does terroir, like utopia, depend less on a defined blueprint for success, and more on the idea that there are different – some better, some worse – ways of making, being, doing?

Utopia

Grounded in Thomas More's literary text published 500 years ago (1516), Utopia is an inherently ambiguous term meaning both an ideal non-existent place (*ou*-topia) and a place of felicity and happiness (*eu*-topia). As utopian representations and studies have evolved over the centuries, and especially since the 1960s countercultural movements, utopia has come to signify the desire for a better way of being in the world, as articulated in as many forms and cultures as can be imagined. Ranging from ecological cohousing to science-fictional cloning, from arcadian self-sufficient farming to postcolonial revolutionary manifesto, the incarnations of utopia today are so varied as to seem almost ubiquitous. And yet at their core they are bound by the desire to make a change, to make life better, to make a new world, rather than simply seek to inhabit and/or exploit the one in which we find ourselves.

Wine, terroir and utopia all encapsulate both a natural foundation and a human construct. They are rooted in nature yet cannot exist without human agency and intervention. Each of these concepts involve human intervention in natural spatial realities to produce positive experiences for humans. Utopia reconceptualises space for a better life; Terroir reconfigures space for a better wine; Wine recasts space for a better grape vine and berry. These qualities can be considered as affirming aspects of their existence and can also be co-opted to cynical or commercial ends. The spectrum for exploration of these concepts is broad and deep. We hope that our multidisciplinary interrogations will help us understand the art and science of making new worlds with wine, terroir and utopia.

Utopian wines

'Wine is one of the most civilized things in the world and one of the most natural things of the world that has been [repeatedly] brought to the greatest perfection' (Hemingway 1932: 5). Papa Hemingway's quote succinctly identifies the dynamic entanglement of natural, physical, material, social and cultural capacities that have marked winemaking through the ages, while the ironic addition of the adverb 'repeatedly' celebrates the incessant evolutions of wine 'perfection' – a state that by definition is necessarily static. Indeed, constant evolutions of climate, seasonality, grape vines, winemaking techniques and wine cellaring means that while some wines are excitedly declared to be legacy, five-star, 100 point vintages, the ideals achieved are only ever transitory and momentary at best. As such even the greatest wines are never perfect. So, while it may appear a thoroughly over-extended bow to proclaim that wine production and consumption is some form of utopian fulfilment (although many wine aficionados would vehemently assert that fine wines are fundamentally utopian in all aspects), it is nevertheless clear that as a product characterized by constantly changing modalities and ideals, wine has a range of potentials that are at the very least utopian-esque. Wine can, therefore, be provocatively analysed for its utopian capacities and possible learnings.

As a product with an inherent capacity for constant and ideally progressive evolution, ephemerality is wine's – and especially good or fine wine's – default mode of being (Howland 2013). Good wines, for example, frequently age well and get 'better' in the barrel, bottle, cellar, and ideally even after popping the cork. As such assertions of a 'good' or 'fine' wine are always a temporally sensitive proclamation and can only ever be a statement apposite to the time and context in which it is uttered. Indeed, many quality assessments and pronouncements are routinely being surpassed by the progressive ephemerality of the wine in question even as the last evaluative syllable fades out. Moreover, wines are typically annual, seasonally dynamic events. No matter how good or ideal this year's vintage is perceived to be, next year's vintage always carries the promise of being even better. Hence ideal wine, even if perceived one season, is possibly going to be surpassed the next and then cast as less-than-ideal in retrospection. Lastly, perpetual variation – oscillating to, from, and around shifting ideals – is literally in wine's DNA and that's without considering the multitude of cultural (*vini-* and *viti-*) modifications and innovations that have enduringly been (and continue to be) brought to hand in the growing of grapes and the making of wine.

It is important to note that wine is only ever truly known (and assessed as good, bad, indifferent, etc via those vacillating, moral-type 'is' and 'ought' questions) when it is drunk. Yet wine is also a product that physically terminates at the point of consumption and when consumed it is always

transformed from the immediacy of corporeality to the political entangle-
ments – the selectivity, partiality, atrophy, embellishment, expansion and
idealisations – of memory and nostalgia. Arguably wine is never 'fixed',
although appears so momentarily in a barrel or a bottle, and its longevity as a
consumable (especially given most wine is drunk with 24 hours of purchase) is
mostly rhetorical – existent within the waxing eulogies of wine writers and the
misty-eyed panegyrics of wine aficionados. Both the finest and worst of all
wines are therefore ultimately lost as corporeal realities as they slip over one's
palate, through one's digestive system and then out to exist primarily within
the vagaries and embroideries of memory. An ideal in wine as a corporeal
reality can only ever be a moment of bliss.

Wine, therefore, is arguably a prototypical utopian modality and especially
if one accepts the perspective that utopian dreaming and enactment is always
provisional and principally exists as a method, an educative process, a disruptive and critical examination, that prompts an ever-striving for the ideal
(Bauman 1976; Bloch 1986; Le Guin 2016 [1989]; Levitas 2013). In this
regard utopia is definitely more aspirational reaching and process oriented
than it ever is conclusive goal or triumphal achievement. Being utopian in
thought and deed is never to rest on one's laurels, is to accept all achieve-
ments or triumphs as momentary at best (illusory at worst), is always to
subject one's dreams and actions to ongoing critical reflection and is to con-
clude that you've constantly come up short (sometimes tantalizingly, other
times woefully, so). But even more importantly, the utopian modality is to be
constantly enriched throughout these processes and experiences so that one's
desire to strive to be better is habitually reaffirmed and enhanced. Utopia is
therefore to knowingly enact 'better' as 'never perfect'.

Grapes have a 'nature capital' (Howland 2019; Taylor 2018) that pre-dates,
pre-empts and anticipates intentional winemaking and which ultimately
transcends our ecological capitals or the known probabilistic limits of science,
folk, experiential and other knowings (historic and contemporary). Grapes
grow on hardy, woody perennial vines, which, eons before the invention of
intentional winemaking around 6000 BCE, grew naturally (typically on and
through tree branches) in areas of the Mediterranean (*Vitis vinifera*), Central
Asia (*Vitis amurensis*) and North America (*Vitis labrusca*) where temperatures
during the growing season range from 13–21°C (55–70°F). Grape vines naturally embody a variety of tolerances to drought and rainfall and can grow in
fertile to very poor soils (Jones 2006), with the latter capacity making them
particularly suitable for cultivation as non-staple (and therefore not competing
with agricultural staples for arable land), yet gastronomically-valued,
plants (Farrington & Urry 1985). Grape vines produce fruits that when
pressed, readily provide a storable, intoxicating, sterile, and transportable
beverage that innately provides a constantly evolving imbrication of complex, nuanced flavours, a beverage that has been asethetically valued since
the wine appellations of ancient Egypt in 2740 BCE (Johnson 2004 [1989];
Unwin 1991).

A key nature capital is the plants' incredible innate propensity toward genetic diversity. It is estimated that currently there are 8,000–10,000 cultivars of *Vitis vinifera* (Gerrath 2015; McGovern 2003), the primary grape species used to make wine. Although this number readily reflects the 'plant's pliable, almost chimeric nature' (McGovern 2003:12), it is actually a suppression of its potential genetic diversity as it also represents a long, intense history of calculated agricultural selection and propagation effectively aimed at maximizing the market production (especially in terms of taste, quality and quantity) of wine (Jones 2006; McGovern 2003). The plants' genetically-diverse propensities are additionally marked by the fact that grape vine growing tips consist of a core and outer epidermal layers with different genetic systems and that, accordingly, new growth (which occurs on new lateral shoots) from the same plant is somatically and genetically different (Olmo 2005: 39).

Other nature capitals include grapes' innate capacity to spontaneously provoke the fermentation of embodied sugars into alcohol (and potentially wine or vinegar), and a highly complex amalgamation of sugars, acids, tannins, esters, lactates, etc that produce fruits and juices that display an unrivalled sensitivity to variations in weather, climate, topography, soil conditions (particularly water availability) and to evolving viticultural and vinicultural interventions. Moreover, constant cultured-inspired evolutions in the 'material capital' of agricultural grape growing and winemaking routinely highlights another innate capacity of grape juice – its pronounced malleability. In fact, grape juice or wine is so malleable that winemakers can either choose to foreground the innate, seasonal and placed-based nuances, complexities and variations of grape juices – that is to articulate, if not valorise, the terroir and typicity of different grape varietals – or they can choose to suppress the same and manufacture wines, typically on a large-scale, highly mechanised basis, that display predictability in taste, quality and profitability year after year.

Wine is therefore typically either a terminating commodity, is being stored and is constantly evolving, or exists within the embellishments, vagaries and atrophies of memory. Whatever the trajectory, wine as an ideal is only ever a fleeting option and one that is constantly being usurped. Moreover, wine is a naturally dynamic substance and as such intentionally reflecting on and striving for the 'better' is a readily anticipated intrinsic reality of wine production and consumption, one that reaches an escalating zenith from the mid-nineteenth century onwards with the emergence of modern wine connoisseurship and the increasing dominance of fine and singular wines (i.e. vintage, vineyard and varietal specific) that operate as benchmarks of quality and distinction (Howland 2013).

Of course, therein lies the rub – just what is considered 'good' or 'ideal' wine, and especially so when one individual's ideal can be another's calamity? Indeed, many wine writers, critics and professional tasters – let alone amateur, albeit enthusiastic, imbibers – claim that all taste is subjective and as for quality assessments of wine, these too are highly subjective matters of 'rating what you like'. The analogy with utopia is obvious, especially as one of its most trenchant criticisms is that there are potentially as many utopian ideals as there are individuals, cohorts or groups and accordingly many will be exclusive, contradictory and conflictual.

Overlooking for moment that it is extremely unlikely that there are currently 8 billion different wine tastes, or indeed utopian visions (let alone billions more of both to account for the tastes and utopian ideals of our ancestors), let us at this juncture simply note that wine tastes tend to 'objectively' cluster around the sweet to mildly astringent (or dry) dimensions (Hanni 2013; Smith 2007) of the human taste spectrum (which also includes bitter, salty, pungent (chili) and umami). Wine also enduringly clusters around other principles and practices (e.g. palatability, hygiene, etc – Howland 2019) that are discussed below in relation to the plural utopias of wine and their desirability, viability and achievability (Wright 2007; 2010). As Smith (2007: 45–46) argues:

> You cannot be sure that someone else will detect the same tastes you do. But there is every reason to think tastes *are* there to be detected.… Sensations are narcissistic in telling us how things are with us. But they are also revelatory: telling us how things are around us.

By comparison utopian visions also tend to cluster around the universalizing objectives – set either in the past, future and/or somewhere else (see Dutton's discussion of the 'four pillars' of utopia and their relation to wine in this volume) – of economic equality, material plentitude, universal democratic governance, social egalitarianism, sexual liberty, relativizing cosmopolitanism, individual autonomy and attenuations of physical suffering caused by illness, disease, natural disasters, aging and/or the exacting burdens of excessive labour. Admittedly there is a slim possibility that 8 billion subjective, wholly unique, experiences of wine tasting (but not wine tastes) exist – including those individuals who exist outside the bio-normative ranges of human taste (especially those experiencing ageusia and unable to physically taste anything at all) and also those who wilfully forgo all alcohol on religious, health or purely personal grounds. Indeed, there is an equally emaciated possibility that 8 billion subjective, wholly unique, experiences of utopian dreaming (but not utopias) also exist – including those anti-utopians, such as (often self-proclaimed) realists, pragmatists or pessimists, who contend that the human condition (and therefore all society) is necessarily doomed to dystopian flaw and failure. However, real wine tastes and real utopias are far more objectively restricted in number and scope.

Wine tastes reflect the 'objective' range and thresholds of wine typicity that are established through a dynamic entanglement of the natural taste characteristics of different grape varieties, the terroir or growing conditions (including site of production, seasonality and varied *vini/viti*-cultural interventions), and the specificities and variations in the bio-historic constructions of taste (Bourdieu 2010 [1984]; Teil 2012). Moreover, wine tastes also vary according to social variables such as the experience and knowledge of the wine drinker (amateur and professional wine tasters have very differently socialized palates with the former typically focused on the immediacies of taste and the latter directing their '*selective* attention' (Smith 2007: 50, author's emphasis) on the unfolding complexities, balances and finesse of fruit, alcohol, acidity, tannins, etc, while young and old wine drinkers also often show marked preferences for sweet and dry wines respectively); via the context of consumption (lightly chilling red wine is a 'must' in hot countries and an abomination in more temperate societies, while a bottle of cheap bubbly might do the trick if the celebrations are exuberant enough, whereas an expensive bottle of champagne might 'fall flat' if the salutations are in any way forced or fraudulent); and/or through the culture or social class of the imbibers and their embodied taste dispositions (in many Latin American cultures the dominant preference is for very sweet wines, while experienced French connoisseurs are noted for their propensity for very dry wines) (Bourdieu 2010 [1984]; Teil 2012; Smith 2007). Such variations are, however, restricted in range and scope, both biologically in terms of the innate taste profiles of grapes and the human physical capacities for tasting, and also socio-culturally in terms of the dialogic relationship between winemakers and predominant (albeit evolving) socio-cultural wine tastes. As Smith (2007: 63, author's emphasis) notes:

> Tastes are real properties of wines even though they bear an essential relation to the subjective experiences of creatures like us.... They are there *for us* to experience. They are not in us, they are in the wine: [while] the pleasures they give us are not in the wine, they are in us.

As with wine tastes, 'real' utopias also arguably share 'objective' criteria that can either confirm or disqualify any pretentions to being utopian. For example, Erik Wright (2010) cogently argues that any proclamatory utopian visions or practices that in anyway seek to restrict or diminish an individual's, cohort's or group's egalitarian access to economic, material, political and social equality are 'objectively' not 'real utopias'. Indeed, according to Wright: '*In a socially just society, all people would have broadly equal access to the social and material conditions necessary for living a flourishing life*' (2013: 4, author's emphasis). Moreover the moral principles of equality, democracy and sustainability (biological, social, economic, political etc for future generations) are cornerstones of all real utopias (see also Bauman 1976; Bloch 1986; Le Guin 2016 [1989]; Levitas 2013).

Any ideals that effectively masquerade as utopian (see Howland's discussion of utopiyin and utopiyang winemaking in this volume), but which do not fulfil Wright's objective criteria above, tend to point to the structural predominance of stratification, proprietorship and territoriality, together with the adjunct tenuousness, unpredictability and deficiencies (real or perceived) of socially-necessary material production, that have marked many (but not all) human societies, especially since the domestication of plants and animals in 5000 BCE and which have resulted in masses of varied, conflictual and vested-interest ideals. It also directs our attention to how we could scale-up and out those egalitarian societies (most notably nomadic gatherer-hunters), gifting economies (often kin/ancestor-oriented) and other similarly democratically inclined institutions (e.g. voluntary/ service clubs etc) (see Diamond 2012; Karatani 2014; Wright 2010). Although it must also be noted that the 'objectivity' of real utopias is definitely a human construct and capital (primarily cultural: moral, ethical and philosophical), whereas the 'objectivity' of wine tastes is a dynamic entanglement of the nature capitals of plant biology (including grape typicity) and human taste capacities, the material capitals of wine (especially the fundamental chemical processes and fermentations of winemaking and the typicity capacities/ranges of different wines), and the socio-historical constructions and distinctions of taste (Bourdieu 2010 [1984]; Smith 2007).

Furthermore, as Wright also notes any individual or social endeavours (e.g. sexual practices, religious beliefs, etc) that do not in any way threaten or diminish anyone's egalitarian access (and flourishing experience of) material, political and social equality are likewise apposite to any utopian situation. Thus, the potential for utopian pluralities and creativity is not only maintained but is practically enhanced by the removal of restrictions engendered by the existence of material, political and social stratifications. To gain an understanding of how this might manifest just think of freely enjoying, for example, the constantly evolving, hyper-eclecticism of music but without being surreptitiously disciplined in matters of taste by the financial interests of Spotify. Moreover, the same principles of egalitarian access could be engaged to assess and facilitate the exclusory use – for example, based on indigenous, ethnic or religious grounds – of everything from churches to sacred lands (Wright 2010).

By way of comparison a 'real' utopian wine also potentially has a number of minimum 'objective' expectations that should be available to anyone inclined to imbibe – that all wines should be palatable, hygienic and equally accessible immediately springs to mind, although clearly the latter is not the case in our current (nor in the many historic) times of commodity, market-based wine production. Indeed, any review of the recorded history of wine will show that it has enduringly been clustered around a number of principles and practices (Howland 2019) that could be considered ideal or utopian-esque. Aside from the valorization of variation, nuance and complexity – or their apparent counters in standardisation and predictability – of wine tastes discussed above, and the palatability and hygiene minima just noted, wine has also long been produced for its intoxicating effects. According to Hugh Johnson (2004 [1989]: 11) wine is 'the most repeatable of mild narcotics without ill effects – at least in the short and medium term', although wine also features in the festival, hedonic excesses of the carnivalesque.[1] Wine has also been enduringly produced and consumed for social reasons – mostly as a facilitating medium of social connectedness (including the commensality and *communitas* of many wine-drinking contexts, the gifting sociality of much household and/or peasant wine production, and even the market parochiality of locally produced wines – see Fournier's discussion of Cirò Marina wine in Calabria, Italy, this volume) and for social status/distinction purposes (the 'best' wines are typically the reserve of the 'best' people). While similarly long histories apply to the medicinal purposes ascribed to wine consumption (current research suggests a glass or two of wine daily has more benefits than exercise for those aiming to live past 70 years – see www.mind.uci.edu/research-studies/90plus-study (accessed 08.02.19)); to its religious purposes (the sacred dimensions of wine consumption from Osiris, through Dionysus and Bacchus, on to the Christian rituals of transubstantiation, are well-canvassed); and to its capacity as a sanitary/hygienic liquid (often as a substitute in times of troubled waters) (Charters 2006; Johnson 2004 [1989]; Unwin 1991).

Aside from the market-based, commodity production of wine and its status, hierarchy and exclusivity conferring modalities, it could be argued that all the other enduring – and thus socially and historically 'objective' – aspects of wine noted above are universally accessible to all who choose to imbibe and therefore wine can at least be assessed as utopian-esque. In this regard many of wine's enduring characteristics and attractions have long met Wright's criteria for morally assessing the utopian potentials and social practicalities of any phenomena – desirability, viability and achievability. Of the three criteria, Wright argues that the problem of viability is the most pressing. Desirability is readily assessed via the moral principles of egalitarian access to material, political and social equality, while achievability is more difficult to assess due to the 'high levels of contingency' that attend the planning for and implementation of any alternative futures, it nevertheless remains an ongoing 'central task for the practical work of strategies for social change' (Wright 2007: 28–29). Assessments (and critiques) of viability of successfully enacting utopian projects rest on analyses of theoretical models and/or empirical studies of how particular social structures and institutions do or could work. While Wright's caution is warranted, when considering the enduring histories and expanding worlds of wine it is clear that its universal, utopian-esque modes of well-being noted above have routinely and readily met all three of his criteria.

Of course, the utopian removal of market-based, commodity production and any accordant social exclusions, stratifications and hierarchies would in no way guarantee universal access to all wines – especially not for those fine wines that are likely to be over-subscribed no matter where on the utopian-dystopian spectrum humanity is positioned – and for this some form of system of lots and/or social credit (earned by undertaking socially worthwhile deeds beyond assisting to provision the necessities of life) would also need to be enacted to ensure the minimum of egalitarian access to the well-being of good wine consumption. The same could potentially apply to ensure utopian access to any other over-subscribed, limited goods (Wright 2010) – say for example, tourist visits to Venice or premium black truffles whenever in season.

Which brings us finally to a consideration of blueprinting or planning for utopian futures. Aside from the perpetual denunciations that utopian dreams are typically unrealistic, impractical, wildly idealistic, and are therefore irresponsible and doomed to fail, another criticism has constantly stalked utopian projects – namely that they are typically over-engineered, over-planned and totalitarian in actual practice, with Stalin's dystopian reign of terror in implementing a socialist paradise in the Soviet Union frequently cited as cause célèbre. Forms of both critiques has led to a contemporary situation where an assertion of utopianism can be a byword for the denigration of any socially, politically or economically transformative projects considered by accusers to be unworthy or unwarranted (Levitas 2010; Wright 2010).

Similar debates about the requisite planning, order and intervention required to produce 'good wine' vex the contemporary wine world, with any disagreements being particularly acute when considering the respective merits and deficits of mass-produced, industrial-scale wines versus boutique, natural wines (see Kaplonski's analysis of natural winemaking in Austria, this volume). In regard of this argument concerning the utopian potentials of wine, perhaps the best response is to adopt the 'Goldilocks'– not too much, not too little, just right – approach. Clearly the production and distribution of palatable, hygienic, readily transported and storable wine has benefitted greatly from the systematic planning and order that has particularly occurred since the rise of industrial capitalism in the mid-nineteenth century and which is readily apparent in contemporary vineyards planted with GPS precision, in wineries resplendent with gleaming, stainless steel, temperature-controlled vats and in the extensive networks of transportation that allow Moët to be as readily drunk in Adelaide as New Zealand Sauvignon Blanc is drunk in London. The question therefore is what utopian wine potential are you attempting to strive for – a natural, terroir and typicity-expressive wine or a year-on-year predictable, standardised, 'plonk'? Either way deploying the requisite Goldilocks' amount of planning, order and intervention required is just fine as long as the particular ideal is momentarily achieved and just as importantly the utopian principles of egalitarian access, utopia plurality, sustainability (environmental and social) and ongoing creativity or striving are in no way compromised. Indeed, somewhat counter-intuitively natural winemaking probably requires far more incremental surveillance, decision-making and consequential interventions (albeit organic) than industrial, large-scale winemaking ever does (Viecelli 2018). So, as far as utopian wines are concerned it is genuinely a matter of whatever planning and engineering works, works.

A utopian reading of wine, or at least a consideration of wine via a utopian framework provides a means for understanding the dialogics of nature and culture that are in constant evolution and negotiation, not only between vineyard and winery, but also between producers, promoters and consumers. Wine potentially becomes utopian whenever it is perceived and valued as a modality that strives for the current ideals of taste aesthetic – and is frequently condemned whenever these ideals are perceived to be sullied through the commercial imperatives of 'bottom-line' commodification. There is, however, no question that wine does exist, as an object, and moreover is tautologically revealed as an ideal discursive of nature and culture whenever a wine is deemed fine. Terroir, on the other hand, is not so clear. 'No such thing as terroir?' is the questioning title of Geneviève Teil's (2012) article, reminding us that Thomas More also coined his ambiguous term to suggest there might be no such thing as 'utopia' either.

Utopian terroir

Detractors of terroir might welcome its association with the more disparaging connotation of utopia *(ou-*topia), as synonym for fanciful, impracticable or downright impossible. Several scholars point to a lack of scientific proof for the existence of terroir (Matthews 2015; Szymanski 2018; Teil 2012) which certainly invites cynicism, but there are also many scientific studies that do support terroir with empirical evidence (Meinert 2018; Goutouly & Hinnewinkel 2015). Essentially, the erroneous notion that terroir = soil, and especially soil minerality that can be tasted in the 'minerality' of the wines, is becoming more and more frequent in popular discourses on terroir. This 'vulgarization' of the concept dilutes terroir to a one-dimensional descriptor for the earth in which grape vines are grown and consequently opens terroir up to attack from sceptics. As Meinert (2018) and others have confirmed, soil is only one of the natural factors linked to place that influences the taste of wine, and its most important quality is not 'minerality' but its capacity for holding and releasing water and nitrogen. Climate is often cited as more influential than soil, as even though we now know that grape vines can grow and wine can be made outside the magical 45th parallel (mostly between the 30th and 50th parallel), the best wines in the world are arguably made within these latitudes. Climate change is also clearly impacting on where, when and how vines are grown and wines are made (Gladstones 2011; Webb et al. 2012). The geographical site – especially its topography – is primordial, as are plant genetics. Terroir is made up of all these elements, and yet its essence is not entirely encapsulated within them.

Making science the centre of proving or disproving the existence of terroir does not tend to bring out its most positive utopian qualities. As described above, it incites polarisation, for and against terroir, dissecting its being to end up with nothingness. Or nothing that has any intrinsic meaning beyond 'environment' or 'provenance' or the various natural elements that contribute to its empirical evidence. Understood as a more interdisciplinary space, combining science with culture, politics with economics, geography with history, terroir takes on dynamic and useful qualities that resonate with those bestowed on the 'best of all possible worlds': the positive *eu*-utopia. Whether this world is accepted with optimistic cheer as Leibniz suggested in his *Essays on Theodicy* (1710) or considered with scorn as in Voltaire's *Candide* (1759) depends more on the perspective of the individual than on the features of the utopia (or terroir) itself.

Although the defining features of utopia – and terroir – are difficult to discern conclusively, they both share some recognizable processes that elucidate how they function in nature and culture. Freed from the traditional blueprint for an ideal, autarkic community, the modern utopia has become a 'spirit' (Bloch 2000 [1918]), a 'game played across lateral possibilities' (Ruyer 1950), a 'spatial play' (Marin 1973). This ludic representation of utopia emphasises its use-value for experimenting with ideas rather than circumscribing a society, which, when applied to terroir emphasises its lighter, more creative aspects. While scientific terroir might be weighed down by blueprints and box-checking, utopian terroir is elevated to a sphere where experimenting with all of the contributing influences in 'place' provides opportunities for dynamic interactions between the natural and cultural environments and the wine.

The French, and many other cultures besides, uphold the importance of terroir, accepted as site-related typicity identifiable in wines. In fact, even French scientists, such as agronomist and ecophysiologist Jean-Pascal Goutouly, defines terroir in progressive utopian-esque terms as 'a project space in perpetual adaptation to its natural, economic and social environment' (Goutouly & Hinnewinkel 2015: 41). For these proponents of terroir-driven wines, the utopian epithet applies a positive charge, indicating that the confluence of certain elements including land, climate, tradition, method and people, is an ideal one, capable of producing the best wines possible if liberated from excessive constraints and allowed to 'play'. However, utopian terroir presents many different permutations, and like utopia – sometimes lauded, sometimes denigrated – terroir has known both fortune and its reversal over the centuries.

Terroir has not always been pronounced in favourable ways in France. From the mid-nineteenth to mid-twentieth century, terroir was a pejorative designation, both generally and with specific reference to wine, indicating an unsophisticated, rustic, 'rude' style rather than a subtle translation of the land and winescape. Interestingly, this period coincides with the most negative time for utopians, when Marx and Engels turned away from *Socialism: Utopian and Scientific* (1880), to dissociate their practical political programmes from less realistic propositions such as eccentric utopian Charles Fourier's suggestion that the axis of the earth might be tilted to make the oceans taste like lemonade (1808). Terroir regained some ground in the early twentieth century with the creation of systematic wine appellations in France that explicitly linked wine production to place, as well as introducing other limits on variety, planting, yield, and viticulture. But then terroir was coopted by the Vichy government who capitulated to and collaborated with Nazi Germany from 1940–1944. War criminal Maréchal Pétain's nationalist propaganda included '*Les Expositions des terroirs régionaux et de la jeunesse*' (Exhibitions of regional terroirs and youth) and '*Travail, Famille, Patrie*' (Work, Family,

Country) alongside an anti-Semitic and pro-Aryan agenda, so that after World War II, terroir was stained by France's shameful collaboration.

The *trente glorieuses* – the 30 glorious years of progress and rebuilding that followed World War II – saw the modernisation of agriculture and heralded the end of peasantry or rural life by the 1970s. This was epitomised by the publication of Eugen Weber's study *Peasants Into Frenchmen: The Modernization of Rural France, 1870–1914* (1976), translated into French as *La Fin des terroirs* (1983). Around the same time, an opposing trend in rural and regional studies appeared including an edited book by Eric Hobsbawm and Terence Ranger (2012 [1983]) called *The Invention of Tradition*, which deconstructed this notion of the end of an era of rustic peasantry and proposed as a counterpoint to read this rise and fall of the peasantry as a folkloric construction. As Gilles Laferté (2006) observes in *La Bourgogne et ses vins: image d'origine contrôlée* [Burgundy and its Wines: Image of Controlled Origin], these two approaches to interpreting the same phenomenon were essentially aligned, though Weber emphasised the end of the old ways, and Hobshawn and Ranger presented a study on the new ways. Terroir followed the same trajectory – torn between these two tensions – on the one hand, it was something dirty, rustic, certainly unappealing in a wine glass and part of the 'truc' old ways – but just as it started slipping away, it was reinterpreted in 'false' new ways as folkloric, nostalgic, and a potent antidote to the destabilisation of May 68 and the social upheavals that followed. Another historical factor influencing the French wine industry at this time was drop in 'French' wine production because before the Algerian war and decolonisation, which resulted in Algerian independence in 1962: Algeria was considered part of France, and contributed over 19 million hectolitres of wine to its production. Much of this Algerian wine was blended, bottled and sold as French wine, both in France and abroad (Meloni & Swinnen 2014).

In the 1970s, the invocation of terroir became a backhanded affirmation of France's 'unadulterated' wine identity, but another event relaunched the folkloric terroir trend on an international scale – the Judgement of Paris – a blind tasting organised by British wine writer Steven Spurrier in 1976 that pitted Californian wines against Burgundian wines – and the Californian wines won. This battle of New versus Old World wines was depicted in the film *Bottleshock* (2008) and is described in detail in Spurrier's memoir *Wine – A Way of Life* (2018). In a reactionary measure against the encroachment of New World winemaking technology and practices in the 1970s and 1980s, terroir became a kind of secret weapon – an unpronounceable and undefinable guarantee of regional Frenchness that was equated at that moment to quality. This weapon was directed as much at the global wine industry as it was turned on its own domestic producers in an effort to encourage them to improve their outputs. Terroir had become inherently utopian, an autarkic tool for protecting and promoting the specificity of a French winemaking idyll in a gesture that resembles a traditional utopia's tendency to separate itself from the rest of corrupted humanity – on an island, in a walled city, or a galaxy far, far away.

The rise of interest in terroir and its potential use value for New World as well as Old World wine producers has launched a wealth of recent publications attempting to circumscribe the subject. The official definition of terroir published by the International Organisation of Wine (OIV) in 2010 reads:

> Vitivinicultural 'terroir' is a concept which refers to an area in which collective knowledge of the interactions between the identifiable physical and biological environment and applied vitivinicultural practices develops, providing distinctive characteristics for the products originating from this area. 'Terroir' includes specific soil, topography, climate, landscape characteristics and biodiversity features.
>
> (Resolution OIV-VITI 333–2010)

The OIV therefore recognises the value of knowledge in discerning terroir, thereby implying a human factor in the mix. The popular 'Wine Folly' website includes a diagram explaining terroir within its range of educational tools and the word 'tradition' is used to evoke the human element of terroir (www.winefolly.com (accessed 24.02.19)). Tradition can be problematic because it can engender value judgements of terroir based on the length of time wine or any other product has been made in a particular place, and consequently the Old World, New World dichotomy is activated, potentially locking terroir back in the French Hexagon again. Knowledge – be it historical (tradition), geographical (climate, soil, slope), or scientific (interacting in multi-species environments) – is a more inclusive yet still definite aspect of terroir terminology today.

Tracing the evolution of scholarly interpretations of terroir in English reveals a fascinating journey from Tim Unwin's cursory mention of the term on page 37 in *Wine and the Vine: An Historical Geography of Viticulture and the Wine Trade* (1991) to Amy Trubek's *The Taste of Place: A Cultural Journey into Terroir* (2008), which presents the first in-depth analysis of the development and spread of terroir from a social and cultural anthropological perspective. Marion Demossier's writings on Burgundian terroir (2010; 2011) and Philip Whalen's (2010) provocative article 'Whither Terroir in the 21st Century: Burgundy's Climats?' began the debate for and against continued promotion of terroir in France, followed up by Zachary Nowak's 'Against Terroir', which declares it nonsense, concluding: 'Place can be important in taste. It can sometimes be very important. But not that important.' (2012: 03). Two more major works appearing in 2015 by Thomas Parker *Tasting French Terroir* and Mark A. Matthews *Terroir and Other Myths of Winemaking* reinforce the case for and against (respectively) terroir's importance in the globalized wine industry. Charters et al. (2017) demonstrate conclusively the aspirational merit of terroir in contemporary wine business and marketing, as place is considered a value proposition in the context of Resource-Advantage Theory. The upward thrust of terroir's trajectory to the current point is overwhelmingly clear, as wine websites all over the world now emphasise their terroir, and the storytellers of wine – from winemakers to media to sommeliers – use the word as shorthand to explain why a wine from one site tastes different to the wine from another. Exaggerations abound, ranging from Tomas Clancy's designation of terroir as the 'God particle of wine'[2] to the ubiquitous claims of 'unique terroir', as though this distinction equates to quality. The dilution and popularisation of terroir has rendered it a banal equivalent of 'soil' in mainstream terms, perhaps in a similar way that the *-topia* suffix has become a reductive signifier for 'paradise' in popular discourse – with examples like Coca-cola's fruit drink 'Fruitopia',[3] J-Topia – for those interested in all things Japanese, and a new Italian film *Youtopia* (2018) by Berardo Carboni about a young woman who sells her virginity online.

Although terroir and utopia have never really achieved semantic stability, perhaps due to their inherent interdisciplinarity, they both actually draw strength from their dynamic mutability and are essentially derailed or corrupted when shackled to a fixed definition or framework. The example of the *Appellations d'Origine Contrôlée* (AOC) as a legislative blueprint for safeguarding terroir offers an interesting experiment in the efforts to pin down and define terroir in the French winemaking context. The AOC system evolved over the first half of the twentieth century, from the shaky first laws of 1905 to the Joseph Capus Law of 1935 with its famous motto of 'local, loyal and constant' to describe the ideal relationship between a wine and the place where it was made. Conceived as a measure to limit wine fraud and fix quality assertions after the phylloxera crisis of the late nineteenth century, which saw European wine production plummet and fake wines or colonial wines (especially from Algeria) flood the market, the AOC drew on geographical notions of terroir to validate place-based naming rights for wine.[4] Violent riots by growers in the Languedoc (1907) and Champagne (1910–11) who rejected imports of lower-priced non-local grapes, must and wine into these regions fuelled the administrative and legislative fires. With the creation of the *Comité National d'Origine* (CNAO) in 1935, which became the *Institut* (INAO) after World War II and changed again to the *Institut national de l'Origine et de la qualité* (2007), the AOC became a regulated, verifiable reflection of the type, quantity, and style of wine produced within a delimited space and a particular place. But the AOC is a fairly rigid system with not much room for innovation in its testing and tasting of 'local, loyal and constant', whereas terroir is constantly evolving, both materially and discursively, more like a process than a product or a system. Teil argues for this more progressive approach to terroir using sociological object theory in her 2012 article mentioned above and has analysed the testing and rejection of terroir driven wines from the AOC in other articles (Teil 2010; 2014). Chris Kaplonski also explores this question in his chapter on natural wine.

The AOC blueprint typology of terroir provokes similar criticism to the 'perfect' utopian society, frozen as if in aspic. This version of utopia may be peaceful and plenteous, but it lacks soul or honesty or the capacity to change – one has only to think of films such as *Pleasantville* (1998) or *The Truman Show* (1998) or indeed Disney's Epcot Centre. The AOC version of terroir is nevertheless much easier to adapt and adopt into wine producing regions outside Europe, under the guise of geographical indications (GIs). The spread of GIs to Canada, the United States, New Zealand, Australia and South Africa has obviously included a corollary interest in identifying, promoting and safeguarding terroir. As Matthews has noted the 'recent and dramatic increase' (2015: 148) of occurrences of terroir relative to wine in digitised books published in English, we can also note its use relative to characterising particular wine regions outside Europe. Douglas et al. foreground 'Canadian terroir' when studying Riesling from Niagara (2001); Brian Croser is resident 'terroirist' in Australia, having educated and influenced generations of winemakers via Charles Sturt University winemaking courses and various other institutions (Croser 2010); Carey et al. plot terroir's role in cultivating Sauvignon Blanc and Cabernet Sauvignon in Stellenbosch (2008). But terroir is not just an untranslatable French code for identifying provenance in the product. Through its forays into new regions, where it is detached from its historical roots, terroir has become an even less anchored 'floating signifier', at the mercy of commercial enterprise and capital gain, as Cross et al. (2017) suggest in relation to Californian viticultural land values, and Charters et al. (2017) confirm in reference to broader market values in their excellent scan of the field.

Where is the true value of terroir? When can it be utopian? Teil employs a musical metaphor to explain the process:

> The task of 'terroir vintners' is to craft the expression of their terroir. To put it in musical terms, they perform a score composed by the terroir; for terroir to emerge, the performance must allow it to express itself rather than conceal it through overpowering practices.
>
> (Teil 2012: 481–482)

Another analogy might allow us to focus more on the wine itself, by comparing it to a crystal prism through which white light becomes a rainbow coloured refraction of light. Like white light exists independently of the prism, all the elements that contribute to the wine (including soil, climate, site and knowledge) exist independently of it but may not be visible. The wine produces a manifestation of all of these elements, recast and reconstituted in such a way that it can be tasted. Terroir becomes perceivable only in the taste of the wine – like the rainbow refracted light, there is no hope of seeing it unless it has passed through the wine.

Utopian terroir can be experienced in winemaking that is constantly striving to translate it better through the wine, via better tasting wines, with more identifiable and relatable links to the terroir. At the 2019 Pinot Celebration Australia, held on the Mornington Peninsula from 8–9 February, after listening to two days of presentations on Pinot Noir clones and wines from around the world, the international guest of honour Thibault Liger-Belair from Nuits-Saint-Georges in Burgundy began his talk with the following: 'I don't make Pinot Noir. I make wine using the tool of Pinot Noir to translate the terroir.' It is a different understanding of the process of winemaking, to be continually seeking better terroir, better understanding of terroir, and better tasting wines.

Clearly these processes are neither entirely natural, nor entirely cultural. Terroir and utopia are not completely natural because they require human intervention to identify and evaluate their contributions to production – of wine and/or of society. They are cultural constructs, devised to distinguish their qualities from the general state of being. Though terroir and utopia often represent an ongoing practice (of winemaking in a certain style in a particular place, or traditional subsistence farming in an eco-friendly environment), they could also be considered countercultural, as they instate boundaries of difference, defining their characteristics in opposition to the established status quo.

On the one hand, the countercultural descriptor may appear more readily applicable to utopia than terroir, given the subversive cast of much social dreaming – from intentional communities to revolutions, inherently critical of the political regime in power and the social norms at play. Thomas Molnar's unforgettable turn of phrase in *Utopia: The Perennial Heresy* (1990) underscores the blasphemous stance adopted when humanists like More projected a paradise created by humans not gods, on earth not in the heavenly afterlife. The recurring dissidence that utopian thought and action have represented across the ages is clearly countercultural, though feminist, ecological, and LGBTIQ movements have become part of mainstream political agendas and capitalism may yet face more challenges from a growing share-economy.

On the other hand, terroir might have its own countercultural charge. Its etymological evolution from simple *terre* – any old earth or land – to *terroir* indicates a process of differentiation based on quality (Matthews 2015). While this stage is a sign that culture, and by extension cultural production of wine, prevail upon nature, the pejorative twist towards *goût de terroir* is an (unintentional) countercultural step back to nature – the natural earthy taste revisits the cultured wine. When terroir's value is (re)instated in the twentieth century, definitively in the 1970s in opposition to New World wine cultures, it is also countercultural – pitting itself against the rising wave of oenological and technological progress, through a return to natural 'talent', an apparently unreproducible taste of place. The role of scientific evidence in viticulture and winemaking has grown to become a powerful force against terroir in the current era. Whether or not terroir is considered countercultural or mainstream now depends more upon disciplinary positioning – Matthews and many other scientists relegate terroir to myth, whereas humanities and social sciences scholars together with much of the popular wine media and many more winemakers are effectively expanding the geographical scope and extending the marketing reach of terroir.

Both terroir and utopia are therefore products of culture as much as nature – despite pretentions to the contrary in both cases. Terroir's current return to nature is like a heretical slap in the face of western society's overwhelming trust in science, yet it remains a cultural product, and furthermore a commercial tool to sell wine's 'unique' properties. Utopia also proposes a return to nature, to ecotopian post-humanism, as rampant technological and scientific progress heralds more dystopian visions of robot wars, climate catastrophe, and the loss of humanity. Turning terroir over and over again in an attempt to find some absolute objectivity seems as redundant as attempting to do the same with utopia. To paraphrase the great Marxist theorist of utopia, Fredric Jameson, utopia is dialectical or it is useless, and then he argues convincingly over thousands of pages that utopia does exist because desire and the idea of potentiality still exist (Jameson 2005). At the end of the final essay of *Valences of the Dialectic*, he affirms:

> from time to time, like a diseased eyeball in which disturbing flashes of light are perceived or like those baroque sunbursts in which rays from another world suddenly break into this one, we are reminded that Utopia exists and that other systems, other spaces, are still possible.
>
> (Jameson 2009: 632)

Let us in turn claim that there is no value to terroir without dialectics, and that terroir exists because wine and the idea of potentiality still exist.

Making new worlds

Wine has traditionally been seen as a product of the Old World, born of winter-buried Georgian grape juice around 6000 BCE in South Caucasus, and spread across the Mediterranean by seafaring Phoenician traders and into Europe by rampant Romans. Much later, the wild *Vitis labrusca* vines of North and South America were domesticated by European migrants in the sixteenth century to make wine, with European *Vitis vinifera* plants sent out with settlers to colonize and 'civilize' the New World. From the Renaissance to the 1970s the Eastern Hemisphere was considered the Old World and the Western Hemisphere plus Oceania the New World, conjectured thus according to Halford John Mackinder's Heartland Theory as expressed in 'The Geographical Pivot of History' (1904). Decolonization and postcolonialism in the 1970s emancipated the New World in many ways, but wine remained tethered to the Old World benchmarks of quality for some decades. Nowadays, the Old World/New World dichotomy is rarely used in any field except the wine industry with New World being code for mass-produced, industrial winemaking, whereas Old World indicates artisanal, terroir-based, traditional methods and produce (Banks & Overton 2010). Even here, there are distinct signs that the winescape has changed again, with debates in *Decanter* and *Wine Spectator* wine magazines,[5] although leading wine economists such as Kym Anderson and Vicente Pinilla maintain the terminology in *Wine Globalization: A New Comparative History* (2018).

Our contributors to this volume do go beyond the winespeak dichotomy of Old World and New World, to unearth innovation in all its forms, whenever and wherever it may emerge. Sites range from nineteenth century Bordeaux, Burgundy and Champagne to twenty-first century McLaren Vale, Martinborough, and Okanagan Valley. To finish this chapter, we briefly outline and comment on their contributions.

The volume is framed by chapters from the co-editors. Dutton begins with an exploration of utopian wine using a classical literary approach to determining the sources of utopia, then applying those categories to wine to determine whether Bordeaux *grands crus* might be considered utopian wines. In the final chapter, Howland leaves the literary last word to Wordsworth, though his analysis of plain-sight utopias using Ursula Le Guin's Utopiyin/Utopiyang dialectic takes an anthropological perspective on New Zealand's fine winemakers.

In the first chapters, the Australian wine imaginary is linked to utopian identity-forming endeavours of the past and present by Julie McIntyre, Mikaël Pierre and John Germov, while William Skinner traces the foundational history of wine in the most utopian of states, South Australia, to reveal the liberty and limits of the McLaren Vale winegrowers. From the Australian context to the French, Marion Demossier examines how, in reaction to increasingly globalised discourses of terroir, Burgundian winemakers have been prompted to situate the notion of *climats* as central to their processes of collective visual re-appropriation, the *mise en héritage* of the site, and to their successful quest for UNESCO World Heritage status. Champagne, Graham Harding argues convincingly, is the first region to translate its terroir into a territorial brand in the late nineteenth century, privileging the cultural over the natural in a marketing model that effectively relaunches the wine region. Steve Charters regards Champagne via Karl Mannheim's dichotomous pairing of ideology and utopia to find that the dominant ideological paradigm of strict protectionism is currently being challenged by the utopian ideal of terroir champagne.

Reinventing wine worlds is the theme that draws together the four chapters that follow: Donna M. Senese, John S. Hull, and Barbara J. McNicol examine ecotopian mobilities in the Okanagan Valley, British Columbia; Kelle Howson, Warwick Murray and John Overton go beyond the veneer of utopianism in the South African wine industry to highlight the dystopian working and living conditions around Cape Town; Vincent Fournier exploits deep fieldwork to explain how utopian narratives of terroir are directing developments in the commercial, social and cultural aspects of winemaking in Cirò Marina, Calabria; Rumina Dhalla focuses on questions of authenticity, identity and utopian terroir in the quest to understand motivations for and experiences of sustainability in the Australian wine industry.

The final chapters veer from the political to the poetic, beginning with Christopher Kaplonski's journey along the utopian itinerary of natural wine in twenty-first century Austria. The road that Moya Costello takes up the hill and toward the past evokes the utopian possibility for young Australian winemakers to return to older methods, while also inventing wholly original ones, and thereby remain reflexively and historically engaged with their evolving processes of terroir and taste. Robert Swinburn conjoins the concepts of (deep) terroir and utopia with Country as understood in Australian indigenous terms, to make ethical sense of winemaking in Southeastern Australia near Geelong.

Wine, terroir and utopia have brought all of these original and diverse perspectives together in a volume that offers new directions in interdisciplinary wine studies. In examining wine and terroir through the frame of utopia, we aim to open up possibilities for innovative thinking about how wine has made new worlds, as well as contribute to making new worlds in wine scholarship.

Notes

1 Arguably if one was to drink to excess and required socially provisioned medical or other harm-reduction services this could be a cost to others. This could occur whenever the energy, labour, etc required to materially provision the required medical or other harm-reduction services created divergences or deficits in the capacities of others to equally access any necessary material resources (e.g. food, shelter, etc). Therefore, moderation (at least so that any 'excess' was not overtly 'detrimental') could be another utopian ideal of wine consumption. The same principles could be applied to assessing the viability of utopian wine production in terms of environmental sustainability and competition with any 'necessary' agricultural production.
2 www.tomasclancy.wordpress.com/2013/03/07/wines-god-particle-the-science-of-terroirism (accessed 24.02.19).
3 www.atlasobscura.com/articles/the-rise-and-fall-of-fruitopia-the-trippiest-beverage-of-the-90s
4 For more information on geographers' roles in defining terroir and the AOC, see Dutton 2019.
5 www.decanter.com/wine-news/opinion/the-editors-blog/should-we-stop-talking-about-old-and-new-world-wine-2291/ (accessed 24.02.19); https://winespectator.com/drvinny/show/id/New-World-versus-Old-World-Wine-Vinny-53983 (accessed 24.02.19).

Bibliography

Anderson, K. & Pinilla, V. (eds) (2018). *Wine Globalization: A New Comparative History.* Cambridge: Cambridge University Press.
Banks, G. & Overton, J. (2010). Old World, New World, Third World? Reconceptualising the worlds of wine. *Journal of Wine Research*, 21(1): 57–75.
Bauman, Z. (1976). *Socialism: The Active Utopia.* London: Allen & Unwin.
Bloch, E. (1986 [1954–1959]). *The Principle of Hope.* Oxford: Blackwell.
Bloch, E. (2000 [1918]). *The Spirit of Utopia.* Stanford: Stanford University Press.

Bourdieu, P. (2010 [1984]). *Distinction: A Social Critique of the Judgement of Taste.* London: Routledge & Kegan Paul.

Carey, V.A., Archer, E., Barbeau, G. & Saayman, D. (2008). Viticultural terroirs in Stellenbosch, South Africa. II. The interaction of Cabernet Sauvignon and Sauvignon Blanc with environment. *Journal International des Sciences de la Vigne et du Vin*, 42(4). doi:doi:10.20870/oeno-one.2008.42.4.809

Charters, S. (2006). *Wine and Society: The Social and Cultural Context of a Drink.* Oxford: Elsevier.

Charters, S., Spielmann, N. & Babin, B.J. (2017). The nature and value of terroir products. *European Journal of Marketing*, 51(4): 748–771.

Croser, B. (2010). Prospects for Australian Smaller 'Fine Wine' Producers. Paper for the pre-AARES conference workshop on The World's Wine Markets by 2030: Terroir, Climate Change, R&D and Globalization, Adelaide Convention Centre, Adelaide, South Australia, 7–9 February 2010. Available online at www.adelaide.edu.au/wineecon/events/2030workshop/pubs/Croser_WC0210.pdf

Cross, R., Plantinga, A. J. & Stavins, R. N. (2017). Terroir in the New World: Hedonic Estimation of Vineyard Sale Prices in California. *Journal of Wine Economics*, 12(3): 282–301.

Demossier, M. (2010). *Wine Drinking in France, An Anthropology of Wine Culture and Consumption in France.* Cardiff: University of Wales Press.

Demossier, M. (2011). Beyond terroir: territorial construction, hegemonic discourses, and French wine culture. *Journal of the Royal Anthropological Institute*, 17(4): 685–705.

Diamond, J. (2012). *The World Until Yesterday: What can we learn from traditional societies?* New York: Viking Press.

Douglas, D., Cliff, M.A. & Reynolds, A.G. (2001). Canadian terroir: characterization of Riesling wines from the Niagara Peninsula. *Food Research International*, 34(7): 559–563.

Dutton, J. (2019). Geographical Turns and Historical Returns in Narrating French Wine Culture. *Global Food History,* 5(1–2): 113–131. doi:10.1080/20549547.2019.1570781

Farrington, I. & Urry, J. (1985). Food and the Early History of Cultivation. *Journal of Ethnobiology*, 5(2):143–157.

Gerrath, J. (2015). Humans and Grapes. In *Taming the Wild Grape: Botany and horticulture in the Vitaceae.* Garreth, J., Posluszny, U. & Melville, L. (eds.), pp. 103–114. Switzerland: Springer.

Gladstones, J.S. (2011). *Wine, Terroir and Climate Change.* Kent Town: Wakefield Press.

Goutouly, J-P. & Hinnewinkel, J-C. (2015). Terroirs et qualités des vins, un lien à l'origine. Mais quelle origine? In *Les vins de Bordeaux: Les itinéraires de la qualité*, book 2, L. Bordenave, J-M. Chevet, J-P. Goutouly & J-C. Hinnewinkel (eds), pp. 9–41. Bordeaux: Vigne et Vin.

Hanni, T. (2013). *Why You Like the Wines You Like: Changing the Way the World Thinks About Wine.* Napa: Hanni Co.

Hemingway, E. (1932). *Death in the Afternoon.* New York: Collier & Son.

Hobsbawm, E. & Ranger, T. (eds) (2012). *The Invention of Tradition.* Cambridge: Cambridge University Press.

Howland, P. J. (2013). Distinction by Proxy: The democratization of fine wine. *Journal of Sociology*, 49(2–3): 325–340.

Howland, P. J. (2019). Enduring wine and the global middle-class. In *The Globalization of Wine*, D. Inglis & A. Almila (eds), pp. 151–170. London: Bloomsbury.

Jameson, F. (2005). *Archaeologies of the Future: The Desire Called Utopia and Other Science Fictions*. London: Verso.

Jameson, F. (2009). *Valences of the Dialectic*. London: Verso.

Johnson, H. (2004 [1989]). *Story of Wine*. London: Mitchell Beazley.

Jones, G. V. (2006). Climate and Terroir: Impacts of Climate Variability and Change on Wine. In *Fine Wine and Terroir – The Geoscience Perspective*, Macqueen, R. W. & Meinert, L. D. (eds.), pp. 1–14. Geoscience Canada Reprint Series Number 9: Geological Association of Canada.

Karatani, K. (2014). *The Structure of World History: From Modes of Production to Modes of Exchange*. Durham, NC: Duke University Press.

Laferté, G. (2006). *La Bourgogne et ses vins: image d'origine contrôlée*. Paris: Belin.

Le Guin, U. (2016 [1989]). A Non-Euclidean View of California as a Cold Place to Be. In *Utopia*, T. More, (1901 [1515]), pp. 128–152. New York: Verso.

Levitas, R. (2010). Back to the Future: Wells, sociology, utopia and method. *The Sociological Review*, 58(4): 531–547.

Levitas, R. (2013). *Utopia as Method: The Imaginary Reconstitution of Society*. New York: Springer.

Mackinder, H. J. (1904). The Geographical Pivot of History. *The Geographical Journal*, 23(4): 421–437.

Marin, L. (1973). *Utopiques: jeux d'espaces*. Paris: Editions de minuit.

McGovern, P. E. (2003). *Ancient Wine: The Search for Origin of Viniculture*. Princeton: Princeton University Press.

Matthews, M. A. (2015). *Terroir and Other Myths of Winegrowing*. Berkeley: University of California Press.

Meinert, L. D. (2018). The Science of Terroir. *Elements*, 14: 153–158.

Meloni, G. & Swinnen, J. (2014). The Rise and Fall of the World's Largest Wine Exporter – And Its Institutional Legacy. *Journal of Wine Economics*, 9(1): 3–33.

Molnar, T. (1990). *Utopia, the Perennial Heresy*. Lanham, Maryland: University Press of America.

Nowak, Z. (2012). Against Terroir. *Petits propos culinaires*, 96: 92–108.

Olmo, H. P. (2005 [1996]). The Origin and Domestication of the Vinifera Grape. In *The Origins and Ancient History of Wine*, McGovern, P. E., Fleming, S. J. & Solomon, H. K. (eds), pp. 29–43. Amsterdam: Taylor and Francis.

Parker, T. (2015). *Tasting French Terroir: The History of an Idea*. Berkeley: University of California Press.

Ruyer, R. (1950). *L'Utopie et les utopies*. Paris: Presses Universitaires de France.

Smith, B. C. (2007). The Objectivity of Tastes and Tasting, In *Questions of Taste: The Philosophy of Wine*, Robinson, J. (ed.), pp. 41–78. New York: Oxford University Press.

Spurrier, S. (2018). *Wine – A Way of Life*. London: Adelphi Publishers.

Szymanski, E. A. (2018). What is the Terroir of Synthetic Yeast? *Environmental Humanities*, 10(1): 40–62.

Taylor, A. (2018). How then could we live? Towards the pragmatic creation of sustainable ecological habitus in cities. PhD Thesis (unpub.). Palmerston North: Massey University.

Teil, G. (2010). Testing terroir: beyond the controversy between scientists and winemakers. Innovation and sustainable development in agriculture and food conference, June 2010, Montpellier, France. CIRAD, INRA, Montpellier Supagro.

Teil, G. (2012). No such thing as terroir? Objectivities and the regimes of existence of objects. *Science, Technology, & Human Values*, 37(5): 478–505.

Teil, G. (2014). Nature, the CoAuthor of Its Products? An Analysis of the Recent Controversy Over Rejected AOC Wines in France. *The Journal of World Intellectual Property*, 17(3–4): 96–113.

Trubek, A. (2008). *The Taste of Place: A Cultural Journey into Terroir*. Berkeley: University of California Press.

Unwin, T. (1991). *Wine and the Vine: An Historical Geography of Viticulture and the Wine Trade*. London: Routledge.

Viecelli, C. (2018). Aesthetics, joy and responsibility: crafting 'natural' wines in Northern and Southern Italy. Paper presented at Wine Worlds, Networks and Scales: Intermediation in the production, distribution and consumption of wine, Université Bordeaux Montaigne, 17–19 October.

Webb, L. B., Whetton, P. H., Bhend, A., Darbyshire, R., Briggs, P.R. & Barlow, E. W. R. (2012). Earlier Wine-Grape Ripening Driven by Climate Warning and Drying and Management Practices. *Nature*, 2(4): 259–264.

Whalen, P. (2010). Whither Terroir in the 21st Century: Burgundy's Climats? *Journal of Wine Research*, 21(2): 117–121.

Wright, E. O. (2007). Guidelines for Envisioning Real Utopias. *Soundings: A Journal of Politics and Culture*, 36: 26–39.

Wright, E. O. (2010). *Envisioning Real Utopias*. London: Verso.

Wright, E. O. (2013). Transforming Capitalism through Real Utopias. *American Sociological Review*, 78: 1–25.

1 The four pillars of utopian wine

Terroir, viticulture, degustation and cellars

Jacqueline Dutton

Introduction

Utopian wine inevitably means something different to each person because whether something is 'utopian' or not is mostly interpreted according to individual tastes or shared values. When the definition of utopia was elaborated as a popular concept – not just referring to the title of a book by Thomas More – in the post-revolutionary fifth edition of the *Dictionnaire de l'Académie française* (1798), it ended with the phrase '*Chaque rêveur imagine son Utopie*' [Every dreamer imagines her/his Utopia].[1] Likewise, we could say, every wine lover imagines her/his utopian wine. It may be a 'natural' wine made from the biodynamically grown vines on one's own land in the Languedoc, drunk with friends from a bottle with no label or price tag; or it may be Domaine Romanée Conti Grand Cru from the Côte de Nuits in Burgundy, which is the most expensive wine in the world.[2] If utopia is in the eye of the beholder, then utopian wine is in the taste and values of the wine lover. The apparent subjectivity of utopia can be problematic for evaluation and analysis: nowhere is this more evident than in the extreme example of Hitler's Third Reich, a utopia for Aryan Germans but an anti-utopia for non-Aryans, especially Jewish and Roma peoples for whom it led to the Holocaust. However, as the definition of utopia has evolved in scholarly studies, new ways of defining and identifying successful utopias have developed, which may also be applicable, by extension, to utopian wines.

In the year 2000, the ground-breaking exhibition entitled 'Utopia: The Search for the Ideal Society in the Western World' that travelled from the Bibliothèque nationale de Paris to the New York Public Library brought together some of the leading researchers on utopia (Schaer et al. 2000).[3] Curatorial advisors and editors of the companion volume Roland Schaer, Gregory Claeys and Lyman Tower Sargent (2000) framed the Renaissance *Utopia* written by Thomas More (1516) with its 'sources' in text and image. These sources for traditional western Judeo-Christian utopias are grounded in four founding myths: the Golden Age of original harmony, the Platonic Republic of order, reason, and justice, the medieval Land of Cockaignian desire, and Millenarian hope for future rewards.[4] In general, western utopian literatures and social experiments have drawn on all four of these founding myths, in differing doses and combinations, to project their images of an ideal society on the crumbling walls of contemporary chaos. They are the four pillars that hold up the structure of utopia with harmony, order, desire and hope. If one or other of these elements is not present in a utopian programme, the chances of appealing to a broad cross-section of readers or social actors is less than likely, and thus the project is not widely recognisable as utopian. As Ruth Levitas notes in *The Concept of Utopia* (1990), utopias often lose their attraction and disintegrate into anti-utopias when desire is not fully explored or otherwise repressed in the narrative – one has only to consider Aldous Huxley's *Brave New World* (1932) or Michel Houellebecq's *The Possibility of an Island* (2006). By digging down to the ancient roots of this literary genre we can therefore distil the essential sources of social dreaming;[5] elements which must be included in these ideal projections if they are to be considered utopian.

Wine also depends upon a range of factors to pursue its ideal, each contributing to the quality and value of the wine produced. Grapes are, of course, fundamental to wine and the diversity of their organoleptic properties elevates them beyond most fruits.[6] The winemaker is at the centre of all winemaking processes, from deciding with vignerons on which sites are best for planting the vines to assessing how long wines should be cellared before release to be drunk. Apart from these cornerstones that grapes and the winemaker represent, the most salient aspects for quality wine production are terroir, viticulture, degustation and cellars. They constitute the four pillars of winemaking that must be present to appreciate wine fully, and without which the product's allure is markedly reduced. When one imagines a wine that is not made to be drunk with enjoyment by anyone who can taste (degustation), it is impossible to envisage such a wine as utopian. Just as utopia's foundations must be firmly anchored in the sources of the literary genre, utopian wine can be recognised only if the essential elements of terroir, viticulture, degustation and cellars are in place.

This chapter will explore the four pillars of utopian wine, first through a theoretical prism, then through a practical example. By tracing the lineage of utopian thought in parallel with the development of these four pillars of winemaking, I will demonstrate the clear yet perhaps unexpected correlations between the two concepts. From Golden Age terroir to the orderly viticulture of Republican reason, from democratised degustation in plentiful Cockaigne to Millenarian cellars full of hope for future enjoyment, the pairing between the four founding myths of utopia and the four pillars of winemaking seems practically perfect. This quasi-chronological approach to comparing the origins and development of utopia and wine, defining their contributions and identifying their pre-modern connections will therefore constitute a theoretical framework to assist in deciding whether a wine might be considered utopian. Focusing then on a case study of Bordeaux *grand cru* wines, I will examine the relative importance of harmonious terroir, ordered viticulture, democratised degustation, and hopeful cellars. In this way, the theoretical framework will be tested via a practical example to establish whether the four pillars of utopian wine are essential to achieve the status of a truly ideal wine.

Golden Age terroir

The Golden Age refers to a past era of harmony, peace, and abundance, where gods and humans co-existed in a bountiful nature before mortal disobedience enacted successive periods of degradation to result in the compromised state of contemporary life (Heinberg 1989; Lovejoy & Boas 1965). Essentially a creation myth, it expresses archetypes such as the perfection of beginnings, nostalgia for paradise lost, and features in most human cultures throughout the world. Judeo-Christian variations include the Garden of Eden and Atlantis, while Amerindian tales of *Eldorado*, Japanese stories of *Tokoyo no kuni,* Hindu visions of *Krita Yuga* and Islamic gardens of *Jannah* all resonate with the same strains of peace, harmony and abundance (Dutton 2010). It is no coincidence that the first mentions of the Golden Age in Greek and Roman texts appear alongside the first western treatises on agriculture and viticulture, which also provide initial indications of the concept of terroir.

The Greek poet Hesiod, a contemporary of Homer writing between 750–650 BCE, begins his most famous epic *Works and Days* with a description of the five ages of humanity, inaugurated by the Golden Age:

> In the very beginning, a Golden Generation of shining-faced humans
> was made by the immortals who abide in Olympian homes.
> They were in the time of Kronos, when he was king over the sky.
> They lived like gods, having a *thumos* without anxieties,
> without labor and woe. Nor did wretched old age
> weigh upon them. Their feet and hands did not change,
> and they had good times at feasts, exempt from all evils.
> And when they died, it was as if they were overcome by sleep. All manner
>   of good
> things belonged to them. And the grain-giving earth, without prompting,
> bore produce aplenty. And they, placidly
> and in serenity, lived off their fields, amidst much material wealth.
>
> (109–119)[7]

Though wine is not an explicit element, 'all manner of good things' for feasting and serenity indicates that wine like food was freely available. According to Hesiod, in the contemporary era of degradation – the Iron Age, these riches can only be enjoyed through working the land, so the way back to the Golden Age is good agriculture and good viticulture. *Works and Days* explains not only the state of original grace, but also presents a guide to reclaiming those benefits lost long ago. As Tim Unwin points out in *Wine and the Vine* (1991), Hesiod advises his brother Perses on the best time for picking grapes in his native Boeotia, as well as on the process of vinification, using a sun-drying method to concentrate the sugars like an Italian *passito* wine:

> But when Orion and Sirius reach the middle of the sky [at dawn],
> and when rosy-fingered Dawn sees Arcturus,
> then it is, Perses, that you should cut off and take home all the grape-
>   clusters.
> Show them to the sun ten days and ten nights.
> Then shade them over for five more, and, on the sixth, draw off into jars
> the gifts of joyous Dionysus.
>
> (609–614)

There are other viticultural directives, like pruning vines before Spring (568–570), and the best times for opening wine-jars and consuming their contents – in Summer, under a shady rock, watering down the 'bright-coloured wine' before drinking it (582–592). Most importantly, Hesiod honours agriculture and viti-culture as a means for accessing the 'god-given' food and wine of the Golden Age, re-establishing a noble connection between humanity and nature rather than deeming labour a curse. This positive symbiotic relationship between farmer and land is key to French agronomist Olivier de Serres' influential *Théâtre d'Agri-culture* (1600) in which he cites Hesiod's philosophy at length, inspiring Thomas Parker in *Tasting French Terroir* to interpret de Serres' (and Hesiod's) approach as an 'ethical construct' (2015: 52): linking god(s), humans and land through the understanding of terroir.

Terroir is more evidently linked to the Golden Age in the writings of the Roman poet Virgil. Much has been made of Virgil's commentaries on viti-culture for quality winemaking in his *Georgics* (29 BCE) including in the work of Tim Unwin (1991), Jancis Robinson (1999), Thomas Parker (2015), and Mark A. Matthews (2015). The idealisation of agriculture observed in Hesiod's *Works and Days* is further enhanced in Virgil's *Georgics*, which depict an 'agricultural golden age' (Johnston 1980), in a lyrical account of farm life that nevertheless reflected Roman viticultural practices (Unwin 1991: 88). In the first book, Virgil mentions that rivers flowed with wine in the Golden Age, stopped by Jupiter in the Iron Age (1.132), and that the earth bore all things needed with no human effort (1.125–128).[8] The second book is addressed to Bacchus, Roman god of wine, describing how to achieve har-mony again by making wine using the best viticultural practices: with vines in aligned rows like a legion of Roman soldiers (2.273–288), noting the right times for planting, pruning, turning the vineyard soil, and clearing other vegetation (2.397–400). Patricia A. Johnston emphasises Virgil's causal links between good winemaking and the coming of a new Golden Age through reference to Saturnus the farmer (2.542) (Johnston 1999: 210).

Virgil's statement '*Bacchus amat colles*' (2.113), meaning Bacchus (wine/vines) likes hills is one of the phrases most quoted by wine writers to demonstrate ancient understanding of how terroir shapes the taste of place.

According to Robinson in *The Oxford Companion to Wine* (1999), Virgil's Golden Age viticulture was already referring to terroir-driven measures: 'A necessary connection between low yields and high-quality wine has been assumed at least since Roman times when '*Bacchus amat colles*' encapsulated the prevailing belief that low-yielding hillside vineyards produced the best wine' (Robinson 1999: 786–787). However, Matthews unpacks this wine meme that took hold in the mid-eighteenth century, placing it back into Virgil's original context which suggests that vines can grow in light loose hillside soils, but produce even more rich and fruitful wine when planted in fertile valleys (Matthews 2015: 14–16). There are subsequent references to intentional low yield, high quality practices in the *Georgics* though, such that vines planted on rich level ground should be planted closer together, and that slopes facing the setting sun should not be planted with vineyards (2.298). Instead of 'terroir', Virgil talks of 'talents' (*ingenia*) inherent in the different soils, and successful winemaking can only result from understanding how site selection and viticultural techniques work together to enhance the quality of wine.

In contemporary terms, minimum intervention, sustainable, natural winemaking might be the closest comparison to Hesiod's and Virgil's directives for reinstating the ideals of Golden Age practices. In regions like Burgundy, terroir rules, and the *climats* have been enshrined by UNESCO classification as world heritage (see Demossier this volume). Tiny parcels of land such as Domaine Romanée Conti are revered for their 'god-given gifts' related to geography, geology, topography, climate, which are tended and enhanced by the delicate touch of the winemaker who works in harmony with the terroir. Winemakers all over the world have embraced this seemingly new yet obviously ancient respect for the symbiosis between natural and human influences on wine.

Writers like Hesiod and Virgil therefore bring together three founding components for ideal wine – natural harmony, human knowledge, and the taste of place – as a panacea for the loss of the Golden Age. Winemakers aim to regain what was originally in balance – the harmony that brought forth wine from nature – through striving to make the best wine possible from the best places available. Whereas Golden Age terroir privileges 'god-given' gifts and human *harmony* with nature, the Republican order promotes an ideal of human *control* over nature.

Republican order in the vineyards

Plato's *Republic*, a philosophical dialogue written in Greece in the late fourth century BCE, presents the western model for an ideal city where order, reason, and justice prevail over chaos, corruption and commercial interests. Like Hesiod and Virgil, Plato refers to a past Golden Age in his works, but unlike these poets who mourn its loss and propose to work in harmony with nature (and terroir) to retrieve a state of happiness, he seems to mock the primitivist notion of paradise, preferring to plan for a new, better organised space where human community dominates nature (Dillon 1992). The ideal city therefore serves as a response to counter the Golden Age idyll, replacing it with positive representations of culture.

Plato hardly mentions wine and the vine, except as examples for arguing the points of restraint in pleasure – controlling consumption of wine[9] – and usefulness and uselessness of specialised tools, such as the pruning-hook for the vine-dresser. Although vineyards are clearly not an integral part of Plato's ideal city, domestication of the wild grape vine and its planting, trellising, pruning, then picking, pressing, fermenting its fruit to make wine for both sacred and profane purposes, are a strong metaphor for the creation of civi-lised order from natural chaos. The Parable of the Vineyard in the Old Tes-tament Book of Isaiah (5: 1–7) develops this metaphor of the orderly, fruitful vineyard that makes fine wine representing the faithful followers of God, and the chaotic overgrown vineyard as those who stray from the path. At the end of the parable, the correlations become explicit: 'The vineyard of the Lord of hosts is the house of Israel, and the people of Judah are his pleasant plant-ing.' This eighth century BCE text offers not only a distinct moral valorisa-tion of human order over natural chaos, but also reliable insights into vineyard maintenance in Israel as confirmed by archaeological research (Walsh 1998).

Republican order has both moral and practical value. It provides organi-sation for the best possible grape growing conditions. This is the practical ideal of the vineyard planted in straight rows, trellised for optimal ripening of the berries and pruned to ensure the most appropriate yield. The highly con-trolled viticulture that has become the norm almost everywhere today is a far cry from the wild grape vine that grows thicker and higher than most other non-tropical vines, intertwines in trees, producing small sparse berries, and mediocre wine with significant human intervention. Roman writers on agri-culture like Cato, Columella, and Varro confirmed the practical advantages of order in the vineyards, stating precise measurements between plants, which have allowed archaeologists such as Jean-Pierre Garcia to identify the begin-nings of viticulture in Gevrey-Chambertin, Burgundy, dating from the end of the first century AD (Garcia 2016). Aerial views of the digs show the rigorous rows and 'clos' (enclosures) that were to become a feature in Burgundy, and the rest of France also followed Roman prescriptions in viticultural order.

As much as these measures were moral and practical, they were also aes-thetic. The notion of highly ordered nature as a symbol of beauty appears from the dawn of agriculture and architecture and reaches its zenith in France in the seventeenth-century garden designs of Le Nôtre for the châteaux of Versailles, Vaux le Vicomte, and many others. Deemed to be a positive sign of progress in western societies, human dominated nature can be just as pleasing to the eye as wild untouched nature, depending on the perspective. Wine tourists, for example, rate the attractive scenery of a wine region, rolling hills striped with rows of vines as one of the top three reasons to visit (Getz & Brown 2006), and wineries have become one of the most popular sites for weddings outside dedicated venues. Viticulturalists and winemakers are equally enchanted to look out on the vineyards and see the order they have created, as Dan Buckle, currently chief winemaker at Domaine Chandon, Yarra Valley, stated in a recent interview:

> In fact there's a very satisfying thing to look out at a vineyard and it's a monoculture growing, a non-indigenous monoculture, growing in straight lines. And this whole order-from-chaos thing about straight lines in agriculture is massively gratifying to the human eye.
>
> (Sexton 2017: 167)

Whether looking out at the vineyards from within a winery or from a plane flying overhead, it is clear that nature has been called to order, in a way that is aesthetically pleasing, practically useful, and reflective of moral control. The Republican contribution to an ideal representation of wine is therefore in the order of viticulture. But where there is order, there must also be desire for the opposite, and this is clearly the Cockaigne impulse that materialises through *drinking* the wine.

Desire and degustation in Cockaigne

The Land of Cockaigne is a mythical medieval alimentary paradise, where food and drink are abundant in nature, not just in their usual forms of fruit, vegetables and animals, but as baked bread and cakes, cooked fish, meats and fowl, and of course wine. It is normally a secular society, where sexual expression – including female desires – is also encouraged and satisfied. Potentially inspired by Greek satirical poets' mockery of the Golden Age as in Lucian's 'Saturnalia' or Pherecratus' comedies, and ironically associated with the Biblical 'land of milk and honey' (Exodus 3: 7–8), Cockaigne appears in European texts from the thirteenth century onwards (Jonassen 1990). The French variant *Li Fabliau de Coquaigne* (c. 1250) seems to be the first written version, followed by *The Land of Cockaygne* in English (c. 1305), with German *Schlaraffenland* or *Kuchenland*, Dutch *Luilekkerland*, and Italian *Cuccagna* all representing the same projection of earthly satisfaction, either translations of the early French and English texts, or with culturally specific modifications, like the parmesan cheese mountain of *Bengodi* in Bocaccio's *Decameron* (c. 1349–1353).

In all these stories, the peasants' paradise diverges from the Golden Age and the Republican order in that it does not depict any transformative process or ideological shift that underpins material wellbeing in this mythical land. There is no balance or harmony, no order or reason, only desire and indulgence in Cockaigne. In the founding *Fabliau de Coquaigne*, the fantastical houses are made of fish and meat, the fences are sausages, and geese roast themselves on rotisseries in the street, basting themselves with white garlic sauce. There is a field of wheat, a sign that food does grow there according to the natural order, but it is fenced with legs of ham and roasted meats. Most importantly, there is wine, the best wine known:

It's a pure and proven truth
That in this blessed land
Flows a river of wine.
Goblets appear on their own,
As do gold and silver chalices.
This river I'm talking about
Is half red wine,
The best that can be found
In Beaune and beyond the sea;
The other half is white wine,
The best and finest
That ever grew in Auxerre,
La Rochelle or Tonnerre.[10]

Everything can be eaten and drunk for free, without remorse, logic or compensation, nor any knowledge of where it has come from. Not only has the cultural order been turned on its head, making rare food and drink normally reserved for aristocrats ubiquitously available, but the natural order has been usurped by culture. When the biological laws of nature are so deranged that animals offer themselves for human consumption, fully prepared and cooked, clearly both nature and culture have been colonised by human desire. As Karma Lochrie describes it: 'Nature in Cocagne performs in drag so to speak, *as culture*' (2016: 63).

Similar inversions of cultural and natural norms are observable in François Rabelais' ode to desire, *Gargantua and Pantagruel* (c. 1532–1564), crystallised in the Thelemites' maxim 'Do what thou wilt' (Book 2, Chapter 57). These inhabitants of the Abbey of Theleme, built by Gargantua, are not just monks but nuns as well, only good-looking ones, living together in joy and distraction instead of hypocrisy and guilt. By indulging their wishes, they become more honest, as the narrator observes in a much-quoted phrase: 'We always long for forbidden things, and desire what is denied us' (Book 2, Chapter 57). Amongst the activities normally frowned upon that are embraced in the Abbey are drinking – as much as one wants – and dancing. Excessive wine drinking is a feature of Rabelais' work, challenging current norms – both the cultural (good manners) and natural (biological capacity). The giant Gargantua consumes huge amounts of charcuterie and mustard followed by 'a horrible draught of white wine for the ease of his kidneys', the narrator adding, 'As for his drinking, he had in that neither end nor rule.' (Book 1, Chapter 21). But Rabelais' descriptions of feasting are not just about excess; he is one of the first French authors to play with notions of terroir. He violates territorial naming rights by attributing wine from Véron, near Chinon in the Loire Valley to the Bretons, who 'take over' this wine by virtue of their preference for drinking it in excessive quantities. As Parker states in his chapter dedicated to Rabelais' Table, 'Such transgression of borders (both geographical borders and the social borders of good taste) ultimately reaffirms the existence of the identities those borders frame.' (2015: 17). Rabelais therefore continues the Cockaigne legacy in *Gargantua and Pantagruel* blurring the lines of nature and culture and challenging any order that they might represent, through the expressions of human desire to consume food and drink.

Contemporary articulations of Cockaigne's topsy-turvy desire to drink in an unorthodox cultural and natural framework can be observed in the development of degustation practices and their subsequent democratisation in wine festivals and public tasting events. *Dégustation* is the French term used for tasting wine, adopted into most European languages as well as English, though in English it is often also understood to mean a long, elaborate meal of many different courses with wines matched to each. Degustations can be professional tastings whereby judges award medals based on quality, or tasters rank the wines for guides, or sommeliers choose wines for their restaurants. In this context, many wines, sometimes hundreds, are tasted, but cultural practice dictates that the natural order of drinking and swallowing is disturbed as the wine is tasted then spat out – even though spitting is a cultural taboo in most western cultures. Obviously, if this unnatural ritual were not observed, another cultural taboo would be shattered by excessive consumption of alcohol and inebriation in a professional forum. Similar norms apply in the case of non-professional degustations for a targeted public in wine stores, or wine tourists in wineries, but transgressions towards consumption and inebriation are more often observed. When degustation is democratised in wine festivals or large-scale public tasting events, there is inevitably much more consumption and therefore inebriation than spitting. The carnivalesque atmosphere encourages breaking the cultural taboo of excessive drinking in a permissive 'Do what thou wilt' situation. The organisation of special transport options to and from and around such events points to a supportive and safe environment for desire and indulgence in wine.

Fulfilment of desire through degustation in Cockaigne and its more recent incarnations depends upon inverting the normal order of things, either with a substitution of nature by culture, or via breaking down cultural norms and democratising access to pleasure, especially wine. Culture's control – or lack of it – over human desire is the key to understanding this pillar of utopian wine. What balances out this unbridled emotion is hope, in the shape of the myth of the Millennium with its guiding hand steering towards future rewards.

Millenarian hope in the cellar

While Cockaigne is based on material wellbeing, the Millennium is inspired by spiritual belief: the hope that if all rules and rituals are observed, when the time is right, salvation will be won. Millenarian mythologies, like the Golden Age, are practically universal, ranging from Indigenous Amazonian Tupi

Guarani peoples' march towards the 'Land-without-Evil' to Jewish messianism. Western Christian Millenarianism combines the suffering of the Apocalypse with the promise of paradise on earth for a period of one thousand years, after the trials have been endured and before the final judgement. The Millennium therefore combines the eschatological 'end of days' with the chiliastic 'second coming' as expressed in the Book of Isaiah (24–27) but it is John's *Apocalypse* (c.70 CE) that detailed the form of the Millennium. Lactantius elaborated upon it in *Divine Institutes* (304–311), describing a return to Golden Age natural bounty:

> the sun will become seven times brighter than it now is; and the earth will open its fruitfulness, and bring forth most abundant fruit of its own accord; the rocky mountains shall drop with honey; streams of wine shall run down, and rivers flow with milk.[11]

Taking textual form in the popular late twelfth century writings of Italian theologian Joachim of Fiore, and his theory of the three ages of the Father, Son and the Holy Spirit, the Millennium is the most temporal of the four founding myths of utopia, both in a political sense and in its essential relationship to the passage of time (Cohn 1970).

Several political movements have modelled their doctrines on this type of desperation versus hope schema, usually involving a rebellion or revolution to enact the end of a repressive regime, like Thomas Münster and the Anabaptists' uprising against a sectarian German government in 1534–35 or Chinese peasant uprisings like the Taiping Rebellion (1850–1864). Religious movements such as the Rastafari, the Mormons and Jehovah's Witnesses are also tied to Millenarian visions for future rewards. Wine has little to no place in these stories of Millenarian hope, though it has surely fired up a few revolutionary spirits.

The Millennium is nonetheless a fundamental pillar of utopian wine, because every winemaker's journey is imbued with hope: hope that the vines will be healthy, that the rain will fall and the sun will shine so that the berries will ripen as they should, that they will be picked at the right time, that the juice will taste good, that the blends are balanced, that the wine will mature as expected. Evidently, great skill and knowledge are required to consistently make the right decisions in viticulture and winemaking, but there is always an element of chance – and therefore hope. Winemakers must also maintain a belief in what she or he is doing, obeying rules and rituals to reap the rewards of the harvest in the shape of a bottle of great wine. However, if winemakers choose not to follow protocols, breaking out of the mould to change the status quo, their actions are tantamount to heresy, revolutionary, seeking a rupture to bring about transformative change. This can and does happen, as seen in the introduction of New World technology in making Old World wines with more emphasis on oenological techniques in the 1970–80s, and the return to more natural viticultural and oenological processes since the beginning of the third millennium in 2000.

Of course, most readers of this book will have lived through the turn of the millennium, heard the prophecies, and experienced the drama of the 'Millennium bug' supposed to shut down global economies through a technology glitch. This did not come to pass but millennial terminology remains relevant today, predominantly used to refer to the generation who came of age around the millennium – the Millennials (b. 1980–1996). Although they do not have a direct relationship with the Millenarian mythologies or movements discussed above, Millennials do have an interesting connection to changing wine styles, leading the charge for natural wine. Much research has been undertaken over the past decade on Millennials' wine preferences and consumption, demonstrating higher consumption at a younger age, new emphasis on innovative labels, and increased interest in health benefits, sustainability, and the potentially deleterious role of additives.[12] Their involvement in wine culture is not concerned with the time it takes to make and mature the product, nor hope for its future rewards, but instead on contemporary pleasure, satisfaction and storytelling, in some ways more linked to the Cockaigne story.

The wine cellar is therefore *not* the domain of Millennials at this point in history. This place for making and aging wines is ruled by time. By regulating temperatures, winemakers can effectively control the times of the various stages of fermentation. By storing wine in barrels and bottles, they can observe the transformation that time brings, releasing the bottles on the marketplace after the rules and rituals of aging have been respected or the taste of the wine meets with the winemakers' approval. In the cellar, all the time spent on the wine from the vineyard to the bottle is condensed into hope for future rewards, and the launch of the wine offers a moment for recognition and compensation.

Researchers from the University of Burgundy have demonstrated that cellaring wine is inherent to two particular cases of winemaking: the *vin jaune* of the Jura, and the red wines of Burgundy (Gougeon et al. 2014). Their experiments show that Jura wines cannot achieve their distinctive taste without undergoing at least six years and three months of aging under a yeast veil (*voile* or flor), but also under controlled temperatures rather than fluctuating ones. More interestingly, they prove that the taste of place – terroir – is not just relevant to viticulture and oenology. Aging is required to identify and enhance the typicity of wine displaying the signature characteristics of the *climats* in Burgundy, as observed over three to five years of cellaring the wine.

The aging process in winemakers' cellars contributes to hope in quality wines for the producer, but there is also an aging process in consumers' cellars that prolongs this hopeful waiting for the best possible experience. The contents of private wine cellars illustrate consumers' willingness (or not) to adhere to the rules and rituals of the correct aging time before accessing the rewards they have 'earned' through waiting. These wine coffers often display immense status and privilege, with some buyers not ever intending to consume their purchases, waiting instead for the financial rewards of selling the mature wines.

Another Millenarian aspect of wine is the futuristic vision winemakers need to embrace in order to forecast changes in taste and to respond to those changes. They can project forward by planting grape varieties better adapted to future climactic conditions, but also to new fashions in taste – perhaps a shift from Sauvignon Blanc to Pinot Grigio, or a renewed interest in rosé. The wines that are aging in their cellars also need to be tasted and assessed in light of changing trends, such as the rise of high-alcohol, fruit-driven Shiraz and Merlot in the 1990–2000s, now losing ground to more subtle blends. Winemaker Anselme Selosse risked waiting nearly 15 years to release his 2005 Jacques Selosse Blanc de Blancs Grand Cru Millésime champagne, but his maverick vision and hope for acceptance of terroir-driven champagne have been rewarded by high praise and prices.

Although the early stories of the Millennium are unrelated to wine, its framing narrative traces a pathway that corresponds to temporal delays and hope required in making wine, especially in the cellaring process. All of these four founding myths of utopia contribute to fashioning a method for imagining an ideal society that is more complete and balanced than each of its constituent parts. Likewise, they also constitute the four pillars of utopian wine, which should possess an ideal mix of harmonious terroir, ordered viticulture, democratised degustation, and hopeful cellars (and sellers). These parameters will now be applied to a brief case study of Bordeaux *grand cru* wines to ascertain whether they are indeed utopian wines according to this schema.

Bordeaux's *grand cru* wines: utopian ideal?

Bordeaux is best known for its *grand cru* wines, which were formally selected in the 1855 Classification for the Paris Exhibition, though similar systems had been in place to evaluate wines up to two centuries before. The 1855 Classification was based on consistent price points achieved across a number of vintages, ranking 61 red wines from the Left Bank, mainly the Médoc region, in five categories from first classed growths at the top to fifth at the bottom, and 26 white wines from the Sauternes and Barsac regions in the same way, except Château d'Yquem stood out on its own as a Superior first growth. There have been no changes to this classification, except the entry of Château Cantemerle, an omission rectified immediately after its launch, and the upgrading of Château Mouton-Rothschild from second to first classed growth in 1973. This classification is in itself utopian, in the sense that it is a fixed blueprint for the ideal wines of the region. It has been capitalised upon to optimise the positive discourse and to increase the desirability of these wines. Delving deeper into the constituent elements of this apparently utopian ideal may, however, reveal different realities at its core, especially in the case of the red *grand cru* wines, which will be the focus here.

Long before the 1855 Classification, Bordeaux was recognised as a producer of excellent wines, mainly for export, and grown initially in the Pessac-

Léognan and Graves regions around the city. The quality of this terroir was due to both natural and cultural influences, but essentially relates to a kind of Golden Age gift steeped in the harmony of natural 'talents' and human industry. Unlike these regions, the Médoc, located on the Left Bank of the Gironde River estuary, was originally a swampy exposed marshland unsuitable for any agriculture until Dutch traders began investing in Bordeaux in the sixteenth century. By the seventeenth century their engineers had drained much of the land to create the terroir that has become so renowned today: a mix of gravelly well-drained top layers with a base of clay then chalk and some limestone and sandy patches. Planting pine forests between the sea and the vineyards that were subsequently established in Médoc also succeeded in mitigating maritime climactic influences on the vines. Bordeaux winemakers are not widely known for biodynamic, organic, sustainable or natural methods. The valuable terroir of Bordeaux *grand cru* wines is therefore not so linked to a harmonious Golden Age balance of nature and culture, but more to human control over nature, as might be witnessed in the Republican order of the ideal city and its surrounds.

Order is paramount in Bordeaux's *grand cru* vineyards. The vines themselves are immaculately planted and pruned, on land that is fairly flat, so rows run in parallel for miles around rather than sculpt themselves around slopes as in Burgundy. An exception within the classed growths is the highest priced wine of them all, Château Lafite-Rothschild, which retails for over 800 euros per bottle, where the name 'Lafite' actually evokes the features of the landscape – it means small hill in old French – *la hite*. The châteaux are equally impressive, dating mainly from the nineteenth century. Amongst the first classed growths Château Margaux was reconstructed in 1812 and Château Mouton-Rothschild's Petit Mouton was not built until 1885. Their elegant gardens are designed *à la française* and manicured to reflect in flowers and hedges the care also taken in the other gardens – of grape vines. Château Mouton-Rothschild's website even shows a photograph of the 'zen-raked pathway' of gravel leading up to the building.[13] Fifth classed growth Château Lynch-Bages is currently undertaking major renovations on its winemaking facilities, maintaining some original features from the nineteenth century, but its most utopian attribute is the regeneration of the Bages village that adjoins the wine estate. Château Lynch-Bages owner Jean-Michel Cazes bought the entire village establishing his own 'ideal city' including a bakery, butcher, gift shop and café.[14] The large profits made on sales of most – but not all – of the Bordeaux *grand cru* wines mean that considerable investment can be made in improving every aspect of the winemaking process. From vineyard to glass, every effort is made to further research and development in areas such as disease management, climate change, oenological techniques, and fraud detection, so that order and reason can be maintained and closely monitored to ensure continued success.

The international reputation of Bordeaux *grand cru* wines certainly evokes desire, the desire for access to the legendary wines of the 1855 Classification.

Economic rather than cultural capital is required to obtain the status of a Bordeaux first classed growth buyer, but insider knowledge can provide opportunities to enter the market at other levels. Fulfilment of this desire is ordinarily reserved for the financial elite and politically powerful: rumour has it that Mayor Alain Juppé was 'tested' by the influential wine elite before his election in 1995 at a Château Margaux lunch where the exquisite 1982 vintage was served by the magnum (Saporta 2014). Degustation of the first classed growths is not offered at the châteaux unless wine tourists take an expensive guided tour and book well in advance. Depending on the status of the other classed growths, entrance and degustation may be allowed, but hardly on a democratised scale, and certainly according to the rules and rituals imposed by the châteaux. There is a more open-access tasting organised by the *Union des grands crus de Bordeaux, Le Weekend des Grands Crus* at the end of May in Bordeaux, and at other dates around the world.[15] At this event, many owners and winemakers serve their wines in a festive atmosphere, so that the public can taste extraordinary wines from the Médoc classification and also the other Bordeaux classifications (excluding first classed growths) for a reasonable entrance fee – around 65/30 euros for full/concession tickets. The democratisation of wine tasting in general, not just Bordeaux *grand cru* wines, really happens at a five-day festival in mid-June on the *quais* of the Garonne River *Bordeaux fête le vin*.[16] This event has a carnivalesque feeling but does not offer access to the highest quality wines of the region. The most publicised yet most elite professional degustation that effectively sets the prices of new Bordeaux *grand cru* wines is the *En Primeur* tasting held in early-mid-April each year to taste the previous year's vintage. Experts from around the world rank and evaluate the wines before they go on sale the following month, in accordance with the trade regulations of the Bourse, with *négociants* (registered traders) buying their allotted amounts from producers via *courtiers* (brokers) who receive a 2% commission. Although a Cockaignian desire to overturn the system and flood the market with Bordeaux *grand crus* wines (or fake wines) or reclassify the 1855 classification itself does exist,[17] there is not much about the degustation of these wines that speaks of democracy and access for all.

Yet the *En Primeur* marketplace is a perfect representation of Millenarian hope for the future. Bordeaux *grand cru* prices are set and wines are sold two years before they will be delivered to clients. At this stage, they taste like tannin and wood more than anything else, yet the experts declare they can detect the promise of the wine to come and have been proved right many times. These wines often need to be cellared for several years to reach ideal maturity, and many of the châteaux have built hypermodern architecturally designed winemaking facilities and cellars to house the precious barrels and bottles that they retain for later release, and their own degustations. Negociants used to have warehouses to store their wine in the riverside quarter of Bordeaux called the Chartrons, convenient for bulk wine deliveries transported by boat from the Médoc, but now trucks transport their stocks in bottles to storage facilities in the cheaper suburbs of the city. This Bordeaux futures stock market has been captured in the 2013 documentary film *Red Obsession*, directed by David Roach and Warwick Ross, and co-produced by Andrew Caillard MW, a key player in the *En Primeur* markets. Both producers' and collectors' cellars are exposed to scrutiny in this film, showing the elevated status that Bordeaux *grand cru* wines afford to those who can purchase and mature them, and the elaborate displays of these wines that may or may not be consumed in the future. The rewards are clear – either financial or pleasurable – if the owners can wait long enough to reap them.

Conclusion

The four pillars of utopian wine, as defined in relation to the prominent features of the four founding myths of utopia, can be identified to a greater or lesser degree in the case of the Bordeaux *grand cru* wines of the Médoc 1855 Classification. There is a certain harmony between nature and culture in the terroir though centuries of geographical and geological manipulation suggest that human control is key to Médoc's successful terroir. Despite the fact that desire plays an obvious role in both production and consumption of Bordeaux *grand cru* wines, there is little sign of democratised degustation in the rarefied world of first classed growths, unless access is considered in an economic liberal sense allowing anyone with the necessary funds to purchase these wines. Both the Golden Age and Cockaigne are therefore marginalised in this case study, whereas Republican order in the vineyards and elsewhere, and Millenarian hope for future rewards dominate the picture. According to this schema, Bordeaux *grand cru* wines would therefore not be considered utopian wines if equal value were attributed to all four pillars. If they were nevertheless claimed to be utopian, it would be like approving a social project lacking in harmony and democracy as a utopian ideal. Such apparent contradictions have occurred, as history has shown in the Third Reich and other 'utopian' experiments. Bordeaux *grand cru* wines have many qualities and great value, but to become truly utopian wines, they must be more socially accessible and in harmony with the natural world. This conclusion resonates with popular opinion on Bordeaux *grand cru* wines, judged as being too expensive and not attentive enough to organic and sustainable principles. Château Latour is the only classified first growth that is organic,[18] and Château Pontet-Canet and Château Palmer are the only *grand cru* biodynamic producers in the Médoc.[19]

Drawing on utopian studies scholarship relating utopia to four founding myths, and research on wine history and contemporary contexts, this chapter has established conceptual connections between the Golden Age and terroir, Republican order and viticulture, the Land of Cockaigne and democratised degustation, and the Millennium and wine cellars. The theoretical framework comprised of these pairings between the four founding myths of utopia and the four pillars of utopian wine enables a more systematic assessment of a wine's utopian status; determining its credibility as a balanced representation of harmonious terroir, ordered viticulture, democratised degustation, and hopeful cellars. The case study of Bordeaux *grand cru* wines demonstrates the alignment between results of the utopian pillars test and general consensus around evaluating these wines.

In the end, the real question may be whether we accept that utopia is in the eye of the beholder, and by extension that a utopian wine is in the taste and values of the wine lover. If a utopia can be whatever we want it to be, then the Third Reich remains on the list. If utopian wine can be made in any shape or form desired, then the natural wine of the Languedoc, which will never be accessible to drinkers on the other side of the world, or those in tropical climates, or to more than just a happy few, also remains in the fold. Much work has been done to determine the parameters of utopia, and this chapter offers a method for shaping the contours of utopian wine. It has confirmed that the four pillars of utopian wine are essential to achieve the status of a truly ideal wine, and a wine that does not exhibit a balanced distribution between these pillars may only be considered as a personal predilection.

Notes

1 *Dictionnaire de l'Académie française,* cinquième édition, éditions eBooksFrance, Paris, 1798, p. 710.
2 Calculated by wine-searcher.com based on highest individual bottle price at auction combined with highest consistent average price range www.wine-searcher.com/most-expensive-wines
3 For exhibition websites: http://expositions.bnf.fr/utopie/index.htm and www.nypl.org/events/exhibitions/utopia-search-ideal-society-western-world
4 These myths are linked to utopia in most studies of utopia, including early French utopologies by Servier (1967); Ruyer (1950); Bouchard, Giroux & Leclerc (1985); as well as more recent English ones by Kumar (1991).
5 Lyman Tower Sargent (1997) defines utopianism as social dreaming in his landmark article 'The Three Faces of Utopia Revisited'.
6 Coffee and cacao beans (both seeds not fruits) are now attracting much attention for their diverse organoleptic properties linked to terroir (Scholer 2018).
7 Translated by Gregory Nagy, https://chs.harvard.edu/CHS/article/display/5290
8 Virgil's fourth *Eclogue* and sixth *Aeneid* are more focused on describing the Golden Age following Hesiod's schema of declining ages related to metals.
9 The etiquette for drinking wine at parties was further elaborated by Plato in his *Symposium* (c.385–370 BCE).
10 Translated by Paul Morris (2007), cited in Hilario Franco Jr. (2013), pp. 33–34.
11 Lactantius, *Divine Institutes*, Book VII, Chapter 24.
12 There is a wealth of research available on this subject (see Teague 2015; Thach & Olsen 2006).
13 www.chateau-mouton-rothschild.com/the-house/the-mouton-style (accessed 29.01.19).
14 www.jmcazes.com/en/jmc/history (accessed 29.01.19).
15 See www.ugcb.net/en/home (accessed 29.01.19). Prices tend to much higher for these tastings outside France.
16 www.bordeaux-fete-le-vin.com (accessed 29.01.19).

40   *J. Dutton*

Several efforts to reclassify the 1855 classification have been made, including by Alexis Lichine in the 1980s, as well as by David Peppercorn (2003).
18 www.forbes.com/sites/karlsson/2016/12/21/top-bordeaux-chateau-latour-goes-orga nic/#15db75e76033 (accessed 29.01.19).
19 www.pontet-canet.com/en/page/biodynamy (accessed 29.01.19); www.chateau-palm er.com/le-domaine/philosophie (accessed 29.01.19).

References

Bouchard, G., Giroux, L., & Leclerc, G. (1985). *L'Utopie aujourd'hui*. Montreal: Presses Universitaires de Montreal.
Cohn, N. (1970). *The Pursuit of the Millennium: Revolutionary Millenarians and Mystical Anarchists of the Middle Ages*. Oxford: Oxford University Press.
Dillon, J. (1992). Plato and the Golden Age. *Hermathena*, 51: 21–36.
Dutton, J. (2010). Non-Western Utopian Traditions. In *Cambridge Companion to Utopian Literature*, Claeys, G. (ed.), pp. 223–258. London: Cambridge University Press.
Franco, H. (2013). *Cocagne: histoire d'un pays imaginaire*. Paris: les Éd. Arkhê.
Garcia, J. (2016). Sur les traces du plus vieux vin de Bourgogne: une image plurielle du vignoble original. In *Rencontres du Clos-Vougeot 2015: Vin et civilisation: les étapes de l'humanisation*, Pérard, J. & Perrot, M. (eds), pp. 95–107. Dijon: Centre Georges Chevrier.
Getz, D. & Brown, G. (2006). Critical Success Factors for Wine Tourism Regions: A Demand Analysis. *Tourism Management*, 27: 146–158.
Gougeon, R., Roullier-Galle, C. & Schmitt-Koppelin, P. (2014). Le rôle de la cave dans l'élaboration du vin. In *Rencontres du Clos-Vougeot 2013: De la cave au vin: Une fructueuse alliance*, Pérard, J. & Perrot, M. (eds), pp. 13–18. Dijon: Centre Georges Chevrier.
Heinberg, R. (1989). *Memories and Visions of Paradise: Exploring the Universal Myth of the Golden Age*. Wellingborough, Northamptonshire: The Aquarian Press.
Johnston, P. A. (1980). *Vergil's Agricultural Golden Age: A Study of the Georgics*. Leiden: Brill.
Johnston, P. A. (1999). Huc pater o Lenaee veni: the cultivation of wine in Vergil's Georgics. *Journal of Wine Research*, 10(3): 207–221.
Jonassen, F. B. (1990). Lucian's *Saturnalia*, the Land of Cockaigne, and the Mummers Plays. *Folklore*, 101(1): 58–68.
Kumar, K. (1991). *Utopianism*. Minneapolis: University of Minnesota Press.
Levitas, R. (1990). *The Concept of Utopia*. Syracuse: Syracuse University Press.
Lochrie, K. (2016). *Nowhere in the Middle Ages*. Philadelphia: University of Pennsylvania Press.
Lovejoy, A. O. & Boas, G. (1965). *Primitivism and Related Ideas in Antiquity*. New York: Octagon Books.
Markham, Jr, D. (1998). *1855: A History of the Bordeaux Classification*. New York: Wiley.
Matthews, M. A. (2015). *Terroir and Other Myths of Winegrowing*. Berkeley: University of California Press.
Parker, T. (2015). *Tasting French Terroir: The history of an idea*. Berkeley: University of California Press.
Peppercorn, D. (2003). *Bordeaux*. London: Mitchell Beazley.

Rabelais, F. (2006). *Gargantua and Pantagruel*. Trans. M. A. Screech. London: Penguin Classics.

Robinson, J. (1999). *The Oxford Companion to Wine*. Oxford: Oxford University Press.

Sargent, L. T. (1997). The Three Faces of Utopia Revisited. *Utopian Studies*, 5(1): 1–37.

Schaer, R., Claeys, G. & Sargent, L. T. (2000). *Utopia: The Search for the Ideal Society in the Western World*. Oxford: Oxford University Press.

Scholer, M. (2018). *Coffee and Wine: Two Worlds Compared*. Leicester: Troubador Publishing.

Serres, Olivier de. (2001). *Le Théâtre d'agriculture et mesnage des champs*. Arles: Actes Sud.

Sexton, A. (2017). Crafting the Image and Telling the Story: A Cross-Cultural Analysis of Winery Identity in France and Australia. PhD Thesis (unpub.). University of Melbourne.

Ruyer, R. (1950). *L'Utopie et les utopies*. Paris: Presses Universitaires de France.

Saporta, I. (2014). *Vino Business*. Paris: Albin Michel.

Servier, J. (1967). *Histoire de l'utopie*. Paris: Gallimard.

Teague, L. (2015). How Millennials are Changing Wine. *Wall Street Journal*, 5 November.

Thach, E. C. & Olsen, J. E. (2006). Market Segment Analysis to Target Young Adult Wine Drinkers. *Agribusiness* 22(3): 307–322.

Unwin, T. (1991). *Wine and the Vine: An Historical Geography of Viticulture and the Wine Trade*. New York: Routledge.

Walsh, C. E. (1998). God's Vineyard: Isaiah's Prophecy as Vintner's Textbook. *Bible Review*, 14(4): 43–53.

2 To wash away a British stain

Class, trans-imperialism and Australian wine imaginary

Julie McIntyre, Mikaël Pierre and John Germov

Introduction

Australia's emergence in the nineteenth century as a New World wine country is the result of a British imaginary to make antipodean colonies in suitable climate zones into new sources of wine for domestic and export trade. In global trade, the Australian wine industry burgeoned as part of the nineteenth century dichotomy of Old World versus New World winemaking practices and business structures. This binary arose as a result of the disruption of traditions of production and trade caused by devastation from pest (phylloxera) and disease (powdery mildew) outbreaks in Europe (Simpson 2009). The world of global wine trade then, as now, was an economic and discursive space in which the Australian wine industry exists, but is not entirely encompassed. Wine industries are conglomerations of businesses in competition with each other within domestic and export markets. Industry histories therefore require statistical data to quantify and explain positive and negative patterns in profit growth and market share. For this reason the qualitative concepts of terroir and utopia are not useful frames for viewing the New World (or settler society) Australian wine industry of the nineteenth century, but they do provide valuable insights into the class-based nature of the Australian wine imaginary.

Australia's colonial period extends from 1788 to 1901, when the British colonies of the continent were constitutionally federated as an Australian nation. This chapter historicises the colonial Australian wine imaginary as a utopian determination to shape a more healthful Australian society by fostering a less British, and more European lifestyle, through the cultivation of wine grape vines and the enculturation of wine drinking habits. Using evidence of this imaginary based on European precedents expressed in publications by key colonial wine advocates, we also historicise attention to defining specialised localities for wine grapes, which had a small part in the language of wine growing advocates but was not then called terroir.

Terroir and utopia are both cultural constructs centred on imaginative narratives that some places or futures are better than others. The origins and transmission of these imaginings offer a window onto desire for change in a particular time and space. Utopia, argue M. H. Jacobsen and Keith Tester, is the philosophical twin of social theories of how to achieve a common good. Yet there remains scant agreement on what constitutes utopia as 'a better place' or where this better place might best exist. What is clearer, attest Jacobsen and Tester, is that the desire for utopia comes at a time of the fear of dystopia, or the experience of it. Dystopia is a place or experience that is (for the viewer or imaginer) unpleasant, perhaps even horrific, as a result of social, political or environmental conditions (Jacobsen & Tester 2012: 1–5).

As for terroir: in the French context, sociologist Marion Fourcade and anthropologist Marion Demossier have successfully parsed the cultural formation of claims that the nonhuman nature of Burgundy, in particular, is divinely-endowed and ideal physical environment for wine grapes (Demossier 2018; Fourcade 2012). In Australia, anthropologists Robert Swinburn and William Skinner, and environmental historian Daniel Honan, have drawn attention to the idea of *terroir* today as the basis of a powerful emotional connection between people cultivating wine grape vineyards, the places they live and the flavour qualities of the wine they make (Honan 2017; Skinner 2015; Swinburn 2013). As we have argued elsewhere, however, *terroir* is a term in wine trade discourse only recently applied to the practices of developing wine regions in Australia (McIntyre 2011a). Any attempt to ahistorically retrofit this idea to the colonial era overlooks the transmission of vine stocks and knowledge that resulted in Australian wine, along with traditions of inter-regional blending. As Jacqueline Dutton has recently shown, *terroir* gained its tenacity in French and international wine discourse as a result of the distinctive disciplinary marriage of Geography and History in the French academy that permitted geographers an authoritative voice on matters of wine history (Dutton 2019).

One of the most interesting features of the development of wine growing in colonial Australia is that it required trans-imperial exchanges of vine stocks and ideas rather than being contained within the British Empire, particularly (but not exclusively) from France. Furthermore, Australian wines were made to in some ways mirror European wines familiar to British middle-class consumers who dominate the historiography of booster literature for wine. This chapter is concerned with contradictions inherent in the Australian colonial imaginary envisaging the transformation of the chiefly British derived working-classes into people of other European nations that were other imperial powers. Elite colonists in New South Wales believed that creating a wine drinking culture among the British-born lower orders and their offspring could recast social behaviour from disorder to more civil drinking practices, and in the 1860s legislated to this end (McIntyre 2011b). This chapter shows that this idea of the transformative qualities of wine also existed in colonial Australia more broadly.

A few words are due on the idea of Australia as a New World wine industry. As an overview: experimentation in growing wine grapes in Australia began at the outset of British colonisation in 1788, with a very small quantity of wine made as early as 1792. By the 1860s the three British wine producing colonies of Australia – South Australia, New South Wales and Victoria – had achieved the economic definition of a wine industry, far from the geographical Old World of Europe. Many family wine businesses competed to sell their products in the domestic market, although vineyards were not yet the sole pursuit of any settler landowner (McIntyre 2012). During this time, unlike the tradition among European imperial powers to refer to the colonised Americas as the New World, Britain did not call Australia a New World, nor did settler Australians refer to themselves in this way. Then, also in the 1860s, powdery mildew and phylloxera were inadvertently transferred from the American New World into Europe's wine lands, and began to spread. By the 1880s, these infestations caused the loss of an estimated two-thirds of Old World wine grape vineyards. This devastation forced increased wine production outside of continental Europe to meet consumer demand, changes which monumentally disrupted pathways and patterns of wine trade (Strachan 2007). Australian wine producers had low volumes available for export until the 1880s (Simpson 2009). Still, once a small flow of wines from Australia entered the globalised marketplace, traders in the northern hemisphere began to discursively configure Australia's, as well as America's, burgeoning wine industries as New World. New World wine was interloping and overly scientific in a competitive dichotomy of style and taste that privileged the Old World as traditional and artistic, which in some quarters persists today.

A British 'stain' of convictism and working-class drunkenness

At the turn of the nineteenth century, British aspirations to cultivate New Worlds were informed by theories of geography and ecology that led imperial authorities to believe wine grapes could be grown there on a commercial basis, along with a multifarious collection of other temperate zone as well as sub-tropical crops (Dunstan & McIntyre 2013). The colony of New South Wales was first established in 1788 on the Country of the Gadigal people of the Eora Nation with 11 shiploads of immigrants from Britain. Approximately half of the close to 1,500 people on the first fleet invasion voyage were convicted criminals sentenced for petty theft to transportation from Britain as labourers in a colonial project, for between seven years and life. The remaining colonists were imperial agents such as colonial administrators or military guards. As many tens of thousands more convicts were transported to New South Wales up to 1840, the idea of the colony as founded by criminals pervaded the imperial and settler colonial imagination. The Australian colonies of Victoria and Queensland were created from parts of the original eastern Australian colony of New South Wales, tarring each of these colonies – if less vigorously than New South Wales (and another colony, Tasmania) – with the unflattering brush of convict beginnings, known as the 'convict stain'. Convict transportation to Western Australia occurred until 1868. South Australia, as a British colony established without convict labour, escaped the convict stain.

This means there are some variances between the eastern states and South Australia in the nature of the wine imaginary as a middle-class desire to correct social disorders among the working-classes, but Australian wine imaginers were usually middle-class. They were professionals or imperial agents and well-educated landowners.

In early eastern Australia, public habits of problem drinking came to be considered to originate in the criminal as well as the working-class character of the founding settlers, although the quantity of alcohol consumed in these colonies per capita peaked in the 1830s and would not again be as high (Fitzgerald & Jordan 2009). Following on from the cessation of convict transportation to New South Wales in 1840, pockets of problem drinking with beer, spirits and even some wine again flared in the 1850s when the New South Wales and Victoria gold rushes spurred tremendous impulsive immigration into and around the colonies. Many failed fortune hunters sought consolation in overconsumption of any alcohol they could obtain. The convict stain, and the subsequent deepening reputation (if not actual dominance) of a colonial working-class drinking problem amid the gold rushes provides the backdrop for continuing middle-class despair at the instability of the lower orders from 1830 through to the 1870s. South Australia, for its part, retained a more settled and civilised social air. Even so, as this chapter shows, some South Australians joined the burgeoning argument for wine as a healthy alcoholic beverage compared with others, an idea appropriated from Britain.

In 1824, young Scottish agriculturalist James Busby immigrated with his parents and siblings to New South Wales. Once established in Sydney, Busby self-published a book called *A Treatise on the Culture of the Vine and the Art of Making Wine* (1825). He declared this to be the first book in the English language to address how to grow wine grapes and make wine from them, which had not taken place in Britain for many centuries (Busby 1979 [1825]). Busby gained his expertise on wine production from reading French publications and as a result of living for some months in the Bordeaux wine region of France. Busby's interest in wine growing did not occur in a vacuum. It proceeded from British government recommendations for colonial cultivation and represented a continuity of English wine drinking culture. Busby, like many lettered Scotsmen of the Enlightenment, attached much value to French wine production and sought to emulate it in new British territories. There were official reports recommending colonial wine production and Busby saw an opportunity to win a reputation that would secure his future through land grants in return for seeding a beneficial colonial export enterprise.

Busby in the *Treatise* believed the 'natural' role of colonies was to send raw materials to the centre of empire – that is, 'intercourse between a colony and its parent state, which consists of the raw product of the one for the manufactured commodities of the other' (Busby 1979 [1825]: iv). Colonial wine, although manufactured in the colonies (though presumably to be blended and labelled by British merchants), could be of great economic benefit.

Soon, however, in New South Wales – when presented with the actuality of very few gentlemen farmers and a greater number of lower-class settlers (often freed convicts) who were predisposed not to wine growing but to heavy alcohol consumption – Busby revised his stance. When he wrote *A Manual of Plain Directions* (1830), he adopted a less florid tone in his prose, in response to criticism from colonists who found the *Treatise* to be pompous and inaccessible, and hoped to appeal to lower-class colonials. He also predicted social and therefore economic disaster if the current level of drunkenness (from all forms of alcohol) continued. It is not certain that Busby intuited that, from a purely economic perspective wine – and as opposed to agricultural products such as sugar – export quality wine was contingent on a domestic scale of production that achieved a variety of wine tastes. He could tell, however, that there would be no wine without more people growing grapes, and more people enjoying wine, and he felt convinced that wine drinking people were more settled in their social habits.

In the *Manual*, Busby's rationale for creating a wine industry metamorphosed into an environmental utopianism to achieve social perfection with economic benefits. This is clearest in his repeated exhortation of a biblical ideal. 'In the state of happiness', wrote Busby, 'which is promised to the people of Israel, by the prophet, he tells them that "they shall sit, everyone under his own vine, and under his own fig tree and there shall be none to make him afraid"' (Busby 1830: 27). A future of bounty and ease would allay fears of failure and suffering. Coursing through this utopian vision is the emulation of what Busby perceived as a French tradition of planting corn and wine on adjacent lands, one for sustenance; the other for pleasure, as articulated by Arthur Young in an account of his tour through France in the late eighteenth century (Young 1794).

While an illogical slippage may be detected in the *Manual* between exactly which grapes New South Wales settlers should grow and for what purpose, Busby believed in the transformation of New South Wales colonists from their present lives of alcohol abuse, squalor and depravity to a more settled state through wine growing and drinking. Busby was not alone in his thinking that the introduction of access to inexpensive, low alcohol wine could encourage sobriety. This theory had a surprising persistence in colonial New South Wales policy making until the 1880s. Yet in Busby's case, the rhetorical shift to social benefits and idealism that occurred between the writing of the *Treatise* and the *Manual* is not as evident in his third book, *Journal of a Tour of Spain and France* (1833). The *Journal* chronicled his journey to collect a varied and largely pointless collection of grape vines which he imported to the colony of New South Wales (Busby 1979 [1834]).

Busby conceived the *Manual* in the most drunken period in Australia history (Dingle 1980). There was genuine cause for concern that social harm from drunkenness threatened social disorder, and that such disorder could in turn endangered the potential of the colony of New South Wales to fulfil its envisaged economic role within empire. Busby, for his part, certainly sought quotidian serenity rather than the looming dystopia of colonial drunkenness and poverty. Although he appears rather fatuous in the *Treatise* and in his letters to colonial officials, Busby's private correspondence reveals that the wellbeing of his extended family was probably his prime motive for intervening to encourage an end to intemperance in favour of the emergence of a prosperous and cultured colonial society (Busby & Kelman MSS1183).

Even so, Busby's efforts led to a brief surge in only elite interest in wine-growing and no discernible effect on the more populous – chiefly British-derived labouring class and small farmers whom he sought to reach (McIntyre 2012). Over the subsequent generation the coalescence of a more stable colonial economy and society again raised hopes for successful wine growing, and the health benefits of wine, and the need for transimperial exchange became bound to the wine imaginary.

A healthy beverage for mind and body

In 1843, colonist George Suttor produced a boosterist manual to encourage British settler capitalists to Australia and New Zealand with the promise (again) of an ease in producing grapes for wine, and oranges. In an instructive tone Suttor advised his less-travelled countrymen that 'the light wines of France are for a warm climate a very healthy beverage; they constitute the chief support of the people of the country' (Suttor 1843: 129). Suttor's observation was a rare public linkage between wine, health and prosperity until a generation later.

In 1867, medical doctor Henry Lindeman, a winegrower in the Hunter and Murray River wine regions of New South Wales, captured an idealism in the benefits to health and social order be gained from cultivation of vineyards for wine. Lindeman wrote:

> How soon our refreshing, exhilarating and restorative wine will take the place of poisonous spirits. We shall then rapidly become a sober instead of a drunken community... and when the law will allow wine to become our national beverage, thousands of acres now encumbered with the 'dreary eucalyptus', will smile with the vine, and another civilising industry will spring up in our midst to employ thousands of families in the light and pleasing labour it requires, and to attract a desirable class of immigrant to our shore.[1]

There are two matters to be drawn from this statement. First, Lindeman believed colonial wine to be a beneficial tonic for the colonial working community, as distinct from other forms of alcohol, including imported wine containing high levels of grape spirit as a preservative during shipping. People were going to drink alcohol, and low-alcohol colonial wines were ideal. Second, not only would the Australian landscape be transformed in a manner Lindeman considered to be desirable but 'a desirable class of immigrant' could be enticed to make a living from winegrowing if colonial regulations encouraged a market for colonial wine. This 'class' of immigrant was presumably not British as people did not have experience in winegrowing in the cold British Isles, although Lindeman may also have meant humble rather than elite settlers from Britain. Either way, he saw a link between settled drinking and an ideal settler society.

Lindeman employed labourers of the lower orders of society and had experienced firsthand the social flux of the eastern Australian gold fields. He desired these goldfields in particular, and the colonies more broadly, to be orderly and healthy, rather than unruly and characterised by what he perceived to be preventative illnesses brought on by drunkenness. Lindeman and other settler colonials were influenced by Robert Druitt, a British medical doctor who wrote on the benefits of good quality yet inexpensive table wines for the drinking public.

Druitt's press columns, later collected in a book, are among the earliest known advocacy for wine as healthful. He held that 'Civilised man must drink, will drink, and ought to drink; but it should be wine'. The moral properties of wine compared with other forms of alcohol were evident in wine as a nutrient. Although alcohol was a cheap drug, Druitt valued that 'one mouthful of Madeira or Burgundy will produce an instant exhilaration, because of the wine flavours, which no quantity of sheer alcohol and water could produce' (Druitt 1873: iii–6).

Like Lindeman in New South Wales, in Victoria, Hubert de Castella, a Swiss-born colonist (naturalized French in 1848 before coming to Australia), also drew on Druitt's works to support his opinion (De Castella 1877: 10). According to Druitt,

A cask or a few dozens of light ordinary wine, as Fronsac, Beaune, or Ofner, some samples of good Claret, Burgundy, Naussa, Vöslauer, or Auldana, and a few of white to match, as dry Ruszte, Hochheimer, Montrachet, or white Bukkulla, should form part of the cellar of everybody that can afford it and desires to keep out of the doctor's hands.

(Druitt 1873: v)

This statement was welcomed by De Castella, as Druitt set on equal footing French, German and Australian light wines for their health benefits.

Moreover, De Castella, like Druitt, thought that access to wine would foster temperance. De Castella used the comparison between working-class habits of wine-producing districts and working-class habits of as yet unproductive agricultural districts to support his argument. 'It is said,' wrote De Castella,

that the people of wine countries are more temperate. This requires explanation. In the provinces of the south of France, of Italy, and other warm countries, where wine is so common that it is – like water – within the reach of all the members of rural families, drunkenness is truly unknown. But drunkenness is quite common amongst the labouring classes in wine countries where wine is dear, and where the wages man cannot supply his family with it. For him and for them the public-house, the wine without eating, the wine with excess, is a tempting feast.

(De Castella 1877: 14)

De Castella echoed Busby and Lindeman that wine should and would become an everyday beverage. 'The day will come,' stated De Castella,

when, in Victoria, every farmer will have his one or two acres of vineyard for the supply of wine for his family, evoking as ideal the self-sufficiency of wine production he perceived as a norm in the south of France, Italy or Spain in the mid-nineteenth century.

(De Castella 1877: 14; see also Busby 1830)

Like Lindeman, De Castella witnessed the social disorder of the gold rushes, noticing that the consumption of spirituous liquors was excessive due to the tough conditions of mining. Nevertheless, De Castella admitted that wine seemed to have no taste or cultural appeal to miners as it was considered too light in alcohol content to achieve sufficient consolation from the hardships of labour. (De Castella 1861: 196)

Samuel Davenport, a South Australian colonist, was peculiarly concerned with the welfare of his tenant farmers (Nicks 1972). He quoted famous French viticultural expert Jules Guyot's report to the French Government in 1868, highlighting Guyot's argument about the wines of Auvergne, central France, whose daily consumption were held to have eradicated endemic sickness for some people.[2] To Davenport, this constituted evidence that wine consumption should be democratized in South Australia; that all classes could benefit from what he perceived as its positive effect on bodies and minds.

In Britain, the denunciation of all fortified wines (those with grape spirit raising alcohol levels to as high as 30 per cent, primarily from Spain and Portugal) as uncivilized began in the 1840s. Light wines from France were seen as the ideal replacement. This led to what Charles Ludington calls the 'great nineteenth-century wine debate,' pitting British middle-class advocates of fortified wines against those preferring light wines (Ludington 2013: 234–237). Social reformers and economic liberals believed that the British preference for fortified wines was politically constructed and that it could be undone by lowering the duties on light wines (Ludington 2013: 239). Richard Cobden, architect of the 1860 Treaty of Commerce with France, argued that the duties so far imposed on French wines favoured the consumption of strong wines with harmful effects on bodies and spirits, and prevented French natural and healthy wines from being consumed in Britain (Nye 2007: 32).

This debate naturally sounded too among the middle-classes in the wider British Empire, and especially in Australia. The same arguments were used there to promote free trade with France. Alexander Charles Kelly, a doctor and winegrower of South Australia who travelled through France in the 1840s to study winegrowing practices, published his first book *The Vine in Australia* in 1861, which met with success and was reprinted the following year. Kelly introduced modern viticultural and winemaking techniques to Australia, but he remarked on consumption habits in the colonies and Britain. He not only deplored the short-termed effects of British protectionist policy against France, but also its long-termed effects, which would have 'vitiated' the British taste in favour of strong wines from Spain and Portugal (Kelly 1980: 2). Eventually, this opinion won the debate in Britain and Kelly hoped that the recent decrease of duties on French wines would encourage light wine consumption in Britain and in the British Empire.

In the 1890s, some commentators continued to rail against the persistent preference for strong wine, beer and spirits in colonial Australia. François de Castella, son of Hubert de Castella, wrote a handbook on viticulture for beginners in 1891, in which he stated

> In Europe strong wines are going out of fashion every day and giving place to lighter ones; people preferring a claret of which they can drink a bottle without inconvenience to a strong wine of port or sherry type, which does not quench the thirst, and of which a couple of glasses may be taken with impunity. In Australia the taste for strong wines still continues, although lighter ones are coming more into favour every day.
>
> (De Castella 1891: 67)

Less optimistic was the opinion expressed in an article of the *Agricultural Gazette of New South Wales* in 1896, pointing out the distinction in drinking habits according to settlers' cultural and social origins.

> It is greatly to be deplored that in a climate like New South Wales, which is very much akin to that of South of Europe, public taste inclines towards stronger beverages than wines, such as beers and spirits. Our wines are certainly appreciated by the German, French and Italian colonists and by a chosen few Britishers, but they are 'caviare to the general'.[3]

Thus, Britishness still represented an obstacle to the rising of an established colonial wine complex and idealised wine-drinking society, on the eve of Federation. Another major concern was the necessity of shaping specific practices adapted to local conditions on the model of European wine districts.

Locale, transimperial transfers and adaptations

In nineteenth-century Australia, while the term *terroir* did not have the same meaning it has accrued in wine appreciation discourse in the present century, some notion did exist of fine wine qualities discernible from the location of vineyard plantings. As shown above, the early Australian wine imaginary was expressed in a colonial society disinclined to both the planting wine grape vineyards and drinking of wine.

In 1865, English geologist William Keene owned a hobby vineyard in the Hunter Valley and was president of the Hunter River Vineyard Association. As a result of residing in France for many years, and owning a hobby vineyard in the Pyrenees, Keene understood the historical geography of that country better than most other colonial Australians. He remarked that French specialisation in grape varieties for wine, vinegar and eating fruit had evolved over a very long time, and that patience must be expected in Australia before specialisations were apparent, although they should also be aimed for.[4] Keene also established a link between the Australian climate and the type of wine to be produced and consumed in the colony. As he explained,

> Now, our own climate and soil are eminently favourable to the production of these harmless wines, and we shall learn to appreciate them rather than despise them, as has been the fashion hitherto. Experience will teach that strong drinks are not adapted to our daily use, but rather those wines which may be partaken of as a beverage to refresh and not inebriate.[5]

Keene expresses here the necessity of re-educating colonial populations and teach them how to drink 'healthy' wine instead of strong fortified wines as a daily beverage. Also, the link between geographical characteristics and the sort of wine to be produced and consumed in a specific region could lead to the idea of terroir.

The physical environment and climate of Australia favoured the planting of vineyards and drinking of wine but not the social environment. In 1843, George Suttor mentioned the suitability of light wine drinking to the climate of New South Wales (Suttor 1843: 129). Later Hubert de Castella regretted that the colonial taste favoured spirituous and liquors, but also that colonists, when they drank wine, preferred strong fortified wines. 'Port and sherry advocates had taken up the movement. The warmest districts were proclaimed as the best to grow vines, and the men who planted in more temperate localities were pitied for their mistake' (De Castella 1886: 83). De Castella is presumably referring to himself and his brother Paul, having established their vineyards in the Yarra Valley, near Lilydale, north-east of Melbourne, a district known for its relatively cool climate. De Castella also admitted that he made some mistakes planting varieties unsuited to the local climate.

In the 1890s, a new generation of colonists and winegrowers in Victoria began to formalise their perceptions of the suitability of grape varieties to certain geographical regions. Hans Irvine, owner of the Great Western winery in western Victoria, described the challenges that were facing Australian viticulturists in comparison with their European counterparts. He explained that the Australian winegrowers had to find their own way to make a wine adapted to local conditions. He also acknowledged that experiences had eventually taught them the best types of wine grapes to plant in a specific district and the quality and taste of the wines which could be produced there. He concluded by saying that

> it may, therefore, be claimed that the first, or experimental stage, is past, and the wine-grower can confidently look forward to reaping an abundant harvest; the result, of course, will depend upon whether the teachings of the past have been taken advantage of.
>
> (Irvine 1893: 2)

The 'teachings of the past' is a phrase that recalls the twentieth century definition of *terroir* by French geographers as a result of long-lasting experiences after the preordained matching of traditional practices with local natural conditions (Dutton 2019). Of course, Irvine did not only talk about natural elements constituting the colony, but also about technical knowledge regarding viticulture and winemaking. Yet he underscored the environment (climate, soil, topography) of each district as integral to the quality and character of the wine from vineyard localities (Irvine 1893).

François de Castella, as Government viticulturalist of Victoria, had a great influence on the wine sector of that colony (and, from 1901, state). He considered that each district should focus on the production of a specific wine, or only a couple of different types of wine, with a few grape varieties cultivated in each area, in order to secure unvarying character and quality (De Castella 1891). De Castella was of opinion that the choice of the *cépage* had less impact on the final quality of the wine than the soil and climate (De Castella 1891: xiv).[6] Furthermore, in his mind, the name of the place where the wine was produced should be indicated on the bottle as the key information.

> Each district now has its Vine-growers' Association. Let all the vine-growers join it, and agree amongst themselves to produce one class of wine, or two at most – say one white and one red – and instead of the host of names mentioned above, the wine will then come to be known by the name of the district in which it is produced. We should have, for example, Rutherglen, Great Western, Bendigo, Mooroopna, and so forth. [...] A man will then have some idea of the contents of a bottle from the label.
>
> (De Castella 1891: 27)

A continuing confusion about grape variety names in Australia was one of de Castella's main motivations for advocating such a system. But more importantly, like his father Hubert, François de Castella had visited France and even studied and practised viticulture and winemaking in some of the great growths of Médoc, near Bordeaux, in particular at the celebrated Chateau Latour during the vintage of 1883 (Hardy 1885: 404). This experience certainly influenced his view on the best model for the Victorian wine industry.

[s]uch districts as Bordeaux, Burgundy, Chablis, Sauternes, Champagne, all produce distinct types of wine, and the names of these districts have become famous throughout the civilized world. At the Cape the depreciation of wine was so great that they had to adopt this system, which has so far been attended with most beneficial results.

(De Castella 1891: xiv)

De Castella highlighted the role of past experiences, adaptations of grape varieties and viticultural practices to local conditions and trade and marketing benefits that represented the commercialisation of colonial wines under the name of the district where they were made. He also established a classification of Victorian districts according to their climate and the types of wine they should produce – in comparison with European districts – with three categories: cool regions, on the southern side of the Dividing Range, most similar to Bordeaux, Burgundy and Champagne; intermediate regions, in central Victoria, corresponding to southern France or northern Italy; and warm regions, in the northern part of the colony, which would be similar to Spain, Portugal and Sicily (De Castella 1891: 21).

John W. Bear, owner of Château Tahbilk, in the Goulburn Valley, Victoria, was also in favour of reorganising the wine sector. He published a book to promote wine growing as an essential industry for the colony in 1894, in which he deplored the presence of what he called 'miscellaneous collections of nondescript wines' on the colonial market and described what would be an ideal region-by-region classification of wines. Like de Castella, he promoted a district-based wine industry on the French model.

Ultimately each locality or district would be known and represented by the particular class or 'type' of wine – whether light or full, sweet or dry – it was fitted to produce, just as is now the case in the different wine-growing districts of France.

(Bear 1894: 57)

Bear called for a more focused type of production in each district, from both economic and environmental points of view. The objective was to adapt production to local natural factors and producer supply to market demand.

Bear seemed mostly motivated by economic concerns rather than agricultural or even *'terroir'* concerns. Victorian wine historian, David Dunstan describes him as one of the most dynamic and intelligent leaders of the late-nineteenth century Victorian wine industry. But Dunstan also acknowledges that Bear was more talented as wine broker and industry organiser than as winegrower (Dunstan 1994: 212). In fact, there is no clear evidence that he or any other winegrowers or colonists wanted to highlight any expression of place or *terroir*. The desire to develop only a few specific wine grapes in each district was mainly the result of quality and trade concerns. Furthermore, other colonists like Paolo Villanis promoted blended wines from different districts to improve poor quality products. More interestingly, Villanis, like Irvine, Bear or De Castella, took France as a model to legitimate his view, pointing out that the practice of blending has been common in this country for centuries to improve wine quality, even in celebrated wine districts like Bordeaux and Champagne (Villanis 1884: 69).

That being so, some colonists' comments highlighted a distinctiveness in Australian wines' taste in relation to environmental factors. In 1890, Adrian Despeissis, an agricultural expert of French origin, became consulting viti-culturist for the New South Wales Government. That same year Despeissis started to publish articles on vine dressing and winemaking in the *Agricultural Gazette of New South Wales*. In one of his articles, he established the distinction between wines made from the same grape varieties but in different places, using the example of Cabernet Sauvignon and Malbec grown in Médoc and Australia. He stated that the Australian wine was 'more heady, less fresh to the palate, and less bouqueted' than its French counterpart due to the difference of climate.[7]

According to South Australian wine businessman Thomas Hardy's accounts of tastings by a wine broker and a wine merchant in Bordeaux, Australian wine bore a distinctive taste of eucalyptus from the species of trees that dominated the Australian landscape while Bordeaux wines of Médoc were infused with a flavour of pine-trees growing near the vines of this district (Hardy 1885: 106). F. de Castella expressed a similar comment about an 'Australian taste' of wine that he attributed to the debris of eucalyptus trees in the soil (De Castella 1891: 75). Some European connoisseurs said Australian wines possessed '*goût de terroir*', literally a taste of soil or earthiness present in poor quality French wines in the late nineteenth century.

Concluding remarks

Out of respect for Australia's first peoples we acknowledge that all Australian terroir exists in Aboriginal Country that has not been ceded by Aboriginal people to settler colonists. The remaking of Australia into a settler society economy and environment from 1788 was above all dystopian for Aboriginal Australians. It is from a settler colonial perspective that making a new colonial world in Aboriginal Country included making a new wine world. Settler colonial desire for a 'good life' entailed access to fine wine as an antidote to the perceived lack of convivial connoisseurship for the middle-class. And, as envisaged by these same colonists: access to ordinary, inexpensive wine served as a working-class alternative to inexpensive, binge-able, beers and spirits.

Much of Australian history is configured as playing out within the bounds of empire. Yet from the outset of colonisation the resources of other empires enabled the repeopling and environmental transformation of the continent, such as the creation of a colonial wine industry (McIntyre 2018). The colonial wine imaginary required the acquisition of knowledge and labourers from beyond British imperial borders through transimperial flows of people and know-how. These imaginers also hoped, in vain, that the colonial Australian working-class would become less British and more European. Australia as a wine country is by origin a combination of influences adapted in circumstances that recast ideas of wine as well as its materiality. By the end of the colonial period in 1901 although little wine was produced relative to other forms of alcohol, a continuing imaginary co-existed with a small but robust industry.

Terroir is not, however, simply a vineyard-facing concept. Its purpose is to inform the stratification or *classing* of certain wine regions in relation to others in the pricing and desirability of wine for consumers. Dutton has made plain the rhetorical origins of terroir among French geographers as apologists for the superiority of classed fine wines as place-based in comparison to ordinary wines from other districts. Following this line of argument, colonial Australia not only lacked sufficient wine customers to warrant the sophistication of classifications of French wines in the nineteenth century. It also lacked both the French scholarly tradition of cognate Geography and History that fomented the construction of terroir as a concept and a class of the academic experts in the disciplines that might have made this possible.

In utopian frameworks, prophets or imaginers 'remind the people that if they carry on as they are doing, the future will be exceedingly bleak'.[8] Those colonials we have discussed above deployed the prospect of a bleak future as their rationale for wine growing and drinking. Still, they were a minority even by the end of the colonial era when the persistent anti-wine culture of a predominantly working-class British people thwarted the vision of the wine imaginers. Ultimately too, structural forces – licencing restrictions due to temperance, economic depression, world wars and some poor government decisions on grape varieties and agricultural subsidies – meant that table wine, and widespread habits of wining and dining, did not become popular in Australia until the 1970s (Kirkby 2006).

Notes

1 Henry Lindeman, Letter to the Editor, *Sydney Morning Herald*, 25 December 1867.
2 Papers on fermentation of grape juice and on vine and olive cultivation, c. 1872–1900, manuscript, State Library of South Australia, Davenport family papers, PRG 40, 20. Actually, Guyot reported the account of the Mayor of Riom about sickness disappearance in the Auvergne's marshes, 'these insalubrious lands,' as he called them, thanks to the introduction of local wines in alimentary habits of the people. See, Jules Guyot, *Etudes des vignobles de France: pour servir à l'enseignement mutuel de la viticulture et de la vinification françaises.*, vol. 2 (Paris: Victor Masson et Fils, 1868), 192.
3 *Agricultural Gazette of New South Wales,* April 1, 1896, vol. 6, no. 12, 407.
4 *Maitland Mercury*, 6 May 1865.
5 *Maitland Mercury*, 6 May 1865.
6 This opinion was also common in late nineteenth-century France and represented a way to distinguish wine districts and growths from each other during the over-production crisis which occurred after the phylloxera plague ended (Dion 1990: 27).

7 *Agricultural Gazette of New South Wales*, vol. 1, no. 1, July 1890, 255.
8 Eagleton cited in Rigby (2012: 151–152).

References

Anderson, K. (2004). *The World's Wine Markets: Globalization at Work*. Cheltenham: Edward Elgar.

Bear, J. W. (1894). *The Coming Industry of Victoria: Viticulture*. Melbourne: Melville, Mullen & Slade.

Busby and Kelman Papers, Mitchell Library MSS 1183, State Library of NSW.

Busby, J. (1830). *A Manual of Plain Directions for Planting and Cultivating Vineyards and for Making Wine in New South Wales*. Sydney.

Busby, J. (1979 [1825]). *A Treatise on the Culture of the Vine and the Art of Making Wine; compiled from the works of Chaptal, and other French writers; and from the notes of the compiler, during a residence in some of the wine provinces of France, 1825* (facsimile edition). Sydney: David Ell Press.

Busby, J. (1979 [1834]). *Journal of a Tour through Some of the Vineyards of Spain and France, 1833* (facsimile edition). Sydney: David Ell Press.

De Castella, H. (1861). *Les Squatters Australiens* [in French]. Paris: Hachette.

De Castella, H. (1877). *Extracts from an English Book on Wine*. Melbourne: Still and Knight.

De Castella, H. (1886). *John Bull's Vineyard* [in English]. Melbourne: Sands & McDougall Limited.

De Castella, F. (1891). *Handbook on Viticulture for Victoria*. Melbourne: Robt. S. Brain, Government Printer.

Demossier, M. (2018). *Burgundy: A Global Anthropology of Place and Taste*. Oxford: Berghahn Books.

Dingle, A. E. (1980). The Truly Magnificent Thirst: An Historical Survey of Australian Drinking Habits. *Historical Studies*, 19: 227–249.

Dion, R. (1990). *Le paysage et la vigne: Essais de géographie historique* [in French]. Paris: Editions Payot.

Druitt, R. (1873). *Report on the Cheap Wines from France, Germany, Italy, Austria, Greece, Hungary, and Australia: Their Use in Diet and Medicine*. London: H. Renshaw.

Dutton, J. (2019). Geographers as Historical Authorities in Narratives of French Wine Regions. *Global Food History*. 5(1–2): 113–131.

Dunstan, D. (1994). *Better Than Pommard: A History of Wine in Victoria*. Melbourne: Australian Scholarly Publishing.

Dunstan, D. & McIntyre, J. (2013). Wine, olives, silk and fruits: The Mediterranean plant complex and agrarian visions for a "practical economic future" in colonial Australia. *Journal of Australian Colonial History*, 16: 29–50.

Fitzgerald, R. & Jordan, T. (2009). *Under the Influence: A History of Alcohol in Australia*. Sydney: Harper Collins.

Fourcade, M. (2012). The vile and the noble: On the relation between natural and social classifications in the French wine world. *The Sociological Quarterly*, 53(4), 524–545.

Guyot, J. (1868). *Etudes des vignobles de France: Pour servir à l'enseignement mutuel de la viticulture et de la vinification françaises* [in French], Vol. 2. Paris: Victor Masson et Fils.

Hardy, T. (1885). *Notes on Vineyards in America and Europe*. Adelaide: Thomas Hardy.

Honan, D. (2017). The Elements Are Against Us: Hunter Valley wine and the paradox of an enduring relationship between people and environment. Honours thesis (unpub), History: University of Newcastle.

Irvine, H. (1893). *The Australian Wine Trade.* Victorian Department.

Jacobsen, M. H. & Tester, K. (2012). *Utopia: Social Theory and the Future.* Farnham: Ashgate.

Kelly, A. (1980 [1861]). *The Vine in Australia.* Sydney: The David Ell Press.

Kirkby, D. (2006). Drinking the Good Life: Australia, 1880–1980, in *Alcohol: A Social and Cultural History*, M. P. Holt (ed.), pp. 203–223. Oxford: Berg.

Ludington, C. (2013). *The Politics of Wine in Britain: A New Cultural History.* New York: Palgrave Macmillan.

McIntyre, J. (2011a). Resisting Ages-Old Fixity as a Factor in Wine Quality: Colonial Wine Tours and Australia's Early Wine Industry as a Product of Movement from Place to Place. *LOCALE: the Australasian-Pacific Journal of Regional Food Studies*, 1(1): 42–64.

McIntyre, J. (2011b). Adam Smith and faith in the transformative qualities of wine in colonial New South Wales. *Australian Historical Studies*, 42(2): 194–211.

McIntyre, J. (2012). *First Vintage: Wine in Colonial New South Wales.* Sydney: UNSW Press.

McIntyre, J. (2018). Trans-'imperial eyes' during British imperial voyaging in the Atlantic, 1787–1791. *History Australia.* 15(4): 674–692.

Michel, E. (1888). *A travers l'hémisphère sud: Ou mon voyage autour du monde* [in French]. Paris: Librairie Victor Palmé.

Nicks, B. A. (1972). Davenport, Sir Samuel (1818–1906). In *Australian Dictionary of Biography*, National Centre of Biography, Australian National University. Available online at http://adb.anu.edu.au/biography/davenport-sir-samuel-3371/text5095 (accessed 13. 06. 18).

Nye, J. V. C. (2007). *War, Wine and Taxes: The Political Economy of Anglo-French Trade, 1689–1900.* Princeton: Princeton University Press.

Rigby, K. (2012). Utopianism, dystopianism and ecological thought. In *Utopia: Social Theory and the Future*, M. H. Jacobsen & K. Tester, (eds), pp. 151–152. Farnham: Ashgate.

Simpson, J. (2009). *Creating Wine: The Emergence of a World Industry, 1840–1914.* Princeton: Princeton University Press.

Skinner, W. (2015). Fermenting Place: Wine Production and Terroir in McLaren Vale, South Australia. PhD (unpub), Anthropology: University of Adelaide.

Strachan, J. (2007). The Colonial Identity of Wine: The Leakey Affair and the Franco-Algerian Order of Things. *The Social History of Alcohol and Drugs: An Interdisciplinary Journal*, 21(2): 118–137.

Suttor, G. (1843). *The Culture of Grape-Vine, and the Orange, in Australia and New Zealand.* London: Smith, Elder & Co.

Swinburn, R. (2013). Rethinking Terroir in Australia. In *Wine and Culture; Vineyard to Glass*, R. Black & R. Ulin (eds), pp. 33–50. London: Bloomsbury.

Villanis, P. (1884). *Theoretical and Practical Notes Upon Winemaking and the Treatment of Wines.* Adelaide: Webb, Vardon and Pritchard.

Young, A. (1794). *Travels During the Years 1787, 1788, and 1789. Undertaken More Particularly with a View of Ascertaining the Cultivation, Wealth, Resources, and National Prosperity of the Kingdom of France*, second edition, Volume 2. London: W. Richardson.

3   Liberty and order

Wine and the South Australian project

William Skinner

Introduction

In January 1840 the Governor of South Australia, Colonel George Gawler, addressed a large crowd of colonists gathered for dinner at an Adelaide hotel. The occasion was to commemorate the founding of the Colony four years prior. For its time, South Australia represented a progressive and even radical experiment in social planning (Bowie 2016; Pike 1967), and Gawler used his speech to highlight some of the utopian ideals around which this colonisation was oriented:

> There are two points essential to the well-being of a country – liberty and order (cheers). Unite these two together, and there is the greatest political happiness which can be obtained in this world. May they ever hold their true proportion in South Australia! – May this be the land of true liberty (tremendous cheers) ... But then the liberty I hope for is social liberty – not independent liberty – not that liberty by which a man says, I will do as I please, whether it is right or wrong – but that liberty which binds man to man, all uniting in social feeling for the good of the community. This is the liberty I hope to breathe in South Australia (great applause).
> (Gawler, quoted in South Australian Register 1840, parentheses in original)

Moving away from existing colonial models that saw Britain's overseas possessions as significant chiefly in terms of their material benefits and burdens to the Empire, the colonisation of South Australia sought to reshape the moral and philosophical foundations of colonial settlement itself. Anchored in Utilitarian social thought that held the maximisation of social good to be a moral imperative, the 'systematic colonisation' of the South Australian model instead offered transformative prospects for society. Colonies were reimagined as 'sites of economic productivity, social amelioration, and civilizational potential' (Bell 2010: 38); in other words, they were to be economically self-reliant, as well as vanguards of civilizational and moral progress.

As the success of the South Australian colony depended on self-sufficiency, the suitability of the land for agricultural production was foremost in the minds of its early planners. With fertile soils, good rainfall and relatively mild climate due to the moderating influence of the sea, the country on the eastern shores of the Gulf St Vincent had been identified as being particularly high-value, and it was here, on the well-watered plains between the sea and the Mount Lofty Ranges, that the town of Adelaide was founded in 1836. The crops that thrived best in this new environment were those cultivated in parts of Mediterranean Europe that boasted similar climatic conditions, including grains like wheat and barley, olives, almonds, figs, stone fruit – and, of course, grape vines.

Guided by this favourable geography, South Australia's wine industry has developed to become the largest in the country, now contributing nearly half of Australia's total wine production (Wine Australia 2016a). But the suitability of the landscape for vine cultivation and wine's potential economic benefit to South Australia only tells part of the story. As another extract from Gawler's speech below shows, wine grapes were themselves also thought to hold a powerful civilizational potential:

> Ardent spirits are truly the root of all evil. They are the origin of more than two-thirds of all the crime which occurs in the British Colonies, and it is a vice for which there is no excuse in a country like this. In a cold country like England there may be some excuse, but in this country it is the height of madness to drink ardent spirits. Look at Spain, Portugal, the South of France, or Italy, and you see nothing of the kind there. The drink they use in these countries is wine, and they are sober countries. Let us then follow their example and be strictly a wine-drinking community, and let all here use their influence to bring this about.
>
> (Gawler, quoted in South Australian Register 1840)

For the early boosters of the South Australian colony wine was a social good, and the cultivation of the vine thus became a moral concern. Drinking wine – rather than the 'ardent spirits' that Gawler sees as its opposite – was the mark of the 'sober' countries of the Mediterranean, and it is to these countries that South Australia, with its comparable climate, must look.[1] The agricultural landscape of South Australia was settled systematically in service of British Utilitarianist social thought, but in a way that drew specific inspiration from the 'civilised', wine-drinking cultures of the Mediterranean. In this chapter, following a brief discussion of the political utopianism underpinning South Australia's founding, I will explore the way the social imagining and practical engagement with the viticultural landscape remains influenced by these interwoven civilizational ideals. Ethnographic data, derived from fieldwork conducted since 2012 in the wine region of McLaren Vale, south of Adelaide, show that conceptions of 'liberty' and 'order' valued by early South Australian colonists remain relevant to present understandings of vineyard space, wine production, and terroir.

Utilitarianism and 'systematic colonisation'

In early nineteenth-century Britain the population growth spurred by the nascent industrial revolution led to a range of social pressures: overcrowding in urban areas, land shortage, and poverty and misery among the working classes. Seeking to find solutions to these problems, and unhappy with the way existing colonies like the Australian penal settlements at Sydney and Van Diemen's Land had developed – reliant as they were on the labour of an enslaved underclass – a number of social thinkers founded the National Colonisation Society in London in 1830. Here, they promoted the idea that a well-planned 'systematic colonisation', in line with theories of John Stuart Mill and Jeremy Bentham, could alleviate these social ills. In Mill's words, 'the planting of colonies should be conducted, not with an exclusive view to the private interests of the first founders, but with a deliberate regard to the permanent welfare of the nations afterwards to arise from these small beginnings' (Mill quoted in Souffrant 2000: 107). In 1833, Robert Gouger and a committee of other radical Members of Parliament established the South Australia Association to push for a new Colony to be formed along these Utilitarian lines, and in 1834 Parliament passed the *South Australian Colonization Act*, paving the way for the founding of the colony in 1836 (Bowie 2016: 36).

South Australia was, from the outset, 'envisaged and established as a model, convict-free colony, founded on principles of democracy and freedom of religion' (Santich 1998: 32).[2] What became known as the 'Wakefield Scheme' of systematic colonisation, after its designer, Edward Gibbon Wakefield, sought to avoid the problems that had afflicted the colonies at Sydney and Swan River, where rampant speculation had led to large swathes of land being bought up at low cost and a shortage of labour necessary to make the land productive (Whimpress 2008: 1–2).[3] While other Australian colonies also relied largely on the availability of convict labour, the South Australian system was designed to avoid the need for indentured labour or for ongoing economic support from Britain. Another key element of the colonisation of South Australia was the commitment to social principles of religious equality and liberty that were not present in Britain: that is, South Australia was to be a model of a new kind of society. Many of the colony's boosters were members of Nonconformist sects and promoted freedom of religious belief, as well as the maintenance of a separation between church and state. For many, then, South Australia represented what has been termed a 'Paradise of Dissent' (Pike 1967). Early settlers in the McLaren Vale region included Wesleyan Methodists, Congregationalists and Baptists (Santich 1998); aside from these British groups, the Colony also provided a haven for other religious groups, notably including the persecuted 'Old Lutherans' from Prussian Silesia, who founded settlements and farmed in the

Adelaide Hills and the Barossa Valley, which would eventually become perhaps the most well-known of all Australian wine regions (Ioannou 1997).

Under the Wakefield Scheme land was sold at a fixed price, high enough to limit speculation and low enough to allow 'small capitalist' émigrés to purchase agricultural holdings in the Colony. Purchasers of land orders were entitled to one town acre and one country section, to be chosen from the Land Office upon arrival in Adelaide once surveying had been completed (Government of South Australia & Primary Industries and Regions SA 2013). This totalising organisation of space represented by surveys of the South Australian landscape enabled an efficient distribution of land among the middle-class 'small capitalist' émigrés who bought 80-acre plots to farm in the agricultural areas surrounding Adelaide. Proceeds from land sales went into an Emigration Fund, to be used to finance the passage of young working-class people of 'good character' for employment in the new colony: 'chiefly agricultural labourers, shepherds, and female domestic and farm servants' (Wilkinson 1849: 89). While the colonisation of South Australia was limited to 'free settlers' and avoided the importation of a British underclass, the system necessitated maintaining a capitalist class and a working class under their employment.[4]

Imagining the landscape

For promoters hoping to attract new settlers to South Australia, the landscape of the new colony was often compared to the pleasant visual amenity and productive capacity of the English countryside: 'The country from Cape Jervis, up the Gulf St. Vincent, viewed from the sea, is exceedingly picturesque, resembling, for the most part, the finest parks in England' (Capper & South Australian Company 1839: 15). In making categorical connections between the 'beautiful' country on the shores of the Gulf St. Vincent and the familiar parklands of Britain, a visual landscape not yet physically 'shaped' by Europeans became encumbered with a thick layer of cultural meaning. Colonial engagement with the land in South Australia has thus been, from the beginning, an exercise in 'imagining landscapes' (Janowski & Ingold 2012) in relation to familiar, shared notions of how agricultural land *should* be. For new arrivals, however, the promised Arcadia remained distant:

> the South Australian landscape looked dreary and hostile; it was a hard land to love, and to their minds it needed to be 'rescued from a state of nature', civilised and tamed to conform, as far as possible, to the landscape with which they were familiar.
>
> (Williams 1974:4)

The first step in 'civilising' the landscape was in its rational quantification and division, achieved through the systematic and totalising processes of spatial survey and division. The second step was to bring it into agricultural production.

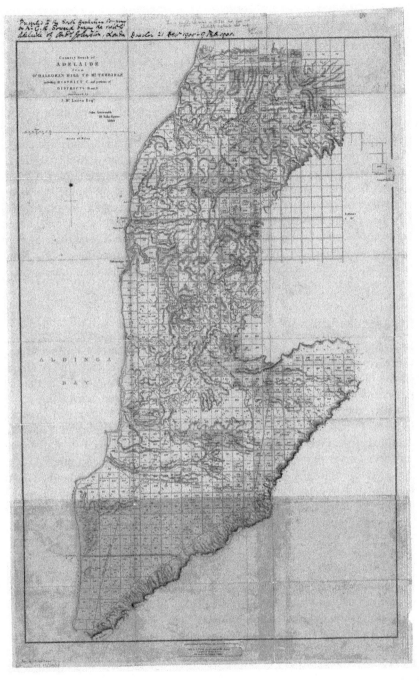

Figure 3.1 Dividing the landscape: survey of the agricultural regions south of Adelaide
(McLaren & Arrowsmith 1840)
(Image courtesy State Library of South Australia)

While comparisons with English countryside ideals were often superficial or misleading, similarities were quickly noted in climate and landscape between parts of South Australia and areas of Mediterranean Europe. Settlers wasted little time in planting the countryside with crops native to the Mediterranean basin: 'wheat, oats, barley, and other grain … plums, peaches, nectarines, vines, olives, oranges and other fruits common to climates in which these flourish' (Sinnett 1862: 21). Colonists identified, especially, the 'peculiar adaptation of our climate' and suitability of soil and terrain to winegrowing. As Stevenson (1840, quoted in Bishop 1977: 11) put it, 'I cannot doubt that the grape will, at no distant period, become one of the staples of South Australia.' Britain's Southern Hemisphere colonies in Australia, New Zealand and South Africa had been long recognised as ideal sources for the wine demanded by consumers 'at home', and indeed the very development of wine industries in these countries was dependent upon the global needs of Empire and those of the home market in Britain (see Anderson & Aryal 2015; Bell 1993; McIntyre 2012).

Most new settlers to the regions south of Adelaide were Britons with little or no winegrowing experience. Often, vineyards were just one element in a mixed-use farm, but some farmers saw economic opportunity in specialisation and 'launched themselves into this new venture with rash enthusiasm', with varying results (Santich 1998: 126). The process of trial and error employed by many of the first vignerons was not always efficient, as A. C. Kelly, a key figure in the early South Australian wine industry, noted in 1861:

> Vines from all parts of Europe, and the most diverse climates, were indiscriminately mixed in the same vineyard…. There are many acres of vineyard in situations as warm as Adelaide, planted with vines of Northern Europe, which proved so utterly worthless that they have been rooted out after ten years trial, to be replaced by the more vigorous vines of the South of Europe.
>
> (Kelly 2008 [1861]:11)

Many of the 'free settlers' attracted to farming in South Australia, however, were members of Britain's middle-classes, possessed some knowledge and appreciation of European wines, and displayed a scientific approach to grape growing and winemaking alongside their romantic idealisation of viticulture. Matthew, the proprietor of a McLaren Vale winery known for its Italian varieties, told me that these settlers 'came to the colonies educated and well-travelled. They would have seen South Australia and dreamed of it becoming like the Mediterranean, with vines, olives, figs.' South Australia therefore provided a framework within which British colonists could imagine and enact Mediterranean agrarian ideals in service of specific colonial-entrepreneurial aims. This was a rational project, the aim of which was to maximise profitability from farming, but one with associated aesthetic dimensions that persist to the present day. Early settlers viewed the landscape with a romantic gaze, overlaying the native eucalypts and kangaroo-grass with visions of Provence,

Tuscany or Portugal. Indeed, authors writing about the district still appeal to its picturesque 'Mediterranean qualities' (see, for example, Santich 1998: vii), and these are drawn upon in the promotional material of wineries and other businesses:

> The first British colonists were fully aware of the similarities between McLaren Vale and the coast of the north-west Mediterranean.... Today McLaren Vale folks like to think that their region on the Gulf St Vincent, patron of viticulturers, has 'the best Mediterranean climate on Earth'.
>
> (Yangarra Estate Vineyard)

Residents and visitors alike in McLaren Vale invoked Mediterranean ideals when describing the landscape. As Kate, a chef and local resident, told me: 'walking in between the vineyards, catching a glimpse of an old farmhouse here or there, the rolling hills, the blue skies ... you could be in Tuscany!' Importantly, this 'Mediterranean' imaginary transcends both the visual amenity of the landscape and its agricultural use. It also included an imagined parallel with cultural ideals, particularly in the integral links between food, wine, family and community. This image of a Mediterranean utopia preceded and informed the material scaping of the countryside, but during the mid-twentieth century an influx of new southern European migrants, particularly from agricultural regions of southern Italy, came to shape the social landscape of the Vale (King 2004). As Alfie, a retired winemaker, told me:

> We've really had a changing food culture since the War, with the new immigrants, the Italians and everything – it's globalisation, I suppose, it's really fantastic, when I was younger people just ate the same thing every day and every week. And it was only with that change that people started drinking wine with their meals – before that it was unheard of!
>
> (Alfie)

Symbolically, the 'Italian influence' in McLaren Vale is an important one. Interlocutors from Mediterranean and northern European cultural backgrounds alike expressed an admiration for the virtues of agrarian life that these migrants supposedly embodied: 'that real southern European thing about getting together and breaking bread, working in the vineyard or the garden, going fishing, making wine' (David).

The landscape conceived and viewed through this romanticised prism of 'Mediterraneanness' becomes one positively associated with an integrity of community, agricultural production, eating and drinking, and conviviality – often in sharp contradistinction to the actual experiences of prejudice and exclusion experienced by migrants upon arrival:

Figure 3.2 A 'Mediterranean' ideal: the McLaren Vale landscape
(Credit: Author)

> Being an Italian in the Vale in the early days was very much an 'us and them' mentality. Racism was quite strong – I was at McLaren Vale Primary School and at that stage I was the only Italian in my class. These days people are a bit more conscious about what's acceptable. It took a long time for the Italians to be accepted but it's happened, it's definitely a new world compared to how it was in the 50s and 60s.
>
> (Claudio)

A Mediterranean culture of temperate wine-drinking, and the association of wine drinking with food and family, has been a recurring trope in South Australian history. In contrast to the 'ardent spirits' that were blamed for many of Britain's own social ills, wine was for the early founders of South Australia the drink of sober nations, said to facilitate civility and conviviality and temperance. The production of wine was therefore represented as crucial for South Australia's *moral* development just as it was for its economic development. While alcohol was often viewed negatively through the upright and moralistic values of the dominant South Australian establishment, exceptions were made for wine, understood in very different terms as a civilising drink. Wine was important for social as well as physical health, as Matthew told me:

A lot of wine was grown for supposedly medicinal purposes. And in the early part of the [twentieth] century there were big temperance movements, but this didn't hurt wine production. I'm from a long line of Methodist ministers, and growing wine grapes was always justified because wine was 'healthy'.

(Matthew)

In McLaren Vale, grape growing and wine production has been successful to the point that it now dominates the region spatially, socially and economically. The reasons for this are myriad, but it could not have occurred without a synergistic match between a physical landscape favourable to the vine and the social and economic conditions that allowed the industry to flourish.

Exploring terroir

The history of winegrowing in South Australia is a history of entrepreneurship within an ordered system of spatial and social regulation, and in this lies an inherent tension between ideals of 'liberty' and a recognition of the need for constraint. This ambivalence manifested in the attitudes of McLaren Vale growers and winemakers to a range of issues during my fieldwork, including wine taxation, governance and management of water resources, land use zoning, and biosecurity regulation around the viticultural pest phylloxera (for the latter, see Skinner 2018). In all these cases, my interlocutors felt that regulatory and policy constraint on individual entrepreneurship was necessary, in the words of one viticulturist and winemaker, 'to save us from ourselves' (Thomas). Unfettered capitalistic freedom is seen as potentially dangerous, and as well as formalised, legal regulations, winegrowing in McLaren Vale is constrained by a range of social norms relating to the acceptability of certain practices. For example, producers' approaches to the use of chemical pesticides or fungicides in the vineyard, or irrigation water, is conditioned by broader sentiment that valorises 'environmentally sustainable' winegrowing; frequently, interlocutors expressed pride at the Vale's perceived status as one of the most 'clean and green' wine regions in Australia.

An important example of the way these community norms manifest in practice is in the success of the 'Sustainable Australia Winegrowing' (SAW) program, a self-assessment system allowing winegrowers to benchmark their practices across a range of environmental, economic and social values with a view to achieving overall sustainability of the wine industry in the region (Santiago-Brown et al. 2015). [5] While SAW is a voluntary program, there is strong uptake across McLaren Vale: 130 growers participate, their vineyards representing 44% of the region's total area under vine. Among my own informants a majority participated in the program and expressed support for its objectives and values, which promotes ecologically sound practices and regional social development, and draws links between these themes and overall strength and wellbeing of the industry and the region. Cohesion around certain practices and normative values such as those embedded in the SAW program is integral to an overall sense of regional identity, and this is seen to provide an important corrective to the potentially damaging forces of economic self-interest.

Grape growing and wine production are in the Vale framed by an implicit ethical dimension, and this extends to incorporate the social bonds between people that would otherwise be competitors. A community-minded coopera-tiveness is said to be central to the district, and producers will often actively promote other businesses that they see as aligning with their own values. During difficult vintages, for example, people will 'pitch in' together, lending equipment and sharing labour. Peter, a winemaker, told me that when he moved back into McLaren Vale to take over the family winery after working for some years interstate, he was helped out materially by his competitors:

> Arthur [another winemaker] immediately said 'Welcome back' and asked me if he needed any help, if there was any equipment I needed to borrow for my winery, and so on – no questions asked. There's a real community bond and sense of cooperation. People here have the mentality that if something is good for the region as a whole, it's good for them.
>
> (Peter)

While McLaren Vale winegrowers' attitudes include a (sometimes grudging) acceptance of the need to work within regulations and policies that exist for 'the good of the industry' generally, and an acceptance of the importance of complying with regionally-held social values, they also embrace the possibi-lities of creative expression and entrepreneurial freedom that are permissible within these structures. In many 'Old World' regions of Europe, where wine has often been made in very specific ways from local grape varieties for many centuries, production is subject to rigid labelling laws that aim to preserve the integrity of emplaced traditions and thus maintain their value (Barham 2003; Demossier 2011). This is not the case in Australia, where there are no restrictions on varieties used in a wine labelled 'McLaren Vale', other than that at least 85% of the grapes used were grown in the region, or in produc-tion techniques other than a requirement to use only prescribed additives and processing aids (Wine Australia 2016b). Interestingly, many of my inter-locutors expressed this freedom not in terms of *transcending* the constraints of place (as, for example, through high-tech winemaking interventions aiming to achieve particular flavours), but instead as a freedom to explore its possibilities.

There can be no construction of shared identity, however, without con-currently defining those values that fall outside its boundaries. While McLaren Vale producers are quick to align themselves with valorised aspects of regional identity, including ecologically-friendly viticultural practices and cooperative social relations, these aspects have their opposites, looming as potentially dan-gerous forces in the Vale's winegrowing imagination. For individual producers, then, the *perception* of alignment with the best interests of the region is impera-tive. Edward, a winery owner aged in his seventies, told me that there was an expectation that people are seen to comply with the generally-accepted values. 'If you don't comply, you'll probably be run out of town!' The degree to which winegrowers can chart their own course in the creative or entrepreneurial inves-tigation of their terroir is constrained by these anxieties.

The McLaren Vale landscape is shaped by diverse factors of climate, geo-graphy and geology: cool, wet winters and hot dry summers, tempered by afternoon sea breezes off the Gulf to the west and overnight 'gully winds' draining off the range of hills to the east; a topography of plains and undulat-ing hills; and an intricate diversity of underlying geologies, incorporating areas of sand and sandstone, clays, alluvial deposits, and ancient bedrocks (Fairburn et al. 2010). This is a physically complex 'terroir', and vignerons thus speak of 'working with' the landscape and growing conditions of the region, over the variations of each growing season, to gain an ever-increasing knowledge of these relationships. This is an ongoing process: 'even after a whole lifetime you don't stop learning about your terroir … we're still trying to best learn what we have' (Chris). This physical diversity is essential to local understandings of the region: McLaren Vale was often referred to as a 'patchwork quilt' of different and locally distinct patches of vineyard land, with their own soils, aspects, ele-vations and microclimates, each of which could offer different qualities for

Figure 3.3 Tasting and blending
(Credit: Author)

winegrowing. In the words of viticulturist Tim, 'I really think of it as an artist's palette – all the ingredients are there, and it's up to the skills and knowledge of the growers and winemakers to learn how to work with the specific conditions.' Other metaphors my interlocutors used to describe the landscape were those of a 'spice rack' from which different flavours could be selected, or a 'laboratory' for creative experimentation.

Terroir in the Vale is thus understood by my interlocutors in terms of an ongoing process of discovery, a creative exploration of the productive potentialities of the landscape to uncover the complex ways grape vines, place, and practice might best fit together. There is a general belief that a micro-level physical variability within a generally benign broader climate allows experimentation with grape varieties and vineyard practices to flourish and permits a culture of creativity amongst producers of the region. As Paxson argues, terroir in many so-called 'New World' settings is 'not an a priori quality to be discovered through selective recuperation of the past; rather, it is something to do to make the future' (Paxson 2010: 445). In the absence of a strong local or regional terroir tradition, producers actively set out to create it. This is both a conscious and an idealistic enterprise, seeking to draw 'meaningful lines of connection among people, culture, and landscapes to invest rural places anew with affective significance and material relevance' (Paxson 2010: 446). The expression of the landscape through the wines of McLaren Vale is expressed not only as a function of the interrelation of the vine with the soil and other elements of physical geography, then, but also of the ongoing activities, practices and decisions of people operating within the particular social and cultural milieu of the region. The true 'terroir' of a site lies not in static, given properties, but instead comes to the fore through its relational synergies.

Experimentation with vineyard and winemaking practices in the exploration and interpretation of McLaren Vale's terroir occurs within a general atmosphere of innovation and creativity (especially relative to many so-called 'Old World' wine regions), but it is tempered and constrained by a broader conservatism said to be part of the social and economic heritage of the region and the state. In the words of Dan, a young winemaker who makes what he calls 'natural, living wines', without fining, filtering, or additions like commercial yeast cultures:

> There is a great heritage of creativity, openness to new ideas, and cultural expression here. There is real creativity happening in wines that are about individuality, expression of site, experimentation. But at the same time we are technocrats, we understand the value of science. On one hand we have great old brands and a strong history and tradition, but on the other hand people are curious about new things and broadening their horizons.
>
> (Dan)

Dan sees contemporary winemaking in South Australia in terms of an interplay between the various 'threads' running through the cultural fabric of the state: a heritage that includes 'progressive' and 'creative' thought alongside conservative, moralising tendencies, as well as an orientation towards scientific rationality.[6] For him, as with many of my interlocutors, terroir – winegrowing *place* – is not just to be understood as a bounded microcosm of vine, soil, vineyard and vigneron, but extends into the broader social relationships and cultural ideals that impinge upon and inform this productive assemblage.

Winegrowers often suggest that the grape varieties that have been planted in large numbers in the Vale have not always been those that are 'best' for the location. From the late nineteenth to mid-twentieth centuries, for example, large tracts of high-yielding grape varieties were planted across McLaren Vale and surrounding districts for the production of bulk fortified wines demanded by domestic and export markets.[7] From the 1960s onwards, with increasing postwar migration to Australia from wine-drinking southern European countries, the associated rise of a domestic culture of drinking wine with meals, at home or in restaurants (Allen 2012), and shifting global tastes, many of these varieties were replaced once more by grapes oriented to the production of dry table wines. In the 1970s and 80s worldwide market trends led to mass planting of varieties like Riesling and Chardonnay in the Vale, grapes less suited to warm climate than the suddenly unfashionable red varieties like Shiraz, Grenache and Mataro that had historically formed the backbone of McLaren Vale's vineyard. A mid-1980s State Government-funded 'vine pull scheme' intended to boost industry competitiveness saw the uprooting of wide areas of these red grapes (Barrett 1989). Red wine quickly regained popularity, however, and it is largely upon these wines – present in the Vale since the earliest vineyard plantings of the mid-nineteenth century – that McLaren Vale's reputation rests.[8] As winemaker Andrew told me,

> I like experimenting with different wines, but I feel that it can steal from your heritage if you're too sporadic and chasing fashions. You should make wine in the style that suits the place. Grenache in McLaren Vale is the variety that probably stands out: it's lighter, quite complex…. It suits the growing conditions in McLaren Vale perfectly, but Shiraz is by far the most popular grape here. Why? Because of our cultural history. And for a while there everyone was planting Chardy [Chardonnay] and ripping everything else out – that's terrible, you have to respect your tradition.
>
> (Andrew)

Here, Andrew addresses one of the tensions inherent in notions of terroir: the tension between its physical/sensory expression (which grape 'best suits' the place viticulturally, or best represents the flavour of the place) and its cultural/historical expression (relating to heritage and the political economies of consumption). In his view, it is important to pursue a 'taste of place', but in a manner that respects extant traditions and remains true to a clear, shared understanding of regional values.

The construction of an idealised South Australian wine landscape, for he and other McLaren Vale vignerons, involves the ability to consciously explore their terroir, experimenting with varieties and wine styles. This exploration is done with an eye to the 'bigger picture' of an integrity of regional purpose, but there is a feeling that, in some ways, the regionally-shared ideals and values promoted by winegrowers in McLaren Vale are fragile and precarious ones. Implicit in this construction of a discrete identity and purpose for the region is a notion that some practices and values fall outside these boundaries. Practices like those relating to environmentally sustainable or historically appropriate viticulture, or cooperation between wineries, are imagined in large part with relation to 'what we are not', with a persistent anxiety that these values may be undermined or weakened by external social influences or economic demands.

Conclusion

The settlement of the South Australian landscape was idealistic and aspirational, a utopian project aiming to regulate and impose a specific form of social order upon what was previously considered an 'uncivilised' wilderness. For the early colonial founders, liberty was a crucial concept: this liberty was not to be found in the lack of regulation of the individual, however, but in the order that brings citizens into community with one another around a set of shared goals and values. These values included industriousness, entrepreneurship, temperance, and – within limits – a socially-minded outlook oriented towards the 'common good'. With connotations of civilizational progress, sobriety, health, and sophistication, and value as a trade commodity, wine was perfectly suited to both the physical and moral climate of the new colony, and also offered opportunity for its economic enrichment. While many of the initial principles of colonisation were eventually modified or abandoned, there remains an acknowledgement within South Australia that these values have, in many important respects, filtered through history to influence present social attitudes. In McLaren Vale, I have argued, vestiges of this are evident in the structuring and practice of the present-day wine industry.

In the Vale's social history, we can see a historical interplay between two forces: the highly planned, bureaucratic division of space and regulation of society that the founders of the South Australian colony implemented when settling the landscape, and the 'freedoms' of creative and entrepreneurial practice that this planning was intended to achieve. Such social planning enabled the development of an industry that is now relatively heterogeneous, encompassing a spectrum of approaches and practices and supporting a coexistence of producers at a range of scales and operational models, from one-person businesses to large multinational joint-stock corporations. But the entrepreneurial freedoms accessible to McLaren Vale winegrowers have limits – in formal, regulatory and legal terms and, importantly, in terms of social expectations. Moreover, few of my informants would consider the removal of these sorts of constraints on practice to be ultimately beneficial for the industry as a whole. Freedom occurs within the bounds of acceptable social practice. This, in McLaren Vale, has a crucial moral dimension: those who seek personal gain at the expense of regional benefits and integrity are looked dimly upon, and it is for this reason that boundaries around acceptable practice are vigilantly monitored, maintained and reinforced.

Notes

1 Cultivation of the wine grapes was seen more broadly as a vehicle for social betterment, as one Victorian pioneer suggested: 'To the Australian Vine! To the Vine which gives prosperity, which makes men sober and kind, which engenders sociability, which employs most hands, which brings the greatest comfort to rural families—to the cultivation of the Vine, the best of all to develop a new country' (De Castella 1886: 78–79).
2 Of course, this paid scant regard to the original inhabitants of the landscape, such as the Kaurna people of the Adelaide region (including McLaren Vale), for whom white settlement brought about radical rupture, displacement, disease and violence (Amery 2016; Williams 1974).
3 Wakefield's models of systematic colonisation were implemented in modified forms in South Australia and, subsequently, Western Australia and New Zealand.
4 Karl Marx, unsurprisingly, was critical of the South Australian project. In fact, Chapter 33 of 'Capital' is almost entirely devoted to a criticism of Wakefield's ideals, which he believed served simply to reproduce the exploitative social conditions of labour in the 'mother country' (Marx & Engels 2011 [1867]).
5 These areas are: soil health, nutrition and fertiliser management; pest and disease management; biodiversity management; water management; waste management; social relations between workers, community and wineries; and economic sustainability (McLaren Vale Grape Wine and Tourism Association 2018). The SAW program established by McLaren Vale winegrowers is now being adopted beyond the region and is often held up as an example of McLaren Vale's national leadership and progress in environmental matters.
6 Twentieth-century developments in wine chemistry, microbiology, and technologies of production, storage and transport helped place Australian wine industries at the 'cutting edge' of scientific winemaking, contributing to an export-driven 'wine boom' from the 1980s to 2000s (Allen 2012; Anderson & Aryal 2015).
7 These included Doradillo, Muscat, Pedro Ximenes and Palomino Blanco
8 The three most important grape varieties now grown in McLaren Vale, by vineyard area, harvest volume, and value, are Shiraz, Cabernet Sauvignon and Grenache (Vinehealth Australia 2017).

References

Allen, M. (2012). *The History of Australian Wine: Stories from the Vineyard to the Cellar Door*. Melbourne: Melbourne University Publishing.

Amery, R. (2016). *Warraparna Kaurna!: Reclaiming an Australian Language*. Adelaide: University of Adelaide Press.

Anderson, K. & Aryal, N. R. (2015). *Growth and Cycles in Australia's Wine Industry: A Statistical Compendium, 1843 to 2013*. Adelaide: University of Adelaide Press.

Barham, E. (2003). Translating terroir: the global challenge of French AOC labelling. *Journal of Rural Studies*, 19(1): 127–138.

Barrett, S. (1989). An assessment of the Vine Pull Scheme: a case study of the Southern Vales of South Australia. *The Australian Geographer*, 20(2): 185–190.

Bell, D. (2010). John Stuart Mill on colonies. *Political Theory*, 38(1): 34–64.

Bell, G. (1993). The South Australian wine industry, 1858–1876. *Journal of Wine Research*, 4(3): 147–163.

Bishop, G. C. (1977). *The Vineyards of Adelaide: A History of the Grapegrowers and Wine-Makers of the Adelaide Area*. Blackwood, S.A.: Linton.

Bowie, D. (2016). *The Radical and Socialist Tradition in British Planning: From Puritan Colonies to Garden Cities*. London: Routledge.

Capper, H. & South Australian Company (1839). *Capper's South Australia*. London: H. Capper.

De Castella, H. (1886). *John Bull's Vineyard: Australian Sketches*. Melbourne: Sands & McDougall.

Demossier, M. (2011). Beyond terroir: territorial construction, hegemonic discourses, and French wine culture. *Journal of the Royal Anthropological Institute*, 17(4): 685–705.

Fairburn, B., Olliver, J., Preiss, W., White, P. & Primary Industries and Resources South Australia (2010). *Geology of the McLaren Vale Wine Region*. Adelaide: Government of South Australia, Primary Industries and Resources SA.

Government of South Australia & Primary Industries and Regions South Australia (2013). The measure of the land [online]. Available online at www.pir.sa.gov.au/a ghistory/left_nav/land_settlement_in_sa/the_measure_of_land (accessed 15. 04. 18).

Ioannou, N. (1997). *Barossa Journeys: Into a Valley of Tradition*. Adelaide: Paringa Press.

Janowski, M. & Ingold, T. (eds) (2012). *Imagining Landscapes: Past, Present and Future*. Farnham: Ashgate.

Kelly, A. C. (2008 [1861]). *The Vine in Australia: Its Culture and Management*. Fitzroy, Vic.: Red Dog.

King, S. (2004). Italians on the land: fruit and vine growers in the Riverland and the Southern Vales. In *Memories and Identities: Proceedings of the Second Conference on the Impact of Italians in South Australia*, D. O'Connor & V. Andreacchio (eds), pp. 167–174. Adelaide: Australian Humanities Press.

Marx, K. & Engels, F. (2011 [1867]). *Capital*, volume I: a critique of political economy. Translated by S. Moore & E. Aveling. Dover Publications.

McIntyre, J. (2012). *First Vintage: Wine in Colonial New South Wales*. Sydney: UNSW Press.

McLaren, J. & Arrowsmith, J. (1840). Country south of Adelaide from O'Halloran Hill to Mt. Terrible including District C and portions of Districts B and D. Map. London: John Arrowsmith. From State Library of South Australia [BRG 42/120/28], available online at www.collections.slsa.sa.gov.au/resource/BRG+42/120/28 (accessed 27.11.18).

McLaren Vale Grape Wine and Tourism Association (2018). Sustainable Australia Winegrowing. Available online at www.mclarenvale.info/industry-development/SAW (accessed 17.04.18).

Paxson, H. (2010). Locating value in artisan cheese: reverse engineering terroir for new-world landscapes. *American Anthropologist*, 112(3): 444–457.

Pike, D. (1967). *Paradise of Dissent: South Australia 1829–1857*, 2nd edn. Melbourne: Melbourne University Press.

Santiago-Brown, I., Metcalfe, A., Jerram, C. & Collins, C. (2015). Sustainability assessment in wine-grape growing in the New World: economic, environmental, and social indicators for agricultural businesses. *Sustainability*, 7(7): 8178–8204.

Santich, B. (1998). *McLaren Vale: Sea and Vines*. Kent Town, S.A.: Wakefield Press.

Sinnett, F. (1862). *An Account of the Colony of South Australia Prepared for Distribution at the International Exhibition of 1862*. London: Robert K. Burt.

Skinner, W. (2018). Presence through absence: phylloxera and the viticultural imagination in McLaren Vale, South Australia. *The Asia Pacific Journal of Anthropology*, 19(3): 245–263.

Souffrant, E.M. (2000). *Formal transgression: John Stuart Mill's philosophy of international affairs.* Rowman & Littlefield Publishers.

South Australian Register (1840). Public dinner to His Excellency Colonel Gawler and in commemoration of the establishment of the Colony. *The South Australian Register*, 11 Jan.

Vinehealth Australia (2017). SA winegrape crush survey regional summary report 2017: McLaren Vale wine region. Available online at www.vinehealth.com.au/media/Regional-report-2017-McLaren-Vale.pdf (accessed 15.04.18).

Whimpress, A.W.P. (2008). The Wakefield model of systematic colonisation in South Australia: an examination with particular reference to its economic aspects. Ph.D. (unpub). Adelaide: University of South Australia.

Wilkinson, G.B. (1849). *The Working Man's Handbook to South Australia, with Advice to the Farmer, and Detailed Information for the Several Class of Labourers and Artisans.* London: John Murray.

Williams, M.J. (1974). *The Making of the South Australian Landscape: A Study in the Historical Geography of Australia.* London and New York: Academic Press.

Wine Australia (2016a). South Australia. Available online at www.wineaustralia.com/discover-australia-wine/south-australia-wines (accessed 17.04.18).

Wine Australia (2016b). Wine Production Standard. Available online at www.wineaustralia.com/labelling/wine-production-standard (accessed 17.04.18).

Yangarra Estate Vineyard (n.d.). McLaren Vale. Available online at www.yangarra.com/mclaren-vale (accessed 22.04.2018).

4 Burgundy's *climats* and the utopian wine heritage landscape

Marion Demossier

As you watch this video[1] – www.youtube.com/watch?v=RFtr6EgM5J4 – against the flowing musical background of *Nightcall* (London Grammar), the viewer's perspective is transported by a drone, above the autumnal vineyards, zooming in and out of a golden, picturesque wine landscape, following rows of vines, a tapestry of hilly plots, walls, villages and the beautiful lake of Geneva. The Lavaux vineyard terraces are presented, according to the World Heritage Sites website,[2] as a '30km stretch of land along Lake Geneva where viticulture has been practised since at least the 11th century'.

In common with Burgundy, which in 2015 was accorded World Heritage status (category cultural landscape) for the *climats de Bourgogne,* the local Benedictine and Cistercian monasteries, who owned the land, were said to have started large scale winemaking here. In a similar vein, but in a more dramatic fashion, another YouTube video[3] presents the legendary terroirs of Burgundy as a treasure for humankind accompanied by a quote of the eloquent former journalist Bernard Pivot: 'In Burgundy when we speak of a *climat* we do not look up to the sky, we keep our eyes to the ground.' The video takes us from the vineyards to the cellar presenting the *climats* as the result of human action. The emphasis here is on the historical and hierarchical construction of the site since the Middle Ages, and culture as well as folklore and religion, feature heavily as the unique peculiarities of this place.

For centuries, Burgundy has been recognised as the home of the world's finest wines and as the self-proclaimed birthplace of a model of terroir connecting taste to place. Burgundy holds a unique place in the French wine industry because of its history, its size and high concentration of small producers, with 4,100 family businesses cultivating 31,500 hectares, 288 negociants and only a dozen cooperatives, most of them located in the South. Burgundy as a wine region is composed of five wine producing areas, from north to south, the winegrowing regions of Chablis and the Grand Auxerrois; Côte de Nuits, Hautes Côtes de Nuits and the Châtillonnais; Côte de Beaune and the Hautes Côtes de Beaune; the Côte Chalonnaise and the Couchois, and finally, the Mâconnais, representing 28,841 hectares under vines, accounting for 3% of all commercial winegrowing in France. The grands crus production concerns only a small band of land in the Côte d'Or which forms the core of the *climats de Bourgogne* UNESCO world heritage site. That terroir concept was given legal form during the 1930s when the French state developed the system of AOC, emphasising the relationship between a given place, its micro-climatic characteristics and the local culture incarnated by wine growers and their traditional techniques. The story of terroir seemed to guarantee the taste of place and to justify the high price of purchase for this closed gustatory experience with a 1945 Romanée Conti bottle sold at a New York auction in 2018 for the astronomical price of US$558,000.

Yet the concept of the *climats de Bourgogne* is a recent local invention, part of an attempt to renew the terroir ideology while positioning Burgundy wines in the context of an ever more globalised world of wine. In this new climate, traditional hierarchies and regions of production are increasingly challenged. The *climats* are defined as Burgundy's own version of terroir, with the term taking on a different sense to that usually associated with soil, exposition and meteorological conditions. According to the dossier,

> The climats are precisely delimited vineyard parcels on the slopes of the Côte de Nuits and the Côte de Beaune south of the city of Dijon. They differ from one another due to specific natural conditions (geology and exposure) as well as vine types and have been shaped by human cultivation.[4]

Following this definition, the *climats* are another term for a historically created exceptional mosaic of vineyards with a hierarchy of crus and an international reputation.

Central to this recent reconfiguration of terroir as *climats de Bourgogne* lies the utopian quest for an imagined perfect place, the viticultural equivalent of the Garden of Eden, as well as a vision for an ideal future detached from the essentially backward looking rural idyll often constructed by the affluent middle-class (Howland 2010). Following Levitas' argument of utopia as a method rather than a goal, 'the advantage of utopian thinking is that it enables us to think about where we want to get to, and how to get there from here' (Levitas 2007: 300), utopia is, for the purpose of my argument, attached to a process of place-shaping defined as a collective reimagining and acting with recognition of provisionality, responsibility and necessary failure (Schucksmith 2018: 165). Utopia becomes a mode of eternal becoming, striving and experimenting in the face of an uncertain world. Through the *climats de Bourgogne* it is hoped, especially by the local elites, wine professionals and politicians that a collective imagining of a quintessential terroir will be underpinned by the reconciliation of sustainability with aesthetics and a moral economy, defined as an economy that is based on goodness, fairness, and justice, as opposed to one where the market is assumed to be independent of such concerns, through the heritagisation of wine landscape[5] seen as central to the place-shaping utopian project. The vision behind the Burgundy terroir story is about history, God – or the monks – and the goodness of the soil (Demossier 2018). The monastic trope guarantees the historical authenticity of the region and its long-lasting search for quality, humility and good taste in the face of an ever-changing wine industry. History, religion and the ties to the soil have all served as the guarantor of the place and its reputation at a time of increasing frauds, investments from external actors and entrepreneurs, as well as conspicuous forms of consumption.

This chapter examines how the notion of wine landscape as a utopia is used, contested and negotiated through the re-imaginings of wine heritage by the local community in Burgundy, especially around the UNESCO world Heritage site. By wine landscape, we refer to the two distinct definitions provided by Eric Hirsch (Hirsch & O'Hanlon 1995: 1) of landscape as a framing convention (from an objective standpoint-the landscape of particular people) on the one hand, and to the meaning imputed by local people to their cultural and physical surroundings (how a particular landscape is perceived by inhabitants) on the other. Barbara Bender (2002: 103) argues that landscape may be defined in many ways depending upon, among other things, gender, class, ethnicity, occupation, physical ability, but all definitions incorporate the notion of 'time passing'. In Burgundy, time is paradoxically fixed through the *climats* narrative which celebrates the Cistercian period crucial to the emergence of a local terroir. Wine landscape is deployed here primarily as a historical cultural landscape and a gastronomic site of embodiment, but it is also lived as land-use from the producers' perspective and visually apprehended as an aesthetic, picturesque and bucolic touristic place devoid of any form of economic exploitation as a source of capital. Place-shaping through the UNESCO heritage landscape recognition offers a platform for the re-negotiation of utopian past, present and futures.

Burgundy, like other wine producing regions, has frequently experienced profound changes in its economic and professional practices. It has also been buffeted by the effects of economic depression as in the 1930s, and by natural calamities, notably the phylloxera crisis of 1880, or more recently by the threat of the esca disease (fungi). Wine landscape is in Burgundy the result of a combination of complementary factors, including periodic place-shaping projects, often centred on the most reputed plots and their place in the world wine hierarchy, and the influence of the market. The vineyards that existed before the phylloxera crisis (when polyculture was part of the local economy), or after the expansion of the popular Gamay grape in the nineteenth century, hardly resemble the *climats* of today. Amongst the educated and wine savants, Stendhal is often cited for his mocking description of the vineyards of the Côte d'Or at the time as 'the dry and small hill of Burgundy'. Until the 1960s the area was concerned with the intensive production of grapes, which were sold by the wine growers to negociants or the larger landowners who actually made and bottled their wine. That traditional division broke down rapidly in the final decades of the twentieth century as the wine growers increasingly became masters in their own houses and mechanised viticulture. Yet they had to share that privilege with the larger landowners who dominated the cultural story.

Wine landscapes have therefore become inscribed in a broader set of frameworks, combining a wide range of characteristics from the historical formation of local viticulture to legal definitions of denomination of origin and the collective sense of ownership attached to them. It also reflects the multiple meanings and social relations attached to them and which are not necessarily shared unilaterally. The historical argument, in the case of Burgundy, is therefore multi-layered, multivocal and has been largely reinterpreted through the contemporary prism of UNESCO heritage status. As Bender has argued (2002: 106), 'Different people, differently placed, engage with the world in different ways'. Wine landscape, defined in terms of *climats,* has become central to processes of collective visual re-appropriation and to the *mise en héritage* of the site. An ongoing struggle to reconcile the ideal and actual productive terroir is now part of the local political, social and cultural place-shaping project. Utopia defined as a 'polyphonal method' (Shucksmith 2018: 165) is used as a trope to explore the paradoxes and contradictions, largely instrumentalised by the main social actors, and inherent to the heritagisation process of wine landscape in an uncertain world. The chapter discusses how the relationship between these utopian futures could address the growing challenges facing wine communities in the broader context of sustainability and climate change.

Reconfiguring the *climats de Bourgogne* as wine landscapes

Over the last fifteen years, a significant number of predominantly Western European viticultural sites have sought recognition as UNESCO World Heritage landscape or cultural sites, a phenomenon that has accompanied the emergence of a new category of perception for consumers that of 'wine landscape'. In Burgundy, the rapid rise in land prices and the globalisation of wine culture in the late twentieth century meant that viticulture became a highly specialised agricultural activity for the wine producers, negocians and landowners. Until then, for most consumers, Burgundy was a gastronomic gustative experience, a landscape constructed through knowledge of the names of its villages and their wines. Both phenomena are part of a broader shift which has transformed wine landscape into another competitive element of differentiation in the hierarchy of value attached to the world of wine. By hierarchy of value, I rely on the concept used by Herzfeld (2004), which refers to 'the implicit global hierarchy of value that wine producers and consumers employ to objectify and communicate the subjective taste knowledge and identity of place' (Jung 2014: 27). It is against the background of international competition that wines are constantly evaluated, ranked, performed and compared, and that wine landscape, as a new value, contributes to this implicit international hierarchy. This process is manifold, messy, ongoing, multi-scalar and fragmented, but remains nevertheless a challenge for historical and emblematic sites such as Burgundy (Demossier 2018).

By becoming a World Heritage cultural landscape and promoting a new reading of terroir, Burgundians are seeking to maintain their hegemonic position in the hierarchy of wine where place, taste and social experience still matter (Demossier 2015; 2018). In this context, the picturesque and bucolic aspects of the Burgundian wine landscapes metonymically represent the historical, cultural, political utopia that needs to become a concrete expression of the place and of its *climats*. Since the 1960s and the introduction of intensive agricultural methods of production such as fertilisers and the use of harvesting machines, the picturesque, bucolic optic disappeared from the local producers' landscape narrative. Yet it would be fair to say that the local wine landscape has never been appreciated for its aesthetic and bucolic values in the local psyche (Bonnot 2002). It was first and foremost for the wine growers a hard land to cultivate and, for the rest of the local population a recreational space.

With the UNESCO heritage stamp, wine landscape is now an established part of the experience attached to oenological tourism and the development of a visual drinking culture. As part of the intense rescaling of the global politics of heritage to suit social and economic development purposes and to create new connections between local and global, wine landscapes have come to fill a central place in the new narrative about global place-shaping. In a recent report published by ICOMOS (International Council on Monuments and Sites),[6] the broader international context which gave 'wine landscapes' an institutionalised meaning is further explained. From a heritage perspective, vineyards are widely recognised to be amongst the most remarkable forms of landscapes created by human activity, both by the mark they make on the territory and by the cultural traditions associated with them even if rarely explicitly defined. So, it was hardly surprising that they found their way on to the World Heritage list almost as soon as the category of cultural landscape was created.

Of the many and varied agricultural landscapes, vineyards are the most commonly protected. UNESCO has accorded World Heritage status to six wine regions in which the landscape is essential and four regions in which it is not typical.[7] There are only two other types of agricultural landscapes that have been recognised as World Heritage sites: those of tobacco crops and rice. Since 1992, when the introduction of the category of cultural landscapes in the World Heritage List took place, three major viticultural sites have been recognised, including those famous for some of the finest vines in the world: the old jurisdiction of Saint Emilion (Bordeaux Grand Cru); the valley of the Upper Douro (Porto) in Portugal; and the slopes of Tokaj (Tokaji aszú) in Hungary. In other cultural World Heritage landscapes, the vine plays a major role (Wachau, Cinque Terre, Val de Loire, the Rhine valley, etc.). Burgundy and the *climats de Bourgogne* joined this list in 2015 as a cultural landscape.

As a result, wine landscape in Burgundy has only recently become a category of collective perception and appreciation in the regional psyche. As pointed out by Gilles Laferté (2011: 685):

The image of a 'cheerful and wine-rich Burgundy' is found in Michelet's *Tableau de la France* (1861), and in *Le tour de la France par deux enfants* (1877), Burgundy is associated with vines and wine production. These are understood to be an invaluable source of economic wealth for France.

According to Laferté (2011: 685): 'vineyards possessed no aesthetic value'. However, the interwar period saw the gradual emergence of the vineyard as picturesque, bucolic scenery to be admired and this became part of the orchestrated attempt by regional entrepreneurs to establish a regional marketing around gastronomy and wine (Laferté 2006). In 1937, a *Route des grands crus de Bourgogne* was inaugurated from Dijon to Santenay along the Route Nationale 74 as part of a broader national touristic development. Marked by colourful roof tiles and local stone monuments, the Burgundian landscape was at the time shaped both by the absence of other nationally and internationally heritage valued landscape registers. The pioneering efforts of the Burgundian wine industry between the wars led to the redefinition of the basis of terroir as an expression and recognition of quality (Laferté 2011: 685). For Kolleen Guy, (2007) who studied Champagne during the inter-war period, the French have traditionally marketed products of the terroir with little reference to the *savoir-faire* of labour, preferring instead to locate the value of terroir products in idealised depictions of place and *savoir-vivre*. In Burgundy, this folkloric marketing was, however, further developed after World War II around the regionalist terroir and gastronomy model for most quality food produce and became a point of reference for the tourism industry as part of the new *mise en scène* of the regions (Laferté 2006). Interestingly, wine landscape formed part of the visual repertoire attached to Burgundy as a touristic region, but

> [e]njoying the sight of vineyards seemed incongruous in the early twentieth century. People formerly saw them as merely indicating productive agricultural land, much as we rarely stop today to admire any field of wheat, rapeseed, or corn.
>
> (Laferté 2011: 712)

The productive and the picturesque optics were therefore rather disjointed in the local understanding of place and this was still the case before the award of the UNESCO status in 2015.

My first encounter with the vineyards as both picturesque landscape and as a site of production dates back to the 1980s and to my years as a doctoral student conducting an ethnography of the *grands crus*. Having been born in Burgundy, I felt like many of my contemporaries that the vineyards were there and had always been there, but there was little aesthetic discourse or pleasure associated with their picturesque presence. The vineyard was mainly defined as a space for long walks or strolls on Sunday afternoons. It was not described as aesthetically pleasing in the local narrative. Instead it was first and foremost a workplace and a site of physical and economic hardship for the wine growing community. I have argued elsewhere how work is central to the local politics of identity in the wine growing community (Demossier 2011, 2018). Wine growers generally saw the vineyards as their patrimony and a way of earning their living while they progressively witnessed the increasing economic value of the land and its products. The landscape was largely fragmented, running in parallel with the nineteenth-century railway network and the National Road 6 which helped to form a barrier to further viticultural expansion. The *Route des vins* was the key touristic feature of the place. If today you were to drive south from Dijon to Santenay, along this road, most of the vineyard would be located on your right-hand side, visually presented as a tapestry or a patchwork of small plots assembled together and organised around a series of densely populated traditional Burgundian villages. As Laferté (2011: 712) rightly stated:

> It is more of a gastronomic landscape, a landscape constructed through knowledge of the names of its villages and their products and through an appreciation for the observable markers of wine quality, vineyard labor, and the portrayal of history.

Yet the prominence of landscape in UNESCO heritage claims has given a new meaning to viticultural landscapes and invested them with a global political and cultural resonance. It has also created a new internationally valued landscape visual register attached to wine heritage and tourism. The *climats de Bourgogne* cultural landscape thus joined the internationally valued heritage landscape registers contributing to the promotion of wine culture and tourism.

The development of wine tourism in Burgundy was spearheaded by a wide range of global networked initiatives which saw the orchestration of new schemes, representations and events in wine regions. In 2006, for example, the United Nations deemed wine so integral to human history that it created and endowed an international chair for wine culture and tradition in Burgundy, which, revealingly, was given to a female climatologist specialising in the physical rather than the social or cultural aspects of the subject. Brock University in the USA and its CCOVI (Cool Climate Oenology and Viticulture Institute) was part of the driving force behind the creation of the chair. Proposed and spearheaded by the University of Burgundy and supported by CCOVI-Brock University, the Chair for Wine and Culture was established by UNESCO after much coordinated strategic lobbying. This facilitated, as a result, deeper engagement with the concept of wine culture and how it could be more productively enhanced through environmentally sustainable practices by local communities and the regional actors. The UNESCO application gave a new impetus to wine culture and the *climats* as a sustainable and moral wine landscape enabling the local elites to place-shape an idealised vision of terroir. Environmental challenges, wine frauds and economic moral concerns were the impetus behind recasting Burgundy terroir as a utopian terroir landscape.

What has emerged triumphantly from those layered processes is the terroir image. It is now a fundamental part of the new heritage strategies put in place to refine the distinctiveness attached to specific sites in the global world of wine and the UNESCO application is yet another stage in recasting Burgundy's place in the world order. As Jacques Maby has argued (2002: 198), it is only recently that a more orchestrated and professional approach to wine landscape as a touristic object of consumption has re-emerged in France and that oeno-tourism has developed on a significant scale. In Burgundy, the first national wine road established in the 1930s pointed in the direction that would be developed much later (after the War, Occupation and immediate post-war reconstruction). More recently, as part of the new global wine heritage strategies, wine landscape as an aesthetic and 'authentic' site has become a key part of oenotourism, adding value to new categories of consumption that link place and taste: 'You can see what you drink, it comes from this plot'.

Such development strategies cannot be fully discussed without referring to the UNESCO heritage categories such as cultural landscape, cultural site and intangible heritage and how they have developed since their inception (Demossier 2018). The recent French initiatives to win UNESCO World Heritage status for a wide range of sites, landscapes and objects such as gastronomy have to be read against the ways in which states can exploit UNESCO conventions in imaginative ways to suit their own purposes (Demossier 2015). The development and ratification of the UNESCO Intangible Heritage Convention (2003), which broadened the scope of an earlier convention act of 1972 by embodying 'a particular understanding and conceptualisation of the nature of both cultural and natural heritage' (Smith & Akagawa 2009: 1), has been highly significant. Moreover, the scope of the UNESCO application goes further by integrating many different categories, including wine, from historical landscapes (Tokaj wine region), cultural sites (Piedmont) and wine routes (Spain). In 2013, the ancient Georgian Qvevri winemaking method was inscribed onto the Representative List of the Intangible Cultural Heritage of Humanity. It is this broader context that provided the background to some of the discussions behind the UNESCO application in Burgundy.

The main protagonists associated with the new visual representation of the region as the land of gastronomy and wine have gravitated around both the *Association pour les climats de Bourgogne* and the BIVB (Burgundy Wine Board). Local politicians, a handful of reputed wine growers as well as the local negociants, joined the project in 2008. This joint venture was inspired by the work of Gilles Laferté cited above and his publication 'La Bourgogne et ses vins, image d'origine contrôlée' (2006). As one of my key informers from the BIVB commented: 'we are working increasingly with the University of Dijon, the History Department and their research has been extremely useful for us'. On the basis of the folkloric economic model described by Laferté (2006), a wide range of connections have been made linking the worlds of entrepreneurs, politicians, the University and wine-producers as well as negociants. The BIVB which has recently been re-organised in management terms is now co-headed by both the negociants and the wine producers, a remarkable step given their history of conflict. Since the award of World Heritage status and after a campaign led by the former president of the *Association pour la reconnaissance des climats de Bourgogne* and famous wine producer, Aubert de Villaine, a series of cultural events have been orchestrated around the heritage site with the latest project being the *Cité des vins de Bourgogne* which aims to connect Beaune with Chablis and Mâcon.[8]

Against this broader context of creating 'wine landscape' as a meaningful category of collective perception and a place-shaping utopia, a wide range of local actors have sought to engage with the new iconography of the *climats de Bourgogne*. The range of new visual initiatives attached to the aesthetic and picturesque dimensions of wine landscape fits into the global awareness of nature, the environment and place as a sensorial category of perception. The visual largely dominates any other sensorial dimensions alongside the gustative experience of tasting. One of the leading local actors, François Desperriers, with his talented photographer friend Aurélien Ibanez, decided in 2010 to create a website devoted to wine and gastronomy with a particular focus on Burgundy and its wines. They joined the local efforts aimed at marketing the *climats de Bourgogne* by filming the emblematic auction of *Les Hospices de Beaune* which showcases every year some of the most reputed Burgundian wines sold through an auction. In recent interviews[9] both wine lovers and social media experts described their adventures. They started from twitter and went onto Facebook, which gave them a broader platform to engage with the world of wine counting up to 3,600 friends and generating debates around viticultural issues.

From this they quickly realised that there was a need for more content and information about the region. They filmed, for example, the iconic *Marche des climats*, working closely with wine producers. The *Marche des climats* is another illustration of place-shaping as it took the local population and visitors through the vineyards retelling the story of the origins. The film shows a gathering of local dignitaries, including leading members of the wine profession and politicians, standing in the vineyards and watching an actor dressed as a monk recount his tale.

Have you asked yourself why and how? Why and how the climats or the terroir were born here? You're thinking about the Romans, aren't you? I am sure the Romans, but not the Benedictines, they arrived after the Romans, just to reorganise everything. They didn't know how to do it amongst the chaos and the ruins they found. They asked themselves, how could we do it? Let's think Greek, and they thought about the great Greek philosopher Aristotle who said that the world can be understood by following the natural lines. The Benedictines understood that and thought about it. They observed the soil and they tasted the soil. They said why does the snow stay here and not here, why does water stagnate here and not here? They asked themselves all these questions and above all they tasted the soil.

(Author's translation)

The newspaper *Le Monde* devoted one of its columns to their success as a wine blog dedicated to novices and amateurs.[10] The work of François and Aurélien has gone from strength to strength and they have now become the point of reference for the regional wine industry and wine lovers. They have worked with several domains in need of featuring their own promotional material against educational and informative presentations of the wines in English. It is also worth noting that Burgundy has occupied centre stage with the success of two films: *Ce qui nous lie / Back to Burgundy* (2017) by Cedric Klapisch and the documentary film *Grand Cru* (2017) by David Eng.

Finally, one of the other major factors in the visual reconfiguration of the wine landscape is part of the rise of internet technology and the new opportunities for producers to tell their own stories. It is only recently that digital communication has come to play an important role for the profession and that clips, images, interviews and writings have started to showcase Burgundy and its *climats* in a more prominent fashion. This digital *mise en scène* of wine growers represents a major shift in the way in which individual stories are told, and it has repercussions for the global world of wine with its paradoxical values such as capitalism versus artisanship, its constant process of imbrication cascading from the local to the national to the transnational and back and forth. The *climats* have become the ingredients of a new story around environmentally friendly practices and a return to a more sustainable and picturesque landscape. Several of the wine growers I have followed over the last decade have contributed to this shift and it is easy to follow this trend by just searching through YouTube videos under Burgundy wines (Demossier 2018). As we have seen, if winegrowers and negociants have started to invest significantly more in the visual production of their own individual landscape, they are also doing it in parallel with the professional associations responsible for communicating on the wines and also more broadly on the attractions of the whole region for tourists and wine lovers. In this process, a specific aesthetic category of wine landscape has come to dominate the heritagisation of the site as well as its touristic gaze (Urry 1990). What results from these individual initiatives is a paradoxical engagement with the site as 'authentic' and invested of a moral economy.

From gastronomic to wine landscape: a new category of aesthetic value?

As part of the broader circulation of wine landscapes attached to UNESCO sites, the main Burgundian social actors created their own visual imaginary taking the *climats de Bourgogne* as a pretext to recreate the terroir ideology and to position the vineyard in the new wine global hierarchy as a sustainable, symbolic and aesthetic place. Prior to this successful orchestration of new visual representations of the place, Eva Bigando (2006) argued that both Burgundy and Bordeaux cultivated what she described as a synecdoche – defined as a device in which a part of something represents the whole, or it may use a whole to represent a part – therefore creating a disjuncture between the realities and the images and representations of the place. Bigando (2006: 91) notes that the high aesthetic value assigned to the Côte d'Or – the core zone of the UNESCO's application – is said to reflect a perpetual search for perfection, which is associated with divine and religious attributes incarnated by the reference to the Cistercians and seeks to guarantee the quality of the wine produced through the authenticity of the site. This mythical construction of the wine landscape contributes to the showcasing of Burgundy and the recent World Heritage veneer has complicated this process of telling a long-lasting story about the place, history and religion.

The central heritage zone – Côtes de Beaune and Côte de Nuits – which represents only 20% of the Burgundian wine region still dominates the visual narratives of the *climats de Bourgogne*. As part of the iconography, history, gastronomy and religion incarnated by the figure of the monk are the new features of the place, emphasising the terroir ideology. What is, however, distinctive is the modern twist encapsulated by the mobile camera or the drone offering the visitor a birds' eye view of the vineyards, working around the light and the seasons, to give a temporality that transcends other media such as postcards that are usually fixed into singular and one dimensional spatio-temporal readings. This modern twist engages the tourist in a new sensorial and fluid visual experience creating emotions and feelings in relation to the landscape and the monumental heritage associated with it. Focusing on specific features of the new wine landscape such as dry walls, fruit trees and bees, the utopian realisation of the ideal wine landscape is showcased. This provides a new distinctive addition to the repertoire of the wine tourist, while it also frames the experience of the place in a different fashion, emphasising the picturesque and bucolic visual rather than the real or enacted. These contrasting perspectives have often clashed such as when wine growers sought to expand their plots by getting rid of the dry-stone walls. The often-cited example of the *colline de Corton* recently sold by the former CEO of the Béjot domaine[11] to the American businessman owner of Screaming Eagle in Napa Valley and Arsenal Football Club in London[12] epitomises the paradoxical machinations of a shifting utopian aspiration, demonstrating that the eco-cultural model has yielded to commercial priorities in this case.

It could be said that the Côte d'Or still dominates the visual narrative incarnated by the *Clos de Vougeot*[13] and the *Hospices de Beaune*[14] as religious historical symbols of the place. In this new wine landscape, the wine growers are almost totally absent from the narrative and there is an attempt to focus on the diversity of the soil, the history and material culture of this story. The *climats* have become the new ingredients of this visual construction of place. Emphasis is put on plots, rows, soil, landscape reminders of past iconographies, crosses and religious sites. There is a taste of *déja vu*, reminiscent of some of the cabinets displayed in the old Museum of Wine in Beaune, a sense of fossilisation and museification of wine culture. Yet the post-modern twist lays with the attempts to make the site lively and attractive for younger generations through a series of events organised locally like, for example, the greeters (volunteers who welcome tourists in their city or region) or the new cycle path.[15] Despite initiatives such as this and others, which are often seen as clashing with the site and its production, there is a real danger of fetishizing the place as the Garden of Eden, the ideal terroir landscape and consequently, of obliterating the diversity and complexity of the wine region, which has a lot to offer beyond the UNESCO World Heritage site. The local wine culture cannot be reduced to a chocolate box by fixing one visual landscape register, namely aesthetic and ideal, to the detriment of the collective land use. The question remains about the heritagisation process and its capacity to generate a more engaged and collective form of heritage in which producers, tourists and locals all benefit from the whole encompassing experience. The political is often described by some of the wine producers as the agent of disorder. Yet due to the exponential growth of demands for fine wines most of the producers remain passive when confronted by the impact of local governance in the UNESCO prescriptive framework.

Beyond some obvious environmental concerns, tensions between the democratisation of the heritage site through touristic development and the site as a productive and highly economically valued place are likely to emerge. Tourists wandering in the vineyards are likely to impact on the environment and clash with the locals as well as with the wine producers. Examples of villages imposing cycle paths and managing their environmental sustainability during periods of viticultural chemical treatments are often cited. The last decade has already witnessed greater restrictions in terms of access to the vineyards as well as a growing regulation of the private and public space. In Beaune, beneath the hill on which the statue of the Virgin Mary is perched, a new street sign indicates that the harvest of grapes is forbidden and will lead to prosecution. According to the local police force:

> to collect grapes in a vineyard is a robbery, an offence punishable by a penalty of three years' maximum imprisonment and a fine of €45,000. Grape theft is not only a crime, but directly affects the productivity of the vineyard and the wine sector already challenged by the climate change.[16]

The landscape has, over the years, seen an increase in policing, explained partially by the decline in the number of grapes harvested, but also more generally by a growing privatisation and securitisation of the plots. Historically until the 1970s, access to plots was collective. These practices have, however, disappeared with the rise of individual landownership. When the annual harvest period starts in early autumn some of the issues described above are likely to become more acute, especially if the vineyards are invaded by coaches, bikes and tourists.

The Burgundy application to UNESCO became more problematic when it started to engage with local politics, especially within the *communes* as explained by one of the main protagonists behind the UNESCO application. The vision attached to the wine landscape promoted by the *Association pour les climats de Bourgogne* and its leader, Aubert de Villaine, focused essentially on the promotion of the ideal terroir landscape as utopian. The *Association* had to negotiate the relationship between rural and urban areas through territorial plans, known as *Schémas de Cohérence Territoriale* (SCoTs – 'Territorial Coherence Schemes'), a landscape plan for the qualitative management of the landscape of the Côte between Ladoix-Serrigny and Nuits-St-Georges and local urbanism plans. The perimeter of the property is fully covered by two SCoTs (the Dijon SCoT and that of the cities of Beaune and Nuits-Saint-Georges) which provide a comprehensive framework for municipal and local development plans: the coordination of their objectives and regulatory tools contributes to territorial management effectiveness through their sectorial planning instruments. The management framework is completed by the signing of a Territorial Charter by the 53 local decision makers. It engages them to cooperate in the governance of the property, which is ensured by the *Association pour les climats de Bourgogne*. Managing the tensions between 'collective good' and private property is a challenge. The value of the land as well as the difficulties attached to land succession, from one generation to the next, has impacted on the ways in which wine growers engage with the site and its so-called restrictive framework. A few wine growers had to change their plans regarding the building of new premises for wine production due to new planning regulations, while some decided to help their children to establish a new vineyard elsewhere. They have also been asked to be more environmentally aware when the tourists are visiting.

Seasons, work and crafting: a utopian place-shaping project?

In a recent article, Maria Gravari-Barbas (2014: 2) argues that 'the new winescape might be seen as a paradigmatic landscape of more general mutations in hyper-modern Western societies'. The author notes a parallel between trends in the winescapes and those that characterise central metropolitan areas or international elite resorts and she cites three significant trends: the era of artist capitalism that is to say the rise of the artisan as a modern feature of global wine culture; the incursion of the marks and labels transforming the winescapes in brandscapes; the role that tourism plays in these transformations by turning the site into a commodity. Central to those trends remains the understanding of the relationship that contemporary societies maintain between culture and nature (Gravari-Barbas 2014). Contemporary societies are characterised by changing relationships between nature and culture, and utopias play a central role in enabling the negotiation of what could be still seen and understood as 'natural' or 'authentic'. An ongoing struggle to reconcile the productive ideal and actual terroir is now part of the local political, social and cultural narrative. In generating a utopian vision around wine landscape as the ideal terroir incarnated by the return to monastic Cistercian time and the construction of an associated bucolic optic, the *Association pour les climats de Bourgogne* seeks to foster a participative and inclusive process of engagement with place-shaping. Yet this visionary process has contributed to the unfolding of multiple social constructions of the territory and the emergence of a polyphonal utopian method for a global world. On the one hand, the process of heritagisation of the site has heightened the constraints, such as dealing with environmental pressures due to climatic changes, under which wine producers engage with nature, creating new challenges which will be addressed in a wide range of ways, from the management of waste water to producing solid organic waste that is often similarly mishandled. On the other hand, vineyards are far from being natural as they are one of the most crafted pieces of agricultural land and managing them is far from a collective and standardised process.

Wine landscapes offer a powerful metaphor for the balance between nature and culture (Maby 2002: 205). The global wine industry has demonstrated that different models of viticultural production can coexist from the artisanal, crafted, niche orientated production to the industrial production, mass consumption wine styles promoted by the big global players. Those models of viticultural production have given form to different types of wine landscapes in which nature is performed visually in a wide range of ways. This theme of a dialectic between nature and culture has found a new resonance through the *climats de Bourgogne* opportunity. Several traditional domains have chosen to produce clips around wine landscapes, the seasons and work conducted in the vineyards and in the cellar. What is often shown is how time and space are both key to the viticultural experience. Traditional methods also often feature as part of the story which unfolds from the time of the pruning in January to the visit to the cellar in December. One example is provided by the promotional clip produced by *Bourgogne Live* for the *Baillage de Pommard*.[17] Behind the background of the village of Pommard, a group of wine growers introduce the skills and tasks attached to wine production throughout the cycle, making visible a few differentiated skills such as some preferring manual labour rather than using the tractor, others having modern press material while a few still press by hand. The emphasis is, however, on artisanal, small scale and environmentally friendly viticulture. This idyllic representation of village life is far from being the norm.

The prestigious vineyards of the Côte de Nuits and Côte de Beaune, which are located in the department of the Côte d'Or, are therefore only one (small) part of Burgundy. Overall issues of knowledge, cultural and social capital and engagement are thus central to the production of excellence, as are good marketing skills. The highly individualised and differentiated Burgundian wine landscape provides a range of economic niches which enable good, and even sometimes bad producers, to achieve distinction and excellence. However, only a small group of wine elites has achieved real economic success and has moved the goalposts of quality since the 1990s by redefining quality and terroir through more ecologically friendly practices and discourses (Demossier 2011). Interestingly, a few wine growers at the margins of Burgundian viticulture have recently joined them in promoting ecological methods in their production (Demossier 2018: 23). This shift has accompanied the utopian vision attached to the Burgundy UNESCO application and it could be seen as an increasingly growing utopianism underpinned by a new ecological collective imaginary constructed around the *climats de Bourgogne* as a wine landscape and also a morality that Burgundy seeks to aspire as an 'authentic' terroir place. Yet the process is far from being univocal.

As a result of this composite social organisation and the increasing individualistic capitalist mode of production the sense of community also remains a mere utopia that is jealously preserved by the profession as an element of authenticity attached to the place. The strong collective values attached to, for example, the old confraternities of Saint Vincent or to the mutual aid practiced at times of major crisis constantly resist the growing individualism that has accompanied the capitalist development of the wine region, but it has become something from the past. These values are constantly advanced in debates at the local level, but they act more as cultural markers of an ideal world rather than demonstrating a real belief that those values and practices can be sustained in our modern age. Terroir thus provides a window onto the mechanisms by which societies are able to use globalisation and modernity to suit their own purposes. The paradox of this is that the global explosion of attention to terroir – or the national conditions of winescapes – conceals human intervention, local land politics and the homogenisation of many wine manufacturing practices in most parts of the world, including France. The chimeric qualities of the concept of terroir imbue wine from Burgundy in particular with a sense of mythological excellence.

In the course of Burgundy's application for UNESCO heritage status, an increasing number of domains decided either to revamp their outdated websites or even to commission short professional documentaries about themselves. This growing *mise en scène de soi* forms part of a broader technological, cultural and environmental shift which is designed to recast the Burgundy story around the new concepts of *climats de Bourgogne*. It is a striking example of the phenomenal success of local elites in disseminating and promoting the *climats* story, rebranding authenticity around new notions such as ecology and nature. Nature here is presented in a specific ecological way and the environmental shift seeks to reposition the wine region in the global hierarchy of value where ecological concerns and associated human stewardship and enrichment have acquired ever greater weight. The UNESCO application and construction around the *climats* as the 'authentic' site of a singular historicised value are part of that process – they are amongst the most expensive wines in the world – and they are not only part of the domain strategy, but they also tell a story about the place and its continuous struggle against the elements. Within the UNESCO application itself, terroir was presented throughout as an ideal of environmental sustainability illustrating a clear attempt to shift the agenda and local meaning about terroir in the new global wine hierarchy. This new strategy represents a way of preserving the equilibrium between people and place and of mediating globalisation at the local level. Yet striking differences still characterize the local situation as far as sustainability is concerned.

Conclusion

Wine landscapes have become a major selling point in the global promotion of wines. They are often showcased through a visual *mise en scène* and promoted through orchestrated communication (Maby 2002) as well as oenological tourism and individual marketing initiatives. Indeed, putting a landscape on a wine is putting a face on a name. Wine landscapes are only part of the touristic oenological experience and an increasing number of visitors to viticultural sites are eager to engage further with the world of wine. UNESCO has played an instrumental role in putting these famous names on the map and as a way of proposing an alternative reading of the Old and New World touristic experiences. History, Tradition and Culture are seen as trump cards in this new competitive orchestration of the world of wine and wine landscape seems to be seen as another way of telling the same story. On 9 January 2018, the Decanter magazine devoted its pages to UNESCO world heritage wine regions by presenting a series of emblematic wine landscapes emphasising their aesthetic appeals. Yet it did not cover the whole story of these modern utopias confronted by fast capitalism and growing frauds or address the issue of a mystical landscape emptied of its human features and the realities of its intensive commodification and economic value. The average price of Burgundy grand cru vineyards rose by nearly 9% in 2014, to 4.35m euros per hectare, according to France's SAFER agency, which governs agricultural land deals. It is said prices ranged from 2 million euros to 10 million euros per hectare.[18] As I hope to have demonstrated, utopian depictions of wine landscape in the context of global capitalism are used and negotiated through the polyphonal re-imaginings and experimentations of wine landscape heritage by the local community, especially around the UNESCO world Heritage site. Yet it creates a disjuncture between the idyllic image circulating and the realities of what it means to live in such highly economically valued and heritagised site on the ground or even to visit it as a tourist. Experiencing the Burgundy winescape today might become a quest for the Holy Grail.

Notes

1 Lavaux, 2014. Les vignes d'Or (Golden vines, canton de Vaud district, Switzerland), short clip produced by Valentin Dubach to introduce the wine landscape of

the UNESCO world heritage site, www.youtube.com/watch?v=RFtr6EgM5J4 (accessed on 06.03.18).

2 www.worldheritagesite.org/list/Lavaux%2C+Vineyard+Terraces (accessed on 06.03.18).

3 www.bing.com/videos/search?q=climats+de+bourgogne&&view=detail&mid= C66DDD37C148F3F0AF8CC66DDD37C148F3F0AF8C&&FORM=VRDGAR (accessed on 06.03.18).

4 www.drvino.com/2015/07/06/unesco-burgundy-climats-champagnes/ (accessed on 27.03.18).

5 For more discussion on moral economy, see the work of Didier Fassin (2005).

6 www.international.icomos.org/studies/paysages-viticoles.pdf (accessed on 06.03.18).

7 Internal research report entitled 'Analyse comparative des climats de Bourgogne', Yves Luginbühl, 2009, 47pp., which was circulated to a small number of members of the scientific committee, including myself.

8 www.cite-vins-bourgogne.fr/fr/un-projet-en-reseau_15.html (accessed on 07.03.18).

9 www.youtube.com/watch?v=Nhx8LSxYwGc (accessed on 07.03.18).

10 www.lemonde.fr/m-styles/article/2012/05/11/les-blogueurs-prennent-de-la-bouteille_ 1699121_4497319.html (accessed on 07.03.18).

11 For more details, see www.decanter.com/wine-news/maison-bejot-vins-et-terroirs-turmoil-suspected-fraud-306395/ (accessed on 05.11.18).

12 See www.decanter.com/wine-news/tension-mounts-corton-hills-mystery-buyer-3537 41/ (accessed on 29.10.18).

13 The *Clos de Vougeot* vineyard was created by Cistercian monks of Cîteaux Abbey, the order's mother abbey and is a wall-enclosed vineyard, a *clos*, in the Burgundy wine region, and an Appellation d'origine contrôlée (AOC) for red wine from this vineyard

14 The Hospices de Beaune or Hôtel-Dieu de Beaune is a former charitable alms-house in Beaune, France. It was founded in 1443 by Nicolas Rolin, chancellor of Burgundy, as a hospital for the poor. The original hospital building, the Hôtel-Dieu, one of the finest examples of French fifteenth-century architecture, is now a museum.

15 The greeters of the Pays Beaunois, for example, are as diverse as the area, depending on whether they live in Beaune or in one of the typical surrounding villages; whether they are farmers, wine growers or other professionals such as teachers, midwives, ICT specialists, housewives or even former town councillors; and whether they have always lived here or, at some point, decided to move from Paris, or even Great Britain, to settle down for good in Burgundy.

16 www.bienpublic.com/cote-d-or/2016/09/28/vendanges-des-vols-de-raisin-et-des-regles-non-respectees (accessed on 07.03.18).

17 www.bailliagedepommard.com/index.html (accessed on 08.03.18).

18 Read more at www.decanter.com/wine-news/burgundy-grand-cru-vineyard-prices-still-rising-259646/#RGAl5Oda3IU30KfC.99 (accessed on 29.10.18).

References

Bender, B. (2002). Time and Landscape. *Current Anthropology*, 43(S4): 103–112.

Bigando, E. (2006). La synecdoque paysagère, une notion pour comprendre les représentations des paysages viticoles bourguignon et bordelais. In *Sud-Ouest européen*, Vol. 21, territoires et paysages viticoles (Coordonné par Michel Réjalot): 83–93.

Bonnot, T. (2002). Des tuiles, des toits et des couleurs : de Beaune à Disneyland Paris, une tradition bourguignonne. *Terrain*, 38(March): 153–162.

Demossier, M. (2011). Beyond Terroir: Territorial Construction, Hegemonic Discourses and French wine culture. *Journal of the Royal Anthropological Institute*, 17(4): 685–705.

Demossier, M. (2015). The Politics of Heritage in the Land of Food and Wine. In *A Companion to Heritage Studies*, Logen, W., Craith, M. N. & Kockel, U. (eds), pp. 87–100. London: John Wiley & Sons.

Demossier, M. (2018). *Burgundy. A Global Anthropology of Place and Taste*. London: Berghahn.

Demossier, M. (2019). Reflexive Imbrications. In *The Globalization of Wine: The Trans-Nationalization and Localization of Production, Leisure and Pleasure*, Inglis, D. & Almila, A. (eds), pp. 47–64. London: Berghahn.

Fassin, D. (2005). Compassion and repression, the moral economy of immigration policies. *Cultural Anthropology*, 20(3): 362–387.

Guillard, M. (2003). De la vigne symbole à la vigne spectacle: l'avènement du paysage viticole. Paysages de vignes et de vin. Patrimoine, enjeux, valorisation. Colloque international Abbaye Royale de Fontevraud: 101–106.

Gravari-Barbas, M. (2014). Winescapes: Tourisme et artialisation, entre le local et le global. *Cultur*, 08(03). Available online at www.uesc.br/revistas/culturaeturismo (accessed 13.02.19).

Herzfeld, M. (2004). *The Body Impolitic: Artisans and Artifice in the Global Hierarchy of Value*. Chicago: University of Chicago Press.

Hirsch, E. & O'Hanlon, M. (1995). *The Anthropology of Landscape: Perspective on Place and Space*. Oxford: Clarendon Press.

Howland, P. J. (2010). Self-gifting and the Metro-rural idyll: An illusion of ideal reflexive individualism. *New Zealand Sociology*, 25(1): 53–74.

Jung, Y. (2014). Tasting and Judging the Unknown *Terroir* of the Bulgarian Wine: The Political Economy of Sensory Experience. *Food and Foodways*, 22(1): 24–47.

Laferté, G. (2006). *La Bourgogne et ses vins: image d'origine contrôlée*. Paris: Belin.

Laferté, G. (2011). Ethno-tourism and the Folklorization of products: the marketing of French luxury wines in the inter-war years. *French Historical Studies*, 34(4): 679–712.

Levitas, R. (2007). Looking for the blue: the necessity of utopia. *Journal of Political Ideology*, 12(3): 289–306.

Levitas, R. (2013). *Utopia as a Method. The Imaginary Reconstitution of Society*. London: Palgrave Macmillan.

Maby, J. (2002). Paysage et imaginaire: l'exploitation de nouvelles valeurs ajoutées dans les terroirs viticoles, *Annales de Géographie*, 624: 198–211.

Overton, J. & Banks, G. (2015). Conspicuous Production: Wine, capital and status. *Capital & Class*, 39(3): 473–491.

Shucksmith, M. (2018). Re-imagining the rural: From rural idyll to good countryside. *Journal of Rural Studies*, 59: 163–172.

Smith, L. & Akagawa, N. (2009). *Intangible Heritage*. New York: Routledge.

Urry, J. (1990). *The Tourist Gaze*. London: Thousand Oaks.

5 Inventing tradition and terroir

The case of Champagne in the late nineteenth century

Graham Harding

Introduction

In 1887 the newly formed trade body representing the 'Grande Marque' houses of Champagne won a decisive victory in the long series of bitterly fought legal actions over the right to use the term 'champagne' on bottles of wine. The *Cours de Cassation* [the French Appeal Court] ruled that the term 'champagne' could only be applied to wine *'récolté et fabriqué'* [harvested and produced] in the region of that name (Hodez 1923). This 1887 judgment, which was confirmed on appeal in 1892, was the fruit of a long campaign of legal action by the *Syndicat du Commerce des Vins de Champagne*, the group of 35 champagne houses that came together in 1882 to secure the principle that *'il n'est de champagne que de la Champagne'* [it's only champagne if it's from Champagne].[1] Victory ensured that only wines that were grown and produced in the French region of Champagne could bear the name 'champagne' on the label. This chapter explores how the champagne industry developed over the next ten to 15 years to consolidate this legal victory and – in the process – created the world's first true territorial or regional brand.[2] The judgement at the Angers *'cours de cassation'* was clear and ultimately conclusive but it had not closed down those producers of sparkling wine from the neighbouring French region of Saumur or the Rhineland who had been using (or abusing) the term 'champagne'. They remained a very significant threat to the Champenois.

This chapter covers four areas. The first is the steps that the *Syndicat du Commerce des Vins de Champagne* (SCVC) took to re-make the image of champagne.[3] I use the term 're-make' because their promotional efforts, which centred around the Paris Exhibitions of 1889 and 1900, involved creating a foundation myth for their wine. The immediate purpose of this myth was to address the perception that champagne was 'fabricated' or manufactured rather than a natural product. Second, it focuses on the ways in which Moët & Chandon exploited and, to a degree, appropriated the territorial brand of 'Champagne' for its own promotional purposes. Third, building on the SCVC initiative and the Moët & Chandon case, it explores the nature of the early twentieth-century link between terroir and the territorial brand and, lastly, it briefly considers the broader implications for the more recent branding of champagne, the issue explored in this volume by Steve Charters.

Central to the image making project of the SCVC was Raphael Bonne-dame, a journalist, editor and publisher based in Epernay, the epicentre of the nineteenth-century champagne industry. He was editor of *Le Vigneron Champenois,* the paper of the champagne trade, author of many books on champagne houses, primary author of the publicity booklets produced for the Exhibitions and assiduous promoter of his native region.[4] I will argue that he played a key role in the creation of the modern branding of champagne.

Though his writing, Bonnedame laid the foundations for both the territor-ial brand of Champagne (that is a brand drawing its authority from a specific, named region) and the cultural 'terroir' of champagne (that is the wine). He did not use the word 'terroir'. At that time, this term had none of the com-plimentary associations it now carries. Rather it invoked a disagreeable sense of rusticity and roughness. But, by invoking Champagne as a region of wit, inspiration, grace and beauty which embodied '*l'esprit Gaulois*' [the Gallic spirit] Bonnedame played a major role in establishing the key elements of twentieth and twenty-first century branding of champagne.

Modern branding theory has come to distinguish many separate kinds of brands (which I will not attempt to enumerate here).[5] By the mid-nineteenth century the term 'brand' was essentially used to denote the products of different producers, for example Veuve Clicquot's champagne or Beecham's Pills (Anderson & Homan 2002: 921–923). The focus is on the house, that is the family of the founder. By the late nineteenth century separate product brands were being created, e.g. Sunlight Soap, in which the name of the producer was subordinated to the name of the product itself. Regardless of type, such nineteenth-century branding took tangible form. The coat of arms or the name on the cork, the product name on the label, the colour of the label or the foil around the neck, the word 'champagne' itself; all these are tangible marks that can be protected from counterfeiters through court action.[6]

However, what modern branding theory and practice has come to recognise is that protecting the tangibles is not enough. Brands are not just marks of identity but also tools to manage meaning. Such meaning is built up over time by con-sistent communication *to* consumers and through the consistent experience *of* consumers. The process is two-way rather than uni-directional and involves not just tangible marks of identity but intangible associations or values. The ima-ginary on which champagne has come to rely owes its strengths both to the aristocratic and hedonistic heritage of champagne and the territorial 'roots' that it acquired in the early twentieth century. As Ghislain de Montgolfier of Bollin-ger noted in 2005, for a luxury product to be more than an 'advertising stunt' ['*un coup de pub*'] it must have roots ['*il doit avoir des racines*'].[7]

The SCVC and Bonnedame were focused in the 1880s and 1890s on a new form of branding which demanded the support of powerful yet intangible symbols. Today we recognise territorial or regional brands as a separate category of brands (Vela 2013). Through a number of different European

Union schemes, protected place names provide the basis for branded products such as Parma ham and Gorgonzola cheese.[8] To be effective such brands need to make a clear link not just with the geographical origin but with the meaning of the place.

Whilst scholarly work on territorial brands and place-name branding has begun to appear in the last decade there has been relatively little historical work in the field (Anholt 2007). The development and exploitation of the territorial brand of champagne in today's marketing practice has been studied in a number of recent articles, notably by Steve Charters and his several collaborators (Charters & Spielmann 2014; Lockshin 2012; Menival & Charters 2014; Smith Maguire & Charters 2011). However, none of these scholars, though well aware of the history, devotes time to origins. The only person to do so is the historian Kolleen Guy, whose 2003 book *When Champagne Became French,* studies the early marketing of champagne, largely through the extensive collection of labels held in the Marne archives (Guy 2003: 235–236).

This chapter draws on two major sets of source material in addition to the more recent secondary literature on the marketing of champagne and other wines, notably Burgundy. The first is the publications written for the *Syndicat du Commerce des Vins de Champagne* and the marketing initiatives of *Le Vigneron Champenois*, which Raphael Bonnedame edited and published for many years after taking over from his father in the late 1870s. Bonnedame's printing and publishing business also published many of the key SCVC documents. I supplement this material with popular guides to the production of champagne written and produced by Bonnedame for the two Paris Exhibitions in 1889 and 1900, the SCVC's account of the 'Palace of Champagne' at the 1900 Exhibition (which re-used material from the 1889 Exhibition) and articles in *Le Vigneron Champenois*. The second set of sources which I have used deal with the marketing and advertising of Moët & Chandon in the British market between the late 1880s and the early 1920s, in particular their pavilion at the 1908 Franco-British Exhibition at London's White City. Moët & Chandon were, by some way, the largest supplier of champagne to the British market and their primary agents, the Simon Brothers, were extremely active in promoting the brand and celebrating its linkage to the Champagne vineyards and the iconic figure of Dom Pérignon.[9]

The information available on Bonnedame himself is scanty and the archives of the SCVC remain hard to access so it is difficult to decide whether he was mainly a copywriter or whether he had a more important role in the deliberations of the SCVC. Nonetheless, as editor of the most important trade newspaper and a practising journalist with a deep knowledge of the champagne houses, whose histories he had written and first published in *Le Vigneron Champenois* in a series called '*Les gloires de Champagne*', he was clearly an influential figure.

The *Syndicat du Commerce* summary of the judges' decision at the 1887 hearing in Angers was that '*les vins recoltés et manutentionnés en Champagne ont seule le droit de porter ce nom*' (1905: 9). In other words, wines grown or vinified outside the area could not use the name 'champagne' on their labels.

A variant of this same line is still used on the official champagne websites.[10] For the *Syndicat* the victory at Angers was '*une consécration de notre droit*' [sacred vindication of our rights] but they recognised that they could not simply rely on the law. In a letter published in *Le Vigneron Champenois* they called on their colleagues to participate in a collective presence at the forth-coming 1889 Exposition Universelle in Paris. They argued that not to do so would be to leave the field open to those 'illicit' competitors who would once again attempt to 'usurp' their place and their name. Not to put on a show would, they said, be an 'abdication' (1887: 1). The proposal for a collective display was accepted and the outcome was what the *Petit Journal* guide to the 1889 Exhibition called an 'audacious' display that represented the history of a bottle of champagne from vine to glass rendered in wax figures at 1/10th scale.[11] Though there is no definitive visual evidence, the heavily illustrated SCVC report of the 1900 display strongly suggests that these figures were re-used (Blondeau 1901). To ensure that the visitors understood the significance of what they were seeing a *Notice historique sur le vin de Champagne* written by Bonnedame (1889) was given to all visitors.

In his booklets written for the 1889 and 1900 Exhibition, Bonnedame had essentially three themes in mind. These were the process of creating cham-pagne, the unique qualities of the region and, third, the revitalisation and popularisation of the legend of the seventeenth century Benedictine monk, Dom Pérignon, whom he portrayed as the 'inventor' of sparkling wine. In exploring these themes, he was addressing three key issues that have under-pinned the marketing of champagne in the last 120 years. First, he attacked the powerful nineteenth-century discourse on champagne that portrayed it as a wine that was 'artificial' or 'manufactured', a discourse that is still current.[12] Second, he played a central role in creating the persistent current imaginary of Champagne as an Edenic (even utopian) terroir. Lastly, he revitalised the foundation myth of Dom Perignon, which, despite its historical inaccuracies, retains enormous potency.[13]

Throughout the nineteenth century, British journalists and wine writers raised the spectre of 'fabrication' over champagne. For the *Morning Post* in 1860, the newspaper of the British elite, champagne was 'the most artificial of white wines. From no grape juice in nature can champagne, as rendered to commerce, be made without collateral mixture'.[14] Fifteen years later, in an article on 'Wine and Wine-Merchants', Matthew Freke Turner insisted that, despite its value in medicine, it was 'artificial', a wine made of an 'imperfectly fermented grape juice [...] sweetened with sugar-candy dissolved in brandy [in which the] want of tannin is supplied by oak shavings' (Turner 1874: 616). Such comments would be repeated throughout the century.[15] Bonnedame's answer to such challenges was, first, to insist that the 'inimitable qualities' of champagne were due not to 'artifice but to the special nature of the soil and geography of the province of Champagne'. He was emphatic that this was not a 'fabricated wine' but that its 'transformations' were based on the 'ingenious use of natural forces' and the 'constant labour of generations' (Bonnedame

1899: 25–6). His own proof copy of his 1893 book on Moët & Chandon insisted that '*Il est de la dernière importance de prouver aux étrangers que nos vins sont naturels; ils sont travaillés, mais il n'entre dans leur composition aucun corps étranger.*' [It is of the utmost importance to show people that our wines are natural; they are worked on but there is nothing added to them.] and in the text he changed '*ils sont travaillés*' [they are "worked on"] to '*ils ont à subir plusieurs manutentions très délicates*' [they are put though very delicate operations] (Bonnedame 1899: 73). This repositioning of champagne as 'natural' echoed the terms of the contemporaneous 1892 appeal judgement which declared that champagne was 'purely natural'.[16]

Second, Bonnedame focused on the unique – even utopian – qualities of the Champagne region. His *Quelques mots sur le vin de Champagne* depicted his homeland as a paradisiacal region which represented the '*l'esprit Gaulois*' or 'Gallic spirit'. He asserted that the wine was responsible for the great number of artists, scientists, writers and generals that Champagne had 'given' to France (*Syndicat du Commerce des Vins de Champagne* 1889: 23). Unlike the Anglophone writers of earlier in the century who depicted the 'peasants' as crafty, suspicious and greedy, the author painted a picture of the Champenois as sober, moral and courteous, whilst the women had all the gifts: 'beauty, grace, wit and warm hearts' (Bonnedame 1899: 21–5).[17] It is probable that, in painting Champagne as emblematic of the best qualities of France and Frenchmen, Bonnedame was drawing on earlier writings about Champagne – the work of both contemporaries and antecedents.

As Thomas Parker's work on the evolution of the idea of 'terroir' has shown, Champagne had been identified with an ideal imaginary of France from at least the eighteenth century. Montesquieu, in a youthful work of 1717, claimed that the '*marne*' (that is the marl or chalk underlying much of the Champagne region) 'is full of volatile spirits that enter into our blood [and the] effect is a certain lightness, a fickleness, this French vivaciousness' (Parker 2015: 124).[18] Such work – or Voltaire's similar remarks – may well have been known to many of the poets who entered compositions for a poetry competition that *Le Vigneron Champenois* had run a few years earlier.[19] The newspaper had appealed to the 'vast federation' of French poets to reflect in verse how 'the wine of Champagne is the wellspring of all the great men and all the noble sentiments that inspire us, the French' and Bonnedame was one of the judges. '*Buvons ce necteur de Cocagne*' [let us drink this nectar of Cockaigne] was the rallying cry of one of the winners, thus linking Champagne to the mythical land of medieval plenty.[20]

Stylistically, the illustrations to Bonnedame's publicity material similarly harked back to the past. They represented vineyard work as it had been fifty years earlier (Figures 5.1 and 5.2).

Though the images and text looked to an arcadian past – for instance, he wrote of the workers singing joyous 'songs of the countryside' as they walked to and from the harvesting each day – Bonnedame did not evoke the countryside itself. There was no description of the land and no reference to its

Figures 5.1 & 5.2 Peasants working in the vineyards of Champagne
These illustrations contrast strongly with advertisement pages of his newspaper (Figure 5.3) which carried detailed drawings of the latest vineyard technology required to spray the vines against mildew or inject them with chemicals in the vain attempt to combat phylloxera.[21]

particular qualities.[22] Hopeful letters to *Le Vigneron Champenois* insisted that its soil would resist phylloxera, the most dangerous vine disease of the nineteenth century. The correspondents were wrong but Bonnedame's powerful depiction of a unique and original 'terroir' (though he did not use that word) still echoes through contemporary champagne marketing.

The third of Bonnedame's themes was that of the man he called the 'inventor' of champagne. His writings, whether for the Exhibitions or in his other works on the champagne houses, rescued Dom Pérignon from almost sixty years of near obscurity. The 1820s mythology of the humble cellarer at the Abbey of Hautvillers who called to his colleagues 'come quickly for I am seeing stars' was revived.[23] In Bonnedame's account he was the 'inventor of champagne' who knew how to make it sparkle. In fact, Pérignon probably

Figure 5.3 Spraying the vines against mildew with late nineteenth-century technology (Source: *Le Vigneron Champenois,* 24 March 1886, p. 1)

spent his working life in the late seventeenth and early eighteenth century trying to eradicate the second fermentation that caused the bubbles but made the wine prone to spoilage. It is certain that Pérignon did not invent the cork. It is a myth that he was blind.[24] The consensus of modern scholars is that he was an expert blender and it is telling that as late as 1884, Paul Chandon de Briailles of the eponymous champagne house, proposed that the chemist whose technical innovations had enabled the creation of modern champagne should be honoured with a statue in Epernay.[25] The proposal came to nothing, instead a statue of Dom Pérignon was finally erected in 1910 (Guy 2003: 28). In 1914, his starring role in the creation of champagne was confirmed by *Le Petit Journal*, which was then one of France's most popular newspapers. Its front cover in June 1914 celebrated the 200th anniversary of Dom Pérignon's discovery of champagne. Not only a founder but a date (*Le Petit Journal* 1914: 1).

This 'invention of tradition' – as Hobsbawm and Ranger famously put it in 1983 – was very convenient for the industry (Hobsbawm & Ranger 1983: 1–14). By the end of the nineteenth century and the early twentieth century champagne was becoming more and more strongly associated with vulgarity, new money and somewhat unrefined carnality. Just two weeks after it celebrated the bicentennial, a short story published in *Le Petit Journal* describes how its anti-hero 'dreamt of nothing other than night-time bars and private rooms [*'cabinets par-ticuliers'*] where, after the champagne, mad orgies were unleashed' (*Le Petit Journal* 1914). The revitalisation of the Dom Pérignon myth was a powerful counter-balance to such stories and to the post-World War One linkage of champagne with *'le jet-set et les restaurants de nuit'*.[26]

An Arcadian terroir?

By incorporating Dom Pérignon into his narrative of both Champagne the place and champagne the wine, Bonnedame gave the industry a powerful foundation myth. But was this a utopian myth? In his critique of Frank and Fritzie Manuel's epic analysis of European utopian thought, J. C. Davis sharpened the Manuels' seven 'constellations' of utopian thought to four fundamental types: the medieval Cockaigne myth ('a world of instant self-gratification' where rivers of the finest wine flow through a landscape of eternal spring and all form of labour is prohibited); the Arcadian world where joyful work applied to nature's gifts ensures that appetites 'are satisfied in a temperate way'; the 'perfect moral commonwealth' in which a 'prescriptive moral order' creates a society capable of enduring hardship and want; and lastly the millennial utopia in which 'nature will be transformed by a force arising and acting independently of the wills of individual men and women' (Davis 1984: 8–10).

Bonnedame's depiction of the champagne harvest is – in Davis' typology – arcadian. The labour is joyful; there is conviviality as grape-pickers in their dormitories chat and sing, implicit sensuality as the girls and boys flirt under watchful maternal eyes. But this social harmony is based on the peasants knowing their place and the rules of social conduct. There is no 'system' of moral enforcement, no sense of the stasis that pervades More's Utopia.

Champagne as an enabler of conviviality and celebration has become a potent theme for the industry in the past century. Guy's work pointed to the drive by Eugene Mercier and other entrepreneurial producers in late nineteenth-century France to promote the use of champagne for domestic celebrations. The series of labels produced by Michel Levy for 'Fiancé' champagne followed by 'Nuptial' and finally 'Bébé' not only cue but pattern the desired celebrations.[27]

Phylloxera had no impact on such celebrations. Though some growers might have believed that the 'unique' conditions of Champagne made it miraculously immune to the ravages of the pest, it made no apparent difference to consumers.[28] The power of champagne's terroir lay not in the soil but in the convivial and celebratory myth that it embodied. To some extent the contributors to the champagne poetry competition were using Champagne as a metonym for France itself. Bonnedame himself explicitly equated *'l'esprit champenois'* with *'l'esprit gaulois'*.[29] France's reputation for *joie de vivre*, wit and sensuality was strongly reflected in the nineteenth-century British take on champagne.[30] Adding Dom Pérignon to the *cuvée* provided the ideal counterweight to fears of hedonism. But Bonnedame was not the only one to incorporate Dom Pérignon into the marketing mix.

Moët & Chandon – integrating territorial and proprietary brand

Central to the revitalisation of Dom Pérignon was the firm of Moët & Chandon. Their appropriation – on the basis of their ownership of some of the vineyards his abbey had possessed – of the claimed creator of champagne started in first years of the twentieth century and continued in the 1920s and 1930s with their launch of Dom Pérignon as a separate premium brand.

By 1900 Moët & Chandon had been established in the British market for more than a century. The Moët name came to prominence in the first decades of the nineteenth century and by 1860 it was probably the best known of all the champagne houses in Britain.[31] However, whilst well known, it was not necessarily regarded as a brand of the highest status.[32] In the period 1875–1905, the price of the Moët & Chandon wines was consistently the lowest of the group of ten premium brands documented by the pioneer historian of champagne, André Simon, in his 1905 book (1905: 184). From the late 1870s onwards, the firm invested, innovated and communicated aggressively to strengthen its position in the British market. Their lack of a true premium wine was addressed in 1879 by launching 'Brut Impérial' as an 'entirely "Brut" [wine] with only its natural saccharine and no added liqueur', and then, in the 1880s, changing the name to 'Dry Imperial' and greatly upweighting the level of advertising.[33] Chiming with the taste of the time, this was a vintage-dated dry wine. Brut Imperial (or Dry Imperial) remained the central wine of the firm until at least the early twentieth century.[34]

The launch of Brut Impérial and the change of name to Dry Imperial was part of a broader British turn in the firm's marketing. Not only was the wine blended to suit the British preference for fully dry wines but in mid to late 1880s they commissioned 'puff pieces' for Brut Impérial/Dry Imperial and donated magnums of this wine to a dinner commemorating the return of the Guards from Egypt.[35] This gesture was reported in identical terms by dozens of newspapers.[36] In another widely reported gesture, they volunteered to absorb the cost of new taxes on sparkling wine rather than passing it on to the consumer.[37]

The advertisements accompanying this British turn increasingly focused on the attributes of the *maison* (or 'house'). In 1889 and 1890 over 350 advertisements in the British press headlined Moët & Chandon's claim to possess 'over 2,500 acres of the finest vineyard land'.[38] Further advertisements on these lines continued into the early 1900s. In 1902, display advertisements for the house headlined 'Triumphs of 1902' celebrated its antiquity ('founded at the beginning of the 17th century'), proclaimed it 'The Triumph of Quality, the Cachet of Popular Approval, and the Choice of the World's Great Nations' and repeated the claim to '2,500 acres of the finest growths'.[39] In 1905 they published a brochure with a strongly Anglocentric perspective written by 'A member of *The Times* advertising staff'. The Moët & Chandon style was described as 'specifically designed to suit the taste of English connoisseurs'. The 'restorative' effects of champagne were supported by the claim that the 'Oxford and Cambridge Eights drink Champagne after rowing a hard course'. The company cast doubt on the quality of some other wines made from non-Champagne grapes and shipped to England under the name of champagne, and once again boasted of their possession of '2,500 acres of the finest Champagne land'. The brochure closed with the reminder that their Dry Imperial was the champagne 'best known in all the Colonies of the Empire on which the sun never sets'.[40]

This claim to the regard of the British elite was reinforced in 1908 but placed within the broader set of champagne values inscribed in the 1900 Paris Exposition. Moët & Chandon co-sponsored the very well-attended 1908 'Franco British Exhibition' held at White City, the newly launched exhibition venue designed by cultural entrepreneur Imre Kiralfy.[41] They erected a pavilion in a prime location next to the 'Royal Enclosure' and took half-page advertisements in a series of 'society' periodicals such as *Country Life, Tatler, Bystander* and *Illustrated London News*. Inside the pavilion, the visitors immediately saw three oil paintings featuring champagne. The first was of 'the Blind Monk who was the first to discover the secret of making Champagne wine "sparkling"'. This appropriation of Dom Pérignon was justified on the basis that they owned his 'original' vineyard.[42] The other two paintings showed champagne drinkers and were, reportedly, 'thoroughly Frenchy and full of life'. Further inside the pavilion was a series of three-dimensional dioramas featuring the 'gathering of the grapes' (again noting the firm's possession of more than 2,500 acres of vineyards), the process of vinification, a general view of the cellars and the 'Grand *Chantier* where the disgorging, final corking and wiring is proceeding'.[43] Moët & Chandon's explicit use of the visual technology and copy strategy of the Paris 1900 Exposition for the British Exhibition is both striking and unique.

In the late 1920s, a series of advertisements in popular journals such as the *Illustrated London News* and the *Sketch* reiterated the claim that Moët & Chandon had the 'largest acreage of vineyards in the Champagne district and are the biggest distributors of that Wine in the World'. The copy continued with the claim that 'they export to this Country a greater quantity of Champagne than any other house'.[44] In 1936, the firm, with the involvement of their London agent Simon Bros, launched the world's first 'prestige cuvée' at double the price of the most expensive vintage champagnes under the name of Dom Pérignon, a brand that they had acquired in 1927 through marriage (Stevenson n.d.).

Dom Pérignon's role in champagne continues to be significant – both as a product brand as a key part of the foundational myth of champagne. No other five-billion-euro industry can trace its origins back to a single 'inventor' – even if the word is increasingly used within quotation marks.[45] For that the *Syndicat* and Bonnedame must take credit. Pierre Boisard, who studied the origins of Camembert, called his article the 'future of a tradition' (Boisard

1991). In their imagining of a natural wine produced from a utopian terroir by a monk of genius, the *Syndicat* – with the marketing support of Moét & Chandon – invented the tradition of their industry and created an enduring marketing proposition based on the definition and evocation of a distinctive territory. But can it be termed a terroir?

Terroir and the territorial brand

I have argued that the SCVC's initiative appears to have been the first time that a region actively set out to develop and promote a territorial brand by promoting and exploiting an image of their region. This went beyond simply asserting the link between place and production. Such basic linkages have been traced back into the eighteenth century but consist of little more than lists of French regions and their notable products – such as '*jambon de Bayonne*', or '*truffes de Périgord*' (Meyzie (2015). Champagne, however, was the first territorial brand to create an image for its region in support of its defence of legal rights.[46] Camembert presents an interesting parallel example but its campaign to create national recognition for a territorial brand followed from its exposure to French troops during the First World War almost a generation later (Boisard 1991: 175). The focus on utopian terroir that the SCVC and Bonnedame pioneered was equally powerful in the long-term as the cultural underpinning of champagne marketing.

Analysis of the current marketing strategies of the champagne houses by Steve Charters and others has shown how both large and small houses project an image of terroir-based authenticity. But the term terroir is highly ambiguous and increasingly contested. The *grande marque* houses researched by Charters and Smith Maguire do not use the same terroir definition as the local grower-producers. In their words, the larger producers 'placed greater emphasis on regional-level geographic terroir, and brand-level cultural terroir, whereas smaller producers were more likely to emphasise highly-localised and personalised land- and cultural-based notions of terroir' (Smith Maguire & Charters 2011: 1, 3, 5–6).

Recent work on the concept and development of terroir has identified many different strands. The earliest dictionary definition, formulated by the Académie Française in the late seventeenth century, focused on the link between land and agriculture and included, in its examples, the notion of '*goût de terroir*' (*Le Dictionnaire De L'académie Française* 1694: 522). This definition remained largely unaltered for at least two centuries, although, as Thomas Parker has shown, the connotations and implications of the 'taste', 'smell' or 'accent' of terroir fluctuated over time. Until the early nineteenth century, the '*goût de terroir*' was literally the 'taste of the soil' and unambiguously the taint of rusticity. Seventeenth-century gourmets such as Saint-Evremond defined the best champagne as that which (in Parker's words) 'left no earthy flavour whatsoever' (Parker 2015: 17, 95; also Parker 2010).

These historical and functionalist definitions of terroir have increasingly been supplemented and challenged by more figurative definitions which give greater weight to the role of men and women in creating and manipulating the land and the landscape.[47] Dominique Barjolle in 2002 noted that French dictionaries continued to focus on '*aptitudes agricoles*' but defined terroir as '*un espace humain caractérisé par une histoire commune qui le raconte* [a human space defined by the human story it tells]' (Barjolle et al. 1998: 8). More recently, Emmanuelle Vaudour has suggested that there are four interlocking components: 'nutriment terroir' (soil, plants, environment), 'space terroir' (environment, territory and historical geography), 'slogan terroir' (advertising and image exploitation) and 'conscience terroir' (identity focused). She notes, too, that 'little attention has been paid to "issues of scale" in terroir' – the point made by Charters and Smith Maguire in their comparison of large and small producers in Champagne (Vaudour 2002: 119–120, 121).

What seems beyond doubt is that terroir has become an instrument of marketing. Arguably, it has been so since the original Bordeaux classification in 1855. This essentially price-based ranking was used by producers to drive sales.[48] Gilles Laferté's seminal articles on the re-development of terroir in the 1920s and 1930s make it clear that, however deep rooted the notion of terroir in Burgundy might be, the development of terroir-led festivals such as La Paulée had a marketing and promotional purpose.[49] Certainly the *Syndicat du Commerce des Vins de Champagne* had a similar goal in mind and, as Guy has noted, the Burgundian producers also appear to have considered an 'aristocratic commercial strategy' at the 1900 Paris Exhibition.[50] However, Charters, Spielmann and Babin's 2017 article was probably the first fully to 'address terroir as a marketing concept'. The authors identify terroir as a 'unique and organic marketing resource' that cannot be duplicated and can be used to justify higher prices in the market (2017: 748–749).[51]

The power of Champagne terroir does not fundamentally lie in the soil but in its capacity to transform an agricultural product into a cultural object.[52] For the growers and producers of champagne, their terroir is a 'source of shared value' from which they can draw individual equity (Spielmann & Williams 2016: 5637). In 1890, the advocate for Moët & Chandon (in their legal suit against Henri Moët for passing-off) noted that champagne was 'entirely exceptional' in the fact that it was brand-driven, that reputation alone determined the choice of the purchaser and that the reputation of any given producer derived not from the 'terroir which produces the wine, as it does for Burgundy or Bordeaux, but from the name of the producer'.[53]

Roger Dion noted over 50 years ago that terroir is not the only source of objective value in wine. He argued that such value depended rather on 'opportunistic elements' such as the location of vineyards close to major population centres or 'communication routes' (Dion 1952: 418, 419–420).[54] The River Marne in medieval and early modern times was such a route, allowing as it did, for easy access to Paris. One could now argue that the success of a given terroir depends less on its functional components and more on its access to modern communication routes – including marketing and advertising. This was the insight that Bonnedame and the wealthy champagne houses that made up the 'Syndicat' grasped more than a hundred years ago. Their invention and communication of a cultural terroir – as other contributors to this volume show – was both powerful and percipient.

Notes

1 See www.maisons-champagne.com/fr/professionel.umc/origines-et-missions/article/les-origines (accessed 16.02.16). For the judgment of 1892, see Hodez (1923: 73).
2 For discussion of what marketers term the regional or territorial brand and economists the collective brand see Menival & Charters (2014: 173).
3 For the proceedings of the Syndicat, see the yearly reports published by Matot-Braine (Syndicat du Commerce 1884–1901).
4 The profiles of the different houses were first printed in his newspaper and later published in book form. See, for example, Bonnedame (1893).
5 For a thoughtful guide to modern branding, see Kapferer (2008).
6 Beecham's Patent Pills were not patented but they were protected as a proprietary trade name. See Corley (2011: 13–14, 52–69). Beecham built his patent medicine business into the market leader primarily through his understanding of advertising and pricing.
7 '*C'est bien, le luxe, mais cela ne peut être qu'un coup de pub, un produit de luxe doit avoir des racines*' [Luxury is all very well but it can't just be a publicity stunt, a luxury product has to have roots]. Quoted by Framery in Pitte (2010: 253).
8 For PDO (Protected Designation of Origin), PGI (Protected Geographical Indication) and TSG (Traditional Speciality Guaranteed) marking schemes, see Thomas (2013: 87–8).
9 Although it focuses primarily on the dynastic and organisational history of the house, and pays less attention to the marketing, the best single book on the firm is Desbois-Thibault (2003).
10 See 'Champagne only comes from Champagne, France' <www.champagne.fr> (accessed 15.10.16).
11 See *Le Petit Journal* guide at www.worldfairs.info/expopavillondetails.php?expo_id=6&pavillon_id=992 (accessed 25.10.16).
12 See Framery who reports that the Mayor of Celles-sur-Ource argued that '*ce n'est pas un secret pour personne que le champagne n'est pas un vin naturel*' [it's no secret that champagne is not a natural wine] (1964: 248).
13 See Guy who precisely articulates the importance of 'the holy origins of champagne [which] helped legitimise a drink originally associated exclusively with the frivolity and decadence of aristocrats' (1999: 229).
14 *Morning Post*, 18 May 1860, p. 4.
15 See Vizetelly (1882: 154–67).
16 Quoted in Framery: '*Que les vins de Champagne [sont] purement naturels d'ailleurs, comme les vins de Bordeaux et de Bourgogne*' (2101: 250).
17 For the mid-century stereotype of the greedy, cunning peasants of Champagne, see Lynn (1858: 53).
18 For the background to Montesquieu's work see '*L'Esprit des lois*' in Benrekassa (2013: 6).
19 For the genesis and results of the poetry competition see *Le Vigneron Champenois*, 26 March 1884, 9 April 1884 and 16 April 1884. Bonnedame was secretary to the jury.

20 For Adolphe Chavance's winning poem see *Le Vigneron Champenois,* 13 August 1884: 3. For the concept and development of the Cockaigne myth, see Pleij & Webb (2001).

21 See, for example, *Le Vigneron Champenois,* 18 May 1887, back page, for a series of advertisements for vineyard technology.

22 The value of the landscape itself as a branding device has been described only recently. See Tomasi et al. (2013); Gyimóthy (2017).

23 The mythology owed its substantive origins to Dom Oudard, writing of a man he never knew. See Gandilhon (1968).

24 For the blindness, see Bullock et al. (1998: 482, 485). The authors note there is no 'substantive evidence' for his supposed blindness and, whilst accepting he may have suffered eye problems in later life, refute the idea that he might have been blind whilst in his capacity as cellarer.

25 *Le Vigneron Champenois,* 2 July 1884, p. 1.

26 *'Une dégradation […] de l'image du champagne devenue le vin de la jet set, des restaurants de nuit et des prostituées'* [A degradation of the image of champagne [which has] become the wine of the jet-set, night clubs and prostitutes]. See Tesson (2015).

27 For the celebratory Marne labels see Guy (1997: 511). The 'Fiancé' label was deposed in the Marne archives on 18 April 1888.

28 *Le Vigneron Champenois,* 4 June 1890, p. 1.

29 *Le Vigneron Champenois,* 3 February 1886, p. 1.

30 See *Bristol Mercury* (24 June 1880: 6) for the link between French 'vivacity' and 'their own champagne'.

31 In the period 1850–59, Moët & Chandon had 135 mentions in the British provincial press, compared to 90 for Veuve Clicquot and 83 for Ruinart. British Newspaper Archive search conducted 6 June 2017.

32 See *Ridley's,* 8 August 1867, p. 8 on the firm getting into 'low company'; see also 12 November 1878, p. 344.

33 For the 1879 launch of Brut Impérial, see *Huddersfield Daily Chronicle,* 21 February 1879, p. 3. In the period 1889–90, there were more than 450 advertisements for 'Dry Imperial' in the British press, spread across 40 newspapers.

34 The terms Brut or Dry have now been dropped in favour of 'Moët Impérial'. See www.uk.moet.com/Our-Champagnes/Moet-Imperial (accessed 29.04.18).

35 In the 1880s the wine was dosed with around 1 gram of sugar per litre; the twenty-first century equivalent has 9 grams of sugar per litre.

36 For the puff in *Hotel Mail,* see *Ridley's,* 12 January 1885, p. 26; for the Guards dinner advertisement see, for example, *Northampton Mercury,* 25 November 1885, p. 5.

37 See, for example, *Sheffield Daily Telegraph,* 11 June 1888, p. 4.

38 See, for example, *Hampshire Advertiser,* 3 August 1889, p. 1. Post World War 1, this claim was changed to the 'largest acreage of vineyard land'. See *Bystander,* 5 December 1928, p. 84.

39 See, for example, *Globe,* 25 November 1902, p. 19.

40 'A Member of The Times advertising staff', *Moët & Chandon* (London, 1905).

41 For the background to Kiralfy's success as entrepreneur and designer and the scale and success of the 1908 Exhibition, see Geppert (2010). For the guide to the Exhibition, see *The Franco-British Exhibition: Official Souvenir,* (London, 1908). Other sponsors were Ardath Tobacco (owners of the 'State Express' brand) and the Australian wine firm of P.B. Burgoyne.

42 *Illustrated London News,* 4 July 1908, p. 24. At that point the firm did not own the 'Dom Pérignon' brand. This was an (under-exploited) property of Eugene Mercier and did not come into the hands of Moët & Chandon until 1927 when it formed part of Francine Durand-Mercier's dowry on marrying Comte Paul de Chandon-Moët. Moët & Chandon did not commercialise this wine until 1935, but it has since become a flagship of the firm. See T. Stevenson (n.d.).

43 For an image of the 'chantier', see *Sketch*, 22 July 1908, p. 32. It is possible that there was also a guidebook of some form to the Moët & Chandon pavilion for visitors, but there is nothing in the firm's archives and I have been unable to locate an example elsewhere.

44 For example, see *Illustrated London News*, 27 July 1929, p. 38.

45 For a recent example of the continuing potency of the Dom Pérignon story, see www.bbr.com/producer-703-dom-perignon (accessed 8.11.16).

46 For a broader perspective on the 'invention of terroir' see the work of Laferté (2012).

47 For a helpful survey of terroir and its link to the French AOC labelling system see Barham (2003: 129–133); Teil et al. (2010).

48 For the importance of the 1855 classification in respecting and regulating pricing see Markham (1998: 52, 96, 172).

49 See Fourcade (2012: 530–531) for the 1855 Burgundy classification by Lavalle. Fourcade argues strongly that 'the geographic entrenchment of status distinctions remains the one constant feature of the French system'; also Laferté (2003: 435; 2012: 6–8). It is worth noting, however, that this 'invention of terroir' apparently received no attention whatsoever in the British press in the inter-war years. Not until 1962 did a favourable reference to terroir in the context of wine appear in the British press. See the *Sphere*, 7 April 1962, p. 27 for a review by 'Ganymede' praising the wines of the Jura.

50 See Laferté (2012: 10) for a discussion of the possible Burgundian marketing strategies at the turn of the century.

51 Spielmann & Williams (2016: 5637) identifies the champagne territorial brand as a 'shared source of value'; the first reference to terroir in the marketing of champagne appears to have been Danay (1991: 37). Stories of the locality or village were identified as one of the potential marketing 'trumps' (*'atouts'*) that could be derived from the local terroir.

52 For a modern take on this process see Faure (1999).

53 Tribunal de Commerce de Reims (1890: 15). '*le vin de Champagne est un commerce d'un genre tout à fait exceptionnel au point de vue de la marque* [...] *c'est la réputation qui seule détermine le choix de l'acheteur, et la réputation ne résulte pas du crû, du terroir d'où il est tiré, comme pour les vins de Bourgogne, de Bordeaux ou autres, mais du nom du fabricant.*' The issue of competing terroir and brand 'logics' has also been explored in a stimulating, if over-prescriptive, form by Croidieu and Monin (2006).

54 For a typically insightful exploration of this issue see Teil et al. (2010: 10, passim).

References

'A Member of The Times advertising staff'. *Moët & Chandon*. London: Moët & Chandon, 1905.

Anderson, S. & Homan, P. (2002). 'Best for Me, Best for You' - a History of Beecham's Pills 1842–1998. *Pharmaceutical Journal*, 269: 921–924.

Anholt, S. (2007). *Competitive Identity: The Brand Management for Nations, Cities and Regions*. Basingstoke: Palgrave Macmillan.

Barham, E. (2003). Translating Terroir: The Global Challenge of French AOC Labeling. *Journal of Rural Studies*, 19(1): 127–138.

Barjolle, D., Boisseaux, S. & Dufour, M. (1998). *Le lien au terroir: Bilan des travaux de recherche*. Lausanne: Institut de l'economie rurale. Available online at www.aop-igp.ch/_upl/files/Lien_au_terroir.pdf

Benrekassa, G. (2013). L'esprit des lois. In *Dictionnaire Montesquieu*, C. Volpilhac-Auger (ed.). Lyons: ENS. Available online at www.dictionnaire-montesquieu.ens-lyon.fr/fr/article/1376478016/fr

Blondeau, F. (1901). *L'exposition du syndicat du commerce des vins de Champagne en 1900: Rapport général, présenté au nom de la commission exécutive.* Reims: Matot.

Boisard, P. (1991). The Future of a Tradition: Two Ways of Making Camembert, the Foremost Cheese of France. *Food and Foodways,* 4(3–4): 173–207.

Bonnedame, R. (1893). *Notice sur la maison Moët & Chandon d' Epernay.* Epernay: Bonnedame.

Bonnedame, R. (1899). *Quelques mots sur le vin de Champagne.* Epernay: Bonnedame.

Bullock, J. D., Wang, J. P. & Bullock, G. H. (1998). Was Dom Perignon Really Blind? *Survey of Ophthalmology,* 42(5): 481–486.

Charters, S. & Spielmann, N. (2014). Characteristics of Strong Territorial Brands: The Case of Champagne. *Journal of Business Research,* 67: 1461–1467.

Charters, S., Spielmann, N. & Babin, B. J. (2017). The Nature and Value of Terroir Products. *European Journal of Marketing,* 51(4): 748–771.

Corley, T.A.B. (2011). *Beecham's, 1848–2000: From Pills to Pharmaceuticals.* Lancaster: Crucible Books.

Croidieu, G. & Monin, P. (2006). *Competing 'Terroir' and 'Brand' Logics and Violating Genetic Codes in the Wine Industry.* The European Institute for Lifelong Learning, Working Papers 2006/06: 1–33. Available online at https://learninghub.em-lyon.com/ EXPLOITATION/Default/digitalCollection/DigitalCollectionAttachmentDownload Handler.ashx?documentId=193934

Danay, J. (1991). *La viticole champenoise,* 545(April): 35–38.

Davis, J. C. (1984). The History of Utopias: The Chronology of Nowhere. In *Utopias,* P. Alexander & R. Gill (eds), pp. 1–17. London: Duckworth.

Desbois-Thibault, C. (2003). *L'extraordinaire aventure du Champagne: Moët & Chandon, une affaire de famille, 1792–1914.* Paris: Presses Universitaires de France.

Dion, R. (1952). Querelle des Anciens et des Modernes sur les facteurs de la qualité du vin. *Annales de Géographie,* 61(328): 417–431.

Faure, M. (1999). Un produit agricole 'affiné' en objet culturel: Le fromage beaufort dans les Alpes du Nord. *Terrain,* 33: 81–92.

Fourcade, M. (2012). The Vile and the Noble: On the Relation between Natural and Social Classifications in the French Wine World. *The Sociological Quarterly,* 53(4): 524–545.

Framery, D. (2010). Le terroir du vin de Champagne: réalités naturelles ou représentations discriminantes entre vignoble et négoce. In *Le bon vin entre terroir, savoir-faire et savoir boire: Actualité de la pensée de Roger Dion,* J.-R. Pitte (ed.), pp. 247–257. Paris: CNRS Éditions.

Franco-British Exhibition (1908). *The Franco-British Exhibition: Official Souvenir.* London: Franco-British Exhibition.

Gandilhon, R. (1968). *Naissance du Champagne, Dom Pierre Pérignon.* Paris: Hachette.

Geppert, A. C. T. (2010). *Fleeting Cities: Imperial Expositions in Fin-De-Siècle Europe.* Basingstoke: Palgrave Macmillan.

Guy, K. M. (1997). Drowning Her Sorrows: Widowhood and Entrepreneurship in the Champagne Industry. *Business and Economic History,* 26(2): 505–514.

Guy, K. M. (1999). Oiling the Wheels of Social Life: Myths and Marketing in Champagne During the Belle Epoque. *French Historical Studies,* 22(2): 211–239.

Guy, K. M. (2003). *When Champagne Became French: Wine and the Making of a National Identity.* Baltimore: Johns Hopkins University Press.

Gyimóthy, S. (2017). The Reinvention of Terroir in Danish Food Place Promotion. *European Planning Studies,* 25(7): 1200–1216.

Hobsbawm, E. J. & Ranger, T. O. (1983). *The Invention of Tradition*. Cambridge: Cambridge University Press.

Hodez, R. (1923). *La protection des vins de Champagne par l'appellation d'origine*. Paris: Les presses universitaires de France

Kapferer, J. (2008). *The New Strategic Brand Management: Advanced Insights and Strategic Thinking*. London: Kogan Page.

Laferté, G. (2003). La mise en folklore des vins de Bourgogne: La 'Paulée' de Meursault. *Ethnologie française*, 3: 435–442.

Laferté, G. (2012). *End or Invention of* Terroirs? *Regionalism in the Marketing of French Luxury Goods: The Example of Burgundy Wines in the Inter-War Years.* Working Paper, 2012/2: 1–20.

Le dictionnaire de l'Académie Française (1694). Paris: Jean Baptiste Coignard. Available online at www.artfl.atil.fr/dictionnaires/ACADEMIE/PREMIERE/premiere.fr. html (accessed 21.03.18).

Le Petit Journal (1914). Supplément Illustré, 14 June. Available online at https://gallica. bnf.fr/ark:/12148/bpt6k717116h.item (accessed 30.06.18).

Lockshin, L. (2012). The Future of the Champagne Brand. In *The Business of Champagne: A Delicate Balance*, S. Charters (ed.), pp.105–118. London & New York: Routledge.

Lynn, E. (1858). Wine, No Mystery. *Household Words*, 17(41): 321–325.

Manuel, F. E. & Manuel, F. P. (1979). *Utopian Thought in the Western World*. Oxford: Basil Blackwell.

Markham, D. (1998). *1855: A History of the Bordeaux Classification*. Chichester: Wiley.

Menival, D. & Charters, S. (2014). The Impact of Geographic Reputation on the Value Created in Champagne. *Australian Journal of Agricultural and Resource Economics*, 58(2): 171–184.

Meyzie, P. (2015). La construction de la renommée des produits de terroirs: Acteurs et enjeux d'un marché de la gourmandise en France (XVIIe–Début XIXe Siècle). *French Historical Studies*, 38(2): 225–252.

Minard, P. (2010). Le bureau essai de Birmingham, ou la fabrique de la réputation au XVIIIe siècle. *Annales. Histoire, Sciences Sociales*, 5: 1117–1146.

Parker, T. (2010). Saint-Evremond and the Case of Champagne d'Ay: Early Modern French Aesthetic Theory Viewed through the Optic of Terroir. *PFSCL*, 38(72): 129–146.

Parker, T. (2015). *Tasting French Terroir: The History of an Idea*. Oakland: University of California Press.

Pleij, H. & Webb, D. (2001) *Dreaming of Cockaigne: Medieval Fantasies of the Perfect Life*. New York: Columbia University Press.

Simon, A. L. (1905). *History of the Champagne Trade in England*. London: Wyman.

Smith Maguire, J. & Charters, S. (2011). Territorial Brands and the Scale of Production: The Example of Champagne. In 6th AWBR International Conference, pp. 1–9. Bordeaux: Bordeaux Management School.

Spielmann, N. & Williams, C. (2016). It Goes with the Territory: Communal Leverage as a Marketing Resource. *Journal of Business Research*, 69(12): 5636–5643.

Stevenson, T. (n.d.). Dom Pérignon Oenothèque, 1966–1996. Available online at www.worldoffinewine.com/news/dom-perignon-oenothque-19661996-4207945 (accessed 21. 09. 2017).

Syndicat du Commerce des Vins de Champagne (1884–1901). *Comptes Rendus Annuels*, Vol. I. Reims: Matot-Braine.

Syndicat du Commerce des Vins de Champagne (1889). *Notice historique sur le vin de Champagne.* Epernay: Bonnedame et Cie

Syndicat du Commerce des Vins de Champagne (1905). *Propriété du nom de Champagne. Arrêts et jugements divers.* Reims: Matot-Braine.

Teil, G., Barrey, S., Floux, P. & Hennion, A. (2010). Le Terroir, Une Cause À Faire Valoir. In *Le bon vin entre Terroir, savoir-faire et savoir-boire: Actualité de la pensée de Roger Dion*, J. R. Pitte (ed.), pp. 227–246. Paris: CNRS Éditions

Tesson, Y. (2015). Les projets de publicité collective dans le Champagne (1931–1939). *Mode de Recherche*, 21: 5–15.

Thomas, A. (2013). Country-of-Origin Marketing: A List of Typical Strategies with Examples. *Journal of Brand Management*, 21(1): 81.

Tomasi, D., Gaiotti, F. & Jones, G. V. (2013). *The Power of the Terroir: The Case Study of Prosecco Wine.* Basel: Springer Basel.

Tribunal de Commerce de Reims (1890). *Chandon et cie contre Henri Moët.* Reims: Imprimerie Coopérative.

Turner, M. F. (1874). Wine and Wine-Merchants. *The New Quarterly Magazine*, 2: 595–619.

Vaudour, E. (2002). The Quality of Grapes and Wine in Relation to Geography: Notions of Terroir at Various Scales. *Journal of Wine Research*, 13(2): 117–141.

Vela, J. D. S. E. (2013). Place Branding: A Conceptual and Theoretical Framework. *Boletín de la Asociación de Geógrafos Españoles*, 62: 467–471.

Vizetelly, H. (1882). *A History of Champagne: With Notes on the Other Sparkling Wines of France.* London: Southeran.

6 Terroir wines in Champagne

Between ideology and utopia[1]

Steve Charters

Introduction

The discourse of the champagne region is full of references to terroir, as a glance at the website of the *Comité Champagne* (CC),[2] or many of the major houses makes clear. This was one of the factors behind the successful recent application for UNESCO world heritage status as a cultural landscape. Yet champagne is produced from a single, large appellation covering a wide range of natural environments: such a vineyard is very different from the notion of terroir in other parts of the world – most classically Burgundy in France, with its focus on small, individual plots.

This traditional *champenois* idea of terroir, which in terms of scale operates generically and without local specificity, sits perfectly with the way champagne is produced and marketed by the large houses which make millions of bottles with grapes sourced from all over the region. More precise interpretations of the concept would undermine their automatic right to claim an underlying terroir for their product. Place offers a level of authenticity which underlies the luxury branding of the wine. Nevertheless, this assumption is under challenge, predominantly from smaller producers, supported by some intermediaries, who increasingly promote 'terroir' champagnes in contrast to the mass-produced, widely available, house brands with their focus on luxury.

To explore these ideas further I will examine the context for the potential for utopian terroir in champagne, looking at both how utopia may be relevant to the region and how the idea of terroir has developed there. This is then supplemented by an examination of the way in which terroir has been presented over the last 20 years, based on personal fieldwork.

Context

Two notions of utopia

Utopia has myriad forms, but it has been suggested that there are two which emerge very clearly. The first of these is in the eponymous book by Thomas More (1973 [1516]). More offers an ideal country, but it is a carefully structured place, subject to the benevolent despotism of old, wise men who govern to ensure tranquillity and access to resources for all. It is not a liberal democracy and has a stringent legal system and severe punishments. Crucially, at least by implication, it is fixed and unchanging.

The second form of utopia is one that has developed as an alternative since More. It is a reinvention over the last 500 years (Sargent 2010). It was clear that More was not proposing that the England of Henry VIII should be remodelled on the lines he had imagined, but that he was using his mythical country as a way of examining socio-political structures. That approach has been revisited over the centuries so that utopia becomes not merely an ideal, but a challenge to the status quo. It is aspirational; the desire to create a better world. To this extent utopianism[3] is positioned against something – an existing world or worldview – and represents an idealised 'other' to be attained, as a response to dissatisfaction with existing social structures.

This dichotomy was given a theoretical context in the twentieth century by Karl Mannheim in *Ideology and Utopia: An Introduction to the Sociology of Knowledge* (Mannheim 1960). Mannheim argued that ideology and utopianism both stem from social conflict. One group may be dominant and cannot or will not contemplate alternative ways of organizing society. Other groups are less powerful and only see what is necessary to transform society, rather than necessarily diagnosing how a society is currently operating (with both strengths and weaknesses). These groups thus focus less on what actually exists, and more on the necessity of achieving something else. Sargent (2010) noted that Ricoeur developed this theme further, arguing that a goal of utopianism is to challenge and ultimately destroy an ideology. This is one of the 'positive' aspects of utopian ideals, as it challenges the hegemony of ideology by offering alternatives. Thus, there is a symbiotic link between utopia and ideology. The latter once had utopianism at its core, an ideal of how the world could be when the belief-system is established, and thus utopia may ultimately become an ideology.

Two notions of terroir

Terroir, of course, has its roots in the claim that the style of a wine is formed by the viticultural environment in which the grapes are grown. There are, however, very different conceptions of terroir in France (Charters 2006; Charters et al. 2017). Broadly these can be split into two types which can be categorised as the Burgundian, and that of Champagne.

Terroir in Burgundy is based on the specific impact of the environment on a wine style. This may be a region, but the most prestigious wines come from a village or an individual site (a *climat*). For this reason, in Burgundy there are 84 appellations, 33 of which represent a single plot of land (*grand cru*); additionally, there are over 600 *premiers crus*.[4] Such a precise structure is predicated on an explicitly defined link between the land exposure, the climate and the soil of the vineyard with the taste of the wine. This has become the dominant paradigm for terroir in much of the world.

Terroir in Champagne operates differently. There is a single appellation for an area of 34,000 hectares spread over a region of around 150 kilometres north to south and 80 kilometres east to west. *Grands* and *premiers crus* exist, but they are villages and not individual plots, and have no appellation of their own (Charters 2012). Most of the wine sold (over 70%) is made by large, well-known brands which source grapes from across the region without distinguishing any sub-regional difference in style.

The development of terroir in Champagne

This focus on the brand does not mean that place is not important; as will be seen, the region uses its terroir to promote its wine. Nevertheless, there was a conflict between 'place' and 'brand' in the nineteenth century which was the result of disputes between the vignerons[5] and the larger houses (or negociants) who sell most of the wine (Guy 2003). Place became the dominant framework for denoting the wine, but brand survived by assimilating the discourse of place into its identity. The foundation myths of the region started to be formulated at the end of the nineteenth century. Raphael Bonnedame, the editor of *Le Vigneron Champenois* trade paper, was fundamental to this. As noted by Graham Harding in his chapter, it was Bonnedame who elaborated the role of Dom Pérignon as the 'creator' of the process of second fermentation. Nevertheless, as Harding also suggests, Bonnedame's starting point for the character of champagne was not history but the geography and soil of the region which gave 'inimitable qualities' to the wine; it was not a 'made' wine. This attention on place was reinforced by the first world war, fought across the region, where as Guy (2003: 187) observes, 'the soil of champagne was watered by the blood of Frenchmen', adding an extra significance to regional terroir.

At this point, the discussion was about the *terroir de Champagne*, not *champagnes de terroir*.[6] The latter only began to become significant from 1918 onwards. The first *champagne de terroir* is generally considered to be Salon, released commercially in 1921, with grapes sourced from various sites in the village of Le Mesnil-sur-Oger.[7] This was supplemented in 1935 by the Clos des Goisses, one selected *monoparcelle* wine from Champagne Philipponnat. Subsequently there was Cattier, from 1951, with Clos du Moulin, followed by Krug (Clos de Mesnil and later Clos d'Ambonnay), then, in the 1990s, others – including Leclerc Briant, Billecart Salmon, and Taittinger (Avellan 2006). Yet, with the exception of Salon, all these houses produce one or a few *champagnes de terroir* alongside wines blended more widely from across the region.

The notion of terroir in Champagne went beyond the primary focus on soil which is evident in Burgundy. It has been argued that terroir extends into the underground cellars carved out of chalk (Wilson 1998). These offer natural cooling which is influential in the process of second fermentation and ageing. Furthermore, the terroir in Champagne has been modified in other ways, which are less publicly discussed. The soil has been altered with lignites and cinders taken from the top of the *Montagne de Reims* to improve its texture (Berry 1990). Further, for a long time at the end of the twentieth century rubbish from Paris, in blue plastic bags, was ground up and spread on the vineyards as a form of fertilizer (Faith 1988). It is still possible to see small fragments of blue plastic in the vineyards: remnants of the bags in which the waste was deposited.

The well-known champagne brands were all the creation of houses - the large companies which dominate the production of champagne. However, from 1929, and particularly after 1945, some growers who sold grapes to the houses also began to sell their own wines, a market which expanded so that today it accounts for over 20% of all champagne, mainly sold in France (Charters 2012). Growers tend to have land holdings in one or a few neighbouring villages. This allows them to produce *monocru* (and even *monoparcelle*) wines.

For a long period, the growers did not necessarily promote terroir. The move towards the appropriation of the rhetoric of terroir by vignerons began in the early 1990s (Verdier 2013). Verdier analysed the use of the word in *La Champagne Viticole* (the vignerons' monthly journal), noting that in 1991 there was a seminal article telling vignerons how better to market their wine in the context of terroir. By 1994 the vignerons' union (the *Syndicat Général de Vignerons*, or SGV) had launched a formal campaign underlining terroir and linking it to authenticity.

Gradually the discourse of terroir moved beyond the soil to include 'savoir-faire' – respect for, but also mastery of, the rhythms of nature to enhance the wine. It also underlined artisanship: the vigneron could express herself or himself by the wine and also the place – both geographic and imagined. This helped to mystify the product. In 1995 the collective brand of *champagne des vignerons* began, with a logo created by the SGV in 1998 (Verdier 2013). Verdier suggests that later there was a move back towards terroir more purely as soil – yet, crucially, its use was the response of a group of small producers (as individuals and organisationally) who saw themselves caught between cheap champagne in supermarkets and the *grandes marques*[8] and identified terroir as the way forward to establish their identity. It has also been noted that the 1990s was the period of the development of production elsewhere by the houses, especially in California (Brochot 2000). This could be seen as a move to develop a 'delocalised' champagne by the big producers (Brochot 2000: 88), and the shift to terroir by the vignerons therefore a reaction, to underline the significance of their own place. More recently it has been noted that, compared to the houses, the vignerons are more likely to use the notion of terroir as a key element of the promotion of wine tourism in the region (Gatelier 2017).

The image of champagne and the idea of terroir

The research on which this study is based is in two parts. First it uses my engagement of over 20 years with the Champagne region including seven years living there. This resulted in a number of interactions with key actors involved with champagne. Of these interactions 137 were recorded in field notes covering a gamut of issues (and ranging widely beyond terroir). Most interactions were concentrated in the period 2007–2015 but there were some in the decade before that and have been others since. The strength of this process has been that it has not focused on terroir (at no point was the topic explicitly raised with informants) so that any comments are top-of-mind and reflect the informant's own view of the importance and character of the concept.

The second form of research has been an analysis of documents (essentially brochures and websites) authored by producers of champagne. This analysis was in two parts; the first was historic (examining brochures produced over the period of 1997 to 2009). The second part was a contemporary snapshot of websites (in both French and English). The websites comprised both those relating to the companies whose brochures had been previously examined (in order to see if there had been any change in approach to the way terroir was projected) and a number of other websites produced by vignerons who were underrepresented in the brochures examined.

Who is talking about terroir?

Informants have been categorised by their role in the champagne industry. The basic differentiation within the Champagne region is between the vignerons and the houses.[9] The former includes the cooperatives (groupings of vignerons who produce wine sold either to other companies or under the cooperatives' own brand); effectively these form a third category of producer. Furthermore, although the houses are seen as a collective set, there is a difference between the largest grouping (LVMH) with a turnover of over 1.5 billion euros p.a., and the smallest with less than a million euros p.a., plus all sizes in between. This smaller type of house is much more aligned culturally, socially and economically with the large growers (but differs in having the right to buy grapes) than to the large champagne producers. As this may affect their approach to a concept such as terroir they have been categorised as a fourth group, the 'small houses'.

As well as businesses making wine there are coordinating bodies for the whole industry (the CC), for the vignerons (the SGV) and for the houses (the *Union de Maisons de Champagne* (UMC)). These are collectively represented as a fifth group - the interprofessional bodies. Beyond these associations there are also other actors; representatives of banks, brokers of grapes and wine, and local retailers, who also have a perspective on champagne. These have been united in a sixth group as 'other actors'.

The field notes accumulated over the last 20 years have thus been split six ways.[10] The largest number is with vignerons (50) and a further ten with cooperatives but there are also 40 with houses and four with small houses (this latter includes one small producer of 60,000 bottles per year which is part of a larger group – but is given effective autonomy within that group, and has a distinct management culture). The final 33 interactions are split between the interprofessional bodies and other actors.

When this is done it is evident that unprompted references to terroir are proportionately most common amongst the (very few) small houses – all of whom raised the topic – and the vignerons. The interprofessional bodies and the cooperatives also made a number of points on the subject, but the houses generally spoke of it very little: less than a half of the proportionate number of references made by the vignerons.

How is terroir characterised?

Analysis of the discourse about terroir produces a number of dimensions of the concept (see Charters et al. 2017; Spielmann & Gelinas-Chebat 2012; Vaudour 2002). Amongst these we can observe the following: environmental terroir; human (i.e. cultural) terroir; viticultural and production terroir (themselves the impact of human activity on environment); stylistic (or taste) terroir – the organoleptic distinctiveness of a wine; marketing terroir (called 'slogan' terroir by Vaudour (2002)) which includes the protection of a terroir in an appellation, and; authenticity terroir (with these last two being a direct result of human terroir).

It is necessary when considering the varying views on terroir within Champagne to stress that there is no simplistic divide between the houses and the vignerons, with the latter being the group which promotes the concept and the former ignoring it. It is also the case that all types of producers and the interprofessional bodies will use the word terroir at times. Having said that, it is clear that the approach of the larger houses is quite limited.

The few references to the topic by representatives of the houses focused very much on the human role in terroir. A video at one large house stated that 'Réné Lalou[11] was a real creator of terroir'.[12] Another puts terroir in the context of tradition, the use of barrels and human respect for the grapes. Soil and/or climate were commonly used but to underline the idea of terroir as aspect of the region itself, rather than a specific, local, environmental factor. What was emphasised was the human dimension – particularly savoir-faire and the refinement and quality of the process of making champagne.

The CC in particular also focuses on the human aspect of terroir; it is regularly linked in their literature and what they have said to savoir-faire, and the understanding of how champagne is made. A very early encounter with the CC (or CIVC as it was then known) included an explanation of how gas and liquid spectrometry could be used to analyse the unique chemical make-up of champagne: 'This is essential to protect champagne'. These chemical structures reflect the terroir of champagne uniquely – but the process was not used to market the uniqueness of champagne but as proof in disputes about the origins of counterfeit champagne. Later, a viticulturist who worked in a research capacity for the region as a whole said 'Humans are artists, who build the terroir', again reinforcing the issue of savoir-faire or production over environment. This emphasis on human or cultural terroir has its roots back in the nineteenth century (see the chapter by Graham Harding in this volume).

Exhibit 1: UNESCO World Heritage Designation

In 2015, after a ten-year campaign, the 'Slopes, Houses and Cellars of Champagne' were awarded World Heritage Status by UNESCO as a cultural landscape. The proposition had initially included all of the vineyards in the appellation, but in the end only a small number of traditional sites in the Marne Valley (totalling just 220 hectares) were selected as representative of all, along with the ancient Roman cellars of Reims still used by some of the houses, and the 'Avenue de Champagne' in Epernay, home to many of the best known brands (UNESCO 2018). Terroir was mentioned twice in the supporting application, once in connection with the chalky rock of the regions and the second time as being something developed by local industry into a mass production of very high quality (*Coteaux Maisons et Caves de Champagne* 2018).

The application thus combined vineyards (terroir) with production and with image and marketing. The committee promoting the application was chaired by a vigneron, but included a great deal of support from the houses, as well as the CC. The local industry was overall supportive, feeling that it would add value to the whole of the region.

At the same time the Burgundy wine region also obtained the same recognition from UNESCO. However, in that case it was the vineyards alone (all of them in the Côte d'Or – over 1,300 *climats*) which were the focus – and UNESCO explicitly titled this designation 'The climats, terroirs of Burgundy'. This was a concentration on the terroir rather than the savoir-faire or marketing.

As noted above, most references to terroir in direct interactions were made by vignerons. They see terroir through all the dimensions outlined previously, with specific comments on its authenticity, production and taste. As one would expect of grape growers, the environmental dimension is very important and referred to regularly.

Furthermore, of equal importance to viticultural terroir for the vignerons is marketing terroir. Regularly, when asked what makes value in champagne, terroir was cited; one defined marketing as 'the image of a *récoltant-manipulant*[13] using the specifics of his terroir; this is the approach which justifies the price'. This focus on marketing was underlined by those members of cooperatives (themselves grape growers) who commented on terroir. When we examine the (very few) brochures from vignerons all of them explicitly used the term terroir to talk of their wines, and they tended to put some emphasis on the specific environmental context of their vineyards. This was reinforced further when the contemporary vigneron websites were analysed. The words 'terroir' and 'parcelle' appear in nearly all of them, as does soil and site.

One vigneron volunteered that terroir is fundamental to their work. He argued that there are good and bad vignerons and negociants 'but when you are a negociant you are a winemaker; a vigneron is a man who is there to interpret terroir'. He was based in the Côtes des Blancs, and is very specific about variations in wine styles from different parts of the area, distinguishing the north of the Côtes as 'feminine and racy' and the south as powerful and structured – 'more smoky, graphite and mineral'. Another, reasonably large, vigneron, making 120,000 bottles per year, commented that 'it's important for us to separate the terroirs ... we have 47 *parcelles* and 15 hectares to keep separate.' Unusually they use indigenous rather than cultured yeast for the first fermentation, as 'it's important to respect the yeast we have in Champagne; it relates to the terroir.' These comments reveal a focus on the micro level and the distinct environmental impact it offers on wine styles.

Exhibit 2: The role of Anselme Selosse

A key actor in much of the discourse around 'new' champagne – whether terroir, or biodynamics, or production method, is Anselme Selosse. The driving force since the 1970s behind the *domaine* established by his father (Champagne Jacques Selosse) he has both reshaped ways of viewing champagne and influenced a new generation of vignerons in the region. At one time biodynamic (although he has moved away from this now) and with a focus on terroir, he trained not in Champagne but in Burgundy which has radically shaped his outlook (Walters 2017). The wines have been described as Burgundian (Faith 2016).

I attended a tasting run by Selosse which was a fascinating insight into his oblique way of understanding champagne. Twenty-two people paid to come – including about six vignerons keen to learn from him. The tasting began not with wine but with water containing various mineral salts. This was necessary to calibrate our palates to the different mineral composition of each of his wines.

According to Walters (2017: 128) 'the significance of what he brought back to Champagne [was] the philosophy that authentic wines are unique wines that reflect their terroir'. Yet Selosse is not a dogmatist; he told the tasting that he prefers Tao to biodynamics. Balance, the middle way, is important. He explained this in terms of the way he may make his wines. Wines with a lower dosage[14] are more clear, very distinct and precise. More highly dosed wines are fuzzy – the mirror is hazy – but sometimes you do need to see yourself as bit hazy, rather than very precise. At the same time he reinforced his commitment to terroir in Champagne and for champagne. 'In California or New Zealand the wine is the handiwork of humans' (i.e. there is no terroir). Yet against this, his pursuit of Tao forced him to underline that 'tradition is something that can evolve... while remaining in the spirit of the wine; the process can change'.

Many of his wines have a traditional (Burgundian) terroir-focus; they come from single vineyards. Others are from different vineyards within a single village. Yet others, however, may cut across three villages. Perhaps ultimately, therefore, his focus is not on terroir precisely but is rather broader. 'Essentially we're of the countryside, and our goal is to give expression to the countryside' (Faith 2016: 155).

Interestingly, the most emphatically traditional position on terroir (i.e. environmentally- rather than human-focused) was provided less by the vignerons and more by the small houses, all of whom mentioned it very specifically as a factor in their wines. Thus, one said that their wine is the opposite of standard non-vintage champagne; they use a single variety from a sole village and just one year. The philosophy is to 'allow the terroir to speak'. Another commented that 'I'm not sure that you can explain what terroir is – you can just taste it', focusing very much on the impact of environment on style. He went on to state that they had decided to put specific vineyard site names on their label, and that their 1996 Avize *grand cru* wine has a map of their vineyards in the village on the label. This is reinforced in both the brochures and the websites from this group, where the word terroir appears regularly and there are many references to the village in which they are based or the specific characters of the vineyards they own.

How are perceptions of terroir changing?

The most evident change in the view of terroir in Champagne is that references to it seem much more common than in the past from all key actors in the region. A comparison of contemporary websites (predominantly from the houses) shows that most now use the word at some point in their presentation. When we look at brochures issued by these same producers, most being ten years old or more, the term was used much less. That does not mean that the concept was ignored previously; *parcelles* were mentioned by some producers (thus showing a recognition of the role of specific sites) and savoir-faire was widely referenced; there is, all the same, no sense that any of these factors needed to be interpreted directly within the paradigm of terroir itself. Now the word is used regularly, at least in passing; where it is not used, it tends to be either very large houses or occasionally a smaller vigneron who eschew it. It is also the case that the interprofessional bodies are now referring to it, whereas in the past this was less often the case. To the extent that it was referenced previously (either explicitly or implicitly) it was more cultural terroir which was indicated.

A further examination was made of a selection of about 20 current websites created by vignerons. Overwhelmingly, these reference terroir directly, as well as talking about their sites, soil and viticulture; it still seems more important for the vignerons than the large houses.

Exhibit 3: Transgressing the Norms

Whilst there may be differences in the presentation of champagne it is rare to see explicit disagreement. However, one producer – a small house – told his story of how he had developed *monoparcelle* wines. The large houses were unhappy with this – even the CIVC was critical because they said that he had no 'clos'[15] and should only make one *monocru* and not three. Nevertheless, his *monocrus* are always blended wines; one of them he talked about came from both the 2005 and 2006 vintages, and was 40%

Chardonnay, 40% Pinot Noir and 20% Pinot Meunier – and this, he felt, put them in the mainstream of champagne styles. He has consolidated parcels with neighbours to get a single six-hectare block in one particular village – losing a bit at each exchange but gaining concentration of ownership. They now use their approach to produce a series of wines labelled 'authentique'. Everything that this producer did was focused on different aspects of specific terroirs; the environment, the production processes, the wine styles and a focus on authenticity. The champagne establishment remained critical; there was an acceptance that there could be monocru wines – but they should not become too dominant. That may well be because they were perceived to threaten the image of terroir as overarching the whole region in Champagne (and thus inherent in every bottle) rather than coming from individual sites (and therefore, by extension, unavailable for the large volume brands).

Discussion

> 'I have always found it much more exciting to make the best possible Ay Vauzelle Terme than to make 3 million bottles.'
>
> (Small House Owner)

Verdier (2013) noted the growth in the idea of terroir in Champagne, from the early 1990s, and located it very much within the discourse of the vignerons. Yet the use of the term seems to have grown further in the last 15 years and spread beyond the vignerons alone. However, it is evident that the way in which the word terroir is employed varies widely. It seems clear from a number of the interviews detailed here that terroir is often mentioned but much less frequently explained. It appears to operate as a shibboleth; a necessary, inclusive term which identifies the user as someone who accepts the regional identity of the wine without needing to adopt the more philosophical interpretations of the word. In this case it is often linked to price or value in private discussion and to regional distinction (focusing on savoir-faire) against other sparkling wines in public discourse. For many this is a terroir 'managed' by the CC, and which supports the widespread production and international marketing of a luxury product. It is institutionalised, part of the regional ideology, and reflects the idea that terroir as a construct is a way of entrenching the wine industry culturally and giving a common language for quality ideals and hierarchies (Demossier 2010). In this context Champagne terroir is basic, a reflex which must be expressed – but true quality comes from things beyond it (particularly around production method and regulations). It is necessarily integrated into the ideological hegemony but not elaborated, as its subordinate role in the UNESCO bid suggests.

The alternative is the terroir of utopianism with its discourse of minerals, single plots and authenticity. There are different lenses we can use to understand the importance and effect of this approach. One is that of the desire for a defined cultural identity; historically this was provided by political difference (predominantly between the more radical vignerons and conservative houses (Guy 2003)). In part this reflected a long-standing internal division in Champagne; the conflict between the (*bourgeois*) towns of Reims and Epernay with their focus on technique and technology and the (*paysan*) villages which emphasise land and nature. As political ideology becomes less significant other beliefs move in to fill the gap between the dichotomous cultural backgrounds of the key actors. This utopianism may also be a response to external circumstances: the luxury marketing of the wine in duty free stores of Singapore, the up-market wine shop in Mayfair or a nightclub in Los Angeles – all of which are the *domaine* of the houses. In none of these does place, the vignerons' environment, matter.

Another, complementary, way of understanding the utopian use of terroir is through the lens of business – and especially marketing. The differences in personal identity noted above play into differences of image, and therefore brand identity. Terroir-focused producers are consequently recreating the parameters of how champagne should be viewed in order to fashion an image for their wine. This image has to offer meaning for what they are doing (and is based on their cultural identity) but it must also offer value to their consumers. In doing this they are essentially aiming to replicate what Bonnedame did over a century ago, to challenge the sense that champagne is an artificial or constructed wine (see the chapter by Graham Harding in this volume), and thus to underline the distinctive and authentic nature of what they make.

In business terms this approach has echoes of a David and Goliath struggle. However, there is a logic to the approach. By fundamentally challenging the concept of what champagne should be these producers are not arguing for ideological evolution, but a utopian revolution in the identity of the wine. This is thus an attempt to disrupt existing business models. As has been noted by Morgan (2009) 'challenger brands' may need to succeed by actively challenging dominant brands rather than just carving out a niche for themselves. This lens – the economic – is not an alternative to the cultural interpretation but the two interact. The cultural is used to give credibility to the brand identity and business success sustains and reinforces the ideological challenge. The two are interdependent.

Firm type has previously been suggested as an influence on how a champagne business markets itself (Smith Maguire & Charters 2011). What is significant from this research is the confirmation that it is less the structural position of the business which is significant in determining its view on and use of terroir (thus vignerons and cooperatives versus houses) and more the size of the business. Small houses and the more dynamic vignerons are more likely to focus on specific terroirs than cooperatives and larger houses, and possibly than small vignerons as well. There is, of course, the economic underpinning to this. The large houses blend their wines from all over the region and must place less emphasis on environmental terroir and more on savoir-faire. The vignerons are more likely to stress environmental terroir, which is the counterpoint when you are small and do not have access to large volumes of grapes, but do have specific and localised plots.

Despite the focus of the proponents of environmental terroir on authenticity, their approach is not a 'rediscovery' of terroir in champagne. Whilst champagne labelled as being from a particular locality (e.g. *champagne de Sillery*[16]) was quite prevalent at times, the idea of terroir as a single plot (even single village) wine almost certainly did not exist in the region before the current period, and until the time of Salon from the 1920s onwards. Bonnedame himself, for all his focus on the significance of the region, did not use the word terroir in his writing (Graham Harding, personal communication). In the period when Burgundy was beginning to focus on the very specific origin of its wines – from about 1900 but especially in the 1920s and 30s (Jacquet 2010; Laferté 2012; Whalen 2009), the ideology in Champagne was fusing soil and climate into a large volume story, based on the skill of the *chef de cave* in blending. Even today it is clear that Burgundy has taken a different approach (Thach et al. forthcoming). As Demossier (2004: 96) suggests, terroir is the 'ongoing construction of a collective representation of the past through the work of producers', and that work in Champagne is of a very recent origin.

Conclusion: creating new worlds

Mannheim (1960: 173) suggested that 'a state of mind is utopian when it is incongruous with the state of reality within which it occurs'. This means the focus is on things which do not actually exist or which do not fit with the established paradigm. He goes on to argue that to be utopian this stance must also stimulate activity which aims to break down the status quo, and replace it with the alternative.

The new interpretation of terroir as an influence with precise environmental specificity, a notion promoted by some of the vignerons and the small houses, fits with Mannheim's comment. Over 72% of all champagne is produced by houses with a regional focus. A further 9% originates with the cooperatives, the largest of which also blend from all over the region. Even many of the vignerons, sourcing grapes from a number of places or with a story that focuses on family history or savoir-faire and specific production techniques, accept the orthodox view of terroir. Laferté (2012) has suggested that, in Champagne, image and belonging are dominant, rather than tradition and identity, which are more significant in Burgundy. Belonging to the group and the cohesive message to the outside world thus trumps individual distinctiveness as core values in the region. This establishment view of terroir is not necessarily anti-utopian, and is indeed utopian in the sense suggested previously of the carefully ordered society, managed by a few 'elders' for the collective benefit of all. In the aftermath of the bitter disputes between vignerons and negociants at the beginning of the twentieth century (Guy

2003) such a carefully managed social order did seem utopian (and it was a precursor to the great success and growth of champagne in the post-war period). The apogee of this approach was the successful UNESCO world heritage designation, which both crystallised the success of the champagne utopia and also fixed the identity and homogeneity of the region as an unchanging, historic unity, locked as much into image and production as environment and certainly not focused on the individual sites; it was the codification of the ideal.

Yet this success, and the tightly controlled way in which it was brought about, became the ideology which the contemporary *terroiristes* in Champagne are now challenging. Theirs is an ideal to be attained, a vision of diversity, of specific *parcelles*, of a village identity and of variety. It is the ideal of a vibrant countryside (against the houses which tend to be in urban centres and focused as much on their caves as the rural source of grapes). This is aspirational; the desire to create a better world, which is not dominated by the uniformity of millions of bottles of the same wine. It also contrasts itself with the perspective of marketers who emphasise the luxury of the product rather than the visceral need to prune vines in the snow in February or harvest the grapes in the rain, something which the smaller producers understand first hand. At the same time, it is not necessarily a carefully thought-out manifesto with a clearly defined theology or programme. As Anselme Selosse demonstrates, as he fluctuates between talking about terroir or minerality to the 'middle way' and even the countryside, this utopianism is a usefully fuzzy dream, allowing myriad interpretations and presentations. Nevertheless, the utopian terroir in champagne is positioned against something – an existing world or worldview – and finally represents an idealised 'other', however ill defined, to be attained.

Notes

1 I want to thank Graham Harding for comments on the first draft of this chapter, and my students Nicolas Altmann, Pierre Nouhaud, Sarah Messouak, and He Xuan for their help with the analysis of champagne publicity.
2 Known until recently as the Interprofessional Committee for the Wines of Champagne (CIVC)
3 This term will be used throughout to define the aspirational, challenging form of utopia in contrast to the existence of a perfect state.
4 These are village appellations which have higher status and can add the name of the vineyard to the name of the commune.
5 A vigneron is a grower (usually very small-scale), member of the category responsible for 90% of all grapes in the region. They may sell their grapes to larger producers and/or make some champagne from their own grapes.
6 Following Avellan (2006), I distinguish two specific localised terroir champagnes; *monocru* (from a single village), and *monoparcelle*, from a single plot of land. These could be seen to equate to commune and *climat* terroir in Burgundy.
7 There was in fact an earlier one – Mont Ferré, near Reims, run by a vigneron, Charles Benoit, from 1888, but this can be seen as an outlier. I'm grateful to Graham Harding for this information.

8 The most well-known of the negociant brands.
9 The key difference between vignerons and houses is that the former can only source grapes to make wine from their own vineyards, whereas the latter can buy grapes from growers or wine from cooperatives to make their champagne. Some of them own no vineyards at all.
10 What follows is a numeric analysis of qualitative research. It is an indicator but was not undertaken with any quantitative analysis in mind, and clearly no valid tests for significance can be carried out.
11 A famous, previous, *chef de cave* of the house.
12 All translations from French made by the author.
13 The local administrative term for a vigneron who sells wine in addition to grapes.
14 The small amount of sugar added to the wine before it is released for sale to balance the acidity in champagne.
15 A walled vineyard, marked off from other surrounding plots, and giving a clear individual identity to a specific wine; it has been used by some negociants – perhaps most notably Krug – to identify a *monoparcelle* wine.
16 A wine from a village close to Reims, possibly a generic term for wines assembled from a number of good villages nearby, with aristocratic associations, and easily accessible due to its proximity to the city.

References

Avellan, E. (2006). Antithesis of Champagne: Single Vineyard Style Wines: Past, Present and Future Prospects. Unpublished Dissertation. London: Institute of Masters of Wine.
Berry, E. (1990). Soil in Fine Wine Production. *Journal of Wine Research*, 1(2): 179–194.
Brochot, A. (2000). Champagne: Objet de culte, objet de lutte. In *Campagnes de tous nos désirs : Patrimoines et nouveaux usages sociaux*, M. Rautenberg, A. Micoud, L. Bérard & P. Marchenay (eds), pp. 75–90. Paris: Editions de la Maison des Sciences de l'Homme.
Charters, S. (2006). *Wine and Society: The Social and Cultural Context of a Drink.* Oxford: Butterworth-Heinemann.
Charters, S. (ed.). (2012). *The Business of Champagne: A Delicate Balance.* Abingdon: Routledge.
Charters, S., Spielmann, N. & Babin, B. (2017). The Nature and Value of Terroir Products. *European Journal of Marketing*, 51(4): 748–771.
Coteaux Maisons et Caves de Champagne (2018). Champagne Hillsides, Houses and Cellars. Available online at www.champagne-patrimoinemondial.org/le-dossier/le-dossier/ (accessed 16.02.18).
Demossier, M. (2004). Contemporary Lifestyles: The case of wine. In *Culinary Taste: Consumer Behaviour in the International Restaurant Sector*, D. Sloan (ed.), pp. 93–108. Oxford: Elsevier Butterworth-Heinemann.
Demossier, M. (2010). *Wine Drinking Culture in France.* Cardiff: University of Wales Press.
Faith, N. (1988). *The Story of Champagne.* London: Hamish Hamilton.
Faith, N. (2016). *The Story of Champagne.* Oxford: Infinite Ideas
Gatelier, E. (2017). De la ressource territoriale 'vin' à l'architecture du service oeno-touristique : Une application au cas du vignoble champenois. PhD Thesis (unpub). Reims: University of Reims Champagne-Ardenne.
Guy, K. M. (2003). *When Champagne Became French: Wine and the Making of a National Identity.* Baltimore: The Johns Hopkins University Press.

Jacquet, O. (2010). Les appellations d'origine et le débat sur la typicité dans la première moitie du XXe siècle : le rôle du syndicalisme vitivinicole bourguignon et la création des AOC. In *AOC, terroirs et territoires du vin*, J.-C. Hinnewinkel (ed.), pp. 117–128. Pessac: Presses Universitaires de Bordeaux.

Laferté, G. (2012). End or Invention of Terroirs. Unpublished manuscript. Dijon: CESAER INEA-Agrosup.

Mannheim, K. (1960). *Ideology and Utopia: An Introduction to the Sociology of Knowledge*. London: Routledge & Kegan Paul.

More, T. (1973 [1516]). *Utopia*. Harmondsworth: Penguin Books.

Morgan, A. (2009). *Eating the Big Fish: How Challenger Brands Can Compete Against Brand Leaders*. Hoboken: John Wiley and Sons.

Sargent, L. T. (2010). *Utopianism: A Very Short Introduction*. Oxford: Oxford University Press.

Smith Maguire, J. & Charters, S. (2011). Territorial Brand and Scale of Production: The example of champagne. Sixth International Conference of the Academy of Wine Business Research, Bordeaux, 9–11 June: Bordeaux Ecole de Management.

Spielmann, N., & Gelinas-Chebat, C. (2012). Terroir? That's Not How I Would Describe It. *International Journal of Wine Business Research*, 24(4): 254–270.

Thach, L., Charters, S. & Cogan-Marie, L. (forthcoming). Core Tensions in Luxury Wine Marketing: The case of Burgundian wineries. *International Journal of Wine Business Research*.

UNESCO (2018). Champagne Hillsides, Houses and Cellars. Available online at www.whc.unesco/ordg/en/list/1465 (accessed 16.02.18).

Vaudour, E. (2002). The Quality of Grapes and Wine in Relation to Geography: Notions of terroir at various scales. *Journal of Wine Research*, 13(2): 117–141.

Verdier, B. (2013). Construction d'une rhétorique professionnelle: La notion de terroir dans la champagne viticole de 1909 à 2010. In *La construction des territoires du Champagne (1811-1911-2011)*, S. Wolikow (ed.). Dijon: Editions Universitaires de Dijon.

Walters, R. (2017). *Bursting Bubbles: A Secret History of Champagne and the Rise of the Great Growers*. Shrewsbury: Quiller Publishing.

Whalen, P. (2009). 'Insofar as the ruby wine seduces them': Cultural strategies for selling wine in inter-war Burgundy. *Contemporary European History*, 18(1): 67–98.

Wilson, J. (1998). *Terroir: The Role of Geology, Climate and Culture in the Making of French Wines*. London: Mitchell Beazley.

7 Ecotopian mobilities

Terroir-driven tourism and migration in British Columbia, Canada

Donna M. Senese, John S. Hull and Barbara J. McNicol

Introduction

The aesthetic ideals and lifestyle identities derived from wine production have driven tourism and migration mobility in many parts of the world. Terroir, an indefinable Gallic term, blends the production of innovative and living products with natural and cultural resources to define unique geographically delimited space (Unwin 2012). As Unwin (2012) explains, in the course of their history, human communities construct an assemblage of distinctive cultural traits, knowledge and practices of interaction between the natural world and human factors that contribute to its existence. At the heart of our research is the desire to answer questions about how the landscapes of terroir, its delimited space, cultural traits and interactions between natural and human interactions have influenced mobility. Use of the term terroir is often associated with wine regions, but has also been linked with food and other forms of agricultural production. Declaration of a unique terroir can create a powerful marketing identity that has influenced the draw of wine regions by tourists and amenity or lifestyle migrants. The process that evolves wine production areas into wine tourism and amenity migration regions is not well understood, but both phenomena are pervasive in the rural regions of industrial economies where agricultural productivity and environmental integrity synthesize into an *ecotopian* brand.

Ecotopia, the ecological dimension of utopian thought, deploys ecological ideals as tools of social and economic organization (Berry & Proctor 2011: 121). Callenbach's influential *Ecotopia* (1975) articulates these ideals (Callenbach 1975 [1990]) and the importance of place in determining them. Set in the North American Pacific Northwest, Callenbach's *Ecotopia* is a forerunner to amenity imperialism of alpine and agricultural rural landscapes of the Pacific northwest that has been blighted through resort gentrification for wealthy corporate tourists and hobby farmers (Travis 2008). Rural destination marketing has a long-standing relationship with utopian nature, imagined with romantic, nostalgic discourses of pristine Edenic natures, seemingly devoid of any influences of humanity (Markwell 2018: xv–xvi).

Using images of a healthy cultural life set in a pristine natural environment to brand destinations is a common marketing tool. The rural idyll of agricultural landscapes has been used to entice colonial settlers to remote, unsettled areas for centuries. Moreover, similar imaginings of a blend of agricultural bounty in ecologically pristine environments has emerged in new world wine regions where terroir figures predominantly in the destination brand. The projection of destination images using food, wine and terroir have been used to portray many symbols of cultural identity, quality of life and status (Williams 2001; Frochot 2003; Murray & Overton 2011; Pratt & Sparks 2014; Bruwer & Joy 2017). The overlapping interests of natural beauty and terroir provoke a nostalgia for natural lifestyles (Pawson 1997) embedded in the rural idyll, and are said to patrimonialise winescapes, embedding traditional place-based productions into modern economies (Gade 2004: 848). Patrimonialized winescapes of the idyll are particularly important to new world wine regions where shared histories of traditional wine production are absent. Despite the long important role of imaging the Okanagan Valley as a rural, agricultural idyll to attract emigrants and tourists, investigations of the relationship between mobility and the commodification of Okanagan agricultural landscapes are rare.

In wine growing regions where the expression of terroir is important to geographical branding, an ecotopian image is often cast that imagines the natural world as splendid, often sublime, and the culture that tends it, hardworking and even heroic. Suitable grape growing regions favour natural conditions such as gravelly soil, slope, elevation and aspect that challenge other forms of agricultural production. These challenges extend to human mobility as obstacles to movement and development. The growing interest in wine producing regions as tourism and amenity migration destinations that exists today, is paradoxical to the difficulties that settlers, tourists and more recent migrants of these regions have experienced. We interrogate a geographic history of mobility to landscapes of wine in the Okanagan Valley of British Columbia as a form of transformative change promoted by ecotopian images of terroir that brand the landscape.

This chapter interrogates the geographic history of ecotopian landscape images of terroir in the Okanagan Valley, and its influence on successions of tourists and migrants. A secondary literature review helps us to understand the factors contributing to the simultaneous growth of agriculture and wine production alongside tourism and amenity migration in the valley. In particular, we examine evidence of increasing tourist and migrant mobility associated with images of terroir as a socio-ecological ecotopia. Second, an exploratory content analysis of historical promotional photographic images used to encourage mobility to the valley are compared and contrasted with contemporary promotional wine industry images to identify themes of a terroir-driven ecological utopia in the Okanagan. Finally, a discussion of the history of transformational change in tourism and migratory mobilities associated with continued growth of wine production in the Okanagan will propose potential future trends in the growing wine region.

Terroir and mobility

When the amenities of wine tourism combine with a nature-based lifestyle and associated outdoor recreation opportunities, as they do in the Okanagan Valley of British Columbia, then amenity driven migration and development is often rapid and conspicuous. Since rapid globalization of the wine industry in the 1980s began, the Okanagan Valley, like many new world wine regions has enjoyed tourism growth, population growth and new residential developments of up-market housing that are attractive for proximity to wine and tasting amenities. This appears as evidence of a transformative paradigm shift in tourism that harnesses the social and environmental consciousness of new travel markets and lifestyles that promote wellness, as well as positive social, economic and environmental change embodied in the caring economy. As a catalyst for broader change, transformative tourism serves as an ecotopian paradigm shift towards socially conscious and ecologically sound economy (UNWTO 2016b).

Tourism mobilities that produce intentional and reflective encounters with culture through culinary resources (Long 2004: 7) have grown in significance and interest among a broad swath of researchers and industry stakeholders (UNWTO 2016a). The branding of terroir in culinary and wine destinations is integral to mobilization of migratory and tourist populations using the idea that place matters in the production of wine, food and an exceptional tourism experience and lifestyle. Wine and food tourism, as part of the experience economy, has been shown to enlighten and educate visitors about a plethora of important issues, such as sustainability and climate change, traditional knowledge and culture, family, and health and wellness. In particular, the impacts of climate change in global wine and food destinations is progressively more evident, as travellers are increasingly confronted with wildfires, droughts, and environmental hazards. This has spurred a demand for more conscious travel (Pollock 2012) and for many of these destinations, travellers are adopting more sustainable, 'slower' forms of travel, reassessing their travel mode choices to reduce their carbon footprint (Dickinson, Robbins & Lumsdon 2010). Calzati & de Salvo (2018: 33) argue that the demand for quality in the experience economy is also about rediscovering local communities and traditional cultures through active experiences that can integrate the spiritual and cultural dimensions of a wine and food destination. Awareness of self and others is of foremost importance as part of a revised 'responsible' relationship between hosts and guests. Wine tourism potentially provides, 'a passport to the heart of these lands, their culture and past, their food, festivals, and people … [to] give wine a human story' (Peregrine 2018: 1). Travel to wine and food destinations is also acknowledged as having the capacity to: make one feel healthier by escaping urban stresses; strengthen relationship bonds with loved ones as it provides a tool for personal and spiritual well-being (Hull 2016; Petrick & Huether 2013).

Amenity migrants are also attracted to wine places by the very elements of terroir that delimit wine and food regions geographically, beauty of the rolling landscapes, pleasant climate, cultural tradition and what is often imagined as a natural life style embedded in the rural idyll (Senese et al. 2016; Senese et al. 2018). Amenity migration destinations include wilderness and protected natural environments (McMahon & Propst 1998; Matarria-Cascante et al. 2010) and landscapes of cultural richness that offer lifestyle migration as an agent of transformation (Abrams et al. 2012; Santiago 2017). The importance of mobility associated with lifestyle changes, barring any extreme economic or second home policy changes, will likely continue to increase and create competitive markets as baby boomers continue to retire and have the means to relocate.

While amenity migration to rural areas is occurring all over the world, regions of wine growing landscapes and services have become increasingly popular as destinations. Wine, food, tourism, culture and the arts collectively comprise the core elements of the wine tourism product and provide the lifestyle package that wine tourists aspire to experience (Carlsen 2004). Also attractive are regions with varied topography and proximity to surface water, such as rivers and lakes, which provide diverse, recreational opportunities (McGranahan 1999). Amenity-driven movements of people are often of a diasporic nature, capturing a need to change landscapes by an identifiable group of people (Ali & Ivanova 2015). Landscape changes are directly linked to the two main types of amenity migration markets: (i) amenity-driven migration of active and entrepreneurial young people for employment and permanency or (ii) a tourism amenity market of affluent and generally educated baby boomers seeking a recreational and/or retirement lifestyle. Amenity migrants who seek permanent residency in communities are usually very different to residents who choose to own second homes and visit only seasonally or on weekends or for monthly stretches at various times. At the same time, retirement for a lifestyle change will be different to permanent residents seeking entrepreneurial opportunities (McNicol & Glorioso 2014).

In the Okanagan Valley, permanent residents living in large and wealthy western Canadian cities such as Vancouver or Calgary, support an accessible counter urban-to-rural migration that has motivated a residential housing boom in and around the cities of Kelowna and Penticton. Movement has been from urban landscapes (of stress and work) to landscapes with a perceived slower pace of life promoting a healthier lifestyle, often accompanying retirement. This mobility captures the movement of people who are seeking to experience landscapes as tourists yet who then reside with intermittent or permanent intent, based on an actual or perceived enhanced environmental or cultural quality over their original permanent place of residence (Glorioso & Moss 2003; Moss 2003; 2006).

The Okanagan: an ecotopian terroir

The Okanagan Valley in British Columbia, Canada has much in common with other new world wine regions, replete with landscape manifestations of white European settlement and mobilities driven by the agrarian rural idyll. However, it is also a place that stands out as unique in many respects, particularly in the way it has been imagined as an ecotopian landscape, an idealized ecological and cultivated rural idyll created to encourage, manipulate and drive both tourism and migration.

The Okanagan is a 200km valley in the interior of British Columbia that runs between the Columbia and Fraser River Watersheds. A series of long linear, deep lakes take up much of the floor of the valley which is surrounded east and west by a series of mountain chains. The Monashee and Rocky Mountains to the east and the Coast mountains to the west provide a rain-shadow for a very hot dry interior valley (30 cm rain annually) that forms the northern extension of the Sonoron Desert to the south (Senese et al. 2012). The Okanagan Valley is the unceded territory of the Okanagan Nation, and has a record of continuous settlement for approximately 11,000 years by the Sylix people who adapted continuously to changing environmental conditions. Access to the valley has never been easy, as it sits surrounded by a huge range of ecosystems that include high alpine forests, long ranging grasslands and sloping valley floors to the lakes (Kyle 2017).

European white movement to the valley began in 1811, however, the first organized European attempt to settle the Okanagan was by French Catholic Missionaries around 1850 who planted vines for sacramental wines as well as other crops to supply food to the growing gold rush. After this initial European settlement, in a very practical sense, government needed to attract settlers to the interior to supply growing demands for food to maintain development and growth of mining in the interior. The natural and agricultural landscape of the Okanagan has been integral to its present existence. Since the late 1800s it has been advertised by railway and steamship companies, governments and boards of trade, as an Eden, an oasis where anything could be grown at a range of elevations (Wagner 2008).

Increasing accessibility of the Okanagan over the last two centuries has also been central to its growth. Completion of the transcontinental Canadian Pacific Railway in the 1880s and steamboats became a lifeline to emerging settlements. In 1908, the communities of Vernon, Kelowna and Penticton were small villages in an immense, sparsely settled valley, with a combined resident population of 1663 residents (Statistics Canada 2018; Central Okanagan Economic Profile for Agriculture 2017; Senese et al. 2012). Growing commercialization of agriculture led to infrastructure development in the early 20th century to support a period of rapid urbanization as the population of the region grew to approximately 12,000 residents by 1921 (Statistics Canada, 2018; Okanagan Basin Water Board, 2013). In 1910, Penticton was selected as the headquarters for the new Kettle Valley Railway (KVR) which brought jobs and more growth as the town's population more than doubled by the time the line was finished in 1915. The railway opened up distant markets to Okanagan fruit and also allowed tourists to visit an area that had long been isolated from the rest of the province (City of Penticton 2018). By 1957 the population of the Okanagan Valley had more than doubled to well over 30,000 residents (Statistics Canada 2018).

Tourism expanded in the 1960s from a summer activity centred on lake-based recreation, to a year-round industry with the development of golf courses and the opening of four ski resorts by the 1970s (McGillivray 2011). Between 1964 and 1974, grape acreage increased from less than 1,000 acres to almost 3,000 acres, driven by consumer trends that saw domestic wine sales in British Columbia triple (British Columbia Wine Institute (BCWI) 2012; Senese et al. 2012). The dry climate and the four distinct seasons, along with the low land and housing prices and easy access from the Lower Mainland, resulted in the first interests in the region as a retirement destination. With the passage of the North America Free Trade Agreement in 1989, new varieties of grape production and new rules permitting the sale of wine from farms, helped to promote a wine tourism industry in the region. Wine industry production and population growth increased simultaneously in this period.

The Okanagan is now recognized as one of the ten best wine destinations in the world by *Wine Enthusiast Magazine* (BCWI 2016). The scenic natural environment, agricultural heritage, and recreational amenities that abound, have produced a valuable tourism economy centred on the wine industry and local rural aesthetic (Senese 2016; Hull 2016). The region welcomes over 3.5 million visitors annually, generating CAD$1.7 billion to the regional economy and employs approximately 15,000 residents (TOTA 2012). The BC Wine Institute (BCWI 2016) reports more than 350 licensed wineries in the province, which annually attract one million tourists, with the industry generating an economic impact of CAD$2.8 billion annually. The legion of amenity migrants, especially retirees, also continues to be significant with the 2011 census reporting a population of 280,784 residents in the valley and one of the oldest populations (26% are 65 years and older) in the province (Statistics Canada 2018). The smaller, rural districts of the Okanagan have experienced the highest relative growth (8.3%) of any municipalities in British Columbia between 2016 and 2017 (BC Stats 2018). The City of Penticton, the southern gateway to the Okanagan wine region and largest producer of wine grapes in British Columbia, experienced a growth rate of 6.4% between 2016 and 2017; while the City of Salmon Arm, the northern gateway to wine country and an emerging wine appellation, saw the largest relative increases in population in the province between 2016 at 9.3% (BC Stats 2018).

Visual methods in terroir

The objective of our research is to identify the images of an *ecotopian* terroir and the associated interplay of idealized natural and agricultural landscapes used to influence mobility in the Okanagan. Terroir is uniquely sensual, that is, the definition of its existence rests explicitly in the human ability to sense its existence. Visual artefacts are widely used, and recognized as a research tool among a range of academics (Crang 1997; 2003). Following Urry's 1990 tourist gaze, visual culture, read through the lens of tourist maps (Del Casino & Hanna 2000, 2006) postcards (Pritchard & Morgan 2000) and tourist photographs (Crang 1997; Scarles 2009) has been used widely in tourism and mobilities research. Studies that examine the visual culture of destinations explore and relate the varied ways that tourists, residents, and the tourist industry itself (re)create and (re)present place. These studies also '[emphasize] the interplay between tourism, landscape, representation and social structures, experiences and identities' (Pritchard & Morgan 2000: 115).

Landscape is a central term in this research, and of enduring interest in geographical studies, because it 'encompasses the relationship between the natural environment and human society' (Rose 1993: 86). *Landscape* 'gives the eye absolute mastery over space' (Cosgrove 1998: 48), 'a cultural image, a pictorial way of representing, structuring or symbolising surroundings' (Cosgrove & Jackson 1987: 96). The term *landscape* is, possibly, the only metaphor in geography that refers to 'both an object and its image, its representation' (Minca 2007: 433). The malleability of the term, therefore, 'has rendered landscape a powerful cultural and political device' (Minca 2007: 437). An important piece of this methodological framework is an examination of the way landscape representations attempt to persuade their observers and produce 'effects of truth' (Rose 2007: 161). Among these effects of truth is the ability of landscape representation to act as an important marker of quality experience and product, and this is an important tool for the wine industry (Tomasi et al. 2013) that allows the consumer to link the product to a specific place (Padgett & Allen 1997). In 2001 Williams published a content analysis of Okanagan winery destination images and identified a shift in landscape image attributes from wine production processes to the aesthetics of lush impeccably cultivated landscapes of leisure and multi dimensional experiential associations. Williams' image attribute findings span the nature-culture nexus of ecotopian terroir that drive tourism mobility.

In order to position our work longitudinally, we have chosen to use the same destination image attributes to conduct a content assessment of archival promotional photographs included in the field reports of the British Columbia Board of Trade and the Canadian Pacific Railway Survey and contemporary promotional images used by the Okanagan wine industry. The photographs used in archival field guides, travel accounts and brochures dispatch impressions of life in nineteenth century British Columbia (Schwartz 1982) to potential tourists in Eastern Canada and emigrants in the United Kingdom. Images projected by the present-day wine industry through social media and web sites are used by wineries to present a brand image, provide interactive information and personalise winery destinations (Cravidão & Reigadinha 2012). The content assessment of contemporary image galleries was conducted on a sample of 65 winery websites (all of those winery websites with image galleries) and 26 Facebook pages. The sample provides geographical representation of all 11 proposed sub appellations (BCWATF 2015) of the Okanagan Valley, which currently contain 277 grape wineries (WineBC.com).

Ecotopian terroir in early promotional photography of the Okanagan

A nineteenth-century public believed that truth was revealed through careful observation and that the camera did not lie (Schwartz 1982). Photographic images promoting a bountiful, cultivated landscape set in a context of ecological beauty promised emigrants the natural, cultural and class attachments of terroir. Photographs were important promotional tools used by governments, municipal boards of trade, and railway and steamship companies to attract tourists and emigrants to the west. The Canadian Pacific Railway (CPR) produced photographic view albums emphasizing the scenic beauties visible from the main line, boards of trade promoted specific locales, and government agencies published guides and literature for immigrants and settlers (Schwartz 1982). The CPR recognized the need to populate the province and portrayed the railway as a civilizing and colonizing force (Schwartz 1982). The dominant landscape theme depicted by the CPR images examined was unspoiled, natural, ecological beauty with images reflecting the Victorian fascination with scenic beauty in wide panoramic landscapes inclusive of a mild parklike foreground and a mountainous backdrop (Cobb & Duffy 1982). Topographical extremes of the natural world are tempered in these images and rugged terrain is pictured in a manner acceptable: 'to the central Canadian and immigrant Englishman to whom the mountains were merely an intriguing landscape novelty' (Tippett & Cole 1977: 49).

A land and population boom in the Okanagan followed completion of the railway in the 1890s, and with it a development of specific terroir characteristics associated with culture, place and product. Images promoted by the CPR and Board of Trade lured emigrants with the cultural imprint of European settlers on the landscape in visons of the rural idyll on 'abundant, available and usable land' (Schwartz 1982). Governor General Lord Aberdeen is often credited with establishment of fruit farming as a way of life in the Okanagan at this time, and he oversaw widespread promotion in England the Okanagan Valley as a desirable place to live (Royal B.C. Museum n.d.). This era marked a change in the promotional images used to draw emigrants as it envisioned an agricultural bounty capable of domesticating the ecological paradise first imagined in the west. Landscape images in Board of Trade advertisements masterfully aestheticized the landscape to show a promising expanse of young crops in the spring; the provider of plenty in the fall, with proud, beautifully dressed farm owners and farm workers (Figure 7.1) (Cobb & Duffy 1982). The climate is tempered in these images without reference to winter or any extremes to imagine a landscape suitable for emigrants from the 'cradle of the greatest nations of the world and therefore the climate best adapted to the development of the human race' (Grand Pacific Land Company Limited 1912: n.p.). Winter is idealized and only appears as an opportunity for recreation, in the form of sleigh rides and skating parties (Cobb and Duffy, 1982). The semi-arid, natural desert landscape of the south Okanagan is avoided

Figure 7.1 Pear blossoms in Mr. Stirling's orchard, Kelowna, British Columbia, 1909 by G.H.E. Hudson.
(Canadian Copyright Collection, British Library. Picturing Canada project. Copyright 21790 904)

entirely in the visual rendering of the valley, with rare exceptions where sage brush land or forested areas are referred to as future townsites or potential orchards (Summerland Land Company n.d.). Any notion of agricultural difficulty is submerged among visions of fruit and promise of prosperity from the placed based product.

The ideal Okanagan lifestyle was now associated with the rural idyll of fruit farming which dominated the promotional images of the valley. A sense of place evolved a lifestyle adapted to the natural environments as images increasingly focused on prosperous communities, prize-winning produce, exhibitions and growing town sites with impressive public buildings, street scenes, and storefronts. Town sites are shown as peaceful inclusions in the sweeping vistas of the natural landscape (Cobb & Duffy 1982) (Figure 7.2). Social, sporting and recreational events were a big part this new cultural imaging characterized with the prevailing vision of the colonies as a carefree atmosphere. Beautiful homes, happy, prosperous people with a British aristocratic aura were depicted and promoted the Okanagan as a fashionable destination for middle upper-class British immigrants (Dunae 1981). Promoters quoted Earl Grey, Canada's Governor General from 1904 to 1911, who recommended that a farm in British Columbia would be a

Kelowna, The Orchard City (Taken 1908).

Figure 7.2 Townsites within sweeping vistas of natural and cultivated landscape (Kelowna, The Orchard City 1908, G.H.E. Hudson, Canadian Copyright Collection, British Library. Picturing Canada project. Copyright. HS85–10–20690)

fine investment, pronounced fruit farmers to be 'par excellence Nature's Gentlemen' and serious settlers of the better class in the appellation of a son of an Okanagan family (Barman 1984: 34). This provides an interesting segue to the ecotopian terroir promoted in more contemporary promotional images where the idea of appellation broadens the leisure idyll presented in early photography, but remains thoroughly fixed in terms of its positioning to a prosperous, fashionable market in ecologically pristine environments.

Contemporary ecotopian terroir

Our image assessment of contemporary promotional photography used by the Okanagan wine industry also characteristically depicts wildlife and wild landscapes in their promotional landscape ideal, though these are secondary to the manicured, cultivated landscape imagery that foregrounds vineyards and which backgrounds the lake and mountains. A variety of native and semi-arid vegetation along with wildlife, from rattlesnakes to deer, bear and predator birds is shown more frequently in the contemporary promotional photographs (Figure 7.3), perhaps to embolden the rural idyll and convince an increasingly urban market of the natural authenticity of the scene. This is a decidedly ecotopian turn in the landscape imagery of this terroir that positions the wine product, and its experience, within the frame of the natural world.

Skyscapes are frequently depicted in contemporary images, and they are consistently blue, indicating clear, unpolluted air and perhaps a promising, positive outlook for a visit to the winery.[1] We also found images of four seasons in contemporary photography, with frequent images of a snow-covered landscape, suitable for ice wine production (Figure 7.4). Ice wine has become the Okanagan wine industry's most important international export and relies on late harvest temperatures in the range of −10°C for production. The inclusion of winter is in marked contrast to the images portrayed to potential immigrants in the 1880s and also with Williams' (2001) content analysis of Okanagan winery destination images from the 1990s. Climate is consistently tempered in the settler imagery as it is in Williams' findings where only subtle and mostly benign differences in temperatures are noted. Williams found that reference to climate is related to warm temperatures and clear air suitable for a lush and thriving grape crop, with little to no imaging of winter scenes. While in the promotional imagery of the early Okanagan, imagined winter scenes are only included as a recreational resource to ski

Figure 7.3 Contemporary promotional images of wildlife and scenic views of natural environment (Photo credit and permissions: Wines of British Columbia).

Figure 7.4 Contemporary winter image
(Photo credit and permissions: Wines of British Columbia).

or skate. These images appear to have much in common with promotional photography of early European settlement in the Okanagan where the natural, uncolonized landscape is omnipresent but tempered to appear accessible to a wide range of visitors and settlers, and manageable under the desire for human mastery (productionist and recreational) over the environment.

The images of production addressed in Williams' work centred on the relationship between the wine, vintners and viticulturalists in the early 1990s labouring in the fields and cellars, and then wine and culinary visitors recreating in tasting rooms and restaurants in the latter part of the decade. Production facilities with heritage features, antiques and cultural reproduction of Old World architecture predominated the images that Williams reported in 2001, though more modern tasting room characteristics were noted by Williams later in the study. The photo galleries of contemporary promotional images depict winery and vineyard laborers more predominantly than was indicated by Williams and represent a sort of realignment to the imagery used in the early settler promotional photography where a substantial workforce, all happy, smiling and well-dressed go about the teamwork in the business of production. Contemporary images of labour insinuate a similar teamwork, family values and commitment to quality production, perhaps a sign of authentic experience or patrimonialization of a budding industry within the rural idyll. Such labour aesthetic was not present in social media photos, however, where mostly white, older prosperous looking consumers, still happy and smiling go about the business of lounging, rather than labouring, in wine agriculture (Peters 2007).

Architecture is an important trope in the production value of the winery images. Similar to Williams analysis in the 1990s, contemporary architectural images ranged from heritage –classical Greek, Germanic, Roman and Tuscan design – to modernist styles. Architecture is the second most dominant image attribute in the contemporary images, as most all of the wineries display an image of their tasting room or other on their property. The architecture is usually displayed in combination with a scenic view, which is deployed to create a secondary, yet vital and terroir-associated environment. The winery building is often shown to be nestled within a vast dominating natural landscape, and careful attention is used to ensure no other human-made structures, technologies or facilities are included in the image to give the feeling of seclusion within a dominating natural environment (Figure 7.5).

Sense of place attributes in the early 1990s used a combination of natural, cultural and production-oriented elements according to Williams (2001), along with a focus on the winery destination depicted primarily as a wine production center. However, Williams noted a change in the latter half of the 1990s as images used were more strongly related to unique natural and cultural characters worth visiting because of their experiential, educational and leisure appeal (Williams 2001: 49–50). The sense of place attributes in the contemporary images used by wineries reflect a stronger association with settler imagery that positions family and social events at the fore of interactions with the cultural and natural environments. In contemporary images, wineries are busy, social places with weddings, tastings, concerts, and a general sense of prosperity, attractive to a middle-class wine tourist and affluent baby boomers seeking a recreational and/or retirement lifestyle. Included are many images of happy family gatherings, and participation of family members in all stages and settings of production. The sense of cohesion, warmth, commitment and unique cultural characteristics embedded in family images, almost always inclusive of the winery dog, is dominant in the unique vision of contemporary wineries in their cultural adaptation to the local natural environment. Where the family name is used to identify the winery, these attributes tend to be prominent in the forefront of the images.

Figure 7.5 Winery architecture and isolated scenic views
(Photo credit and permissions: Wines of British Columbia).

Conclusion

In summarizing the geographic history of the Okanagan Valley in the central interior of British Columbia, it is evident that ecotopian images, the nexus of nature-culture collusion in the agricultural landscapes in the region have driven settlement, tourism and the growth of the wine industry in the region for over two centuries. Applying Williams' (2001) destination attributes as representative of the nature-culture nexus of ecotopian terroir, the content analysis of photographic images reveals that the themes of landscape, climate and environment, facility, and sense of place support transformative changes in the promotion of the region, branding of the landscape, and ultimately the settlement and development of the region. In the nineteenth century early CPR images portrayed a Victorian landscape – unspoiled, scenic and panoramic in park-like settings with mountainous backdrops. The Board of Trade at the time aestheticized the climate and environment of the valley offering a pastoral landscape for farming and as an accessible and desirable place to live for families.

By the early twentieth century promotional images depicted the Okanagan lifestyle through images of the built environment and of the importance of the sense of place. The Okanagan Valley offered settlers a carefree atmosphere attractive to immigrants adopting lucrative fruit-farming operations. Images of beautiful homes, happy, and prosperous people depicted the region as a fashionable destination for visitors and amenity migrants from middle and upper-class families. By the end of the twentieth century, with the growth of wineries in the region, images focused on the lush, manicured vineyard landscapes in a moderate climate with little attention to the wildlife or naturalized landscapes. The landscape is portrayed as accessible to visitors and settlers to be managed or as a recreational resource for tourism. Winery images by the beginning of the twenty-first century focused on the architecture of the tasting rooms or production buildings in combination with scenic views. Unique natural and cultural characteristics tied to sense of place were highlighted in contemporary images showcasing the activities at wineries – weddings, tastings, and concerts – along with images of the unique cultural characteristics embedded in family images.

The centrality of place as a social, cultural and ecological marker has been a major influence on mobilities associated with oeno-gastronomic consumption as place determines the value consumers associate with gastronomic regions and their terroir. In this way, value directly depends on a socially mediated, carefully curated image of a given place that allows certain wine regions to stand out in a highly competitive global market (Picard et al. 2018: 527). Images of oeno-gastronomic consumption extend to the social customs associated with consumption and forge, in visual form, meanings as well as personal and cultural identities (Taylor & Keating 2018: 309) that have been highly influential in directing tourists and amenity migrants to wine regions such as the Okanagan Valley. Promotional images based in oeno-gastronomic consumption reflect aspirational ideals (Taylor & Keating 2018) and desires

(Bright 2017) associated with an ecotopian landscape. The aestheticized images act as a 'contemporary tool to define social belonging, demonstrate aspirational social standing, and display cultural capital' (Bourdieu 1984 cited in Taylor & Keating 2018) of a socio-ecological utopia imbedded in conceptions of terroir.

Future research will be aimed at understanding the new images of terroir and nature that now brand the landscape in the region that are presently attracting an increasing number of tourists and second homeowners. Concerns about sustainability and the resilience of the region are of increasing concern as the population continues to urbanise the region and challenge the historic rural idyll that has served to draw settlers and visitors for two centuries.

References

Abrams, J. B., Gosnell, H., Gill, N. J. & Klepeis, P. J. (2012). Re-creating the Rural, Reconstructing Nature: An International Literature Review of the Environmental Implications of Amenity Migration. *Conservation and Society*, 10: 270–284.

Ali, N. & Ivanova, M. (2015). Diasporas and Identity: Tourism, Being and Becoming. *Tourism, Culture and Communication*, 15(3): 169–171.

Barman, J. (1981). The world that British settlers made: Class, ethnicity and private education in the Okanagan Valley. In *British Columbia: Historical Readings*, P. Ward & R. McDonald (eds), pp. 600–626. Vancouver: Douglas and McIntyre.

Barman, J. (1984). *Growing Up in British Columbia: Boys in Private School*. Vancouver: UBC Press.

BC Stats (2018). 2017 'Sub-Provincial Population Estimates.' Demographic Analysis Section, BC Stats, Ministry of Jobs, Trade and Technology, Government of British Columbia.

Berry, E. & Proctor, J.D. (2011). Guest Editors' Introduction: Imagining Ecotopia. *Journal for the Study of Religion, Nature and Culture*, 5(2): 121–125.

Bourdieu, P. (1984). *Distinction: A Social Critique of the Judgement of Taste*. Cambridge: Harvard University Press.

Bright, S. (2017). *Feast for the Eyes: The Story of Food in Photography*. New York: Aperture Foundation.

British Columbia Wine Institute (2016). *Annual Report*. Kelowna: British Columbia

British Columbia Wine Task Group (2016). *Final Report from the Appellation Task Group*. Kelowna: British Columbia.

Bruwer, J. & Joy, A. (2017). Tourism destination image (TDI) perception of a Canadian regional winescape: a free-text macro approach. *Tourism Recreation Research*, 42(3): 367–379.

Callenbach, E. (1975 [1990]). *Ecotopia*. Berkeley, CA: Banyan Tree Books.

Calzati, V. & de Salvo, P. (2017). Slow tourism: a theoretical framework. In *Slow Tourism, Food and Cities: Pace and the Search for the' good Life'*, Clancy, M. (ed.), pp. 33–48. New York: Routledge.

Carlsen, J. (2004). A Review of Global Wine Tourism Research. *Journal of Wine Research*, 15(1): 5–13.

Central Okanagan Economic Profile for Agriculture (2017). *Central Okanagan Economic Profile for Agriculture*. Kelowna: Regional District of Central Okanagan.

City of Penticton (2018). Our History. Available online at www.penticton.ca/EN/main/community/about-penticton/our-history.html (accessed 16.09.18).

Cobb, M. & Duffy, D. (1982). A Picture of Prosperity: The British Columbia Interior in Promotional Photography, 1890–1914. *BC Studies*, 52: 142–156.

Cosgrove, D.E. (1998). *Social Formation and Symbolic Landscape*. Madison: University of Wisconsin Press.

Cosgrove, D. & Jackson, P. (1987). New Directions in Cultural Geography. *Area*, 19(2): 95–101.

Crang, M. (1997). Picturing practices: research through the tourist gaze. *Progress in Human Geography*, 21(3): 359–373.

Crang, M. (2003). The hair in the gate: Visuality and geographical knowledge. *Antipode*, 35(2): 238–243.

Cravidão, M. & Reigadinha, T. (2012). Emarketing for wine tourism. *Enlightening Tourism*, 2(1): 1–22.

Del Casino, V. J. & Hanna, S. P. (2000). Representations and identities in tourism map spaces. *Progress in Human Geography*, 24(1): 23–46.

Del Casino, V. J. & Hanna, S. P. (2006). Beyond The 'Binaries': A Methodological Intervention for Interrogating Maps as Representational Practices. *ACME: An International E-Journal for Critical Geographies*, 4(1): 34–56.

Dickinson, J.E., Robbins, D. & Lumsdon, L. (2010). Holiday travel discourses and climate change. *Journal of Transport Geography*, 18(3): 482–489.

Dunae, P.A. (1981). *Gentlemen Emigrants: From the British Public Schools to the Canadian Frontier*. Vancouver: Madrona Publishers.

Feighey, W. (2003). Negative image? Developing the visual in tourism research. *Current Issues in Tourism*, 6(1): 76–85.

Frochot, I. (2003). An analysis of regional positioning and its associated food images in French tourism regional brochures. *Journal of Travel & Tourism Marketing*, 14(3–4): 77–96.

Gade, D. W. (2004). Tradition, territory, and terroir in French viniculture: Cassis, France, and Appellation Contrôlée. *Annals of the Association of American Geographers*, 94(4): 848–867.

Glorioso, R. S. & Moss, L. A. G. (2003). Amenity Migration to Mountain Regions: Current Knowledge and a Strategic Construct for Sustainable Management. *Social Change*, 37: 137–161.

Grand Pacific Land Company Limited (1912). *Kelowna British Columbia*. Winnipeg: n.p.

Hines, J. D. (2009). Rural Gentrification as Permanent Tourism: The Creation of the 'New' West Archipelago as Postindustrial Cultural Space. *Environment and Planning D: Society and Space*, 28: 509–525.

Hull, J. S. (2016). Wellness tourism experiences in mountain regions: the case of Sparkling Hill Resort, Canada. In *Mountain Tourism*, H. Richins & J. S. Hull (eds), pp. 25–35. Oxford: CABI.

Matarrita-Cascante, D., Stedman, R. & Luloff, A.E. (2010). Permanent and seasonal residents' community attachment in natural amenity-rich areas: Exploring the contribution of landscape-related factors. *Environment and Behaviour*, 42(2): 197–220.

Kyle, C. J. (2017). *Lost Landscapes of the Market Gardeners: A Qualitative Historical GIS Examination of the Demise of the Chinese and Japanese Market Gardening Industries in the North and Central Okanagan Valley, British Columbia, 1910s–1950s*. Kelowna: University of British Columbia Press.

Long, L. M. (ed.). (2004). *Culinary Tourism*. Lexington: University Press of Kentucky.

McGillivray, B. (2011). *Geography of British Columbia: People and Landscapes in Transition*. Toronto: University of British Columbia Press.

McGranahan, D. A. (1999). Natural Amenities Drive Rural Population Change. Agricultural Economic Report Number 781. Washington, DC: USDA Economic Research Service.

McMahon, B. & Propst, L. (1998). Park Gateways. *National Parks: The Magazine of the National Parks and Conservation Association*, May/June, 72(5–6): 39–40.

McNicol, B. J. & Glorioso, R. S. (2014). Second home leisure landscapes and retirement in the Canadian Rocky Mountain Community of Canmore, Alberta. *Annals of Leisure Research*, 17(1): 27–49. doi:doi:10.1080/11745398.2014.885845

Markwell, K. (2018). Foreword. In *New Moral Natures in Tourism*, B. S. R. Grimwood, K. Caton & L. Cooke (eds), pp. xv–xvii. New York: Routledge.

Matarrita-Cascante, D., Stedman, R., & Luloff, A. E. (2010). Permanent and seasonal residents' community attachment in natural amenity-rich areas: Exploring the contribution of landscape-related factors. *Environment and Behavior*, 42(2): 197–220.

Minca, C. (2007). The tourist landscape paradox. *Social & Cultural Geography*, 8(3): 433–453.

Moss, L. A. G. (2003). Amenity Migration: Global Phenomenon and Strategic Paradigm for Sustaining Mountain Environmental Quality. In *Sustainable Mountain Communities*, L. Taylor and A. Ryall (eds.), pp. 19–24. Banff: The Banff Centre for Mountain Culture.

Moss, L. A. G. (2006). *The Amenity Migrants*. Wallingford: CABI International.

Murray, W. & Overton, J. (2011). Defining regions: The making of places in the New Zealand wine industry. *Australian Geographer*, 42(4), 419–433.

Okanagan Basin Water Board (2013). *2013 Annual Report*. Kelowna: Okanagan Basin Water Board.

Padgett, D., & Allen, D. (1997). Communicating experiences: A narrative approach to creating service brand image. *Journal of Advertising*, 26(4): 49–62.

Pawson, E. (1997). Branding strategies and languages of consumption. *New Zealand Geographer*, 53(2): 16–21.

Peregrine, A. (2018). Why wine tourism is booming in 2018 – and the best destinations to visit. *The Telegraph*, 1 Februrary 2018. Available online at www.telegraph.co.uk/travel/food-and-wine-holidays/best-destinations-for-wine/ (accessed 25.01.18).

Peters, G. L. (2007). The changing cultural landscape of El Paso de Robles. *Yearbook of the Association of Pacific Coast Geographers*, 69(1): 74–87.

Petrick, J. F. & Huether, D. (2013). Is travel better than chocolate and wine? The benefits of travel: A special series. *Journal of Travel Research*, 52(6): 705–708.

Picard, D., Nascimento Moreira, C. & Loloum, T. (2018). Wine Magic Consumer Culture, Tourism and Terroir. *Journal of Anthropological Research*, 74(4): 526–540.

Pollock, A. (2012). Conscious travel: Signposts towards a new model for tourism. Contribution to the 2nd UNWTO International Congress on Ethics and Tourism, 12 September, Quito, Ecuador.

Pratt, M. A., & Sparks, B. (2014). Predicting wine tourism intention: Destination image and self-congruity. *Journal of Travel and Tourism Marketing*, 31(3/4): 443–460.

Pritchard, A., & Morgan, N. (2000). Constructing tourism landscapes – gender, sexuality and space. *Tourism Geographies*, 2:115–139.

Rose, G. (ed.) (2007). Researching visual materials: Towards a critical visual methodology. In *Visual Methodologies: An Introduction to the Interpretation of Visual Materials*, pp.1–27. London: SAGE.

Rose, G. (1993). *Feminism and Geography.* Minneapolis: University of Minnesota Press.

Royal B.C. Museum. (n.d). Ethnic Agricultural Labour in the Okanagan Valley: 1880s to 1960s. Available online at www.royalbcmuseum.bc.ca (accessed 25.10.19).

Santiago, C. M. (2017). Lifestyle Migration and the Nascent Agro-ecological Movement in the Andean Araucania, Chile: Is It Promoting Sustainable Local Development? *Mountain Research and Development,* 37(4): 406–414.

Scarles, C. (2009). Becoming tourist: Renegotiating the visual in the tourist experience. *Environment and Planning D: Society and Space,* 27(3): 465–488.

Schwartz, J. M. (1982). The Past in Focus: Photography and British Columbia, 1858–1914. *BC Studies,* 52: 5–15.

Senese, D. M. (2016). Transformative Wine Tourism in Mountain Communities. In *Mountain Tourism: Experiences, Communities, Environments and Sustainable Futures,* H. Richins & J. S. Hull (eds), pp. 121–129.

Senese, D. M., Randelli, F. & Hull, J. S. (2016). The Role of Terroir in Tourism Led Amenity Migration. In *Proceedings of the XI International Terroir Congress,* G.V. Jones & N. Doran (eds), pp. 189–194. Oregon: Willamette.

Senese, D. M., Wilson, W. & Momer, B. (2012). The Okanagan Wine Region of British Columbia, Canada. In *The Geography of Wine. Regions, Terroir and Techniques,* P. H. Dougherty, (ed.), pp. 81–94. London: Springer.

Senese, D., Randelli, F., Hull, J. S., & Myles, C. C. (2018). Drinking in the good life: Tourism mobilities and the slow movement in wine country. In *Slow Tourism, Food and Cities: Pace and the Search for the "Good Life",* M. Clancy (ed.), 214–231. London and New York: Routledge

Statistics Canada (2018). *Census Profiles 1921–2011.* Ottawa: Statistics Canada.

Summerland Land Company (n.d.) Brochure – *Kaleden (Beautiful Eden).* Southern Okanagan, BC: Summerland Heritage Museum.

Taylor, N. & Keating, M. (2018). Contemporary food imagery: food porn and other visual trends. *Communication Research and Practice,* 4(3), 307–323. doi:doi:10.1080/22041451.2018.1482190

Tippett, M. & Cole, D. (1977). *From Desolation to Splendour: Changing Perceptions of the British Columbia Landscape.* Vancouver: Clarke, Irwin and Company Limited.

Thompson Okanagan Tourism Association (2012). Embracing our Potential: A Ten-Year Tourism Strategy for the Thompson Okanagan Region. *Kelowna, BC: Thompson Okanagan Tourism Association.*

Tomasi, D., Gaiotti, F., & Jones, G. V. (2013). The Role of Landscape in the Productive Context and in the Quality of Prosecco Wine. In *The Power of the Terroir: the Case Study of Prosecco Wine,* pp. 235–248. New York: Springer.

Travis, W. R. (2008). *New Geographies of the American West: Land Use and the Changing Patterns of Place.* Washington, DC: Island Press.

Unwin, T. (2012). Terroir: At the Heart of Geography. In *The Geography of Wine. Regions, Terroir and Techniques,* P. H. Dougherty (ed.), pp. 37–48. London: Springer.

UNWTO (United Nations World Tourism Organization) (2016a). *Global Report on Food Tourism.* Affiliate Members Global Reports, 4, Madrid: Spain.

UNWTO (United Nations World Tourism Organization) (2016b). *Global Report on the Transformative Power of Tourism: A Paradigm Shift towards a more Responsible Traveller.* Affiliate Members Global Reports, 14. Madrid: Spain.

Urry, J. (1990). *The Tourist Gaze. Leisure and Travel in Contemporary Societies.* London: Sage Publications.

Wagner, J. R. (2008). Landscape aesthetics, water, and settler colonialism in the Okanagan Valley of British Columbia. *Journal of Ecological Anthropology*, 12(1): 22–38.

Williams, P. (2001). Positioning wine tourism destinations: an image analysis. *International Journal of Wine Marketing*, 13(3): 42–58.

Wines of British Columbia.WineBC.com (accessed 15.07.18).

8 Certified utopia

Ethical branding and the wine industry of South Africa

Kelle Howson, Warwick Murray and John Overton

Introduction

Cape Town horror-rap act Dookoom had a hit in 2014 with their track
'Larney Jou Poes' (Boss, you're a c***), a rage-filled, visceral portrayal of
the life of a worker on a South African wine farm. The monochromatic,
reeling, and decidedly dystopian video features frontman Isaac Mutant
driving a tractor surrounded by workers carrying farm tools, rifles, and
tyres, and getting drunk from *papsacks* (cheap wine in bags commonly
associated with 'coloured' wine-farm worker drinking culture).[1] The video
culminates in the burning of the word 'Dookoom' into the side of a hill on
the farm. Mutant raps:

> I always push shit, workers know that kind of living
> 'cos the boss makes it harder, harder, impossible to live
> Fed up of being tired
> […]
> My soul and body's fighting, I'm feeling crippled
> I'm thinking 'fuck you, I'll burn your farm down, now you can work it
> like I do.'[2]

The chorus features actual farm employees chanting to camera 'Fuck you
boss man, I won't do what you tell me'.

Mutant goes on to reference the colonial history of the Western Cape –
the area encompassing the South African Winelands. He touches on the
appropriation of indigenous land, and the subjugation of the Khoikhoi and
San peoples into indentured labour:

> Bra, remember you came here in 1652,
> You was a skollie [thief] too, you was fucking sentenced with a convict
> crew
> You robbed and screwed the natives, now who's the savage?
> In 1657 the National Party was established

[...]
Your constitution was born from cons abusing,
No bomb defusing, my shit is lit, no calming this Bushman[3]
[...]
My family spreaded over the plantations, and by the way, who the fuck is you to call my frustrated ass a racist?[4]

The last line is somewhat prescient. After the album's release, Afrikaner nationalist lobby group AfriForum accused Dookoom of hate speech. AfriForum submitted a complaint to the South African Human Rights Commission, claiming that Dookoom's track was racist towards white people. The debate that ensued saw predictable polarisation, as the heated racial politics that pervades every aspect of South African public discourse momentarily spotlighted Dookoom. Activist Steve Hofmeyr, well known for his spurious claims regarding the existence of a 'white genocide' in South Africa, tweeted 'Romanticising violence & glorifying anarchy in the most violent country in the world? Grow up & man up Dookoom. Get a family, job & responsibility' (Hofmeyr 2014).

Indirectly in response, writer Zethu Gqola commented: '"Larney" has become the anthem for the freeing of the shackled farm worker, and thanks to its raw, unfiltered and menacing lyrics, a lot of governmental personalities, farmer's unions and anyone who isn't black, basically, are pissed off' (Gqola 2014). Much of the contemporary racial politics underpinning these strong reactions is fuelled by myth, misconception and fear, informed by a deep 'colonial unconscious' rendered invisible by powerful narratives of post-racialism (Fanon 1967; Hudson 2013; Levin 2016).[5] The twenty-first century assumption that the playing field has been levelled in South Africa in fact serves to obscure apartheid's legacy of inequality and disenfranchisement, allowing groups like AfriForum to un-ironically accuse Dookoom of racism. The director of the video for *Larney Jou Poes*, Oliver Hermanus, said: 'Despite our grand national obsession with post-racial, post-apartheid, post-anger, post-blame bullshit, I still have that anger and that rage. If it upsets people – great!' (City Press 2014).

Dookoom's track and accompanying video was undeniably provocative. As Benjamin Fogel wrote for progressive platform *Africa is a Country*, Dookoom was 'drawing on the imagery of apocalyptic fantasies of natives rising up against the colonizer in a frenzy of bloodlust that pervades the colonial imagination' (Fogel 2014). The track certainly tapped into some deep sensitivities. The threat of violence on farms evokes images of the experience of Zimbabwe, the violent and well-publicised farm attacks that have occurred in South Africa. Less visceral than that, though perhaps almost as threatening, is the depiction of disobedience. The power of the simple assertion 'I won't do what you tell me' cannot be understated in the context of the South African wine farm, and arguably did as much to elevate *Larney Jou Poes* to the subject of national controversy as any violent imagery. However, as Fogel pointed out at the time, discussions of the working conditions on wine farms were conspicuously absent from the debate.

Dystopian divisions

Wine has long been a cultural and political symbol in South Africa. The industry in the apartheid decades can be seen as a microcosm of the country's violent racial, social and economic divisions. It enjoyed an international reputation for wretched working conditions and exploitation (Brown et al. 2004), and was sustained by a series of formal and informal institutions which artificially ensured the dependency of labour, and the prosperity of farmers. Formally, since 1918, the state-instituted cooperative *Koöperatieve Wijnbouwers Vereniging* (KWV) had controlled every aspect of wine production, determining plantings and varieties, subsidising production, disposing of surplus and setting prices. Relations between farmers and workers operated in much the same way as they had two centuries earlier, when the new British-ruled South African Union emancipated slaves, but instituted subtler measures for retaining and disenfranchising workers. The vicious 'dop' system is the most infamous example: a ubiquitous institution in which workers were paid a portion of their wages in cheap alcohol, meted out throughout the day, to ensure the addiction and therefore retention of labour on farms under competition for labour from the mines further North (Williams 2016). The dop system has contributed to a contemporary rate of foetal alcohol spectrum disorder (FASD) at between 13.6 and 20.8% amongst first grade students in 2013 (May et al. 2013: 9), the highest rate in the world by a significant measure.[6]

At the time of slave emancipation, labour relations in South Africa became thoroughly and explicitly racialised. Skin colour arose as the key determinant of economic status. In recent years, South African critical race theorists have described the construction and legislation of race in South Africa as having the explicit objective of European wealth accumulation at its heart (Frankental & Sichone 2005; Modiri 2012). This can be viewed as a process of 'racialisation of labour' (Bonacich et al. 2008); ensuring European businesses were not exposed to black competition, and securing white control of land, capital and workers. In the wine industry, this resulted in hard delineations being drawn between master, and worker – between white, and black. These colour-based divisions were so powerful that, as South African scholar Andries Du Toit documented in 1993, wine farmers often simply referred to their workers as *ons kleurlinge* [our coloureds], while workers referred to their employer as *ons witman* [our whiteman] (Du Toit 1993: 322).

The implication of mutual belonging, or ownership, indicated by the use of 'our' is revealing. As Du Toit asserted, this is a discursive example of the deeply paternalistic nature of the wine industry, a reality which has endured and evolved since the importation of the first slaves to the Cape for wine cultivation. Du Toit's influential discourse analyses of the world of the wine farm in the 1990s painted a comprehensive picture of the 'micro-politics' of race in the South African wine industry, and the entrenched culture of racialised mastery and servitude which pervaded industry relations and underpinned and informed more visible and well-known expressions of rural apartheid. Since the wine industry's inception, workers have lived on farms, creating insular, isolated communities.

Farm paternalism enshrined the farmer's total control over his workers, with the law of the land essentially giving way at the farm gate (Du Toit & Ally 2003). Paternalism entrenched the attitude that coloured workers were juvenile, irresponsible and untrustworthy. The dystopian South African wine farm has been increasingly exposed to modernising pressures since the collapse of apartheid and the transition to democracy, and has experienced both change and continuity in its recent evolution. Though stakeholders have been concerned with projecting an idyllic or utopian image of South African wine production, the question of how that utopia is imagined – and by and for whom – remains deeply political.

Since the conclusion of the apartheid regime in the early 1990s, much energy has been directed towards re-conceptualising the identity and image of South African wine. This effort has been driven by various actors and imperatives, reflecting at different points political, commercial, social and environmental priorities. However, it can be understood as a fundamentally utopian mission. This is both in the active sense of constantly striving for improvement based on collectively held ideas of 'good', and in the underlying effort to re-imagine and communicate those conceptions of what is good in the context of the South African wine industry. Utopia can be understood, as Levitas (2010), has suggested, as a desire for a better way of doing things which, limited by the constraints of present imagination, is never fully achievable. Peter Howland, in this volume, conceives that 'the utopian impulse is therefore an attempt to rehabilitate past mistakes by striving for a better future while embroiled in a defective present' (p 235).

This view of utopianism is useful in understanding the South African wine industry, haunted as it is by past mistakes. As industry actors strive to communicate the value of South African terroir to global consumers, the tensions between the industry's troubled past and its utopian future remain at the fore. Utopianism in the South African wine industry inherently opposes a still influential dystopia. This project has seen the emphasis of one particular characteristic of South African wine in marketing strategies: that it is *ethical*. Social and environmental ethicality is now central to the construction and communication of the South African terroir in the broader sense, wherein terroir is an expression of both local human and environmental factors which stamp a wine. Defining and authenticating ethical practice in the shadow of an unethical past is thus central to creating a South African wine utopia.

Post-apartheid upheaval

The 1990s were a decade that laid the foundations for a significant transformation in the South African wine industry. In advance of the general election of 1994, the industry began to anticipate changes it needed to make and the ending of the boycott on, or resistance to, South African wines on the global market. This coincided with widespread trade liberalisation, increased exports by New World producers such as Australia, Argentina, Chile and New Zealand, and a growing appetite by wine consumers worldwide for new and interesting wines.

Prior to 1994, under the KWV model, the wine industry had predominately supplied the domestic market, favouring the production of brandy and fortified wine (Ponte & Ewert 2009). The cooperative pool system in which grape growers supplied a small number of producer cellars and were rewarded for volume over quality meant that the industry was ill-prepared for the requirements of quality-appreciative global buyers when market liberalisation arrived. Production had been highly labour intensive, technological advancement had stalled, and the industry trailed the rest of the world in process and product standards (Ponte & Ewert 2009).

Gradual reform, which had begun in the late 1980s and accelerated after 1994 started to undermine KWV's monopoly. Vertical de-integration dismantled the co-operative system and separate wine companies could operate and sell their wines independently of KWV (Cusmano et al. 2010). Producers could develop distinct products, tapping in to the demand for distinct and recognised varietal wines (particularly those with European associations) and for wines with regional characteristics. Moves towards basic labour protection in the late 1980s had also paved the way for the industry to anticipate the sea-change in policy following the democratic transition (Vink et al. 2004). After 1994, exports began to climb steadily (Figure 8.1). Identifying and communicating the meaning of a South African terroir for the global market emerged as an imperative. Utopian political and social aspirations for the progressive, post-racial society were encompassed in the slogan 'Variety is in our Nature' which came to serve as shorthand for this South African terroir.

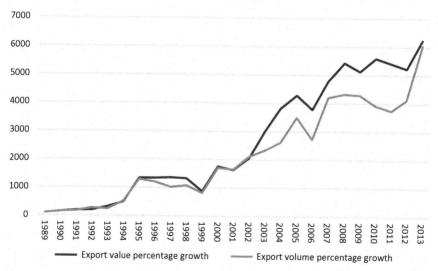

Figure 8.1 South African wine exports: volume and value index comparison 1989–2016 (1989=100%) (Data source: SAWIS, 2016)

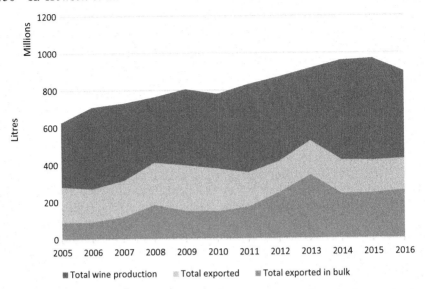

Figure 8.2 Total exports and bulk exports as a proportion of total wine production 2005–2016 (litres) (Data source: SAWIS, 2016)

Alongside increasing export orientation, there was a re-orientation towards higher-value cultivars, largely responding to international demand for red varietals (Bek et al. 2012). Before the 1990s, white varietals dominated South African wine production, with Chenin Blanc as the flagship grape. However, new plantings of Cabernet Sauvignon, Shiraz, and the distinctly South African Pinotage increased significantly, and red wine grew from 16% to 45% of production from 1990 to 2015 (Ewert et al. 2015; SAWIS 2016). Between 1992 and 2002, the total area under vines increased 17% to 108,000ha, while total production volume dropped 5% from an average 815 million tonnes of grapes, to an average 806 million tonnes. In that period, the gross value of wine outputs increased 3.5 times, from R594 million, to R2.1 billion (Vink et al. 2004: 240). This qualitative shift and rise in value-added were significant, yet the transformation remained partial and patchy. The continued availability of cheap labour and land meant that the former approach to bulk wine production could persist. Indeed, South Africa was well placed to tap into demand for cheaper bulk wine (albeit a highly competitive and relatively stagnant market segment), despite the industry's ambitions to compete in the higher quality end of the market. As Vink and colleagues warned in 2004, South African producers 'have only partly escaped the industry's legacy of producing large quantities of standard, high-yielding grapes on irrigated vineyards to make large quantities of cheap wine for which demand is declining' (Vink et al. 2004: 239). Today more than 80% of local wine sales are priced at less than R26 (approx. $US2) per litre (Loots 2017).

Utopian visions

In 2009, following a prolonged period of ad-hoc growth which lacked cohesive strategy, Wines of South Africa (WOSA), the export promotion agency of the South African wine industry, unveiled the branding strategy, DNA SA: A Brand Blueprint for South African Wine. Central to the brand is the oft-repeated slogan 'variety is in our nature', which has been a key aspect of WOSA's branding since 2004. This simple statement contains a multi-dimensional imagery, communicating volumes about the social, spatial, and institutional landscapes of South African wine production. 'DNA' and 'Variety' reference both the vast biodiversity of the Cape Floral Kingdom (a key symbolic element of the industry's self-differentiation), and the cultural diversity of South Africa's Winelands; something that economic actors in South Africa have attempted to positively leverage in order to shed the negative associations of apartheid. Redolent of Archbishop Desmond Tutu's description of the 'Rainbow Nation', celebrations of diversity are front and centre in attempts to generate images of an authentic South African wine utopia. 'DNA SA' has evolutionary underpinnings, evoking genealogical rememberings which interweave land, identity and history into communications of terroir.

WOSA's branding vocabulary for the cornerstone of production integrity

Vocabulary for

Production integrity

ethical   dignity   integrity   traceability   sustainable
responsible   transformation   conservation in action
triple bottom line   transparency   trustworthy   certified
≠hannuwa*   reliable   independently audited

Wine

natural   unique   quality standard   eco-friendly
wines with guaranteed integrity and authenticity   Fairtrade
honest   ethically produced   sustainably produced

*≠hannuwa:
the gathering of good fortune through living in sustainable harmony with our natural environment

(Adapted from Birch 2009: 14)

Within their blueprint, WOSA provide a vocabulary guideline for wine producers, with regards to production integrity. The list of sanctioned terminology is shown in Box 8.1. This encompasses what has come to be understood as a South African wine utopia – for marketing purposes at least. Its construction hinges on the themes of diversity, ethicality, and integrity. These are of course born out of the ongoing process of contending with the industry's dystopian history.

In order to lend weight to claims of integrity, trustworthiness and ethicality, an array of codes of compliance and ethical labelling initiatives have been adopted since the early 2000s. These include both homegrown and international initiatives which set standards for and certify terroir (local origin), labour rights (based on local regulations and ILO standards), empowerment (against measures of black economic participation), and environmental management. This market-driven ethical trade discourse invokes symbols of local natural heritage such as the protea and the sunbird, as well as stylised images of happy workers, in order to communicate positive messages about the South African wine industry context to consumers, and to assign value to the unique environmental and social characteristics of the Winelands.

The most recognised of the ethical certifications active in the South African wine industry are the well-known Fairtrade International, and the industry-governed Wine Industry Ethical Trading Initiative (WIETA). Both initiatives set minimum labour standards, as well as providing for collective association and attempting to provide platforms for dialogue between owners and workers. Fairtrade also channels a 'premium' directly to workers, to be spent on community development projects. As of 2015, 48% of wine grapes produced were certified by either Fairtrade or WIETA.

In large part, the adoption of ethical certifications is in line with the emerging idea in the wine industry that modernising labour relations is good business. Du Toit and Ally (2003) argue that the foundational narrative of 'progressive' industry initiatives coming into the 21st century has been increased economic efficiency:

> To put it crudely, 'racism' was seen as 'inefficient'. It was increasingly being argued that transcendence of the inequitable labour relations of the past made business sense: 'empowering' workers, respecting their rights and offering them better salaries would serve to increase the capacity and competitiveness of the labour force, and hence of the sector as a whole.
>
> (Du Toit & Ally 2003: 5)

Industry-driven ethical certification has been a key strategy for promoting increased competitiveness. This 'ethical' positioning has arguably provided the South African wine industry with a much-needed point of difference, allowing South African wines to reach, and be positively valued by, a growing base of reflexive ethically-minded consumers in Northern markets (Beckett & Nayak 2008; Bek et al. 2012). It has been hoped that ethical labelling would allow producers to retain more value, by enabling them to resist the disembedding processes associated with globalisation (Harvey 1990; Ponte 2009; Raynolds 2000). However, the extent to which consumers are willing to pay more for socially or environmentally certified products remains in question (Carrington et al. 2010; Chatzidakis et al. 2006; Cluley & Dunne 2012). Nonetheless, it could be argued that the enthusiastic adoption of voluntary ethical certification and auditing in the South African wine industry has enabled producers not only to address the image deficit stemming from consumer awareness of their troubled history, but to in fact turn it into a competitive advantage – using it to create a unique utopian positioning for South African wines – one that celebrates physical and social diversity.

Scratching the utopian veneer of certification

However, the moves by the South African wine industry to re-engage and re-embed in global wine markets in the immediate post-apartheid years soon became problematic. Whilst trade embargoes were removed and South African wine could be exported relatively freely to the British market in particular, the new-found integrity of the South African brand, riding the euphoria of majority rule and the election of the ANC government, was contested almost from the start.

Labour unions representing workers on vineyards had more political space after apartheid ended and they were able to highlight how exploitative labour practices persisted. One organisation – Sikhula Sonke – was particularly effective. Founded in 2001, Sikhula Sonke focused on women farm workers, many of whom worked as seasonal and contract workers, often not as members of an established trade union. Women formed a key element of the wine industry labour force. The organisation learned that many apartheid-era labour practices had continued and that employers turned to the use of contract labour to avoid new labour laws. In particular they found vineyard workers being paid below the legal minimum wage, illegal dismissals of seasonal workers, evictions from farm workers' housing, and the use of harmful chemicals by unprotected workers (War on Want 2009). Sikhula Sonke was able to achieve some improvements through collective bargaining but its more significant contribution was through international advocacy. Teaming with the British-based War on Want organisation, a report (*Sour Grapes: South African Wine Workers and British Supermarket Power*) was published in 2009. This report brought stories of South African wine farm worker abuse to the notice of British wine consumers in a campaign that proved very successful. It argued:

Cheap wine comes at a cost. While British consumers benefit from … discount purchases at supermarkets, wine workers in countries like South Africa are left to pay the price. To make a profit from promotional sales, supermarkets transfer the costs down the supply chain to farm owners, forcing them to keep wages low, extend working hours or even lay off workers.

(War on Want 2009: 12)

The campaign urged British consumers to seek out Fairtrade certified wine: 'If you wish to shop ethically, the Fairtrade label provides consumers with a guarantee that the producer is paid a fair price for its wine and that workers are better paid and treated more fairly' (War on Want 2009: 12). What the Sour Grapes campaign was able to do was to implant reminders of the dystopian apartheid wine industry in the minds of consumers but it also linked this image to the considerable power of supermarkets and their buying and marketing practices: 'It is South African workers who pay the price for UK supermarket power and greed' (War on Want 2009: 5). The South African wine brand remained tainted. The campaign and growing consumer awareness of continued poor post-apartheid labour conditions seemed to arrest the growth of the South African wine industry. The substantial growth of wine exports after 1990 (Figure 8.1) appeared to plateau in 2007 then fell between 2009 and 2011. This may in be in part attributable to the global financial crisis although it is clear that the industry remains sensitive to changing consumer preferences

The Sikhula Sonke/War on Want campaign was followed by a damning Human Rights Watch report in 2011 entitled *Ripe with Abuse*. This revealed severe shortcomings in labour standards, and showed that workers faced poor housing, occupational health and safety risks, including pesticide exposure and a lack of access to clean water, and persecution from employers for belonging to a union (Human Rights Watch 2011). An ILO report in 2015 confirmed these findings (Visser & Ferrer 2015). A 2016 documentary by Danish journalist Tom Heinemann, entitled *Bitter Grapes: Slavery in the Vineyards,* focused particularly on labour rights abuses on WIETA and Fairtrade certified farms, alleging instances of wage-docking, pesticide exposure,

Figure 8.3 Wine farmworker housing from *Bitter Grapes*

lack of access to amenities including toilets, running water and electricity, and discrimination by employers against union members. The documentary was widely viewed in Europe and prompted one Danish retailer to remove one of South Africa's largest wine brands, Robertson, from its shelves.

More recently, intense flashes of industrial unrest have taken place which expose the hollowness of the South African terroir utopia. From August 2012 to January 2013, strikes and protests spreading out from the wine farming towns of De Doorns and Worcester saw violent clashes, with three workers killed by police and private security agents. The action involved multiple unions, including the Food and Agricultural Workers Union (FAWU), COSATU, and the BAWSI Agricultural Workers' Union of South Africa (BAWUSA). Workers were primarily demanding that daily wages be increased from R69 (barely above starvation level) to R150. As a result of the strikes, a pay review was eventually undertaken and pay increased to R128.26 per day. However, workers still say this is too little, and have made allegations of pay-docking for goods such as uniforms (Evans 2016). Following the strike, unions advocated for a moratorium on dismissals of workers, but this was not granted, and numerous workers reported being retributively fired by their employer for taking part in strikes (Fogel 2013).

Fairtrade and WIETA are both fundamentally focused on empowering workers. Fairtrade attempts this in part through the provision of a premium for community development projects. The premium is managed by a committee of workers, and has typically been spent on projects such as creches for workers' children, access to healthcare, housing repair and upgrades, and transport to farms. In the course of qualitative interview-based research conducted in the Western Cape in 2016 and 2017,[7] serious questions were raised as to the autonomy of workers' committees, and the level of managerial influence in channelling premium allocations into projects which ultimately save farmers money. Also, on some Fairtrade certified farms, workers' access to training in areas such as financial management and labour rights (which is a key component of Fairtrade certification) was alleged to be insufficient. In the South African model, the majority of this training is supposed to be provided by the farmer or farm management.

Governance and process issues were also identified in the WIETA model, in which some participants claimed that landowners and cooperative interests had disproportionate power in supposedly democratic and representative standards-setting bodies. Furthermore, a reliance on infrequent audits to measure aspects of fairness and empowerment was revealed to be inadequate in both ensuring sustained compliance with standards, and generating meaningful progressive change in industry relations – which in itself is very difficult to audit and quantify. Another key issue with the potential of ethical certification to contribute to structural transformation is that both the WIETA and Fairtrade labour standards for the most part simply mirror national labour legislation. Though WIETA and Fairtrade have performed a much-needed role in encouraging compliance with labour law, interview participants questioned why nongovernmental bodies would be enforcing labour law in place of the Department of Labour and why they should pay to essentially demonstrate that their operations were legal. This finding also raises questions about the level of legal compliance amongst non-certified wine industry operators.

Ethical certification in the South African wine industry has been criticised as neo-paternalism, 'in that paternalist managerial styles are reinforced rather than challenged' (Bek et al. 2012: 148). Rather than driving real transformation, ethical certification may preserve the status quo, and constitute a new form of performative progressivism designed to placate consumers and mitigate against trade unionism on the ground. Seen in this light, ethical certification in the South African wine industry may serve to facilitate the de-politicisation or commoditisation of what are and should be political discourses of empowerment, equality and labour relations (Du Toit 2002).

While it was hoped that ethical certifications would allow producers greater power to retain some profit and control in global value chains, increasingly it seems that compliance with often multiple ethical codes has become a minimum requirement of European retailers for access to shelf space (Bek et al. 2012). Retailers, too, are concerned with protecting their brand reputations under increasing scrutiny of their sourcing standards. Rather than offering a premium for producers, certification is now imposing an added cost in many cases, cutting into profit margins rather than expanding them. The fees associated with compliance with standards and regular auditing can be prohibitive for producers already struggling under price squeezes resulting from oligopsonistic or producer-heavy trade environments. Some have pointed out that under these conditions, ethical certification can be interpreted as a form of value-chain governance (Gereffi et al. 2005), by which lead firms (distributors and retailers) require compliance with an ever-expanding range of technical and ethical production standards while transferring the costs of the monitoring of that compliance upstream to the supply base, and capturing the value-added through improved ethical quality (Du Toit 2002; Ponte 2009). Through the lens of global value chains analysis, it possible to view ethical certification as a product of the neoliberalisation of wine industry relations – that to a large extent the regulation of social and environmental responsibility has been transferred to the market, driven by accountability to consumers who have access to limited information, and therefore limited power, and available for co-optation by the most powerful actors within production networks.

Ethical certification and the neoliberalisation of network governance has also failed to solve many of the problems faced by producers. Post-apartheid changes have had both lucrative, and undesirable impacts. The power of supermarket buyers to drive value chains, impose costly compliance regimes and disproportionately capture value led Ponte and Ewert in 2007 to describe the situation as *An Industry in Ferment*. The authors show that the expensive upgrading efforts that have taken place have simply gained South African producers entry to European markets, that the industry has 'caught-up' by fulfilling the minimum requirements of buyers, that those requirements continue to multiply as retailers become more accountable to reflexive consumers concerned with quality, traceability and sustainability, and that improvements in product and process have just kept up with market demands but have failed to result in increased returns (Ponte & Ewert 2007).

A decade later, these challenges have been compounded by the threat of climate change and serious water crisis in the Western Cape (Booysen 2017). Downwards price pressure caused by lock-in to low price points, continued reliance on a comparatively large labour force now afforded (modest) minimum wage and housing protections, continuing industrial action, and dependant value chain relationships with profitability at the top have facilitated a decline in land under wine grapes, from 102,146 ha in 2006 to 95,775 ha in 2016 (SAWIS 2016: 9). Many landowners are transitioning to alternative crops, with climatic and market conditions favouring citrus in particular. Of those that continue to grow wine grapes, some producers with access to the necessary capital have flourished in the very high-value premium market, while amongst middle and low value producers recent talk has been of pivoting towards less ethical-quality oriented markets in Africa and Asia; and increasing efforts to target the emerging Black middle class in South Africa (Basson 2017).[8] Additionally, the industry has attempted to diversify into areas such as wine tourism (Bruwer 2003; Demhardt 2003), and the supplementary production of artisanal products such as cheese.[9]

While the wine industry has responded successfully to deregulation by most measures: making strides in product and process upgrading, investing massive efforts in marketing and positioning, and becoming internationally competitive in a relatively short space of time, it faces ongoing challenges in retaining value and viability. Furthermore, the industry has a long way to go in addressing the colonial unconscious which still pervades its institutional make-up, the legacy of apartheid clearly visible in racially-delineated ownership patterns, and the poverty, precariousness and powerlessness still experienced by the majority of wine workers (Brown et al. 2004; Du Toit & Ally 2003; Human Rights Watch 2011; War on Want 2009).

Certified dystopia – conclusions

A capitalist market for ethical certification exists, and its correlate is that 'ethics' can be bought and sold to the highest bidder. While market-led ethical responses characterise utopian visions for the South African wine industry, and have gone some way to building a coalition of value chain actors for the implementation of minimum standards, utopian marketing messages serve to disguise existing inequalities, and perpetuate unconscious discourses of power. We observe that the neoliberalisation of conceptualisations of a post-apartheid utopia in the wine industry continues to limit the agency of historically marginalised parties in generating change. Local power relations have been in some ways further entrenched by the increased value chain pressure resulting from trade liberalisation, as producers find themselves subject to further erosion of margins and lock-in to low value market segments, passing on new pressures to labour. The market rules supreme, and ethical certification becomes a tool co-opted by corporations in order to govern the chain, capture value-added, and perpetuate the circuits of capital in their favour. In this sense ethical certification merely tinkers at the margins of the deeply unethical capitalist system within and beyond South Africa.

The ethical discourse that is constructed and applied in order to sell South African wine in export markets is, in effect, strategic in nature. On a global level it works to convince consumers that participatory governance exists with the network, whilst simultaneously reproducing the highly skewed power relations that allow the continued exploitation of labour and some producers that has characterised the industry since its colonial inception. The colonial unconscious and the legacy of farm paternalism is embedded in new utopian narratives of social upliftment in which workers remain largely passive recipients of quantifiable empowerment metrics, and more radical, antagonistic or messy forms of transformation are prevented. Scratching below the veneer of utopia in the South African industry, we see a significant dystopia revealed and one which is unwittingly sustained by consumers who, unaware of the gross inequities that exist, exert market power through ethical discourse mechanisms that in fact obfuscate this reality.

This deeply unethical outcome is driven at the global scale by European supermarket retailers who shift the costs of supply-chain monitoring onto the supply base through the requirement of certification, while capturing the value added by guarantees of the wine's utopian origins. In the face of such intricate technologies of discourse that are co-optable and can be captured by global capital, it is hard to see how ethical global ethical consumerism might resist, let alone subvert, this system whilst operating from within it. It might be that we are reaching the limit of consumers' ability to drive local justice in far-away places.

Government has been largely absent from the construction and implementation of strategies for meaningful reform in industrial relations, with the Broad-based Black Economic Empowerment (B-BBEE) policy framework widely acknowledged to have achieved little more than creating a small black bourgeoisie whilst deepening overall inequality. However, following the forced exit of President Jacob Zuma and his replacement by Cyril Ramaphosa, the ANC faces increasing pressure to acknowledge the perceived failures of the transformation, and the lack of promised redistribution. At the time of writing, state movement to expropriate some white-owned land appears increasingly likely, although the detail and extent of this policy change remains uncertain. In the near future, the government may once again have a large role to play in revolutionising wine production in South Africa, and the status quo which has persisted in part because of ethical certification strategies faces serious threat. While these winds of change will be deeply threatening to those who have benefitted from long standing racially delineated power structures, for the majority of wine industry participants, they have the potential to herald real justice. In the South African wine industry, the marketisation of ethics has betrayed those who have been historically marginalised, and in some ways their continued oppression has been more insidious than ever – masquerading as freedom. It is markedly dystopian, not utopian, and this dystopia requires an entirely new and alternative system of regulation and re-distribution if the gross inequities of history are ever to be subverted. This must be a system that does not merely conjure up false hopes of a diverse utopian terroir within the limits of South Africa's colonial unconscious, but one that can actually deliver a utopia in spite of those limits.

Notes

1 'Coloured' refers to a distinct culture and identity that developed in South Africa's Western Cape as diverse slave communities and, ultimately lineages, came to mix with both Khoisan and settlers. The South African coloured community might be referred to as Creole in other parts of the world. This group is disproportionately represented in the population make-up of wine-farming areas (comprising 49% of the Western Cape population, and 62.12% of the Cape Winelands, compared to 8.8% of South Africa as a whole (Statistics South Africa 2011: 21)). The 'coloured' designation was legally codified and discriminated against in the National Party's Population Registration Act of 1950, though the term had been a feature of popular vocabulary long before this (Frankental & Sichone 2005). The label is problematic and contested. Through the crude categorisations of apartheid, 'coloured' has been defined in a reductionist way in relation to the binary classifications of whiteness and blackness, as something in between the two. However, the term coloured remains in widespread use in contemporary South Africa and describes a complex though undeniable commonality and shared experience amongst those of mixed ancestry in the Western Cape.
2 Original in Afrikaans – YouTube closed caption translation into English.
3 A derogatory term used by the colonists for the indigenous peoples of the Cape.
4 Original of this section in English.
5 The concept of the colonial unconscious comes from Frantz Fanon's (1967) *Black Skin, White Masks*. Fanon wrote that colonialism rested on the social construction of whiteness and blackness, or colonizer and colonized. These oppositional categorizations only held meaning in their relation to one another. Fanon, a psychiatrist, believed that blackness was unconsciously rendered 'abnormal' through colonialism and in relation to whiteness, for both black and white members of the colonial unconscious society. More recently, Peter Hudson (2013) has examined this concept in the context of South Africa, to understand how it has driven resistance to the democratic transition in subtle ways.
6 Similar studies have found rates of 1–1.5% in the US, 1% in Canada, 3.5% in Italy, and 1.8% in France (Olivier et al. 2016: 104). No other country has been shown to have rates of prevalence approaching South Africa's, with the closest being a rural indigenous community in Australia, which was found to have 12% prevalence among primary school entrants in 2015 (Fitzpatrick et al. 2012).
7 Field research was conducted in the Western Cape by Howson for eight months between August 2016 and April 2017. Research involved semi-structured interviews with 44 participants including producers, certifiers, experts, agents, civil society, industry bodies, unions and government.
8 Much attention was given to this latter objective at the Nedbank Vinpro Information Day in January 2017. Speaker Lebo Motshegoa of the market research company Foshizi spoke at length on marketing to Black South Africans. His key insights for reaching this market included the need to pitch wine as an 'aspirational'

product with connotations of status and trend-setting (in the vein of luxury brands such as BMW and Gucci), and the need to associate wine with events in the 'Black calendar' such as *lobola* (bride price) negotiations and funerals (Motshegoa 2017).

9 A prominent example is the Fairview Vineyard and Goat Farm, which in addition to wine, produces cheese, yoghurt and baked goods, hosts a restaurant, deli, and wine tasting room, and is a popular destination for wine tourists.

References

Basson, R. (2017). *Unlocking Value WISEly*. Paper presented at the Nedbank Vinpro Information Day, 19 January, Cape Town.

Beckett, A., & Nayak, A. (2008). The Reflexive Consumer. *Marketing Theory*, 8(3): 299–317.

Bek, D., McEwan, C. & Binns, T. (2012). The South African Wine Industry: Meeting the challenges of structural and ethical transformation. In *The Geography of Wine*, P. H. Dougherty (ed.), pp. 137–157. Netherlands: Springer.

Birch, S. (2009). *DNA SA: A Brand Blueprint for South African Wine*. Stellenbosch: Wines of South Africa.

Bonacich, E., Alimahomed, S. & Wilson, J. B. (2008). The Racialization of Global Labor. *American Behavioral Scientist*, 52(3): 342–355.

Booysen, J. (2017). Wine Makers Hit By Drought. *IOL*, 10 February. Available online at www.iol.co.za/business-report/companies/wine-makers-hit-by-drought-7692953 (accessed 09.02.19).

Brown, M., Du Toit, A., & Jacobs, L. (2004). *Behind the Label: A Workers' Audit of the Working and Living Conditions on Selected Wine Farms in the Western Cape*. Western Cape: Labour Research Service, Women on Farms Project and the Programme for Land and Agrarian Studies, UWC.

Bruwer, J. (2003). South African Wine Routes: Some perspectives on the wine tourism industry's structural dimensions and wine tourism product. *Tourism Management*, 24(4): 423–435.

Carrington, M. J., Neville, B. A. & Whitwell, G. J. (2010). Why Ethical Consumers Don't Walk Their Talk: Towards a framework for understanding the gap between the ethical purchase intentions and actual buying behaviour of ethically minded consumers. *Journal of Business Ethics*, 97(1): 139–158.

Chatzidakis, A., Smith, A., & Hibbert, S. (2006). Ethically Concerned, Yet Unethically Behaved: Towards an updated understanding of consumer's (un)ethical decision making. In *NA-Advances in Consumer Research*, C. Pechmann & L. Price (eds), pp. 693–698. Duluth: Association for Consumer Research.

City Press (2014). Dookoom: AfriForum Will Take Legal Action. *News24*. Available online at www.news24.com/Archives/City-Press/Dookoom-AfriForum-will-take-legal-action-20150430 (accessed 09.02.19).

Cluley, R. & Dunne, S. (2012). From Commodity Fetishism to Commodity Narcissism. *Marketing Theory*, 12(3): 251–265.

Cusmano, L., Morrison, A. & Rabellotti, R. (2010). Catching Up Trajectories in the Wine Sector: A comparative study of Chile, Italy, and South Africa. *World Development*, 38(11): 1588–1602.

Demhardt, I. J. (2003). Wine and Tourism at the 'Fairest Cape': Post-Apartheid trends in the Western Cape Province and Stellenbosch (South Africa). *Journal of Travel & Tourism Marketing*, 14(3–4): 113–130.

Du Toit, A. (1993). The Micro-Politics of Paternalism: The discourses of management and resistance on South African fruit and wine farms. *Journal of Southern African Studies*, 19(2): 314–336.

Du Toit, A. (2002). Globalizing Ethics: Social technologies of private regulation and the South African wine industry. *Journal of Agrarian Change*, 2(3), 356–380.

Du Toit, A., & Ally, F. (2003). *The Externalisation and Casualisation of Farm Labour in Western Cape Horticulture: A survey of patterns in the agricultural labour market in key Western Cape districts and their implications for employment justice.* Western Cape: Centre for Rural Legal Studies, Programme for Land and Agrarian Studies, UWC.

Evans, J. (2016). De Doorns farmworkers still unhappy about pay, rights. *News24*, 20 July. Available online at www.news24.com/elections/news/de-doorns-farmworkers-still-unhappy-about-pay-rights-20160720 (accessed 09.02.19).

Ewert, J., Hanf, J. H., & Schweickert, E. (2015). Strategic Challenges Facing South African Wine Co-operatives: Upgrading or bulk production? *Journal of Wine Research*, 26(4): 287–303.

Fanon, F. (1967). *Black Skin, White Masks* (C. L. Markmann & C. Farrington, Trans.). New York: Grove Press.

Fitzpatrick, J. P., Elliott, E. J., Latimer, J., Carter, M., Oscar, J., Ferreira, M., Carmichael Olson, H., Lucas, B., Doney, R., Salter, C., Peadon, E., Hawkes, G., Hand, M.. (2012). The Lililwan Project: Study protocol for a population-based active case ascertainment study of the prevalence of fetal alcohol spectrum disorders (FASD) in remote Australian Aboriginal communities. *BMJ Open*, 2(3), e000968.

Fogel, B. (2013). Tensions Remain Following Dismissals of Workers in De Doorns. *Ground Up*, 30 January. Available online at www.groundup.org.za/article/tensions-remain-following-dismissals-workers-de-doorns/ (accessed 09.02.19).

Fogel, B. (2014). Done 'debating' Whether 'Larney Jou Poes' is Free Speech? Let's talk about the conditions of farmworkers. *Africa is a Country*, November 3. Available online at www.africasacountry.com/2014/11/afrikaner-farms-race-relations-and-the-new-south-africa/ (accessed 09.02.19).

Frankental, S., & Sichone, O. (2005). *South Africa's Diverse Peoples: A Reference Sourcebook.* Santa Barbara: ABC-CLIO.

Gereffi, G., Humphrey, J. & Sturgeon, T. (2005). The Governance of Global Value Chains. *Review of International Political Economy*, 12(1): 78–104.

Gqola, Z. (2014). Dookoom: Screaming about injustice. *GroundUp*, 15 October. Available online at www.groundup.org.za/article/dookoom-screaming-about-injustice_2352/ (accessed 09.02.19).

Harvey, D. (1990). Between Space and Time: Reflections on the geographical imagination. *Annals of the Association of American Geographers*, 80(3): 418–434.

Hofmeyr, S. (2014). Tweet, 13 October. Available online at www.twitter.com/steve_hofmeyr/status/521525610339131392 (accessed 09.02.19).

Hudson, P. (2013). The State and the Colonial Unconscious. *Social Dynamics*, 39(2): 263–277.

Human Rights Watch (2011). *Ripe with Abuse: Human rights conditions in South Africa's fruit and wine industries.* New York: Human Rights Watch.

La Cour, L. (2016). Photographs Free of Use. In *Bitter Grapes: Slavery in the Vineyards*, documentary written, directed, produced by Tom Heinemann for DR, SVT and NRK.

Levin, R. (2016). Society and the Colonial Unconscious. *New Agenda: South African Journal of Social and Economic Policy*, 62: 6–9.

Levitas, R. (2010). *The Concept of Utopia*. Bern: Peter Lang.

Loots, J. (2017, January 20). State of the Wine Industry. Available online at www.vinpro.co.za/state-sa-wine-industry/ (accessed 09.02.19).

May, P. A., Blankenship, J., Marais, A. S.Gossage, J. P., Kalberg, W. O., Barnard, R., De Vries, M., Robinson, L. K., Adnams, C. M., Buckley, D. & Manning, M. (2013). Approaching the Prevalence of the Full Spectrum of Fetal Alcohol Spectrum Disorders in a South African Population-Based Study. *Alcoholism: Clinical and Experimental Research*, 37(5): 818–830.

Modiri, J. M. (2012). The Colour of Law, Power and Knowledge: Introducing critical race theory in (post-) apartheid South Africa. *Power and Knowledge: Introducing Critical Race Theory in (Post-)Apartheid South Africa*, 28: 405–436.

Motshegoa, L. (2017). Don't ignore consumer insight. Paper presented at the Nedbank Vinpro Information Day, 19 January, Cape Town.

Olivier, L., Viljoen, D. & Curfs, L. (2016). Fetal Alcohol Spectrum Disorders: Prevalence rates in South Africa: the new millennium. *South African Medical Journal*, 106 (Supplement 1): 103–106.

Ponte, S. (2009). Governing Through Quality: Conventions and supply relations in the value chain for South African wine. *Sociologia Ruralis*, 49(3): 236–257.

Ponte, S., & Ewert, J. (2007). South African Wine: An industry in ferment. *Tralac Working Paper*, 8.

Ponte, S., & Ewert, J. (2009). Which Way is 'up' in Upgrading? Trajectories of change in the value chain for South African wine. *World Development*, 37(10): 1637–1650.

Raynolds, L. T. (2000). Re-embedding Global Agriculture: The international organic and fair trade movements. *Agriculture and Human Values*, 17(3): 297–309.

Sargent, L. T. (2010). *Utopianism: A Very Short Introduction*. Oxford: Oxford University Press.

SAWIS (2016). *SA Wine Industry 2016 Statistics* (Vol. 41). Paarl: SAWIS.

Statistics South Africa (2011). *Census 2011: Census in brief*. Pretoria: Statistics South Africa. Available online at www.statssa.gov.za/census/census_2011/census_products/Census_2011_Census_in_brief.pdf (accessed 09.02.19).

Vink, N., Williams, G. & Kirsten, J. (2004). South Africa. In *The World's Wine Markets: Globalization at work*, K. Anderson (ed.), pp. 227–251. Cheltenham: Edward Elgar Publishing.

Visser, M., & Ferrer, S. (2015). *Farm Workers' Living and Working Conditions in South Africa: Key trends, emergent issues, and underlying and structural problems*. Commissioned by The Pretoria office of the International Labour Organization.

War on Want (2009). *Sour Grapes: South African wine workers and British supermarket power*. London: War on Want.

Williams, G. (2016). Slaves, Workers, and Wine: The 'Dop System' in the History of the Cape Wine Industry, 1658–1894. *Journal of Southern African Studies*, 42(5): 893–909.

9   The commercial basis of terroir utopias in Calabria

Vincent Fournier

Introduction

Italy is among the most important wine countries in the world. The richness and diversity of Italian wines reflect the historical depth and cultural diversity of each Italian region. Some regions have significant production and are internationally renowned for their wines, like Piedmont and Tuscany, while others have only minor production that receives little attention from international markets. Calabria is one of these less recognised wine regions. Although at the time of Herodotus (c. 440 BC) that part of the Italian peninsula was called 'Enotria', which is normally translated as 'land of wines', Calabria is today among the Italian regions with the smallest wine production volumes and its wines are not well-known outside of Italy. But there is an exception: the town of Cirò Marina, where the Cirò DOC (*Denominazione di origine controllata*) wine is produced. This *Denominazione* accounts for 75% of all DOC wine produced in Calabria and has a certain international notoriety as a quality wine. Local producers and the population alike are aware of this uniqueness and are justifiably proud of their wine.

Locally, we find vernacular (historic and contemporary), and yet also increasingly globally generic (Howland 2019; Inglis 2019), discourses and ideal imaginaries of terroir, 'fine' and distinction-conferring wines, idyllic vineyards and of leisured, hedonic and aesthetically appreciative wine consumption being deployed to demarcate and authenticate Cirò grape-growing, winemaking and wines as 'unique' and of high quality. As is argued in this chapter, these narratives can be regarded as utopian because they convey the producers' desires and aspirations to create ideal understandings of, and accordant producer, tourist and consumer' engagements with, a local context that is demarcated as 'unique' (or at least non-replicable) and particularly in the assertions of its terroir and history and traditions of production that are perceived to spontaneously impart tastes and quality to local wines. Just as importantly, such narratives also function as calls or prompts to transform local realities so that they are aligned in value and practice with these narrative idealisations of place and product. This form of hermeneutical loop is a long-standing, very common practice in modern marketing and advertising

(Williamson 1978). Essentially pre-existing cultural and social values are pro-motionally attached to specific commodities (think *Coca Cola* and having youthful fun in the sun as being the 'real thing'), which are then 'sold back' to consumers with the promise that lifestyle consumption of these now value-laden, and consequently highly desirable, commodities will ensure their personal experience of the same-self values, ideals and practices (Lears 1994; Leiss et al. 2005; McCracken 1990, 2005; Schudson 1984; Williamson 1978). Although with the recent Cirò adoption of terroir and the promotion of highly localised speci-ficities of place, product and people (especially those concerned with historical and traditional modes of production), the loop is more of a hermeneutical spiral (Motahari 2008) that draws on, references and/or aligns with a range of histori-cally and spatially differentiated, yet also convergent and generic, practices of terroir and of other associated modalities (e.g. appreciative consumption of fine wines, vineyards set in and generative of the rural idyll, etc.) that are circulating within increasingly globalized flows of commercial wine production (Charters 2010; Howland 2019; Inglis 2019).

From this vantage therefore, I define utopia as an idealisation of existent, imagined and aspirational realities, which importantly also has the capacity to transform and improve these realities (see Bloch 1986; Levitas 2010, 2013; Le Guin 1989). Terroir products can also be regarded as utopian because they are subject to similarly idealised narratives that possess the capacity to transform reality and society. But as this chapter will also demonstrate, this utopian aspect of wine, and of terroir products in general, is linked to the way these types of commodity are marketed (Beverland 2005; Charters 2010; Guy 2011; Moran 2016; Paxson 2010). I believe that the utopian dimensions of certain wine narratives, and of other terroir products, are linked to the commercial characteristics and compulsions engendered by this type of place-based and time sensitive commodities. These narratives highlight, and fetishize (Four-nier 2018; Meneley 2004; Paxson 2010), very precise elements, mainly the demarcated, non-replicable *territory* or place of production, together with similarly invented (or at least idealized) vernacular histories and traditions of production. These elements, as this chapter will show, are central to the terroir utopias and just as importantly have been structured, legitimated and disseminated through codified legal systems regulating wine production and commercialization (Charters 2010), see for example the *Appellation d'origine contrôlée* (AOC) in France (c. 1935) and the *Denominazione di origine con-trollata* (DOC) in Italy (1966) (Fournier 2018).

Terroir products are utopian because they are subject to idealised narrati-vization that possesses the capacity to transform reality and society. This chapter will demonstrate that it is the case in Cirò Marina in Southern Italy. We'll begin by outlining how wine producers imagine, idealise and then describe local reality through the marketing of terroir utopia, by analysing the discourses presented on different wineries websites. Following that, we then survey the ethnographic evidence to offer a more complex understanding of local wine production that allow us to put into comparative perspective the utopian market-oriented version of terroir being presented on the websites. Finally, we look at why it is important that these terroir utopias be intimately linked to the ways commercially produced wine is marketed both locally and globally. Many contemporary narratives on wine, especially the ones created by the producers themselves, must be seen as a specific and vested-interest form of commercial discourse that promotes idealised interpretations of reality designed to provoke consumer desire and their consequent (ideally profit generating) wine purchases. Many consumers and producers alike view these utopian terroir interpretations as real and authentic and believe they either transcend or are not necessarily influenced by the producers' commercial goals. This has the double effect of hegemonically casting both the winemakers' utopian terroir aspirations and ideals, and their commercial practices of wine production, as somehow natural, even apical, expressions of human endeavour, as historically enduring, and consequently as socially validated and even noble pursuits. In respect of the terroir utopia this is done directly by articulating and foregrounding the various entangled ideals of place, product, history and people noted above; while with regard to the commercial production of wine it is done by effectively over-looking, deflecting attention away from, or by muting the vested, often contra-dictory, competitive and exploitative interests of market and commodity-based wine production, which has the backgrounding effect of similarly framing this also as a natural aspect and expression of humanity. Accordingly, the producers, by offering idealised versions and seemingly truthful or genuine interpretations of their wine production realities, adroitly turn commercial means into utopian ends that are to be nobly striven for and hopefully attained. And as such they effectively transform the local reality for both themselves and for experiencing others such as wine tourists and consumers.

This chapter is based on anthropological fieldwork conducted in Cirò Marina for almost a year in 2000 and 2001, with two subsequent shorter visits in 2004 and in 2016. During these stays, I conducted formal and informal interviews with different people linked to the wine industry: producers, grape growers, teachers and public officials. The information presented in the following section is based on a content analysis of the websites of the local wineries and undertaken in 2018.

The terroir utopias of Cirò Marina

Cirò Marina is a town of about 15,000 residents, situated in the province of Crotone in Calabria, in southern Italy. There are about 15 wineries in Cirò Marina. There is a public wine cooperative which is open to all grape grow-ers, while there are also private wine cooperatives that are usually established around one or two families and open only to the members of these families. The latter typically comprise of few members, between ten and thirty, with a majority descending from ancient local landowner families. Finally, two thirds are private wineries own by individual families. Some of these wineries pro-duce between two and four million bottles per year, while others produce between 75,000 and 200,000 bottles a year. Some sell their wines on different international markets, mainly Germany and Switzerland,[1] through agents and representatives, while others limit their sales to Calabria and don't work with agents. Besides these wineries, there are about 1,500 winegrowers, generally descending from the families of *braccianti* who received plots of land through land distributions. They produce wine, but only for their domestic needs. If they don't sell their grapes to private wineries, they will typically take these to the public wine cooperative or sell it to buyers from different places in Calabria who resell the grapes to individuals producing their own wine at home.

From the 15 or so wineries producing wine in the Cirò DOC area, 13 have websites. I have undertaken a qualitative content analysis of these thirteen websites, searching to identify the type of information and key tropes deployed to frame and explain the local wine reality. No quantitative methods were used, for example to numerically assess word or topic distributions. The approach was interpretative and was based on my ethnographic knowledge and experience used to identify the common themes deployed by these different websites. On the websites, wineries offer a deliberate and highly idealised image of the local context of wine production. They construct definitive truths (Rose 2017) and distinctive images by putting emphasis on specific aspects of their collectively constructed history, territory and wine traditions. Although these websites and their information are public, I have chosen for ethical reason not to indicate the URL address of these websites and to change names to ensure anonymity.

On these websites, the territory is described and presented as an idyllic rural space: 'Awash with sea green, illuminated by a clear sun under an ever-blue sky and surrounded by colourful hills, the Cirò Marina territory' (see Carmichael 2005; Howland 2008; Williams 2001; and Senese et al. this volume, for the deployment of similar tropes in Okanagan, Canada). This aesthetically valued territory is also linked to equally desirable cultural and human characteristics of the place: 'Our land elegantly combines nature, history, art, gastronomy and folklore.' Finally, the territory is linked to different agricultural productions such as citrus, bergamot, liquorice plant, chilli pepper and 'ancient olive tree groves which originates an excellent golden-yellow extra-virgin olive oil', that together form a broader food landscape that is said to characterise and authenticate Calabria as an appealing gastronomic destination.

Added to these descriptions, all websites offer magnificent photos and images of the surrounding countryside with pictures primarily of verdant vines and vineyards, olive trees, cows, bucolic country landscapes, and the ever calm, beautiful turquoise sea and clear blue sky.

Finally, that territory is depicted as a theatre of idealised rural reality that exists in opposition to the turbulence and stresses of contemporary urban ways of life: 'Far away from the chaos and city's stress, in an environment which seems to block time with a slower pace of life.' Not surprisingly, the territory as an idyllic landscape frames and authenticates the high quality of the wine and trustworthiness, passion and genuineness of its producers. The apparent natural and historical qualities of the landscapes are thus transmitted to wine tastes and quality. There are, however, no images of the town. While Cirò township is mentioned in accompanying texts, the geographic fact that most wineries are actually situated within the boundaries of the township, on its periphery or along the connecting highway, is significantly absent from the promotional images. Although, in responding to that imagined ideal, some wineries have actually started to move and build new facilities in the countryside, surrounded by vineyards, thus illustrating the concrete transformative power of terroir utopias in Cirò Marina.

Along with the territory, history and tradition are also abundantly presented on these websites. An important element found on all websites is an idealisation of historical antiquity. Ancient history, to which a direct link is established through wine, plays a pivotal role in the local terroir utopia. Indeed, everybody I met during the study mentioned it. Although historical evidence is scarce, according to the producers and the population in general, local wine production dates back to Calabria's Greek colonies of the antiquity. Filiation to the Magna Grecia (seventh century BC), a time prior to Rome itself, is a common identity claim in Southern Italy.[2] Through wine production, inhabitants of Cirò Marina are apparently able to trace a direct link to that glorious past. Following terroir utopias' emphasis on the endurability of space and time, the links to that period serve as claims for the durability and quality of the local space for producing quality wines:

> The first Greek settlers who disembarked on the Calabrian coast were so impressed by the fertility of the land that was rich with vineyards that they called it 'Enotria', that is, 'land where they cultivate the best grapes of the land'.

The links to this period also serve as the cornerstone of their winemaking tradition, with a direct reference to grape varieties:

> The Greek peasants brought their new wine-making techniques and new vines to plant: there are in fact, some types of grape, still present in Calabria, that are probably of Greek origin, hence the Gaglioppo, the Greco Bianco and the Mantonico, to name but a few.

Finally, this period of time serves to entrench the antiquity of local production and the consequent qualitative and commercial fame of the local wines:

> The wines from Cremissa (the name of the local Greek colony) quickly became very popular among traders, and they were of such a high quality that they were offered as a gift to athletes who were returning victorious from the Olympics, such as the great wrestler Milo of Croton.

Considering the long, rich and varied history of Calabria, it is interesting to note that almost all the other historical periods are absent from the producers' promotional discourses. Only one website mentions briefly the Roman and Byzantine periods, but in a very elusive way. There is no specific mention of the Kingdom of Naples (thirteenth to the nineteenth centuries), the unification of Italy in 1861 or the twentieth century. All the emphasis is on the Greek antiquity, a powerful utopia as much for the West in general as for the history of wine in particular, and for the producers and inhabitants of Cirò Marina.

The more recent past is mentioned by certain wineries, but in especially subtle ways that emphasise and celebrate the genealogical and kinship links of their own families, and which serve to ground their families in specific agricultural traditions. This is notable, for example, in promotions foregrounding the descendants of 'ancient families' of large landowners: 'The Fràncica family have been the land owners since the 1600s. They have always devoted themselves to the cultivation of vines and olives.' For others, whose ancestors weren't part of these prominent families, the claims are situated within wine production and commercialisation: 'Nicito has been producing its wines here since 1870' or 'With more than 160 years of history, the Perrotta winery is the oldest winery existing today in Calabria', or 'It is here that we have been cultivating vines for four generations'. This enables them to construct the longevity of their family's involvement in equally durable traditions of wine production.

Tradition is explicitly and regularly invoked. First, the varieties of grapes used locally objectively define tradition: 'We started from tradition; Gaglioppo, Greco, and the large number of native varieties present in the region.' Second, tradition is used to indicate various cultural or historical aspects, but without necessarily defining them: 'To safeguard a real heritage of tradition, culture, taste, style and history that are the real essence of our peasant way of life.' Finally, there is an idealisation of traditional methods of (especially hand-crafting) production and to articulate apparent natural, embodied and historical linkages with contemporary methods:

> The Archilione (a local billhook) is the keystone of the concept of 'terroir' which is the sum of the land, the climate, the vines and the hand of the man, his work, responsibility and sensitivity towards the environment around him. [...] I am still fascinated when I see an elderly pruner at work. Every vineyard is treated depending on the climate and the wine to be obtained. That is exactly the way I imagine my wine: from the vineyard to the cellar: the work at the cellar is the direct result of daily work practised in the vineyard.

This idealisation of tradition is amplified by lessening or overlooking the importance of the use of modern technologies: 'Our work is mainly done through craft practices' or 'Winemaking is conducted through traditional methods, with the exclusion of any industrial process'. In reality, all wineries use modern technologies such as hydraulic or pneumatic press, pumps, stainless-steel and temperature-controlled tanks and contemporary oenological science, although some may have older structures and equipment, like cement tanks dating back to the 1970s. Only the grape growers producing wine for their domestic needs actually have production practices that could be qualified as artisanal and hand-crafted in method and scale. That being said, nobody produces wine with the methods that were locally used in the nineteenth and the beginning of the twentieth centuries, for example, with grape crushing directly in the vineyard with very short or no skin maceration. Only the must was carried into town cellars for the fermentation process (Fournier 2014).

These websites all serve a primary marketing function. They present commercial discourses that are meant to promote the wineries, their wines and the places of production as a quality region. As such they offer an idealised view and understanding of place, product and people. Nonetheless, they are representative of the type of utopian discourses on wine and terroir. Together these wineries offer a homogeneous, coherent view and understanding of the local idealised reality, which can be explained by the fact that winery owners actually share and believe in these specific constructed imaginaries not only as ideals, but also as actual and/or aspirational realities. For them, the ideal constructions of reality presented in these promotional discourses, although slightly embellished (a skewing perhaps 'allowed' to highlight a higher order of transcendent truth), is real and authentic. It is the dominant way to constructively and apparently empathetically understand the local wine reality, moreover it is an understanding that is significantly influenced by the legislation systems that codify and legitimate specific forms wine production and commercialisation, and by broader wine consumption cultures (local, historical and increasingly globalised) in which wine provenance is paramount. Constructed space and time, through idealised demarcations of place, history and tradition, are the building blocks of terroir as defined and legitimised by the laws of AOCs or DOCs. By being seen as real and actual by the producers, they offer utopian understandings and notions of 'good' production techniques and wine tastes, typicity and quality that both promotes and enables the transformation of the local spaces and practices, by imagining a better past, and helping invent a better present and future:

> For four generations we have been steadfast supporters of our land and of its richness. We strongly believe in what it represented in the past, what it represents today and above all what it will represent in the future for the world of wine. [...] We now know that our original intuition was a good one, and that some of the most beautiful pages in Calabria's winemaking history have yet to be written.

Without formal collusion, Cirò Marina winery owners produce quite a unified and coherent image of the idealised local reality, illustrating the increasingly globalised (Charters 2010; Inglis 2019) resonance and utopian power of terroir. The elements discussed here are those at the foundation of the definition of terroir, and are enshrined in the regulations on AOCs or DOCs, i.e. place, history and tradition. In contrast with these narratives, the ethnographic reality I encountered was far more ambiguous.

Wine production in Cirò Marina

Compared to the idealised version presented on wineries websites, the reality of wine production in Cirò Marina is more complex and contested and not necessarily as harmonious. In the space available here, I can only highlight and mention a few dimensions of local production I observed during my research. There were, for example, important rivalries between wineries which paradoxically almost impeded the development of concerted actions. During my first stay, there had not been any official association of wine producers since the 1980s. I was told that producers, and people in general, were too individualistic to maintain such a representative association and that in the South, there wasn't a 'culture of collaboration' similar to the one people assumed existed in the North. For the same reason, I was told, small grape growers weren't loyal to the local public wine cooperative.[3] During my stay in 2004, there were two wineries associations, that represented two factions of opposing wineries, and each competing for official recognition. In 2016, there was, however, one official association, but in which some producers were defiant.

There was also opposition between wineries and the small grape growers. Small grape growers felt they were marginalised within the production and commercialization processes and felt they were not receiving a fair share of the revenues produced by the industry. Producers were criticising some of the grape growers for their inability to consistently produce quality grapes, thus justifying why they bought their grapes at lower prices, or didn't buy them at all. The role of these small producers was then paradoxical. As the descendants of the winegrowers of the past, they were also the bearers of tradition. But at the same time, their wine wasn't recognised as a quality wine by the industry standards. For the small grape growers, and the local resident population in general, a good wine was a strong wine. The higher the alcohol, the better the wine, reaching around 17% of alcohol. The grape growers' discourses also emphasised the purity of their wines, which for them was more *genuino* [genuine] because they do not add any chemicals such as sulphur, nor did they submit their wines to any technological interventions such as filtration. Furthermore, grape growers did not typically make any claims regarding the taste of their wines, but rather foregrounded and idealised their artisanal or hand-crafted processes of production. Accordingly, their wine was simply better because they had made it themselves; by the same reckoning, food prepared at home is better than what you buy ready-made at the supermarket – and the small grape growers celebrated their wines through such ideals linked with homemade foods. Winery owners, however, were critical of this way of winemaking as being full of defects, like higher acidity, and for producing unstable wines that turned to vinegar within a year and which accordingly would be improper to put on the market. By contrast, winery owners were defining the quality of their wines in the same manner as wine connoisseurs, wine journalists and other wine intermediaries do around the world (Smith Maguire & Zhang 2016), mentioning precise qualities of colour, aromas, tastes and balance, and emphasising the typicity expressions of local grape varieties and local terroirs.

This illustrates how the past and the tradition were idealised in order to validate and frame the present. The importance accorded to the apparently utopian past of Greek Antiquity was omnipresent, celebrated and fore-grounded by winery owners, grape growers, civil servants and the general population alike. Everybody I encountered and talked to explained to me the link between the present wine industry and the assumed quality of the wine production of the Greek colony of Cremissa. The utopian quality of the past was also explained by invoking tradition and artisanal know-how of small producers of the nineteenth century. But, as discussed above, this know-how was not contemporaneously ascribed to the actual grape growers. This also illustrates a transforming effect of the idealised terroir utopia, albeit via the absence of recognition and valuing of wine produced on the margins of mainstream commercial production.

During my research in 2000–2001, there was a specific awareness about quality. All the commercial producers said that the quality of local wine had deteriorated during the 1970s: 'Before the 70s, there was here an artisanal wine production. While in the 1970s, we start producing too much quantity and we have industrialised the production.' In order to start producing quality again, many explained how they needed to revert to small scale, artisanal production. This utopian framing of the past and of artisanal practice was a response to the difficulties that producers were experiencing with foreign markets. It can be considered utopian because it was an idealisation of the past, offering a solution to the present context, while at the same time the comparable practices of con-temporary small and artisanal grape growers were not considered to offer any alternative solutions. Furthermore in 2016, a new trend toward natural wine emerged. It was a strategy used by some small and new producers to market their wines, although they were using older equipment. As mentioned in the previous section, they were themselves invoking artisanal and traditional meth-ods as a guarantee of quality, which clearly appears here as a utopian framing.

During my research, the value that local producers assigned to their wines was contested by the responses they received from outside markets. Put simply by one producer:

> The problem comes from globalisation. Before, here as everywhere else, people were drinking the local wine and everybody was happy. Today, it's not like that anymore. When I sell to CiboSì (supermarket), when I sell in Germany or when I sell in America, I have to take into account consumers' taste and preferences.

For them, the local wine was a quality wine. But it was not the feedback they were receiving from international markets: 'At the time, the wine of Cirò was the best in the world, because Calabria was our world. Today, people here have understood that our wine is the best in Calabria, but not the best in the world anymore'. This influenced the judgements that local producers were placing on their wines and also on themselves as a producing region.

Winery owners were increasingly sensitive to the judgement of foreign markets. The pressure of the markets and the terroir utopia were compelling them to improve the quality of the local wine to meet internationalised standards. Many producers told me how they were working on attaining higher quality, through better grape selection and through investment in technology such as temperature-controlled tanks, pneumatic presses and French oak barrels, as a response to appease foreign markets. The terroir utopia was thus having a transformative effect on the local production and, in the eyes of local commercial producers this was for the best.

The commercial aspect of terroir utopia

Terroir products are normally seen as traditional and authentic, while in fact they are a specific type of commodity that exists primarily through trade (Trubek 2008). For that reason, the cultural meanings associated with terroir products can also be seen as directly influenced by trade. Many contributors in this book (Charters, Dhalla, Howland, Howson et al.) provide evidence of the commercial basis of different wines utopias. Wine, as any other terroir product, has to be conceived and understood as a commodity. The growing interest that people have for terroir products has been for example interpreted and analysed by researchers as a reaction to the globalisation of the industrial agribusiness (Barham 2003; Mutersbaugh et al. 2005; Murdoch et al. 2000; Pratt 2007; Sylvander et al. 2006; Winter 2003). Therefore, terroir products are a specific form of commodities, but are not perceived as such; their specificity is actually symbolically constructed in opposition to mass industrialised food or products (Trubek 2008). Terroir products are utopia commodified.

Historically, it is through trade that the place of origin of certain products has become important and used to define them. It was the case in ancient Greek and Roman times (McGovern 2003; Unwin 1991) and more recently for Porto (Shaw, 1998), Madeira (Hancock 2009) and Bordeaux (Ulin 1996). The importance of trade in the very definition of terroir products is also illustrated by the emergence of the *Appellations d'origine contrôlée* (AOC) system in France. These laws were at first developed to counter commercially damaging frauds that had emerged, especially during the equally commercially troubling times of the phylloxera crisis (c. 1880) and the economic crisis of 1929 (Lachiver 1988). Through the AOC laws the concept of terroir was legally defined and codified during the first half of the twentieth century, thus legitimising terroir, along with place and tradition as central defining features of wine tastes and quality.

The subsequent development of technical and scientific discourses in the 1960s put an additional emphasis on environmental dimensions such as soil compositions and climate conditions, to endow terroir with a scientific, objective basis, but without being able to explain entirely the variations of taste and quality between wines by these factors alone (Moran 1993). The historical, cultural and human characteristics of specific places, combined with definitive foci on accordant unique traditions, served to expand the reasons and logics that were deployed to explain the inimitability, and thus exclusivity, of each terroir product (Barham 2003; Bérard & Marchenay 1995, 2004; Delfosse 1997; Demossier 2011; Trubek 2008). But at the same time, these elements also hid, or least deflected critical attention away from, the enduring commercial character of wine (Howland 2019) and terroir products by distancing them from industrialized commodities, which nonetheless continue to influence their meanings. Finally, discourses on terroir seem more similar to national identity and ethnicity discourses, especially in the romanticized, highly selective and inventive invocations of place and history evident in the definition of the identity of each product. For the producers, discourses on wine are actually, in part, discourses about themselves (Fournier 2013).

Yet, this process of identity construction of terroir products is ultimately deployed to serve commercial ends: to distinguish what would otherwise be undifferentiated products in markets, which is still the case today for many agricultural products. As a specific form of commercial discourse, they lead to highly idealised interpretations. Many scholars have studied how commercial promotions, together with accordant rituals of commodity purchase and possession, produce idealised framings and interpretations of reality (Schudson 1984; Lears 1994; Leiss et al., 2005; McCracken 1990, 2005; Williamson 1978). For Baudrillard (1968, 1970), the whole cultural universe of contemporary society consists of a utopian illusion of simulacra and simulation that is structured by and through a global system of value-generating things and symbolic meanings directly linked to the capitalist production/consumption of lifestyles and identities. In that perspective, commercial communications continually offer us the multiple utopias of capitalism (see Howland and Swinburne this volume): individual happiness, fulfilling social and family life, joyful public spaces and workplaces, pristine environment and, of course, the solution to all our problems through the consumption of commodities, services and events. In that respect, discourses about terroir must be seen as a specific form of commercial discourse that offer idealised, seemingly grounded or natural, and utopian interpretations of the realities of wine production, consumption and associated identity, sociality and distinction constructs.

But in the case of wine and terroir products, especially when compared to the artifice and anonymity assigned to the production of mass-produced industrial commodities and advertising, these discourses are perceived as true and authentic. These discourses are collectively produced by a multitude of actors and in different global and historical settings, notably the producers themselves, but also professional associations, promotion agencies, officials, cultural intermediaries, researchers and media (writers, journalists, critics, bloggers, etc.). All these actors offer quite coherent and integrated discourses on terroir that predominantly mobilise elements valued as being 'authentic', like artisan producers, inimitable places of production, distinct traditions and histories.[4]

This idealised reality leads the producers to have specific interpretations and responsive practices about their presents and their pasts in order to produce the best image of themselves, their reality and their products. As such these discourses of idealised authenticity have the power to transform the contexts and practices of production through producers actually believing and investing in their own idealised realities and thus moving them toward the routine, even banal, creation of their utopian dreamings. The idealised images that they create about themselves can become aspirational goals to attain, thus compelling and enabling accordant transformations and enhancements of daily reality. It is actually the case in Cirò Marina where increasingly globalized terroir utopias have created spaces that prompt and sanction producers, and the local population alike, to practically recreate ideal images and discourses of their past, present and future in ways that similarly promote and advance the commercial utopias of terroir.

Conclusion

In Cirò Marina, wine production has a long history of transformative effects. It is an important economical asset for this town. It is an important source of money for the local economy. It is also central to the image and identity of the town as perceived by its own inhabitants. The local wine industry is a source of pride. But as this chapter has presented it, wine – both local and drawing from within the flows of an increasingly globalized industry, markets and consumption cultures – also generates opportunities and compulsions for producers and the local population to construct and enact vernacular terroir utopias, starting with the commercial promotional possibilities of envisioning their wine realities as better.

Today, the commodification of wine is ubiquitous, as it is of terroir products in general, yet it is a specific form of commodity that is cast as true, authentic, grounded and natural, especially in opposition to the anonymity and artifice of mass-produced, industrial products. In this context, narratives created around wine and terroir must in part be seen as constituting a form of commercial discourse that offers highly selective and idealised interpretations of reality that essentially privilege the commercially viable and consistent production of wines considered palatable in international markets. This was evident in the rejection of the wines and winemaking practices of local small grape growers – who although still situated within historical traditions of artisan-like, hand-crafted and minimal interventions akin to current trends in natural wine production, were nevertheless regarded as producing inferior and unstable wines that did not warrant commercial release into local, let alone international, markets. Moreover, this selective idealisation of terroir and of accompanying idyllic landscapes and heroic historical/ tradition associations was quite obvious on the wineries' websites. Yet because producers and consumers alike believe in the existence of terroir, these discourses are not solely commercial discourses. They become routinely, even banally, authentic and true, and although idealised interpretations of reality, they appear compelled to be turned into utopias and as such everyday practices increasingly come to reflect and substantiate the rhetoric.

We have seen how the local context of production was complex and contested. We have also seen how the markets pressured winery owners, leading them to develop specific understanding of their own wine. Finally, we can ask why the mercantile dimensions of wine production and consumption tend to be hidden by terroir discourses and utopias. Commercial dimensions – both direct or even suggestive – were wholly absent from the utopian discourses of the winery websites, yet we have seen how these are central to the ideas and practices of producers have about their wine, their places and themselves. This, I believe, should heighten our attention to local and global commercial influences and the market-orientated goals, structures, possibilities and constraints that are endemic in the production of wine as a commodity and also in the diffusion of contemporary cultural representations and values associated with wine, terroir and utopia.

Notes

1 The most important international markets for the Cirò DOC wine because of the emigrants from Calabria.
2 Visible, for example, in Versace's Medusa logo and garment style.
3 The public wine cooperative is seen as a public entity. It is not valorized and is seen as a last resort when unable to sell your grapes elsewhere.
4 That is so, I believe, because the different legal systems encompassing wine production that regulate and define terroir have served and still work as a general frame of intelligibility which enable the symbolic construction of terroir, mainly through the demarcated uses of space (places) and time (history) and which have deeply influenced the way people think about terroir (Fournier 2014).

Bibliography

Barham, E. (2003). Translating terroir: the global challenge of French AOC labelling. *Journal of Rural Studies*, 19(1): 127–138.
Baudrillard, J. (1968). *Le système des objets*. Paris, Gallimard.
Baudrillard, J. (1970). *La société de consummation*. Paris: HEC.
Bérard, L. & Marchenay, P. (1995). Lieux, temps et preuves. La construction sociale des produits de terroir. *Terrain*, 24; 153–164.
Bérard, L. & Marchenay, P. (2004). *Les produits du terroir. Entre culture et réglements*. Paris: CNRS.
Beverland, M. B. (2005). Crafting brand authenticity: The case of luxury wines. *Journal of Management Studies*, 42(5): 1003–1029.
Bloch, E. (1986). *The Principle of Hope*. Oxford: Blackwell.

Carmichael, B. (2005). Understanding the wine tourism experience for winery visitors in the Niagara region, Ontario, Canada. *Tourism Geographies*, 7(2): 185–204.

Charters, S. (2010). Marketing terroir: A conceptual approach. Refereed paper – 5th International Academy of Wine Business Research Conference, 8–10 Feb. Auckland: New Zealand.

Delfosse, C. (1997). Noms de pays et produits du terroir: enjeux des dénominations géographiques. *Espace géographique*, 26(3): 222–230.

Demossier, M. (2011). Beyond terroir: territorial construction, hegemonic discourses, and French wine culture. *Journal of the Royal Anthropological Institute*, 17(4): 685–705.

Fournier, V. (2013). Les effets de la règlementation de la culture: l'exemple de la production de vin en Calabre. *Revue de la culture matérielle-Material Culture Review*, (77/78): 123 138.

Fournier, V. (2014). *Le vin comme performance culturelle. Le cas du Cirò DOC en Calabre*. Montréal: Del Busso.

Fournier, V. (2018). La mondialisation du vin. Entre circulation transnationale de la culture et représentations locales du vin à Cirò Marina en Calabre (Italie). *Anthropologie et société*, 42(1): 271–287.

Guy, K. M. (2011). Silence and Savoir-Faire in the Marketing of Products of the *Terroir*. *Modern & Contemporary France*, 19(4): 459–475.

Hancock, D. (2009). *Oceans of Wine: Madeira and the Emergence of American Trade and Taste*. New Haven: Yale University Press.

Howland, P. J. (2008). Martinborough's wine tourists and the metro-rural idyll. *Journal of New Zealand Studies*, 6–7: 77–100.

Howland, P. J. (2019). Enduring wine and the global middle-class. In *The Globalization of Wine*, D. Inglis & A. Almila (eds), pp. 151–170. London: Bloomsbury.

Inglis, D. (2019). Contemporary Wine Globalization: Longer-term Dynamics and Patterns. In *The Globalization of Wine*, D. Inglis & A. Almila (eds), pp. 21–46. London: Bloomsbury.

Jung, Y. & Sternsdorff-Cisterna, N. (2014). Introduction to Crafting Senses: Circulating the Knowledge and Experience of Taste. *Food and Foodways*, 22(1–2): 1–4.

Lachiver, M. (1988). *Vins, vignes et vignerons. Histoire du vignoble français*. Paris: Fayard.

Lears, J. (1994). *Fable of Abundance. A Cultural History of Advertising in America*. New York: Basic Books.

Leiss, W., Kline, S., Jhally, S. & Botterill, J. (2005). *Social Communication in advertising. Consumption in the mediated marketplace*. New York: Routledge.

Le Guin, U. (1989). A Non-Euclidean View of California as a Cold Place to Be. In *Dancing at the Edge of the World: Thoughts on Words, Women, Places*, pp. 80–100. New York: Grove Press.

Levitas, R. (2010). Back to the Future: Wells, sociology, utopia and method. *The Sociological Review*, 58(4): 531–547.

Levitas, R. (2013). Some Varieties of Utopian Method. *Irish Journal of Sociology*, 21(2): 41–50.

McCracken, G. (1990). *Culture and Consumption: New Approaches to the Symbolic Character of Consumer Goods and Activities*. Bloomington: Indiana University Press.

McCracken, G. (2005). *Culture and Consumption II: Markets, Meanings and Brand Management*. Bloomington: Indiana University Press.

McGovern, P. E. (2003). *Ancient Wine. The Search for the Origins of Viniculture*. Princeton: Princeton University Press.

Meneley, A. (2004). Extra virgin olive oil and slow food. *Anthropologica*, 46(2): 165–176.

Moran, W. (1993). The wine appellation as territory in France and California. *Annals of the Association of American Geographers*, 83(4): 694–717.

Moran, W. (2016). *New Zealand Wine: The Land, the Vines, the People*. Auckland: Auckland University Press.

Motahari, M. (2008). The Hermeneutical Circle or the Hermeneutical Spiral? *The International Journal of Humanities*, 15(2): 99–112.

Mutersbaugh, T., Klooster, D., Renard, M.-C. & Taylor, P. (2005). Certifying rural spaces: quality-certified products and rural governance. *Journal of Rural Studies*, 4(21): 381–388.

Murdoch, J., Mardsen, T. & Banks, J. (2000). Quality, Nature and Embeddedness: Some theoretical considerations in the context of the food sector. *Economic Geography*, 76(2):107–125.

Paulson, E. & O'Guinn, T. (2012). Working-Class Cast: Images of the Working Class in Advertising, 1950–2010. *The Annals of the American Academy of Political and Social Sciences*, 644(1): 50–69.

Paxson, H. (2010). Locating Value in Artisan Cheese: Reverse-Engineering Terroir for New World Landscapes. *American Anthropologist*, 112(3): 442–455.

Pratt, J. (2007). Food values. The local and the authentic. *Critique of Anthropology*, 27(3): 285–300.

Rose, G. (ed.) (2007). Researching visual materials: Towards a critical visual methodology. *Visual Methodologies: An Introduction to the Interpretation of Visual Materials*, pp. 1–27. London: SAGE.

Schudson, M. (1984). *Advertising. The Uneasy Persuasion*. New York: Basic Books.

Shaw, L. M. E. (1998). *The Anglo-Portuguese Alliance and the English Merchant in Portugal, 1654–1810*. London: Routledge.

Sonnino, R. (2007). The Power of Place: Embeddedness and local food systems in Italy and the UK. *Anthropology of Food*. Available online at http://journals.opene dition.org/aof/454 (accessed 05.03.18).

Smith Maguire, J. (2010). Provenance and the liminality of production and consumption: The case of wine promoters. *Marketing Theory*, 10(3): 269–282.

Smith Maguire, J. & Zhang, D. (2016). Shifting the Focus from Consumers to Cultural Intermediaries: An Example from the Emerging Chinese Fine Wine Market. In *Consumer Culture Theory* (Research in Consumer Behavior, Volume 18), N. Özçağlar-Toulouse, D. Rinallo, & R. W. Belk (eds), pp. 1–27. Bingley: Emerald Group Publishing Limited.

Sylvander, B., Allaire, G., Barjolle, D., Thénevod-Mottet, E., Belletti, G., Marescotti, A., & Treagear, A. (2006). Qualité, origine et globalisation: Justifications générales et contexts nationaux, le cas des indications géographiques. *Canadian Journal of Regional Science-Revue Canadienne des Sciences Régionales*, 29(1): 43–54.

Trubek, A. B. (2008). *The Taste of Place. A Cultural Journey into Terroir*. Berkeley: University of California Press.

Ulin, R. C. (1996). *Vintage and Tradition. An Ethnohistory of Southwest French Wine Cooperatives*. Washington: Smithsonian Institution Press.

Unwin, T. (1991). *Wine and the Vine. An Historical Geography of Viticulture and the Wine Trade*. London: Routledge.

Williamson, J. (1978). *Decoding Advertisements: Ideology and Meaning in Advertising*. London: Marion Boyars.

Winter, M. (2003). Embeddedness, the new food economy and defensive localism. *Journal of Rural Studies*, 19(1): 23–32.

10 Ideals for sustainability in the Australian wine industry

Authenticity and identity[1]

Rumina Dhalla

Introduction

It is becoming increasingly clear that the global wine industry is facing a wide range of established and emerging eco-certifying programs, and sustainability in viticulture has become a critical challenge for the global wine industry (Sellers 2015). Much of the impetus for sustainability has emanated from the pressures of the global market where competition has increased, and the number of sustainability certifications for wines are growing and gaining acceptance in the global wine industry. It is also becoming accepted that sustainable practices are a necessary and integral component of the increasing consumer preference for 'green' products (Castellini et al. 2017). For example, the Research Institute of Organic Agriculture (FiBL & IFOAM) suggests that global demand for organic products continues to rise strongly, and sales of organic food products have climbed to over US$80 billion, up from about US$18 billion in 2000 (FiBL & IFOAM 2017). The 2017 Market Report from Australian Organic found that consumers seek out and consume organic products which are predominantly perceived to be chemical free, additive free, hormone and anti-biotic free, non-GMO and cruelty free and are perceived to have health benefits (Lawson et al. 2017).

There has recently been a surge of interest in sustainable, organic and biodynamic wines from consumers, and it is expected that this demand will continue to grow (Miller 2017). Much of the impetus for these wines comes from consumers who are becoming more aware and seeking products that do not harm the environment and are perceived to be healthy. Consumers, as powerful constituents, are thus influencing an increase in the supply and demand for wines that reduce harm to themselves and the environment (Forbes et al. 2009). In Australia, the demand for organic products is rising, and organic grape production saw an increase of 120 per cent between 2011 and 2014, with continued increase in domestic and international demand for Australian organic wine (Winemakers' Federation of Australia 2017). Popular media promote sustainable (also referred to as 'eco' or 'green'), organic and biodynamic wines as 'better for you' (Bell 2014), and there are growing numbers of biodynamic and organic wine producers who are acknowledging these changing expectations and needs of their consumers, and certified organic and biodynamic wines are a growing niche (Wine Australia 2017).

Eco-certifications and related eco-labelling have become a ubiquitous part of the institutional environment across many industries, and in particular, consumer-facing industries (Delmas & Grant 2014). Consumers view eco certification as a signal of sustainable growing and production processes (Schäufele & Hamm 2017). Eco certifications have also been linked to better economic results for certified vineyards (Giacomarra et al. 2016) and improved reputation (Delmas & Grant 2014). However, it was evident from the initial exploration of practitioner and academic literature that despite the growing interest in certifications that identify wines as sustainable, organic or biodynamic, and the potential for increased markets and improved performance, not all producers in these domains opt to get certifications. I was thus curious to see what drove sustainable, organic and biodynamic viticulture, that is, why some producers opted to engage in eco production. In particular, I wanted to explore the influence of organizational identity in the impetus for sustainable viticulture and the adoption of sustainable, organic and biodynamic certifications in Australian vineyards. I hypothesized that the identity of the vineyard would influence the decision to adopt sustainable, organic or biodynamic practices and pursue eco-certification.

I set out to explore the influence of organizational identity on drivers and strategies in becoming sustainable through conversations with wineries, the industry association and the institutional intermediaries such as wine writers and analysts. In particular, I focused on the influence of organizational identity in becoming a certified sustainable, organic or biodynamic vineyard. I argue that all three forms of sustainable production explored in this study promote a utopian vision for wine production through reduction of harm, sensibility for good health, and guardianship and protection of terroir. I also argue that successful adoption of utopian ideals will require an organizational identity that is authentically sustainable, that is, the essence of the organization is about the utopian ideals of causing no harm and flourishing forever (Clegg et al. 2012; Hopkins 2009).

Identity, utopia and strategy

There is limited information available on utopia in organizational settings (Clegg et al. 2012). There is some indication of environmental considerations related to utopia in sustainability literature. For example, de Gues (2002) uses the term 'ecotopia' in relation to environmentally related utopia while Gray (1992) refers to environmental considerations in accounting as 'green utopia'. Clegg et al. (2012: 1738) explain utopia for organizations from a 'what could be' perspective. They draw on examples from Khmer Rouge and argue that utopia would represent removing the violence and evils and replace them with happiness and peace; where actions for benefit of the individual are replaced with actions that benefit the collective (Clegg et al. 2012). An insightful perspective is offered in *The Tragedy of the Commons* by Hardin (1968) who explains that a finite world has finite resources, and cannot support self-interested consumption that depletes collective finite resources. A utopian ideal would be a world where common resources are protected for common benefit. Thus, in this study I understand an organization with utopian ideals as one that adopts processes and practices that cause no harm to people or the environment, uses resources that regenerate thus reducing resource dependence and impact on finite resources, and protects the terroir.

In management literature, organizational identity is understood as that which is core, enduring and distinctive about an organization (Albert & Whetten 1985). As with much of the literature in this field, in this paper I understand organizational identity as the response to the question, 'who are we as an organization'; the response to that question is that which is core, enduring and distinctive about an organization (Albert & Whetten 1985). Organizational identity has been shown to influence organizational strategy and organizational member action (Dutton et al. 1994; Dutton & Dukerich 1991; Elsbach & Kramer 1996; Stimpert et al. 1998). Furthermore, identity is shown to have a strong link to the reputation of the organization (Benjamin & Podolny 1999; Dhalla 2008; Whetten & Mackey 2002).

It is important to mention that for this study, I used Whetten and Mackey's (2002) 'social actor' conception of organizational identity, that is, identity 'of' the organization and not identity 'in' organizations. Whetten and Mackey (2002: 395) explain that there are two conceptualizations of organizational identity: organizational identity as 'shared perceptions' among organizational members and organizational identity as 'institutionalized claims' available to members. The conceptualization of organizational identity 'of' the organization, as understood in this paper, is at the organizational level, where the organization is the social actor, and the 'we' in the 'who are we as an organization' (Albert & Whetten 1985) represents agents and information that speak on behalf of the organization as a social actor, the identity 'of' the organization (Whetten & Mackey 2002). This study is undertaken from a perspective that organizational identity is institutionalized and is articulated as claims about what is core, central and enduring about the organization (Whetten 2003). This is consistent with the perspective of organizational identity 'of' the organization.

In extant literature, organizational identity is understood as the organizational DNA (Schultz 2016), or the 'essence' of the organization (Albert & Whetten 1985). In the context of this study, I argue that a utopian view of organizational identity would be one where identity, that is, who you are (Albert & Whetten 1985) is congruent or authentically linked with what you do (your strategy) (Dhalla 2007). There is no confusion about organizational DNA (Schultz 2016); it does what it is hardwired to do. Thus, an organization that embraces and acts on utopian ideals of sustainability has a strong sustainability identity and organizational members who are driven to support identity-congruent organizational action (Dutton et al. 1994; Elsbach &

Kramer 1996). Congruence, or authenticity, is described in identity literature as being true to the internal self (identity) and external expression and practice (Dutton & Dukerich, 1991; Roberts & Dutton 2009). Congruence between self-defining claims and action is valued by consumers who are willing to pay a premium for authenticity (Kovács et al. 2017). Authenticity will compel organizational members to see the organization as part of themselves, and form a psychological attachment to the organization (Dhalla, 2007; Dutton et al. 1994). Organizational members tend to promote organizational action that supports this identity (Dutton et al. 1994) and defend the organization against external threats (Elsbach & Kramer 1996). Organizational action that is not true or authentic to this essence of the organization leads to negative organizational outcomes such as mistrust, fragmented organizational identity, and increased reputational risk (Dhalla 2011). Thus, authenticity yields benefits for consumers, organizations and organizational members. Wine literature also recognizes the importance of congruence between claims and action. Authenticity, sincerity, and being the 'real' thing is a valuable consideration for wine consumers (Beverland 2005; 2006) and goes beyond impression management and marketing claims (Kovács et al. 2017).

Context

There are limited studies exploring the role of organizational identity of the vineyard in wine literature. Of the little information that is available, much is focused on the geographic identities of the wine regions or nations. My prior studies have revealed that organizational identity strongly influences organizational responses to external pressures and expectations of powerful institutional constituents (Dutton & Dukerich 1991; Dhalla & Oliver 2013). I was thus interested in understanding the role of identity of the vineyard in relation to the response to pressures for adoption of eco-practices and eco-certification. In particular, I was interested in self defining identity claims (Whetten 2006) made by the vineyards about their ideals as expressed through their identity related to sustainable viticulture. To explore this, I conducted in-depth conversations with respondents who are active in the Australian wine industry ranging from industry associations, vineyard representatives, and wine writers, to explore the industry's impetus for involvement in sustainability initiatives and the perceived challenges and benefits. I also analysed the websites of the vineyards and the industry associations, searching for identity statements.

Data for this paper was collected primarily from interviews conducted with sustainable, organic and biodynamic winemakers and grape growers from three wine regions in Australia – Margaret River (Western Australia), McLaren Vale (South Australia), Hunter Valley (NSW). Thirty-eight semi-structured interviews were conducted with insiders in the wine industry. These included twenty-eight interviews directly related to the vineyard with grape growers, winemakers, and viticulturists from sustainable, organic or biodynamic vineyards.

Ten additional interviews were conducted with Australian wine industry representatives, as well as wine writers and analysts, to gain insights on trends on sustainable, organic or biodynamic wines in Australia.

In addition, the websites of each of the interviewed vineyards, the certification agencies and the industry associations were examined for self-defining claims. The intent was to look for statements of claims about the identity characteristics. A search was conducted for self-defining claims about who they are, focusing on sections such as 'profile', 'at a glance', 'who we are', 'about us' and 'overview'. The analysis did not include any vision statements about who they 'wanted' to be; only statements of claims about the organization as it currently was were included.

For example, one biodynamic vineyard's identity claim was posted on the website:

> Not only are our wines certified biodynamic, every aspect of our [region] vineyard and farm is managed in a biodynamic, organic, wholistic and sustainable way which is evident in the individuality and superior quality of the wines.
>
> (Biodynamic Vineyard, Australia)[2]

From the above, we can see that the identity of this vineyard is its biodynamic certification, its connection to the region, the organizational focus of using biodynamic and holistic practices, and the superior quality of its wine.

I was also interested in understanding the Australian eco-certification bodies and their identity claims. For example, the following identity claim is from the website of Entwine Australia:

> Entwine Australia is the wine industry's national environmental assurance program. It provides Australian winemakers and wine grape growers with formal certification of their practices according to recognised international standards.
>
> (www.wfa.org.au/entwineaustralia-old/ accessed 23.01.19)

This statement indicates Entwine's identity as the *national* program for *certification* of *environmental practices* based on *international standards*.

Another example from the Sustainable Wine Growing website:

> The Sustainable Australia Winegrowing (SAW) Program is the result of a series of initiatives developed by McLaren Vale Grape Wine and Tourism Association (MVGWTA) since the early 2000s. [...] Sustainable Australia Winegrowing was developed to maximise growers and regional overall sustainability, and aims to minimise environmental impacts.
>
> (www.mclarenvale.info/industry-development/sustainable-australia -winegrowing (accessed 23.01.2019))

Identity claims made by SAW include its roots in the McLaren Vale Grape Wine and Tourism Association, establishment in since early 2000s as an indication of tenure, focus on regionality, sustainability and minimizing environmental impact of the wine industry.

The two separate sources of data of interviews and websites in the public domain provided increased validation, triangulation and confirmation of the identity claims.

Background on eco-certifications in viticulture in Australia

Eco-certifications generally refer to processes that integrate sustainability considerations and standards. There are eco-certifications in a number of industries in Australia. For example, the Eco Tourism Program, a tourism related eco-certification program through which providers can get certified for Eco Tourism, where the products are certified to be eco-friendly and tourism has minimal impact on the environment (Eco Tourism Australia 2018) and the Australian Forest Certification Scheme which certifies that the timber and wood products were sustainably sourced. Some global certification programs related to the food and beverage industry, familiar to many inside and outside Australia include Fairtrade®, which certifies that products such as coffee, nuts, sugar and fruit carrying the Fairtrade® mark meet their standards for trade following environmental, economic and social considerations (Fairtrade International 2018). Eco-certifications are generally understood to be products that are produced using practices that are codified by a recognized entity and validated as adhering to the accepted sustainability standards of management and production (Delmas & Grant 2014).

Scholars have been exploring this growing trend through a number of lenses. For example, researchers examining the marketing value of sustainability initiatives have found a link between sustainability certifications and premium pricing (Delmas & Grant, 2014; Loureiro et al. 2002). As well, there is growing literature about the reputational, marketing and economic value of eco-certifications (Atkin et al. 2012) and the strategic implications of certifications for the wine producers. Some argue that eco-certifications are particularly important in the wine industry due to the complexity and range of choices available to wine drinkers (Schäufele & Hamm, 2017). For example, organic certifications can have a stronger impact on consumer choice than knowledge of the intrinsic qualities of the wine through a positive halo effect that organic products generate, influencing consumer perceptions (Wiedmann et al. 2014).

Wine certifications in Australia

The escalating number of 'sustainable' or 'eco' certifications certifying agencies and corresponding logos can give rise to growing confusion about what are considered authentic sustainability related initiatives in the wine industry, how they relate to environmental initiatives, and in particular the link between sustainability initiatives and organic and biodynamic growing and production. The growing number of eco-certifications and eco-labelling have given rise to consumer confusion and created perceptions of green washing (Delmas & Burbano 2011; Delmas & Lessem 2017).

In the wine industry in Australia, there are several certification programs, some regional and others national, some government supported and others independent and globally recognized. There is substantial confusion around the use of the term 'sustainable' wine within Australia and in the following section, I briefly outline the major programs and related certifications. This is followed by a discussion on the findings of this study.

Sustainable wine

Sustainable wines, which are variously referred to as 'eco' wines or 'green' wines, generally refer to wines that have been produced with an environmental sensibility. The umbrella certification in Australia is Entwine Australia, which was developed by the Wine Federation of Australia in 2009 (Entwine & Winemakers' Federation of Australia 2015) with support from the Australian government. Entwine Australia certifies growers and winemakers who embrace sustainability (environmental, social and economic) in their business models and strategy. Operationally, growers and winemakers can become Entwine certified by meeting the requirements of the recognized sustainability certifiers in Australia, which as of 2019 are ISO 14001 (International Organization for Standardization – Environmental Management[3], FreshCare Environmental – Viticulture,[4] FreshCare Environmental – Winery,[5] FreshCare Environmental Viticulture Code of Practice,[6] FreshCare Environmental Winery Code of Practice[7]) and Sustainable Australia Winegrowing (SAW), a sustainable wine certification program that originated in McLaren Vale, South Australia and expanded to regions outside McLaren Vale and made available for growers across Australia since 2014 (McLaren Vale Grape Wine & Tourism Association 2014; WVJ 2019). SAW is a sustainable assessment program established to assess and improve sustainability in vineyards using the triple bottom line of environmental, economic and social benefit approaches (Sustainable Australia Winegrowing, 2019). There are seven specific areas of assessment under SAW: Soil Health, Nutrition and Fertiliser Management; Pest and Disease Management; Biodiversity Management; Water Management; Waste Management; Social Relations (workers, community and wineries) and Economic Sustainability (Sustainable Australia Winegrowing 2019). Data is collected through self-assessment workbooks completed annually by the farmer and submitted to the McLaren Vale Grape Wine & Tourism Association (McLaren Vale Grape Wine & Tourism Association 2018). In addition to the self-assessment workbook, the farmer also agrees to random third party certification audits. Third party audits are conducted in 10% of the participating vineyards that are randomly selected (Sustainable Australia Winegrowing 2018). The farmer receives scores based on both the self-assessment and the audit. The resulting certification has five categories: Blue (excellent, or most sustainable), Green (very good), Yellow (good), Red (needs attention, or least sustainable) and finally Purple (needs urgent development, or not sustainable) (Sustainable Australia Winegrowing 2018). The vineyard also receives access to the report with regional benchmarks and information on improving practices (Sustainable Australia Winegrowing 2019).

According to Entwine Australia, as of June 2016, there were around 650 registered members, which covers around 30% of Australia's vineyard area (The Australian Wine Research Institute 2018). One of the key benefits of Entwine is improved international access through recognition as a sustainable product for high-density buyers such as Marks & Spencer (The Australian Wine Research Institute 2018). Researchers are finding that consumers will pay a premium for sustainable wine (Sellers 2015), that is wine produced using environmentally sensitive or 'green' production processes (Forbes et al. 2017; Pomarici & Vecchio 2017).

My findings indicate that much of the impetus for getting a sustainability related certification was in response to competitive and economic pressures. Respondents were generally in agreement that sustainable certifications were becoming a necessity for export of Australian wine to the global market. In particular, when competing with the wines of the southern hemisphere such as sustainable wines from New Zealand, Argentina, and South Africa and both old world and new world wines from Italy, France and California. It is also being recognized that consumers are willing to pay a premium for sustainable wines (Sellers 2015). The largest winery I spoke to was a significant exporter of Australian wine and they considered sustainability certification a baseline requirement for export of their wine. The smaller wineries and vineyards we interviewed expressed a somewhat different opinion, in that, while they perceived a benefit of sustainable certification in terms of competitive advantage, they indicated they struggled to meet the costs, which run at about $110 per year for membership (The Australian Wine Research Institute 2019) and fulfil the reporting requirements associated with obtaining the eco-certification that would be recognized in export markets. For Entwine certification, vineyard members must annually report volume of grapes produced, production method (for example, organic), electricity purchased and generated, total use of water, petrol, diesel, or LPG used, total nitrogen applied, irrigation type and source, vineyard floor management, vineyard biodiversity area, and contractors used (The Australian Wine Research Institute 2019). Certified members also commit to triennial third-party audits (The Australian Wine Research Institute 2019).

It was largely understood that sustainable practices generally focused on reducing waste and emissions and reducing use of resources, thus reducing costs. This is consistent with Entwine's reporting requirements against business metrics: for vineyards, metrics include generation/purchase of electricity; purchase/use of petroleum, diesel and LPG; and production volume. For wineries, business metrics include production volumes; electricity purchased/generated; use of petroleum/natural gas/diesel, and LPG; waste water generated/treated;

and solid waste produced/treated (The Australian Wine Research Institute 2019). None of the wineries or vineyards I spoke with expressly mentioned social issues such as ethical employment conditions as part of their sustainability initiatives. This is consistent with the reporting for Entwine, which does not include metrics for social issues (The Australian Wine Research Institute 2019).

There was also no indication of sustainable practices in the marketing, packaging or distribution of the wine other than the eco-certification certifying that the grapes were grown in a sustainable vineyard and the wine was produced in a sustainable winery. One finding that was consistent was the acknowledgement that the popularity of sustainability certification in Australia was growing, particularly with the launch of the McLaren Value Sustainability Program, the regional program SAW, discussed in detail above.

Organic wines

The main certifying bodies for organic wine in Australia are the Australian Certified Organic owned by Australian Organic and the NASAA Certified Organic (NCO) administered through the National Association for Sustainable Agriculture, Australia. Organic wine generally refers to wine made from organically produced grapes. While the standards differ slightly across jurisdictions, organically produced wines are produced free of toxic pesticides, chemical fertilizers, fungicides and herbicides (Morganstern 2008). They contain minimal, or are free of, sulphites. The International Federation of Organic Agriculture Movement (IFOAM) defines organic production, as 'a production system that sustains the health of soils, eco-systems and people'[8]. In Australia, to be considered organic, the wine must be certified by a government approved certification body (Wine Australia 2017)

Organic wines are also gaining popularity in the consumer market. The Guardian U.K. recently reported that while the whole organic market is performing well, organic wine 'is a runaway success' (Smithers 2017). They suggest that this success can be attributed to the perception that organic wine exemplifies responsibility to the environment and that the wine appeals to the consumer taste for more natural, less synthetic tasting wine (Smithers 2017). This trend is confirmed in Australia, and Wine Australia stated that consumers' interest in organic foods and drinks is the top consumer trend in 2017 (Wine Australia 2017).

I explored the impetus and challenges for organic production of wine with vineyards and wineries that were certified, in the process of being certified, or practicing organic without certification. I found that there were a number of drivers for adopting organic production methodology: consumer preference for organic wines, the reduction of costs associated with spraying and use of synthetic products on the grapes, and a belief that organic production was conducive to long-term sustainability of the operation and the terroir for future production. There was also general agreement that organically produced wine is generally perceived to be healthier in the eyes of the consumer and this understanding is confirmed by literature (Mann et al. 2012). It was interesting to note that similar to sustainable production, none of the organic farmers I spoke to have any processes in place regarding conservation of water or sustainable practices related to packaging, marketing or distribution of the wine.

All the organic vineyard owners and winemakers I spoke with expressed concern related to the effort to remain organic if neighbouring farms continued conventional practices of spraying due to the transfer of chemicals across farms. Other challenges cited in becoming organic included the problem of changing consumer preferences that included the potential contradictions of the availability of conventional wine at a reasonable cost and fluid values regarding the benefits of organic products including organic wine. Others discussed the problem of changing consumer preferences that shifted from availability of conventional wine at a reasonable cost and fluid perceptions regarding the benefits of organic products including organic wine. Organic producers were also quite concerned about variances in the weather particularly in relation to rainfalls as they were constrained from using conventional methods to maintain the health of the grapes.

The majority of organic vineyard representatives I interviewed also explained that while they were practising organic growing, they were reluctant to become certified due to the constraints it would place on them in case they needed to use conventional methods to save their crop, for example, spraying fungicides or pesticides due to excess rain or pest infestation. They were hedging to mitigate potential loss. I thus found that identity congruence with organic farming had a tipping point – while the organic vineyards were committed to organic practices and believed that organic wine was a healthier alternative to conventional wine, they were also reluctant to commit to a certification which could potentially preclude their ability to use conventional methods to save the crop. Therefore, it did not support the utopian ideal of a healthy product and environment.

One message was consistent, however: that regardless of whether they obtain certification or not, my respondents believed that organic farming was a superior way of producing grapes due to the reduced reliance on synthetic fertilizers and herbicides. Results indicate that with organic vineyards in this study, while organic practices were important, the pragmatism of economic sustainability was more salient. This caused incongruence between the grape grower's identity and conviction of organic being the superior practice and the economic need to be viable and survive.

Biodynamic wines

Biodynamic is referred to as organic plus or an 'extreme evolution of organic' (Castellini et al. 2017). It is understood as production without synthetic fertilizers and chemical herbicides, as well as the inclusion of organic practices such as composting, but also a focus on lunar rhythms and use of preparations from cow manure (Parr et al. 2017). Practitioners explain that biodynamic viticulture is a holistic manner of viticulture that predates organic production and is based on the biodynamic agriculture movement started by Austrian philosopher, Rudolf Steiner (Mullen 2016). Steiner was consulted by a group of European farmers who were concerned about decline in crop and animal health (Demeter 2012; Tippetts 2012). Steiner outlined biodynamic techniques in a series of eight lectures that viewed the farm as a self-contained, self-living organism (Demeter 2012) to farmers in Poland in 1924 (Demeter 2014; Paull 2011). Biodynamic practices are distinct from organic and other farming in that biodynamic farming requires the use of eight distinct preparations guided by the teaching of Steiner (Ohmart 2001). The eight preparations are given numbers from 500–508 and each of these preparations is made in a specific way. For example, Preparation 500 is made from dairy cow manure packed into a cow's horn and buried for the winter. It is dug up in the spring, mixed with rainwater and sprayed onto the soil (Ohmart 2001). Preparation 501 is made up of ground quartz and rainwater, packed into a cow horn from a young cow, buried in a sunny spot through summer and dug up and sprayed directly on plants in the autumn (Ohmart 2001). Preparations 502–508, each one discrete, are made out of various plants substances and made into compost. For example, 502 is yarrow, packed into a stag's bladder, 503 is chamomile flowers fermented in soil, 504 is stinging nettle, 505 is oak packed in the skull of a domesticated animal, 506 dandelion flower heads packed in a cow's mesentery, 507 extract from valerian flowers, and 508 horsetail tea (Chalker-Scott 2013). The amounts used are quite small as they are thought to work 'dynamically' (Ohmart 2001).

Biodynamic agriculture is certified by Demeter, an international organization, whose first Chapter was formed in the late 1920s in Germany following Steiner's series of lectures (Steiner 1958) and when the first standards of quality control for biodynamic production were established (Demeter 2014). The first cooperative to sell biodynamic produce was formed in Germany in 1928, and the first standard and the Demeter symbol was established at that time (Demeter Association 2019b). According to the Demeter Association, there were 1000 biodynamic farms in 1931 (Demeter Association 2019b). In 2019, there were 45 certification organizations in the world (Demeter Association 2019b). In Australia, biodynamic wines are certified through the Australian Demeter Biodynamic certification, which was established in 1967 through the Biodynamic Research Institute (Demeter 2017).[9] Biodynamic certification can also be acquired through the Biological Farmers of Australia. While Steiner's biodynamic practices were not widely accepted and were largely dismissed by agriculture science community, they are seen to be making a return in wine (Tippetts 2012).

One of the biodynamic wine producers I spoke with described their first foray into biodynamic wines as a 'leap of faith' but indicated that once they got engaged with biodynamic viticulture, they were certain they would never revert back to conventional winemaking. They used terms like 'killing the earth' when referring to the use of chemicals and spraying, and spoke about 'bringing life' or 'adding life' when referring to biodynamic practices. They referred to homeopathic strategies and a custodial commitment to the land to sustain life. Conventional farming, in their view, was about control and killing things and frequently required killing that which was unnecessary; they referred to biodynamic techniques as fostering life. The goal is to create a self-sustaining eco-system. They also explained that biodynamic viticulture is about not being in control or being scared of the living things in the vineyard. This understanding that fostering life and flourishing forever is a fundamental tenet of sustainability as described by John Erhenfeld, who suggested that sustainability is about life flourishing forever and that flourishing required the whole system to work together (Hopkins 2009). In my exploration, biodynamic production was shown to be about the whole system functioning holistically and in harmony.

At one biodynamic vineyard, the winemaker reminisced that while the impetus to adopt biodynamic techniques may have emerged from the need to survive during economic downturns, the choice of going biodynamic emerged from the core identity of the family of founder of the vineyard. Having once made the choice, the winemaker and farmer I spoke with wondered why they did not adopt the techniques earlier as they were so right for the vineyard. The vines were flourishing despite the strong heat of the summer. They indicated that the soil seemed to be back to its original state and the wine produced is sought by their customers. The choice of certifications was also sought from a certifier that embodied the values and intent of the vineyard; the vineyard selected the Biological Farmers of Australia certification, as it was much more in line with their own pragmatic approach. While they acknowledged that biodynamic techniques are often perceived to be holistic and spiritual, they felt their vineyard was more in line with the pragmatism of conventional farmers and their need to be perceived to be a practical operator. They adopted the biodynamic approaches first in their vineyard to get the grapes right and then the winery and both are now fully biodynamic. One biodynamic vineyard indicated that they faced scepticism from their network of conventional producers; however, they tended to disregard such appraisals with the evidence of their flourishing and successful vineyards. This scepticism is explained by Parker (2002: 299) who suggest that some view utopian ideals as unworldly or impractical. Others argue that in contemporary economic environments, utopia is 'a daydream—a dangerous, romantic, and unfeasible fantasy' (de Geus 2002: 187). Findings in this study show that biodynamic vineyards in this study are driven by a resolute belief in biodynamic farming practices and principles. Their identity was not a daydream or fantasy, but rather a reality of their vineyard and wines, and I found little evidence that there was an extrinsic drive for profit.

In a recent systemic review article by Castellini et al. (2017) investigating studies on the biodynamic production system in viticulture and winemaking process, researchers studying the potential for premium pricing of sustainable wines found that while consumers were willing to pay a premium for organic wine versus conventional wines, there was no known premium gained for biodynamic wines (Castellini et al. 2017).

This was confirmed by the biodynamic wineries who indicated that their primary goal was to produce a wine they were proud of, and which they knew would not harm the plants, the soil and thus the planet. This was who they were, and they chose to practice biodynamic viticulture because they believed it was core to their, practices and identity. One winemaker at a biodynamic winery indicated that in the years the weather conditions did not yield a quality crop they required for their wines, they opt to drop the crop and instead of producing wine, they use it for food and other food products at a loss. This loss was preferable to producing wine using conventional practices to save the grapes. It was clear that biodynamic practices were being used because the vineyard and the winemaker strongly believed in biodynamic farming and the teaching of Rudolf Steiner. I thus found a tight, authentic link between the self-defining values and claims of their identity and their practice strategies.

Castellini et al. (2017) explain this authenticity poignantly in their review. They say

> Biodynamic agriculture is founded on the anthroposophy theory, which states that the human being is in the middle between the earth and cosmos rhythms, bridging a gap between spiritual and material world. Soil, man, plants and all the natural and cosmic elements take part in a holistic view typical of biodynamic agriculture. Growers embrace this philosophical approach and it guides them in daily agricultural practices. Considering this vision of agriculture and the role of biodynamic farmer in the universe, it is clear why biodynamic discipline sometimes appears more as a belief than as a cultivation technique.
>
> (Castellini et al. 2017: 2)

The owners of, and winemakers at, the biodynamic vineyards I interviewed were gravely concerned with the health of their consumers as well as the health of the planet and the cosmos. They indicated that since they did not use chemicals in their processing, their wine was 'fresher' and 'cleaner' and thus better for their consumers. One winemaker pointed to the lunar calendar and the spirituality inherent in the biodynamic techniques as a oneness between the soil, the grapes, the people involved, the wine, the planet and the universe. They saw an inherent connection between who they are, what they do and their impact thus they indicated a joyous and sombre responsibility in not just their viticulture practices but also their processing, packaging and distribution practices.

Researchers indicate that biodynamic viticulture is more resource intensive than other modes of viticulture (Castellini et al. 2017), however the vineyards in this study were far more focused on the authenticity of biodynamic techniques than the potential of making high levels of economic profit. The quality of biodynamic wines is credited to both the farmer's intrinsic role as custodian of the land and the biodynamic techniques (Carter 2017). The wine writers I interviewed were similarly convinced that biodynamic techniques were a premium for wine production. As one writer described in an interview, biodynamic wine is filled with energy and freshness due to the high touch, resource intensive viticulture, which inevitably led to a high-quality wine.[10]

Biodynamic ideals

I found that identity of the vineyard greatly influenced the production methods deployed. Sustainable wineries in this study were predominantly preoccupied with competitive pressures, market positioning, cost reduction and environmental practices related to resource use optimization and waste management systems. They generally identified their organizations as successful, efficient, cost effective organizations vying for competitive positioning. They were optimistic that their sustainable wines will garner the green consumer's loyalty and potentially premium pricing. Extant research confirms that sustainable viticulture practices, particularly those with an environmental, social and economic focus will increase consumer knowledge about sustainable wines and influence choice (Schäufele & Hamm 2017). Positioning the winery as sustainable has positive impact on the winery's marketing and branding strategies (Sellers 2015).

Organic producers were concerned with the perceived health benefits of viticulture, potential for a premium value in the market place, and ensuring survival of the vineyard. They also raised concern about the challenges of certification and hedging their risks in case of climate challenges. While they identified with organic viticulture as more sustainable, there was general agreement that organic certification was not necessarily required as much as organic practices. Organic and biodynamic techniques are linked, an important distinction made by authors in this field is that while organic viticulture is governed by an official set of rules, biodynamic regulation is largely voluntary (Castellini et al. 2017). Also as noted above, Castellini, et al. (2017) found that while studies indicate that organic wines are able to attract premium prices, there is no information they have found that biodynamic wines are able to attract premium pricing. This study adds to this finding by confirming that attracting premium pricing was not the predominant driver for the biodynamic producers in my sample.

I found a strong link between the identity of biodynamic viticulture and wineries and biodynamic production of wine, expressing utopian ideals connecting place, people and products. I found that there was little interest in premium pricing or competitive position. The goal of biodynamic farming is to embrace an ideal that the farm regenerates without requiring infusion of external resources, thus reducing impact on finite resources and, thus sustainable (Demeter Association 2019a). This is congruent with the understanding of sustainability as flourishing forever (Hopkins 2009) – sustainably, holistically and generatively for the collective good. For the biodynamic farmers in my study, the primary preoccupation was to stay true to biodynamic practices. They comfortably spoke about holistic viticulture, homeopathic strategies, spirituality and the preparations as simply the right way, the utopian way, of doing viticulture. There was a strong relationship between their identity and the production of biodynamic wine, and I found congruence between identity and action. Their identity as courageous custodians for future generations was evident in their identity claims and that the biodynamic approach to viticulture was based on care rather than fear. There was no other way for them.

Biodynamic winemakers promote healthy practices and take a custodial view of the soil. The biodynamic producers in this study indicated they produced biodynamic wine because that was 'who they were'. If utopian ideals reflect a strong desire not just for being better for the world, but doing better in an authentic way, with a view to flourishing forever, then biodynamic farmers and winemakers reflect utopian ideals.

Notes

1 The author thanks all the participants in this study for generously sharing their time, expertise and knowledge with the author.
2 Name and source withheld to protect the identity of the vineyard
3 The ISO 14000 family of standards provides practical tools for companies and organizations of all kinds looking to manage their environmental responsibilities (www.iso.org/iso-14001-environmental-management.html)
4 ENV VIT 2nd Edition, provides wine grape growers with an industry specific environmental program to assist them in gaining certification to a recognised environmental standard (www.freshcare.com.au/standards/environmental-viticulture/)
5 ENV WIN 2nd Edition, provides a set of elements which outline specific practices that must be implemented and maintained in order to achieve continuous environmental improvements in wine production (www.freshcare.com.au/standards/environmental-winery/)
6 The Freshcare Code of Practice – Environmental Viticulture offers wine grape growers a comprehensive, easy to follow and outcomes based environmental assurance program, specifically designed to aid in achieving and demonstrating real environmental outcomes (www.freshcare.com.au/standards/environmental-viticulture/)
7 The Freshcare Code of Practice – Environmental Winery was developed by the Australian wine industry in conjunction with Freshcare, to sit beside the Freshcare Code of Practice – Environmental Viticulture. The Freshcare Code of Practice – Environmental Winery provides winemakers with an industry specific environmental program to assist them in gaining certification to a recognised environmental standard (www.freshcare.com.au/standards/environmental-winery/)
8 www.ifoam.bio/en/organic-landmarks/definition-organic-agriculture
9 http://demeter.org.au/certification.htm
10 From a personal interview with a wine writer. Name withheld to protect identity

References

Albert, S. & Whetten, D. A. (1985). Organizational Identity. In *Research in Organizational Behavior*, Staw, B. M. & Cummings, L. L. (eds), pp. 263–295. Greenwich: JAI Press.
Atkin, T., Gilinsky, A., Jr. & Newton, S. K. (2012). Environmental strategy: does it lead to competitive advantage in the US wine industry? *International Journal of Wine Business Research*, 24(2): 115–133.

Benjamin, B. A. & Podolny, J. M. (1999). Status, Quality, and Social Order in the California Wine Industry. *Administrative Science Quarterly*, 44(3): 563–589.

Beverland, M. (2005). Crafting Brand Authenticity: The case of luxury wines. *Journal of Management Studies*, 42(5): 1003–1029.

Beverland, M. (2006). The 'Real Thing': Branding authenticity in the luxury wine trade. *Journal of Business Research*, 59(2): 251–258.

Carter, F. (2017). What's the truth about biodynamics? *Meininger's Wine Business International* (3). Available online at https://www.meininger.de/en/wine-business-interna tional/whats-truth-about-biodynamics (accessed 01.02.19).

Castellini, A., Mauracher, C. & Troiano, S. (2017). An Overview of the Biodynamic Wine Sector. *International Journal of Wine Research*, 9: 1–11.

Chalker-Scott, L. (2013). The Science Behind Biodynamic Preparations: A Literature Review. *HortTechnology*, 23(6): 814–819.

Clegg, S. R., Pina e Cunha, M. & Rego, A. (2012). The Theory and Practice of Utopia in a Total Institution: The Pineapple Panopticon. *Organization Studies*, 33(12): 1735–1757.

de Geus, M. (2002). Ecotopia, Sustainability, and Vision. *Organization & Environment*, 15(2): 187–201.

Delmas, M. and Burbano, V. (2011). The Drivers of Greenwashing. *University of California, Berkley*, 54(1), p. 54–87.

Delmas, M. & Grant, L. E. (2014). Eco-Labeling Strategies and Price-Premium: The Wine Industry Puzzle. *Business & Society*, 53(1): 6–44.

Delmas, M. A. & Lessem, N. (2017). Eco-Premium or Eco-Penalty? Eco-Labels and Quality in the Organic Wine Market. *Business & Society*, 56(2): 318–356.

Demeter (2012). Biodynamic(R) Agriculture: At a Glance. In *Association USD* (ed). USA.

Demeter (2014). Steiner's Impulse for Agriculture. Available online at www.demeter.de/ sites/default/files/article/pdf/demeter_90-jahre_steiners-impulse_english_biodynam ic_160224.pdf

Demeter (2017). History of Demeter Bio-Dynamic: About. Available online at https:// demeterbiodynamic.com.au/history-of-demeter-bio-dynamic-2 (accessed 01.02.19).

Demeter Association. (2019a). *Biodynamic Principles and Practices.* Available online at www.demeter-usa.org/learn-more/biodynamic-principles-practices.asp (accessed 01.02.19).

Demeter Association (2019b). *History.* Available online at www.demeter-usa.org/a bout-demeter/demeter-history.asp (accessed 01.02.19).

Dhalla, R. (2007). The Construction of Organizational Identity: Key contributing exter-nal and intra-organizational factors. *Corporate Reputation Review*, 10(4): 245–260.

Dhalla, R. (2008). *The influence of organizational identity, image and reputation on organizational strategic responses to institutional pressures.* Schulich School of Busi-ness, OBIR area. Toronto: York University.

Dhalla, R. (2011). Incongruence between organisational identity, image and reputa-tion: implications for corporate social responsibility. *International Journal of Busi-ness Environment*, 4(4): 330–352.

Dutton, J. E. & Dukerich, J. M. (1991). Keeping An Eye On The Mirror: Image and identity in organizational adaptation. *Academy of Management Journal*, 34(3): 517–554.

Dhalla, R. & Oliver, C. (2013). Industry Identity in an Oligopolistic Market and Firms' Responses to Institutional Pressures. *Organization Studies*, 34(12): 1803–1834.

Dutton, J. E., Dukerich, J. M. & Harquail, C. V. (1994). Organizational Images and Member Identification. *Administrative Science Quarterly*, 39(2): 239–263.

Eco Tourism Australia (2018). Eco Certification. Available online at www.ecotourism. org.au/our-certification-programs/eco-certification/ (accessed 01. 02. 19).

Elsbach, K. D. & Kramer, R. M. (1996). Members' Responses to Organizational Identity Threats: Encountering and countering Business Week rankings. *Administrative Science Quarterly*, 41(3): 442–476.

Entwine & WFA (2015). Environmental Sustainability in the Australian Wine Industry Consultation Discussion Paper. ACT: Entwine Australia and Winemakers' Federation of Australia. Available online at www.agw.org.au/assets/entwine/DISCUSSION-PAPER-Environmental-sustainability-FINAL-web.pdf (accessed 01.02.19).

Fairtrade International (2018). What is Fairtrade? Available online at www.fairtrade. net/about-fairtrade/what-is-fairtrade.html (accessed 01. 02. 19).

FiBL & IFOAM, (2017). The World of Organic Agriculture 2017: Another record year for organic agriculture. Nürnberg: Research Institute of Organic Agriculture (FiBL) and IFOAM – Organics International.

Forbes, S. L., Cohen, D. A., Cullen, R., et al. (2017). Consumer Attitudes Regarding Environmentally Sustainable Wine: An exploratory study of the New Zealand marketplace. *Journal of Cleaner Production*, 17(13): 1195–1199.

Giacomarra, M., Galati, A., Crescimanno, M., et al. (2016). The Integration of Quality and Safety Concerns in the Wine Industry: The role of third-party voluntary certifications. *Journal of Cleaner Production*, 112(1): 267–274.

Gray, R. (1992). Accounting and Environmentalism: An exploration of the challenge of gently accounting for accountability, transparency and sustainability. *Accounting, Organizations & Society*, 17(5): 399–425.

Hardin, G. (1968). The Tragedy of the Commons. *Science*, 162(3859): 1243–1248.

Hopkins, M. (2009). Flourishing Forever. Big Idea: Leading Sustainable Organizations. An Interview with John R. Ehrenfeld. *MIT Sloan Management Review*, 51(1): 1–4.

Bell, K. K. (2014). Why Biodynamic Wines Are Better For You: Six To Try Now. *Forbes.com*. Available online at www.forbes.com/sites/katiebell/2014/04/22/why-bio dynamic-wines-are-better-for-you-six-to-try-now/ (accessed 01.02.19).

Kovács, B., Carroll, G.R. & Lehman, D. W. (2017). The Perils of Proclaiming an Authentic Organizational Identity. *Sociological Science*, 4: 80–106.

Lawson, A., Cosby, A., Bez, N., et al. (2017). *Australian Organic Market Report 2017*. Research by the Australian Centre for Agriculture and Law (AgLaw Centre) and the Mobium Group. Commissioned by Australian Organic Ltd. Funded by Horticulture Innovation Australia Ltd using voluntary contributions from Australian Organic Ltd. Nundah, QLD: Australian Organic Ltd

Loureiro, M. L., McCluskey, J. J. & Mittelhammer, R. C. (2002). Will Consumers Pay a Premium for Eco-Labeled Apples? *The Journal of Consumer Affairs*, 36(2): 203–219.

Mann, S., Ferjani, A. & Reissig, L. (2012). What Matters to Consumers of Organic Wine? *British Food Journal*, 114(1): 272–284.

McLaren Vale Grape Wine & Tourism Association (2014). *2014 Regional Results*. McLaren Vale.

McLaren Vale Grape Wine & Tourism Association (2018). Sustainable Australia Winegrowing (SAW) Program. In *Association MVGWT*. McLaren Vale.

Miller, C. (2017). Sustainability Research. *Wine Opinions Trade Panel 2016*. San Francisco: California Sustainable Winegrowing Alliance (CSWA). Available online at www.

sustainablewinegrowing.org/amass/library/7/docs/CSWA%20Trade%20Survey%20Summary.pdf (accessed 01.02.19).

Morganstern, A. (2008). What is Organic Wine: Learn. *Organic Wine Journal*. Available online at www.organicwinejournal.com/index.php/2008/03/what-is-organic-wine/ (accessed 01.02.19).

Mullen, T. (2016). Why Biodynamic Wine is the Future. *Forbes.com*. Available online at www.forbes.com/sites/tmullen/2016/10/26/why-biodynamic-wine-is-the-future/ (accessed 01.02.19).

Ohmart, C. (2001). Vineyard Views. *Wines & Vines*, 82(11): 138.

Parker, M. (2002). *Utopia and Organization*. Oxford: Blackwell.

Parr, W. V., Valentin, D., Reedman, P., et al. (2017). Expectation or Sensorial Reality? An Empirical Investigation of the Biodynamic Calendar for Wine Drinkers. *PLoS ONE*, 12(1): 1–18.

Paull, J. (2011). The Secrets of Koberwitz: The Diffusion of Rudolf Steiner's Agriculture Course and the Founding of Biodynamic Agriculture. *Journal of Social Research & Policy*, 2(1): 19–29.

Pomarici, E. & Vecchio, R. (2017). Millennial Generation Attitudes to Sustainable Wine: An exploratory study on Italian consumers. *Journal of Cleaner Production*, 66: 537–545.

Roberts, L. M. & Dutton, J. E. (2009). *Exploring Positive Identities and Organizations: Building a Theoretical and Research Foundation*. New York: Psychology Press.

Schäufele, I. & Hamm, U. (2017). Consumers' Perceptions, Preferences and Willingness-to-pay for Wine with Sustainability Characteristics: A review. *Journal of Cleaner Production*, 147: 379–394.

Schultz, F. (2016). Organizational DNA. In *The SAGE Encyclopedia of Corporate Reputation*, Carroll, C. E. (ed.), pp. 521–522. Thousand Oaks: SAGE Publications, Inc.

Sellers, R. (2015). Would You Pay a Price Premium for a Sustainable Wine? The voice of the Spanish consumer. Sustainability of Well-Being International Forum 2015: Food for Sustainability and not just food, Florence.

Smithers, R. (2017). Grape Britain: UK merry on organic wine as sales soar. *The Guardian*, 3 April. Available online at www.theguardian.com/environment/2017/apr/03/grape-britain-uk-merry-on-organic-wine-as-sales-hit-nearly-6m (accessed 01.02.19).

Steiner, R. (1958). *Agriculture Course: The Birth of the Biodynamic Method*. Forest Row: Rudolf Steiner Press.

Stimpert, J. L. L., Gustafson, L. T. & Sarason, Y. (1998). Organizational Identity within the Strategic Management Conversation: Contributions and assumptions. In *Identity in Organizations: Building Theory Through Conversations*, Whetten, D. A. & Godfrey, P. C. (eds), pp. 83–98. Thousand Oaks: Sage Publications.

Sustainable Australia Winegrowing (2018). What is Sustainable Australia Winegrowing? In *2018 SAW Customer Facing Flyer*, Association MVGWT (ed.). McLaren Vale.

Sustainable Australia Winegrowing (2019). The Sustainable Australia Winegrowing (SAW) Program. Available online at www.mclarenvale.info/industry-development/sustainable-australia-winegrowing (accessed 01.02.19).

The Australian Wine Research Institute (2018). Entwine Australia: What is Entwine FAQs. Available online at www.awri.com.au/wp-content/uploads/2016/07/Entwine-FAQ.pdf (accessed 01.02.19).

The Australian Wine Research Institute (2019). Entwine - What's Involved? Available online at www.awri.com.au/industry_support/entwine/membership/ (accessed 01.02.19).

Tippetts, J. (2012). The Science of Biodynamic Viticulture. *Gastronomica*, 12(1): 91–99.

Whetten, D. A. (2003). Organizational Identity. Corporate Identity and Marketing Conference. Hamilton, Ontario.

Whetten, D. A. (2006). Albert and Whetten revisited: Strengthening the concept of organizational identity. *Journal of Management Inquiry*, 15(3): 219–234.

Whetten, D. A. & Mackey, A. (2002). A Social Actor Conception of Organizational Identity and its implications for the Study of Organizational Reputation. *Business and Society*, 41(4): 393–414.

Wiedmann, K.P., Hennigs, N., Behrens, S. H., *et al.* (2014). Tasting Green: An experimental design for investigating consumer perception of organic wine. *British Food Journal*, 116(2): 197–211.

Wine Australia (2017). Organic and biodynamic wines: a growing niche market for Australian wine exports. *Market Bulletin*, 55. Available online at www.wineaustralia.com/news/market-bulletin/issue-55 (accessed 01.02.19).

Winemakers' Federation of Australia (2017). *Pre-Budget Submission: Backing the Australian Wine Industry*. Available online at https://static.treasury.gov.au/uploads/sites/1/2017/06/C2016-052_Winemakers-Federation-of-Australia.pdf (accessed 26.03.19).

WVJ (2014). Independent investigation announced by WFA into 'incomplete letter'. *Wine & Viticulture Journal*, 29(5): 6.

11 Utopia regained

Nature and the taste of terroir

Christopher Kaplonski

Introduction

As China Mieville reminds us in his introductory essay to a re-issue of More's *Utopia* published to commemorate its 500th anniversary, the island Utopia 'is not by nature an island at all' (2016: 4). It was once part of the continent that it neighbours, now separated by an artificial channel. Mieville also notes 'it is not a long voyage to get there' (2016: 3). I note these observations for they seem to strike me as reflecting both terroir and natural wine as well. Much like Utopia, a different terroir can quite literally be a few steps away: a hop over a stone wall, or a quick scramble up to the next terrace. Yet there is supposed to be no mistaking the different terroirs. So too with natural wine, although this time, I suggest, often more philosophically than sensually.

To turn one more time to Mieville: he also recalls to our attention that the channel that was dug was done at the command of a conqueror. 'The splendid – utopian – isolation is part of the violent imperial spoils' (Mieville 2016: 4). Natural wine and its relation to terroir are not part of imperial spoils, yet they do hint, like Utopia's dark origins, at secret tensions and paradoxes. It is these that I explore here. In brief, the reception that natural wine is often accorded by the wider wine world of connoisseurs, critics and judges reveals a hostility to the new utopian struggle it embodies.

Natural wine is a disruptive movement, one that seeks to overthrow an orthodoxy, to ferment (sic) a revolution. It does this through the guise of a return to a past, a prelapsarian moment of beauty and truth in liquid form. Make no mistake, however, this is a disruptive search for beauty and truth, as perhaps all such searches, and Utopias are.[1]

Defining nature

Before exploring these issues in more depth, let me pause to consider what 'natural wine' is. The short answer: there is no legal definition, nor is there a widely agreed upon definition. 'Natural wine' is best viewed as a field or genre, rather than a single definition. The underlying philosophy behind it can be summed up by an alternative name: 'low-intervention'. The result is a wine that is said to be alive, and reflective of the place it was made, much more so than conventionally produced wines. Unfiltered and unfined, natural or low-intervention wines can be cloudy, rather than the clear, bright wine expected by wine judges. Based on local native yeasts, rather than standard, commercial cultured ones, and often with little sulphur added, they can taste as different as they look. They upset expectations, and can require adjustment of what one thinks wine should be. But for their proponents, that is precisely the point.

The idea behind these at times radically different wines is that one should do as little to the grapes as possible, to let them and their terroir speak for themselves. This includes a range of actions or often, more precisely, inactions. In the vineyard, this includes whether to spray fungicides, pesticides and so forth, and if so, what to use. At the extreme end of natural winemaking, the goal is to not spray at all, but both organic and biodynamic farming methods allow the use of certain chemicals.[2] Even most natural winemakers I have talked to, however, concede that in some years, if they are to make wine at all, steps such as spraying to combat pests or mould may be necessary. Such measures are preferably avoided as they belie the low-intervention philosophy. The winemakers' point is simply that sometimes intervention is an economic necessity and without such interventions, the crop would fail.

In contrast, 'conventional' wine production will most likely include regular spraying of the grapes by a range of pesticides and fungicides, perhaps including glyphosate (Roundup). Synthetic fertilisers may be used. Even here, however, people experiment with different approaches, such as the use of sensors in the vineyard to allow more precise spraying in particular locations, rather than treating the whole vineyard.[3]

The low-intervention approach in the vineyard may well also include letting other plants such as grass, clover, wildflowers and even traditional medicinal herbs (Legeron 2014: 52–53) flourish in the vineyard, whether intentionally or not, and even not taking many steps to curb wildlife incursions, such as fences or netting over the vines to protect them from birds. This is an extreme end of the non-intervention spectrum, it must be noted. Other followers of the general low-intervention approach I have worked with partake of local group efforts, particularly in regards to scaring birds, which included hiring a pilot to buzz vineyards and birds, or having local hunters drive around discharging shotguns in an effort to scare the birds. I have talked to natural winemakers in Austria who have at times lost 20 to 50% of their grape crop to wildlife, but they viewed this as a price they were willing to pay for their philosophy: the vineyard is part of a larger integrated ecosystem. One of these winemakers did not only not mow the grass between the rows of vines, a relatively common practice, but even let saplings spring up, viewing them as an integral part of the ecosystem, and arguing that such competition for nutrients among the plants ultimately made for stronger vines and better wine.

Such a variety of approaches to low-intervention continues in the wine cellar, where the grapes are pressed, and the juice turned into wine. Even among the 'do as little as possible' approaches, there is a range of things that can be done, or not. One universal, however, is the use of wild ferments. This is the term applied when the yeasts found on the grapes, rather than purchased cultured yeasts, are allowed to start the fermentation process. Little to no filtration or fining to remove dead yeast and other particles that can cloud, alter the wine tastes and/or prolong storability, takes place. Removing such particles is an intervention, and thus a step away from a 'natural' wine. The juice from the grapes, known as 'must', is allowed to settle: to sit for a few days which allows large scale matter, or MOG (matter other than grapes), to separate out from the grape juice.

Other additives and processes – reverse osmosis (a process which can be used to lower alcohol levels or increase them), balancing acidity through the addition of tartaric acid (to increase acidity) or a form of carbonate (to remove acidity) – are also avoided. For many, a defining hallmark is the use of minimal added sulphur (a preservative that kills or inhibits unwanted yeasts and bacteria and which protects wine from oxidation) or, ideally, none at all. Even more radical versions may do away with temperature control on the fermentation vessels.[4] Whatever a particular winemaker adopts as their practices, a key point is that 'natural wine' is about what happens in the winery, not in the vineyards. Having said this, the grapes themselves will have been farmed organically or biodynamically, since as originally mentioned, many see the grapevines as part of a larger ecosystem, and choose a form of agriculture they feel respects this. (For a good discussion on natural wine, see Goode and Harrop's *Authentic Wine: Toward Natural and Sustainable Winemaking* (2011). For a more advocacy-based approach, see Isabelle Legeron's *Natural Wine* (2014).)

There are numerous, and often overlapping, reasons why winemakers choose to go down this path. Some may be following a more philosophical bent, following a belief in biodynamics to what can be viewed as the next logical step. Others have done it for what they describe as health reasons, whether through the lack of chemicals, or because of the energy inherent in the wine. (I will return to the concept of 'energy' below, but in biodynamic farming, common in low-intervention winemaking, many of the practices are undertaken to harness and focus the 'cosmic energy' that surrounds and permeates us.) Others still approach natural winemaking as a logical step of evincing concern for the larger ecosystem that their vineyards are part of. Yet a good many others adopt a low-intervention approach to allow the grapes to express themselves and their relation to the land to their fullest. This is wine as it is meant to be, and by implication, the truest reflection of terroir. This is the Utopia they seek.

Seeking, and defending, terroir

Let me turn to terroir, for here we start to see Utopia's dark secrets. Terroir seems to invite as many understandings as there are people who think about wine. Some versions and variations can be seen in the other contributions to this volume, as well as Patterson and Buechesenstein's recent edited work, *Wine and Place* (2018).

There is also a debate over whether terroir can exist at all, and, if so, what it is attributable to (e.g. Bohmrich 1996; Maltman 2008, 2018; Matthews 2015; Meinert, et al. 2018; Teil 2012, 2014). Although we should acknowledge this debate, it can safely be set aside. What matters here is not that terroir is something that may or may not objectively exist, that can be explained through geology, plant biology or other means. Rather, and this seems incontestable, it is something that many winemakers pursue, and to this end, it exists as a goal and a social fact.

For now, let us use Amy Trubek's gloss of terroir as 'the taste of place' (2008). What I am interested in, as with natural wine, is not what the term means, as much as the work it is called upon to do, as well as the implications and problems that arise from this. The 'taste of place' provides us enough clarity to move forward. It is this taste, one specific to a place, recognised as such, that most winemakers seek to achieve in some form or another. (I say 'most' as some wines, particularly high-volume brands, will be more inter-ested in consistency of taste then a reflection of terroir.)

But here a complication sets in. Terroir, it turns out, is not just separated from the mainland by a channel. It also has heavily guarded borders. If one wants to call one's wine a Burgundy, or a Chateauneuf-du-Pape, it is not enough that it is grown and made in the appropriate place. There are numerous regulations. The broad term for these regulations is Geographical Indications, and in the EU such regulations protect 20 categories of items, including hay, lavender, cheese and wine (EU 2012). Much like Anna Tsing's wholesalers and sorters of matsutake mushrooms destined for Japan, the regulations and those who apply them exist to make a judgement, and assign the mushrooms (or wine) 'relation-making powers: the power of quality' (Tsing 2015: 124).

The most famous classification in regards to wine is undoubtedly the French *appellation d'origine contrôlée* (AOC) system, instituted in 1935, but based on centuries of precedent. Most wine-producing countries have similar schemes, many based on the AOC approach. There is no need to rehearse here the full complexity of the AOC system, which itself is only one part of wine classifications in France. Whatever the specific details, such regulations stipulate which grape varieties may be used (often in what proportion), as well as restrictions like the maximum yield of the grape vines. Some may also sti-pulate the particular ways the vines may be pruned, or to what extent, if at all, sugar may be added to the juice of the grapes to increase the final alcohol level, or whether the acidity may be adjusted, and to what extent.

Most importantly here, the wine must pass a taste test. It must exhibit typicity. There are competing definitions of typicity, some of which think it only need to reflect the grape variety, while others, which I want to focus on, include regional and climatic aspects. A wine must be typical, in short. In other words, a Burgundy must taste like a Burgundy, and not a Bordeaux.

There is a range of taste allowable, of course. Not all Cotes-du-Rhône wines taste the same. Some may smell and taste more of red berries (raspberries, for instance) than black ones, depending on the proportion of the different allowed grape varieties that are used. There may be a more evident vanilla aroma from the greater use of oak barrels, which imparts the characteristic. A wine from a hotter year will generally have a fuller body, and a bit more alcoholic heat or bite to it than one from a cooler year. There must be, however, a family resemblance. You need not be a trained wine-taster to recognise the resemblance. Simply drinking enough different Cotes-du-Rhône wines will help you build up a sensory memory of such wines, learning in time to recognise them almost by intuition. What this taste memory is, I would suggest, is another way of describing terroir at a fairly general level, an assigned and hence recognisable taste of place.

Here lies the paradox. Terroir is presented as reflecting the true taste of a place, but that 'true taste' is a heavily regulated one. Terroir is supposed to represent nature, but in truth, in its officially recognised incarnation, it is the construct of bureaucracy.

At this point, some may be tempted to wonder: so what? We're often reminded that what we consider as 'nature' is just another cultural construct, an artificial distinction between Us and Everything Else (e.g. Descola & Palsson 1996; Strathern 1980). There may be a real world out there (and I personally would argue so) but it is riven with human-made classifications and distinctions. Why should terroir be different? This, to be blunt, misses the point, which is not the constructedness, but what is effectively the attempt to claim a monopoly on determining terroir. Once we accept that the 'taste of place' has value, as the EU (and many others) have done, the question becomes is: how is this taste determined, and how should it be?

The short answer is that the taste is determined by a tasting panel that has the power to reject wines it feels does not conform to the expected typicity. While this occurs with each vintage, wines are not often denied the right to use the particular appellation label they are seeking based solely on taste. The *Institut national de l'origine et de la qualité* (INAO) claims that 10% of wines submitted for any particular designation (Burgundy, Pouilly-Fumé) are denied the label, condemning them to be sold as a 'lesser' wine, perhaps even a generic 'table wine', but others claim fewer wines fail to pass (Teil 2014: 110, n. 11). This, critics argue, is not a sign that the wines reflect, or fail to, the local terroir, but a sign of an increasing sameness. 'Rather than blaming the typicity of their wines, on the contrary, the "rejected" vintners challenge the competence of juries to recognise the expression of terroir' (Teil 2014: 100). Others claim that given the inability of vignerons to consistently identify their own wines blind they are playing it safe by accepting most wines (Teil 2014: 110, n. 8). While this may seem surprising – the inability of a winemaker to know their own work – similar stories have been told to me by trusted sources who were present at blind tastings where exactly this has happened.

The problem as presented by some winemakers, in other words, is that the tasting panels, through a process of what we can term sensorial drift, have shifted away from defending terroir to defending an increasingly homogenised, industrialised product. The wines that are rejected, the argument against the tasting panels implies, are the ones that truly reflect terroir. Natural wines often fail these standards of typicity, and, their proponents argue, in doing so truly reflect terroir.

The debate in France over terroir and typicity is explicit and ongoing. It is about regulations as much as taste. It is, to continue the metaphor, a struggle to determine where Utopia is, how to reach it, and once there, what rules to instil and what passages back to the mainland are allowed. This explicitness is not always present in such debates, but that does not make it any less important.

Let me now shift location, both physical and metaphorical, for a time. My own fieldwork on issues of sustainability and taste, which has been focusing on low-intervention wine, has been based mostly in two regions of Austria, Burgenland and Steiermark (Styria), with additional fieldwork in the UK. Along with my project partner, Julia Leijola, we have been interviewing and working alongside Austrian winemakers who embrace a range of positions towards low-intervention wine. All practice it, but to what extent and for what reasons vary. Nonetheless, all are united in their opposition to sensorial drift, and in their support and practical search (struggle) for true (utopian) terroir

One important caveat must be noted – the people I work with do not usually speak of terroir. This is an analytic I've overlaid on our discussions and their approaches. I do this because it serves as a useful heuristic. It may not occur often, or ever, in some discussions, but it is clearly applicable. I have not had the opportunity to probe deeply into the use, or non-use of the specific term, but it is possible to put forward a number of educated guesses. Perhaps the most likely is simply that it isn't an important term to them. It is, after all, a French term co-opted into English language wine discussions. It is known in German wine language, and particularly winemakers who speak English and visit trade fairs in English-speaking countries are familiar with it, and sometimes use it. I have not yet met anyone who did not know the term. Rather, the people I have talked to tend to talk more specifically about the environment – rainfall, elevation, exposure to sunlight or wind – or the particularities of the soil and the bedrock it sits upon. They also talk of letting the grapes speak for themselves. In other words, perhaps terroir is too vague for the connection they feel and seek to express in their wines. Whatever words they choose, arguably, what they are talking about can be encompassed by the notion of terroir, and so I retain it here, hopefully without doing too much violence to my interlocutors' beliefs.

A Utopian itinerary

Our first stop on our Utopian itinerary is the north-eastern corner of Burgenland. About an hour south of Vienna by car or train, we are headed the part that lies between the eastern shore of Lake Neusiedl

(Neusiedl See) and the Hungarian border. The gently rolling hills are dotted with vineyards, farms and wind turbines. It is a region of winemakers and vineyards, with one village, Gols, population 3,700, boasting about 125 winemakers. Gols, in addition to producing wine, has historically been something of a Protestant enclave within Catholic Austria. Intermarriage among the Protestants was common, resulting in multiple wineries with the same surname.

One of the winemakers in Gols is Maria. (As is standard in anthropological literature, I have used pseudonyms for the people I have been working with.) She has run her winery since 2001, taking it over from her parents. Her father is still involved, serving as vineyard manager, and her husband also works there, largely in the winery. As Maria put it once herself, she provides the vision. Since 2007, that vision has been biodynamic, and it increasingly is low-intervention. Maria, who has about 15 hectares (ha) of vineyards, but also buys in grapes, produces a variety of wines. Some qualify as *qualitätswein*, and bear the distinctive Austrian-flag capsule or screw-cap. A *qualitätswein*, or 'quality wine', is a classification similar to the traditional German system. The grapes must come from a single region, although this is often broadly defined. All of Burgenland, for example, a little over 13,000ha, is one region. A *qualitätswein* also must meet certain standards for must weight (sugar content of the grape juice) and final alcohol level of the wine.[5] The grapes must also come from a single district. Many, if not most, Austrian wines carry this designation.

Other wines that Maria makes, however, simply have their cork covered in wax. The use of wax, while no means universal, seems to be a growing trend among Austrian low-intervention winemakers. Whether this is a conscious trend is not clear, but it does serve as a handy, if not infallible, rule of thumb when seeking such wines in a shop. These are wines that run afoul of the classification system, and hence are technically *landwein*, a lower category of Austrian wine. This is not quite 'table wine', but is the equivalent of the EU's general 'wine with geographical indication', a less restrictive category. In Maria's winery, as elsewhere, this should not be taken for a statement of quality. Rather, these are the wines where she pushes winemaking in search of Utopia. Some of these will be unfiltered and unfined, giving them a cloudy appearance, and even possibly bit of grape skin or other particles visible in them, disqualifying faults in conventional wine-tasting and judging, but hallmarks of low-intervention wines.

In a conversation in her winery, as we worked the harvest one year, Maria said that her wines were as low-intervention as they could be. This was to turn out to be a common refrain wherever we talked to winemakers for more than a few minutes. Making wine is, after all, a business. Ultimately, an adherence to a philosophy irregardless of the quality of wine is not something most people I know pursued. This is not to say they feel themselves bound by expectations of taste that have been honed by the larger wine industry and its marketing machine. Rather, I refer to the pragmatics of winemaking. I was surprised when one low-intervention winemaker remarked off-handedly that in cooler years they would chaptalise (add sugar to) the grape must, which allows it to ferment to the desired alcoholic strength. When I queried this – seemingly a violation of a major tenet of low-intervention philosophy, their response was straightforward: if they didn't chaptalise, they wouldn't be able to make wine at all some years, as the grapes had not ripened enough. Similarly, a winemaker may profess strict adherence to biodynamic principles. This should, ideally, include harvesting and other actions taking place in accordance with phases of the moon and other cosmic influences. Yet this is not always possible. Grapes are a crop, after all, and imminent rain or frost that threaten the crop trumps blind adherence to philosophy.

An organic winemaker in the UK echoed this point. He was organic and starting to flirt with biodynamic techniques. Whether they would ever be adopted wholesale was uncertain. But with his use of wild ferments, and organic farming, he was clearly moving along the spectrum towards low-intervention wines. He made wines as naturally as he could. Like my Austrian interlocutor, John said that he would use sugar if needed, but he would never de-acidify the wines. A process to reduce the acidity levels – the zestiness or 'freshness' one can taste in many white, and some red, wines – de-acidification is a fairly common practice in cooler climates, which tend to give higher acidity levels. John did not object to de-acidification on philosophical grounds, but rather, he said, because the process gave wines that are not balanced, and never could be.

There is a limit to what boundaries could be pushed, what technologies and techniques could be dispensed with and still result in a wine they would be proud of. The perfect wine, like Utopia, remains a lucid dream.

People did at times attribute the pursuit of philosophy above all else to others and linked this to what was too often a lack of quality in the wines. One winemaker in Burgenland, Hans, claimed that many French natural wines were faulty, but fewer Austrian ones were so, a difference that Hans linked to a pragmatic flexibility in the philosophy and practices of natural winemakers in Austria. Such faults would include oxidised wines, which are usually described as 'flat' – duller in colour than usual and tasting duller than they would otherwise be, and microbial contamination, which can lead a variety of tastes usually considered unwanted, perhaps most commonly, 'mousiness', said to be reminiscent of mouse urine.[6] Biodynamics, Hans said, was at heart an anti-dogmatic approach. It had to differ from place to place, time to time. One took what worked and left out what didn't. This approach has been backed up by fieldwork. One of the things that struck me most after conversations about biodynamics and natural wine was what a broad church it was. All adherents were looking to make quality wine, wine that showed a connection to the region and the soil, yet how they pursued that goal often differed, at times drastically.

Many also talked about the 'energy' of the wine. This is worth a short comment, as it links us back to the larger philosophical and cosmological principles at hand. 'Energy', when used by different winemakers, like pretty much most terms, can mean different things. Some were clearly referring to the cosmic energy they held their biodynamic methods had instilled in the wine. 'I can taste the energy with just a drop', claimed one biodynamic adherent, perhaps best described as a 'true believer' (they could near enough quote chapter and verse on Steiner's *Agriculture Course* (1958 [1924]), the foundational text of biodynamics). Others were a bit more circumspect, using energy to refer to a vaguer sense of a something inherent in the wine. It was quite possible they also were referring to the energy of the cosmos, but it is just as possible they were using 'energy' as a catch-all term to contrast their approach to wine with the mass-produced, industrial product of the large-scale wineries. Those wines, most people we talked to would claim, were dead, lifeless, uninteresting.

How the various winemakers we know and have talked to strove to reach these multiple ideals of Utopia and the wine they wanted to make differed. Let me turn now to consider some of these approaches, their maps to Utopia, as it were.

Mapping Utopia

They would all doubtlessly agree with Franz, a winemaker in Steiermark, a region in southern Austria, with scenic mountains and winding roads framed by vineyards and forests on the slopes. Franz remarked that we've gotten away from what wine 'really is', and that is something we need to get back to. For him, this is a deep understanding of the land and the grapes as a living plant. They are part of a larger, vibrant, integrated ecosystem. Conventional winemakers, in contrast, view grapes simply as a product to be produced, with as much control and standardisation as possible.

He told us, however, that there was another driving force behind his change from conventional to biodynamic and low-intervention winemaking. That was for health. Franz is sure that low-intervention wine is healthier, as well as being more reflective of the land and environment. Natural wine, according to Franz, was also more fulfilling, and as a result, you tended to drink less than you would with an industrial wine. His wines were served in some of the top restaurants in the world, and they ran a range of characteristics. All that I have tasted, I would say, are definitely more interesting – a wider range of aromas, tastes and even textures, than the vast majority of wines.

Franz is keen on reducing not only the use of fertiliser and other sprays – he farms biodynamically – but also the use of biodynamic preparations. He did not explain why, as the conversation veered off in another direction. But even this fact, seeking to reduce the key preparation used in biodynamics, known as BD500, essentially manure that has matured in a buried cow horn, hints at the radicalness of his underlying philosophy. It is important in this context, as well, that Franz's wine cellar was largely gravity based. The juice is moved from one stage of the process to the next without the use of pumps, which many low-intervention winemakers would argue 'bruise' the juice, leading to inferior wine. Perhaps most intriguing was Franz's attitudes towards emotions. What impacts the grapes the most, he said, is your attitude – what you bring to the vineyard. So, if you are enthusiastic, you'll have healthy grapes. If you view it as a chore, you won't. That doesn't matter if you are biodynamic, natural, or conventional. So, in sum, for Franz, an ideal wine would be the end result of grapes grown in a setting that is closely integrated into the ecosystem and moved through the winemaking process as gently as possible, with as little intervention as is feasible to make a product he believes in, and people will buy.

Peter, who also makes wine in Styria, adopts a similar philosophy, but if anything, takes it to a further extreme. He not only sees the vineyard as part of the surrounding ecosystem but welcomes the world among his vines. When touring his vines on a September afternoon one year, Peter pointed out to Julia and I where a deer had bedded down the night before. His point wasn't 'oh, no, deer have gotten into the vineyard', but rather to highlight the close relationship between his vines and the surrounding countryside. Peter also took the no-tillage or no-mowing approach one step further than most, and proudly pointed out the occasional sapling growing in the rows between his vines. This was not only an example of the continuation of a larger ecosystem but had a symbiotic effect. The roots of the saplings were in competition with those of the grape vines, Peter said. This led to stronger, healthier vines, and, ultimately, better wine. His point was clear – wine should reflect and incorporate the larger ecosystem as much as possible.

With such an approach, it came as no surprise to learn that Peter was a member of *Les Vins Sans Intrant Ni Sulphites* (S.A.I.N.S., Wines Without Additions or Sulphur), a low-intervention organisation that eschews all additives not only in the winery, but also those sprays and preparations permitted by organic or biodynamic farming in the field.

The view that biodynamics was too much intervention was not unique to Peter. Tobias, a low-intervention winemaker from Burgenland, working not far from Maria and Franz, wasn't biodynamic, since people who followed such principles intervened too much in the vineyard. 'They are always out spraying', he said, while he sprays as little as possible, maybe only two or three times a year. Tobias himself did not elaborate (he said he was in a rush when we arrived for our interview) but others had highlighted that Bordeaux mixture[7] requires more frequent and heavier application than modern, synthetic fungicides. They also point out that even biodynamic preparations, such as fertilisers, or a chamomile tea preparation (said to help vines deal with stress) are a form of intervention. Well-meaning intervention, perhaps, but still an intervention.

There is a limit to how far some are willing to push the low-intervention search for Utopia, and once again, this is a somewhat paradoxical limit. To return to Hans in Burgenland, he made an interesting claim. Despite the move of natural winemakers towards less and less sulphur (more specifically, sulphur dioxide, SO_2), and some doing away with it entirely, under the belief that it contributed to lifeless wines, he claimed it was necessary. Not for the usual reasons of preservation, but rather he argued that without the careful use of a bit of SO_2 the influence on taste and aroma of the yeasts will overwhelm the terroir aspects in the wine.

The approach these winemakers adopt could arguably be taken as symptomatic of a larger, Austrian approach. My research partner, Julia, talked to a winemaker in Switzerland, who remarked 'In Austria people seem to view the grapes as the ultimate queens and kings of the procedure and themselves as the servants of taste'. Yet servants, I would argue, is the wrong word, even if the winemakers themselves might agree. The first time we met Maria, we asked her what or who had more influence, the winemakers or the vineyard. Despite an approach that seeks to showcase the grapes and their environment, Maria was clear: it was her as the winemaker that ultimately had the final say in the wine. Even if the winemakers saw their role as shepherding the wine, or a servant of the grapes, this was an act of interpretation. Rather than servants of taste, perhaps we should see the winemakers as chamberlains, or ministers, wielding a quiet power behind the scenes, influencing what does and does not reach the public, seeing themselves as acting in the best interests and wishes of the grapes themselves.

Conclusion

There is an opposite argument to be made, but as far as I am aware, the California winemaker Clark Smith is the only one to make much of it (Smith 2013). If we remain with our equation of the expression of terroir as the route to Utopia, if not Utopia itself, Smith takes a radically different approach. He believes that it is technological intervention, not the lack of it, that enables the truest expression of terroir. Technology should be embraced, and such techniques as reverse osmosis and spinning cone technology, used to remove alcohol from a wine, can lead to better overall balance, he argues. 'Balanced wines not only taste better, they better reflect their place of origin as well' (Smith 2013: 268). In other words, terroir can best be realised through the use of more technology, not less. While some may be tempted to dismiss this view as problematical at best – how is terroir being understood in this instance, and why – it is worth noting in the current context that it does parallel Ursula K. Le Guin's observation: 'Thomas More's secular and intellectual construct *Utopia* was still an expression of desire for something lacking here and now – rational human control of human life' (2016: 195).

Where then, do these explorations into the utopian drive of low-intervention winemaking lead us? We are left largely where we started, with two competing visions of Utopia. Terroir, as recognised through geographical indications (the AOC and similar systems), is an administrative, rational Utopia, that is at odds with the philosophical Utopia the low-intervention winemakers call their own. It has its own gatekeepers, its own moats and channels delineating a destination that most winemakers strive for.

Most, but not all. The low-intervention, or 'natural' winemakers I have been writing about refuse to see the AOC-sanctioned utopia as Utopia at all. For them, rather, it is the mainland. It is the starting point, not the goal. Utopia is a rejection, a disruption, a refusal. So too here. It is, in fact, a triple refusal. It is first a refusal of the sameness of most wines, the sensorial drift of typicity into lifeless blandness. In this sense, it is More's Utopia, close to the mainland, but purposely and violently cut off from it. Second, it is a refusal to rest. None of the winemakers I have worked with and talked to thought they had yet made the perfect wine. I strongly suspect none of them will ever think they will, but it will remain an elusive goal they will chase. In this sense, perhaps natural wine is utopian in the pejorative sense – an unachievable perfection, a fool's errand. Third, and most radical of all, the natural wine movement seeks converts. More's Utopia was isolated, guarded, a land conquered and controlled. The natural wine Utopia in contrast, welcomes all who are willing. It would be happy to be a conquering force once again, invading the mainland and bringing a proselytising ideology with it. It continues to be disruptive. Many proponents may be happy to simply follow their own way, but in doing so, they are overturning, intentionally or not, the isolation of Utopia.

Ultimately natural wine's search for Utopia is like all such endeavours almost certainly fated to fail. It is fated to fail, however, only if we insist on seeing arriving at Utopia as the point. For 'my' winemakers, it isn't. The journey is the point, and the understanding the journey engenders. For this, natural wine is already a success.

Notes

1 I am loath to raise a point that I am unable to follow or develop in this chapter, but it would be possible to argue that the natural wine movement is a revitalization movement in Anthony Wallace's formation: 'a deliberate, organised, conscious effort by members of a society to construct a more satisfying culture' (1958: 265).

2 Organic farming supports a sustainable approach to agriculture, although the term 'sustainable' can be interpreted in many ways. The key point here is that organic farming prohibits the use of what its proponents and regulators see as 'modern' or 'synthetic' fertilisers and pesticides. However, compounds such as Bordeaux mixture, a fungicide of copper sulphate and slaked lime, are allowed. Biodynamic farming, introduced by Rudolf Steiner in 1924, and predating the formalisation of organic farming, follows similar prohibitions, but also works to channel 'cosmic energy' through the use of various preparations (see Steiner 1958; Joly 2008).

3 It has been pointed out by a colleague of mine, a chemical engineer, that modern pesticides and herbicides are designed to break down quickly after application, unlike copper sulphate, which accumulates in the soil. His argument was that more frequent spraying is not necessarily as harmful for the environment as it may appear, since the sprayed products do not linger.

4 The use of temperature control on fermentation dates to the first part of the twentieth century, and is seen by many as a key step in the consistent of production of quality wines. Temperature control can help in the extraction of colour and flavour compounds in red wine and the retention of volatile aromatics in white. For a good, not excessively technical look at the fundamentals of winemaking, see Bird (2010).

5 The Austrian system, much like the German wine classification system it is based
   on, characterises wine based on the sugar content of the grape must before fermentation. A *qualitätswein* must have a must weight of >15KMW (Klosterneu-
   berger Mostwaage – a system for measuring the amount of sugar in the must), and
   at least 9% alcohol by volume.
6 Like many such descriptions of wine and its aromas and tastes, one is left to ponder
   just how the originator of the description knows (or thinks they know) what mouse
   urine tastes like.
7 Bordeaux mixture (also called Bordo Mix) is a preventative fungicide of copper
   sulphate ($CuSO_4$) and slaked lime ($Ca(OH)_2$). It is used to prevent infestations of
   mildew (downy and powdery) and other fungi.

Acknowledgements

Thanks are due to the editors for their invitation to submit a chapter to this
volume, as well as their infinite patience in my actually getting it to them.
Extra thanks are due to Peter Howland for his endlessly helpful feedback.
Thanks are also due to the numerous people in Austria and the UK who have
shared their time, insight and wine. Particular thanks are due to Julia Leijola,
a peerless research partner. Part of the fieldwork which this is based on was
funded by a Cambridge Humanities Research Grant.

References

Bird, D. (2010). *Understanding Wine Technology: The Science of Wine Explained.*
   Newark, Nottinghamshire: DBQA Publishing.
Bohmrich, R. (1996). Terroir: competing perspectives on the roles of soil, climate and
   people. *Journal of Wine Research*, 7(1): 33–46.
Descola, P. & Palsson, G. (eds.). (1996). *Nature and Society: Anthropological Perspec-
   tives.* London: Routledge.
EU (2012). *Regulation No. 1151/2012.* European Parliament and of the Council of 21
   November 2012 on quality schemes for agricultural products and foodstuffs. Avail-
   able online at https://eur-lex.europa.eu/eli/reg/2012/1151/oj (accessed 23. 01. 19).
Goode, J. & Harrop, S. (2011). *Authentic Wine: Toward a Natural and Sustainable
   Wine Making.* Berkeley: University of California Press.
Joly, N. (2008). *Biodynamic Wine Demystified.* San Francisco: Wine Appreciation Guild.
Legeron, I. (2014). *Natural Wine: An Introduction to Organic and Biodynamic Wines
   made Naturally.* London: Cico Books.
Le Guin, U. K. (2016). Utopiyin, Utopiyang. In *Utopia*, Thomas More. London:
   Verso Books.
Maltman, A. (2008). The role of vineyard geology in wine typicity. *Journal of Wine
   Research*, 19(1): 1–17.
Maltman, A. (2018). *Vineyards, Rocks, & Soils: The Wine Lover's Guide to Geology.*
   New York: Oxford University Press.
Matthews, M. (2015). *Terroir and Other Myths of Winegrowing.* Berkeley: University
   of California Press.
Meinert, L. D. (ed.). (2018). Terroir: Science related to Wine and Grape Quality.
   Elements, 14(3).

Mieville, C. (2016). Introduction. In *Utopia*, Thomas More. London: Verso Books.

Patterson, T. & Buechsenstein, J. (eds). (2018). *Wine and Place: A Terroir Reader*. Berkeley: University of California Press.

Smith, C. (2013). *Postmodern Winemaking: Rethinking the Modern Science of an Ancient Craft*. Berkeley: University of California Press.

Steiner, R. (1958). *Agriculture Course: The Birth of the Biodynamic Method*. Forest Row: Rudolf Steiner Press.

Strathern, M. (1980). No nature, no culture: the Hagen case. In *Nature, Culture and Gender*, MacCormack, C. & Strathern, M. (eds), pp. 174–222. Cambridge: Cambridge University Press.

Teil, G. (2012). No such thing as terroir? Objectivities and the Regimes of Existence of Objects. *Science Technology and Human Values*, 37: 478–505.

Teil, G. (2014). Nature, the CoAuthor of Its Products? An Analysis of the Recent Controversy Over Rejected AOC Wines in France. *The Journal of World Intellectual Property*, 17(3–4): 96–113.

Trubek, A. B. (2008). *The Taste of Place: A Cultural Journey into Terroir*. Berkeley: University of California Press.

Tsing, A. L. (2015). *The Mushroom at the End of the World: On the Possibility of Life in Capitalist Ruins*. Princeton: Princeton University Press.

Wallace, A. (1958). Revitalization movements. *American Anthropologist*, 58(2): 264–281.

12 Utopia is just up the road and toward the past

Young Australian winemakers return to ancient methods

Moya Costello

Australia is a New World wine producer, a long way from sites where wine grapes originated in Europe and the Middle East. Land masses on Earth once formed a supercontinent, but those land masses have been splitting up for millions of years – one result being Australia as an island, but large enough to be a continent, floating in the southern hemisphere with no large land mass between it and Antarctica, from which it broke away. To its north is the deep ocean rift between two shelves of Sunda and Sahul, one of the great biological boundaries in this part of the world. The rift became a barrier to the passage of animal and plant life. Hence, Australia is home to the platypus, the koala, and eucalypts as landcover. But it has been inhabited by its Indigenous peoples for tens of thousands of years. Australian Aborigines formed many nations with different languages within a complex culture of deep spirituality notably linked to country (the land). To ancient Europeans, this southern land mass was a mythic place. Northern hemisphere peoples such as the Dutch and French, and fisherpersons from Australia's northern neighbour, Indonesia, visited before the British settled/invaded it as a colony.

Being 'local', then, includes being open to what is beyond the local, to the global, to 'the possibility of shared purpose as the concerns of *here* are linked to *there*' (Campbell 2016: 5). Amid globalisation which tends toward placelessness, localism combined with a return to traditions (from there) is a utopian practice (McIntyre, J. personal communication).

As 'Australian winegrowing emerged from *mobilities* of vinestock and ideas, the classifications of location-based terroir in the French-dominated global wine world did not serve Australian wines well' (McIntyre, J. personal communication – my emphasis). Terroir as a term was originally exclusively invested in a locale, in the local geology, geography and climate. Contested over time, terroir has come to include culture – the viticulturist and the winemaker – because 'the human perspective is fundamental to understanding the ways in which bonds are created between food and places' (Hedegaard 2018: 67).[1] 'The desire to create an Australian wine industry can be dated to the voyage of colonisation to New South Wales under the command of Arthur Phillip' in the late eighteenth century. 'The First Fleet carried wine ... wine grape vine cuttings' and 'conceptions of the ... value of vine cultivation and wine drinking' (McIntyre 2011: 44). There was a nascent sense of terroir in colonial Australia as evidenced through the work of the early colonist James Busby who wrote on viticultural practices, noting the importance of grape varieties finding the soils that best suit them (McIntyre 2011: 49).

But 'perhaps … thinking in Australia about terroir just got waylaid for a time' (Costello et al. 2018: 55). Geographical Indications (GIs) (Halliday 2018), Australia's appellation system for wine growing areas (recognising super zones, zones, regions and subregions as mapped geographical spaces), were first completed relatively recently, in 1996. This is, perhaps, the closest Australia has come to similar European standard-setting, such as the Italian *Denominazione di Origine Controllata e Garantita* (DOCG: controlled designation of origin), denoting controlled production methods, permitted grape varieties, and guaranteed quality.

In Australia, broadly speaking, grape varieties are not linked to place: all regions usually grow a mix of varieties, depending, of course, on geographical and climatic conditions. Moreover, a wine brand or company may have vineyards across zones, and also commonly blend grapes from different regions, and different varieties. Penfolds is an example of a wine company being more important than place. For Penfolds, 'whose Grange is currently Australia's national flagship wine, the practice of blending from different areas is … a way of maintaining a uniformity of style' (Costello et al. 2018: 60). While the place is most often named on an Australian wine bottle's label, that place or wine company doesn't necessarily stand for only a single grape variety nor for the only place where the grape variety is grown.

This is different to 'Old World' wine. In Italy, for example, Soave – a *comune* or township in northern Italy – stands in for the name of the grape, primarily Garganega, though Garganega can also be combined with Trebbiano di Soave (Verdicchio), Chardonnay, Pinot Bianco (Chenin Blanc) and Trebbiano (Ugni Blanc). In *The Oxford Companion to Wine* (Thomases & Gleave 2006: 634), 'Soave' is stated to be a dry, white wine. In Australia, we don't say 'Barossa is a … wine'. Barossa is a wine zone where a large variety of grapes, both red and white, are grown. Another example is the French Vouvray, a *comune* in the Loire, 'where Vouvray is Chenin Blanc and Chenin Blanc … is Vouvray' (Robinson 2006: 759). Liselotte Hedegaard (2018: 66) investigates this phenomenon in her article, '(Re)tasting Places' in *Gastronomica*, pointing initially to the novel *Babette's Feast* where Babette refers to a wine via a place, Clos Vougeot, and is not understood by her co-conversationalist. Further, on a trip to Verona, Collioure and Madrid in 2017, I asked incommodiously, with excessive ignorance and abundant gauche naivety, waiting staff in wine bars and salespersons in bottle shops what the grape variety was in a glass or bottle of wine. 'Why isn't the grape variety on the label?' I asked them, my face scrunching up in annoyance, frustration, and confusion. But I did assume Albarino in Madrid, and Grenache Blanc, alone or in a mix, in Collioure. In Verona, our tour guide explained that there is no need to put the grape variety on the bottle – everyone knows what it is (given the region the wine comes from).

Increasingly, though, in Australia, particular regions have become known as the best match for a particular grape. A representation of these matches has been made literal by the large, commercial wine company Baily & Baily's (n.d.) labels in its Folio series that 'recognised and celebrated winegrowing regions by way of [their] featured varieties'. The labels:

> assertively and proactively privilege the perceived best place for grape match. Their label tells this story textually and visually. A vine leaf is digitally warped to resemble Australia, with a Southern Cross star over the wine-producing area specifying place in the different bottled varieties – for example, the south-west corner of Western Australia for Margaret River Chardonnay, and south-east South Australia for Adelaide Hills Sauvignon Blanc, and Coonawarra for Cabernet Sauvignon.
>
> (Costello et al. 2018: 60)

The Tasmanian Zone is touting itself as one of the best, if not the best, places for making 'Sparkling' (understood as champagne)[2] in Australia, 'equal to anywhere in the world', by virtue of climate and latitude, and then 'the nature of … blends, how much oak [is] used and which vineyards produce the best … wines' (Effervescence 2018). The Strange Bird wine trail, launched in the Granite Belt Region, Queensland Zone, in 2007 (Granite Belt Wine Country n.d.), aims to be educative about making 'wines better suited to place' (Barnes quoted in Allen 2010: 421), by distinguishing itself through alternative grape varieties[3] – such as the whites Viognier and Vermentino, and the reds Tempranillo, Petit Verdot, Barbera, Nebbiolo, Nero d'Avola and Tannat – and re-educating the palate. Granite Belt winemakers recognise that Australian wine drinkers do have an attachment to place and grape variety, such as the Barossa Valley and McLaren Vale Regions for Shiraz.

In the development of an Australian terroir, it is increasingly common to see 'single vineyard' or 'estate grown' on Australian wine labels. Respected Australian wine journalist Max Allen (2010: 20) says that wines coming from 'quality-focused' winemakers celebrating single-vineyard, single-site winemaking are 'terroir-driven': 'more and more people … are thinking … about growing grape varieties and making wine in a way that better expresses their unique patch of country' (Allen 2010: 5).

For 23 years, I lived in Adelaide, the state capital city of South Australia (SA), arguably Australia's central home of winemaking (Halliday 2018), given the internationally known Barossa Valley and McLaren Vale Regions. I became very 'statist', drinking only SA wine. When I moved interstate for work, to New South Wales (NSW) far North Coast/hinterland, I found myself in the Northern Rivers, a subtropical rainforest and a biodiverse region characterised by long hours of sunlight, high rainfall and good soil. 'Region' here means 'all of the towns, small cities and areas that lie beyond the major capital cities' (Regional Australia Institute 2017). I looked around for local wine, and it wasn't, with one exception, in the immediate vicinity.

The climate encourages mould, not conducive to wine-grape growing. Chambourcin, a tough-skinned grape, features in the Northern Rivers Zone's wineries. So, yes, Northern Rivers is a wine zone, but with wineries clustered much further down the coast, around its single region the Hastings River. If I wanted to be a 'locabiber', drinking only local wine, I'd have to include the Northern Slopes Zone (again with a single region: New England Australia) and the Granite Belt Region, both closer to the Northern Rivers than the single region in the zone of its namesake (see Costello & Evans 2013 for distances within and between these wine regions/zones).

But just up the road from where I live, in the village of Clunes, in the Byron Bay hinterland, are the post office, general store, café, bottle shop, and cellar on the main road between Lismore (the central town of the Northern Rivers), and Byron Bay (an internationally famous tourist destination, Australia's most easterly point). These businesses were taken over by the enterprising Dixon family who made a feature of selling local produce: for example, bread from The Bread Social, an artisan bakehouse at The Farm, Byron Bay.

Perhaps going from Australia's well-established wine regions to emerging wine regions such as the Hastings River, New England and Granite Belt is to go to Utopia.[4] The move to the Northern Rivers enabled the young winemaker of the Dixon family, Jared Dixon, to have the pleasures of beaches – Byron Bay, Lennox Head and Ballina – and a suitable terroir nearby for his favourite grapes: Nebbiolo and Tempranillo. That terroir is New England, specifically viticulturalist Mark Kirkby's Topper's Mountain vineyard. The ancient, volcanic red soil is suited to Nebbiolo and Tempranillo, and wild ferment, because of the abundance of wild yeast. A first wine of Dixon's was the 2012 New England Jilly Nebbiolo. Dixon aimed to make his own wine from single regions, wine that he'd like to drink, food-friendly wines, made with minimal intervention – such as discarding filtering/fining. Moreover, the Northern Rivers is a region with a substantial history of developing countercultures (see Garbutt 2014), so 'organic' and 'natural' are commonplace and highly valued descriptors. And in a whole-earth context, natural and organic are considered advantageous for our biosphere's survival.

Besides the reds mentioned, Dixon likes the dry, minerally Chablis-style Chardonnay – a French influence. Another early Jilly wine was the 2013 F.I.F. O. Margaret River Chardonnay. The Margaret River Region, South West Australia Zone, has perfect growing conditions for a Chablis-style Chardonnay, with a Mediterranean climate of cool wet winters and long dry summers, and gravel loam from ancient lateritic soils, with the grapes selected by Dixon grown on gravel lime in Upper Wilyabrup, a sub-region.

Here is a young Australian winemaker thinking about an Australia terroir, perhaps imagining it, calling it into being. The winemaking practices of Jared Dixon of Jilly Wine can be used as an exemplar of a developing Australian terroir and startling utopian moves in Australian winemaking, in a performance that honours both ancient traditions and innovation. Like the 'hipster' phenomenon, what is attractive about a return to the past is that it consists of embellished reinvention, not simple repetition. Dixon believes winemaking is a creative process. Kirkby thinks it is one of the 'dark arts' – alchemical, featuring mystery, chance, science, and creativity.

Dixon works on selected projects with a colleague, Daniel Graham – both alumni of Charles Sturt University, the original home of vintner education in Australia. Graham is based in the Barossa. Their wine education is broad and varied, national and international. Dixon has worked with French chefs in French kitchens; with Houghton Wines, Swan District Region, Greater Perth Zone, Western Australia; and with Heathcote Winery, Heathcote Region, Central Victoria Zone. Graham has worked for the large Australian commercial winery Yellowtail, but also for the smaller Hope Estate, Hunter Valley Region.

Like Dixon, Graham made his first wine in 2012, under the Sigurd label. Their respective labels are named from particulars of their individual family histories, an example of respect for traditional ties. Dixon's paternal grandfather had a lost love, Jilly, a maid below his station (think Cumbria, in northern England, rather than Cornwall in the south, and a more lamentable Demelza not making it with Poldark). Sigurd is a mythic hero from a Norse saga: Graham had a maternal Norse grandfather who came to Australia seeking a new world.

Dixon liberally subtends a variety of aliases or nicknames to Jilly, some still referencing his grandfather, such as White Wolf of Cumbria and Dick Dixon. He subtitled his 2016 Jilly Dick Dixon New England Shiraz Nebbiolo 'addicted to the unknown'. The alias of F.I.F.O., or fly in and out, is a reference to Australia's flying-in-and-out mining workers from a city to a region. He titled a 2015 New England Petit Manseng, Roman Giallo, and used gold wax to drip over the cork luxuriously down the bottle, with the label a leather lookalike, mimicking Roman solder uniforms or shields. Dixon said the Giallo fought through to its fine end, like the Roman soldiers, the fighting force of that ancient empire. For wild ferment can be unpredictable; such an experimental process can include 'interesting' failures, as, for example, Murray Bail, Australian writer, suggested of the painter Ian Fairweather that 'even his failures were distinctive and often demanding' (1981: 214), or, as Australian scholar and writer Astrid Lorange (2014: 31) wrote, 'to experiment is to experience by trialling; to essay; to make an attempt'. And for a cork-and-wax revolution, potentially the first such experiment is retrieving your discarded corkscrew, given most Australian wines are now under stelvin/screw cap. The three strategies – wild ferment, nonfiltering/nonfining, and bottling with cork and wax – complement Dixon and Graham's genuine commitment to the natural, and, where possible, organic and sustainable.

The labels – and bottles, for Dixon imports French bottles – of these independent winemakers speak to both tradition and experimentation. Without ownership of a vineyard, but with enthusiasm and commitment to wine's history and aesthetics, Dixon and Graham are utopian, inventive yet practical creatives: they work by hand with what is at hand. A one-man, hand-made operation is their labour-intensive style, from picking grapes, to pressing them, and then impressing bottles with 'hand-drawn' labels, designed by friends or close associates. Dixon's wines have also featured cloth labels of a hessian or denim lookalike, relating to work in the vineyard. The hand-made 'signature' of the wines underpins the artisan profile of the winemaking. While there are arguments that centre on provenance – the foregrounding of wine's 'origin, mode of production and heritage' (Smith Maguire 2013: 368) – as a marketing tool to capture the authenticity-obsessed, effete consumer-as-a-wine-elitist (McIntyre & Germov 2018: 84), Dixon's and Graham's methods are based in a *jouissant* celebration of the singular pleasures of wine, ancient in origin. Because the wines are boutique-made, they are not cheap in terms consumer-cost. Made in small batches, many of the vintages have sold out.

Natural wine has been described in Australia as the 'new (but actually very old) frontier of wine' (Boys 2018). Experimentation in any art form requires that the consumer learn to understand and appreciate anew. In literature, for example, Lorange (2014: 31) wrote of the American experimental writer, Gertrude Stein, as challenging the very assumptions 'that make reading possible'. Daniel Graham notes that 'Australian wine-drinkers are used to clean, single-dimensional wines' (D. Graham, interview, 2013).[5] He wants to put the wines in front of people who have an experimental inclination. But a young winemaker in Corte Mainente winery, Soave, said to me that you give 'natural' wines to someone you want to convince to be a beer drinker! For me, particularly in white wines, 'the natural'/unconstructed wine results in the impossibility of distinguishing easily one grape from another. However, in the case of Dixon and Graham, the whites still can have the most extraordinary colour, making you think of a dense, golden honey, sometimes with a hallucinatory bronzed-pink tinge. They can be distinct and pleasurable even luscious wines, but at the same time have restraint, elegance and intrigue. At the very least, minimum intervention and filtering make for food friendly wines, which are Dixon's forte.

To develop the local palate for their wines, Dixon and Graham hold local-produce luncheons at the Clunes café and wine-tastings outside the Clunes bottle-shop door. At the café luncheons, Dixon and Graham feed the wine drinkers snapper, rabbit, mushrooms, artichokes and greens. At the bottle-shop door, Dixon and Graham are voluble. Both dark-haired, curious and energetic, they fix the wine-drinker with the glittering eye of the Ancient Mariner to regale him or her with impassioned narratives about their wine. And the wine drinker is captivated, just like the wedding guest by the Ancient Mariner – or the Sultan by Scheherazade's story-telling.

The bottle shop is like walking into Dixon's private cellar, his own Aladdin's Cave. He stocks wines of interest to him, that he likes to drink, whose makers he knows or that he has had a hand in making, or that are 'natural'. Jilly and Sigurd are both stocked in this eclectic wine store. There's wine from Italy, France and Spain, from the Granite Belt and New England and from other small, independent Australian winemakers, who are similarly appearing in fine-dining restaurants, and often producing 'natural' wines, unfiltered/unfined, such as: the Italian Petracavallo (n.d.), avoiding pesticides, and 'undergoing spontaneous fermentation without added yeast'; Konpira Maru Wine Company (2018) similarly touting minimal intervention; Simão & Co (2018) 'from the best vineyards in the five regions of North East Victoria'; Ochota Barrels (n.d.) with the philosophy of going back to basics; and Commune of Buttons (Wine Australia n.d.) 'who do things the old fashioned way, working hard to farm organically', and with 'minimal intervention, letting the fruit (rather than artifice) do the talking'.

Dixon and Graham have co-produced the cheeky label Sud de Frank, initially as a Rosé. Frank is an imagined Australian character. The full naming can be read as a laconic swipe at authority (a very Australian, 'larrikin' thing to do, or a European Bakhtinian common peoples' irreverent, *carnivàle* gesture), and as an acknowledgement of Dixon and Graham's *amour du vin français*, given *Sud de France*'s reputation for luscious Rosés, and with the Sud de Frank label and cap brandishing the French flag colours.

Dixon and Graham didn't name the year, grape variety/ies, the region or the winemakers on the label of their first Sud de Frank in 2016. Julie McIntyre (personal communication 2018) notes that:

> The Australian tradition of naming wines for varieties emerged in the past half-[twentieth]century. Prior to that Australian wines were named for colour and ... styles adapted from European traditions.... The primary use of grape varieties in labelling began in the 1980s. Even in wine shows until that time, wines were judged in classifications that were not delineated by grape variety. Although winegrowers spoke to each other in terms of grape varieties, the nature of varieties was still being untangled (and to some extent still is). With some rare exceptions (in NSW in the 1960s and early 1970s), it was the emergence of single varietal wines from named places as premium rather than ordinary wines that led to the communication of named grape varieties ...

However, both Jilly and Sigurd labels can be exceedingly voluble about their red and white grape mix. For example, in the 2016 Jilly Field Blend, the list of grape varieties – handwritten on the label – is like the chants of Easter Catholic liturgy: the reds being Nebbiolo, Shiraz, Tempranillo, Tannat, Pinotage, Tinta Cão, Touriga, Barbera, and the whites being Gewürztraminer, Chardonnay, Viognier and Petit Manseng. Dixon took the grapes for this blend from the first rows of Kirkby's Topper's Mountain 'fruit-salad' vine plantings, there to deliberately attract, disconcert and confuse birds in the nearby bush, that would normally attack the main vines. Of interest here is the jostling mix of influence on wine production, between soil/climate, viticulturalist and winemaker. Kirkby himself uses winemaker Mike Hayes of the Symphony Hill label in the Granite Belt to make his Topper's Mountain wines. Dixon's Field Blend's almost unimaginable combination of grape varieties makes of Utopia a fiction. Yet the wine label graced one of Australia's leading food-commentary publications, the *Sydney Morning Herald's Good Food Guide* (Good Food Guide 2016). The 2016 Field

Blend label featured a greyscale, alert hare, sitting up, ears vertical, scanning and ready to scamper off in the opposite direction from what they are perceiving, just like a bounding wallaby. And Dixon's wines have been on the wine menus of leading restaurants in his locale (Town (Bangalow), Harvest (Newrybar), The Farm (Byron Bay)) and in boutique fine-wine bottle shops and more restaurants across Australia (Brisbane's Cru Bar and Cellar, Melbourne's Blackhearts and Sparrows, Sydney's Annandale Cellars, and the Merivale Group of Australian restaurants and hotels). Despite the whites and because of big red-wine grapes, the colour of the 2016 Field Blend was a deepish ruby-crimson. Its palate was, not unexpectedly, surprising: at the beginning, where the whites were strong, was citrus, and in the middle came the Turkish delight of the reds, and at the very end was the citrus again. It may continue to be a wine that glides across borders.

Graham can operate similarly. His 2015 Sigurd White Barossa Valley Blend was a combination of Gewürztraminer, Marsanne and Garganega. Although unusual, Graham's mixture was well judged to a fine balance, which is proving to be a characteristic of his wines. The 2015 Sigurd White, wild fermented, and unfiltered/unfined, was the most extraordinary colour: think medieval mead and, if you can hallucinate, you might think of pink. Further, you might think of a white-pink gold. The perfume was of toffee, jube, honey, maybe some caramel or even liquorice. And on the palate it was Scheherazade telling stories, not overnight but on a summer afternoon, with the smell of salt water from the Persian Gulf or Caspian Sea. This was an extraordinary wine, something of a revelation that was entirely about pleasure. Think of silken sherbet, gold brocade, white curtains shifting in the breeze, and you have the idea. Graham has sold into Brisbane's equally discerning Craft Wine Store and Sydney's Moncur Cellars.

The eclectic, utopian mixing of grape varieties by Dixon and Graham may well be going mainstream in Australia, which has a long tradition, for example, already of mixing Semillon with Chardonnay and Sauvignon Blanc. But as I write, a most recent, adventurous – and delicious – white mix from a venerable Australian wine company, De Bortoli, founded in 1928, is their 2017 new label, positioned at a relatively low price point, Down the Lane, with Pinot Gris, Arneis and Vermentino. Of the latter two Italian varieties, Fred Swan (2018), an American wine writer and wine educator, said of Californian developments that 'one [his] favourite trends of the past decade [was] the steady improvement in California wines made from Italian varieties'. So here are utopian moves by old(er) companies of the New World.

In his fourth novel, *The Pages*, about a putative or wanna-be philosopher, Bail (2008) has his narrator say: 'we cannot help being' (199) but 'we end up becoming' (195). This is what shapes existence for an Australian terroir: it is to be 'cautiously but continually negotiated and determined' (Costello et al. 2018). For both young makers, Jared Dixon and Daniel Graham, this experimental phase is more like a permanent philosophy powered by the desire to tell another story in Australian winemaking.

Notes

1 See Costello and Evans (2013) for a discussion of meanings of 'local' and 'terroir'.
2 'Because of mixed vineyards in any region, and the original, non-Australian source of the grape, Australia cannot use a town or region title for a wine variety' (Costello et al. 2018).
3 Classified by Allen (2010: 80–84, 86–88) as major and minor alternative grape varieties.
4 New England Australia and the Hastings River Regions are the only regions in the Northern Slopes and Northern Rivers Zones, respectively.
5 For this chapter, I am drawing on interviews I conducted with Jared Dixon, Daniel Graham and Mark Kirkby in 2013 and following.

References

Allen, M. (2010). *The Future Makers: Australian Wines for the 21st Century.* Melbourne: Hardie Grant.

Bail, M. (1981). *Ian Fairweather.* Sydney: Bay Books.

Bail, M. (2008). *The Pages.* Melbourne: Text.

Baily & Baily (n.d.) Our Range. *Baily & Baily.* Available online at www.bailyandbaily. com.au/our-range (accessed 19. 04. 18).

Boys, C. (2018). The Grape Debate: Setting the Record Straight on Natural Wine. *Good Food,* May 15. Available online at www.goodfood.com.au/drinks/wine/set ting-the-record-straight-on-natural-wine-20180511-h0zxig (accessed 13. 10. 18).

Campbell, N. (2016). *Affective Critical Regionality (Place, Memory, Affect).* New York: Rowan and Littlefield.

Carlin, D. (2018). Essaying as Method: Risky Accounts and Composing Collectives. *TEXT,* 22(1). Available online at www.textjournal.com.au/april18/carlin.htm (accessed 02. 12. 18).

Costello, M. & Evans, S. (2013). *Bibere Vinum Suae Regionis*: Why Whian Whian Wine. *Locale: The Australasian-Pacific Journal of Regional Food Studies,* 3: 133–154.

Costello, M., Smith, R. & Lane, L. (2018). Australian Wine Labels: Terroir without Terror. *Gastronomica: The Journal of Critical Food Studies,* 18(3): 54–65.

Effervescence (2018). Tasmanian Sparkling Festival 2018. Available online at www. effervescencetasmania.com (accessed 30.04.18).

Garbutt, R. (2014). Aquarius and Beyond: Thinking through the Counterculture. *M/C Journal.* Available online at www.journal.media-culture.org.au/index.php/mcjourna l/article/view/911 (accessed 02.12.18).

Good Food Guide (2016). Fresh Australian Wines for the Park This Spring. *Good Food Guide.* Available online at www.goodfood.com.au/drinks/wine/nine-fresh-a ustralian-wines-for-the-park-this-spring-20161019-gs5sw5 (accessed 02.12.18).

Granite Belt Wine Country (n.d.). Strange Bird Overview. *Granite Belt Wine Country.* Available online at www.granitebeltwinecountry.com.au/pages/strange-bird/ (accessed 12.10.11).

Halliday, J. (2018). Wineries: South Australia. *Halliday.* Available online at winecompa nion.com.au/wineries/south-australia (accessed 19.04.18).

Hedegaard, L. (2018). (Re)tasting Places. *Gastronomica: The Journal of Critical Food Studies,* 18(1): 66–75.

Konpira Maru Wine Company (2018). About. *Konpira Maru Wine Company.* Available online at www.konpiramaru.com.au/about/ (accessed 01.04.18).

Lorange, A. (2014). *How Reading Is Written: A Brief Index to Gertrude Stein*. Middletown, Connecticut: Wesleyan University Press.

McIntyre, J. (2011). Resisting Ages-Old Fixity as a Factor in Wine Quality: Colonial Wine Tours and Australia's Early Wine Industry as a Product of Movement from Place to Place. *Locale: The Australasian-Pacific Journal of Regional Food Studies* 1: 1–19.

McIntyre, J. & Germov, J. (2018). Who Wants To Be a Millionaire? I Do: Wine, Gendered Culture and Class. *Journal of Australian Studies*, 42(1): 65–84.

Ochota Barrels (n.d.). Craft. *Ochota Barrels*. Available online at http://ochotabarrels. com/ (accessed 29.04.18).

Petracavallo (n.d.). Chi siamo. *Petracavallo*. Available online at http://petracavallo. wine/it/ (accessed 02.12.18).

Regional Australia Institute (2017). *What Is Regional Australia?* Available online at www.regionalaustralia.org.au/home/what-is-regional-australia/ (accessed 30.11.18).

Robinson, J. (2006) Vouvray. In *Oxford Companion to Wine*, J. Robinson (ed.), p. 759. Oxford: Oxford University Press.

Simão & Co. (2018). *Simão & Co*. Available online at www.facebook.com/pg/Simaoa ndCoWines/about/ (accessed 29.04.18).

Smith Maguire, J. (2013). Provenance as a Filtering and Framing Device in the Qualification of Wine. *Consumption, Markets & Culture*, 16(4): 368–391.

Swan, F. (2018). Seghesio 2017 Arneis and Vermentino. *NorCal Wine: Articles, Wine Reviews & Events by Fred Swan*, 24 August. Available online at www.fredswan.wine/ 2018/08/24/seghesio-2017-arneis-vermentino/ (accessed 02.12.18).

Thomases, D. & Gleave, D. (2006). Soave. In *Oxford Companion to Wine*, J. Robinson (ed.), p. 634. Oxford: Oxford University Press.

Wine Australia (n.d.). Commune of Buttons. *Wine Australia*. Available online at www. wineaustralia.com/jasper-button (accessed 02.12.18).

Wine Australia (2018). Geographical Indications. *Wine Australia*. Available online at www.wineaustralia.com/labelling/register-of-protected-gis-and-other-terms/geograp hical-indications (accessed 02.12.18).

13 Deep terroir as utopia

Explorations of place and country in southeastern Australia

Robert Swinburn

Introduction

The term 'terroir' contains a multivocality that is often overlooked by popular, and often simplified, notions of the term. In its basic form, terroir refers to local factors, mostly environmental, which work to make wine and other agricultural products unique. Within the literature, however, the multiple meanings of terroir have been appropriately acknowledged, including how – as mentioned in the Introduction to this edited collection – terroir is an ambiguous term with meanings that have evolved through time and across space. As many authors have pointed out (Demossier 2010; Ulin 1996), such changes are due to reasons not always benign and include the complex intersections between political dominance, social class, and economic monopolisation. Yet even considering this literature, other possible meanings of terroir have still to be fully explored. This chapter calls for one such exploration. I argue that the deployment of terroir not only emerges from political domination, historical classism, and the marketing strategies of profit-maximising entrepreneurs; terroir also expresses something deeper. In previous work, I called this aspect of terroir, 'deep terroir' (Swinburn 2013), and – in this chapter – I suggest that it is a utopia.

By 'utopia', I have a specific definition in mind. Ghassan Hage points out that throughout the history of modern western thought, the notion of utopia has come to be clustered together with terms such as 'romantic', 'idealist', and 'sentimental', implying that utopian thought lacks a connection with reality (Hage 2011: 7). However, drawing on the work of Bruno Latour and Eduardo Viveiros de Castro on multi-naturalism, Hage suggests that what we generally refer to as reality is, in fact, just the dominant reality, and that there are always minor realities in which we are enmeshed (Hage 2011: 8). Hage notes that, 'utopia, rather than being a space inspired by an idealised past that has disappeared, or a future-oriented imagining of that which has no existence, is metonymic of minor and repressed spaces in which we already dwell in the present' (Hage 2011: 8). To restate Hage's argument, utopia is distanced from its popular characterisation as an idealised, non-existent place and as synonymous with feelings of felicity and happiness, both of which conjure associations with the imagined rather than the real. Rather, utopia consists of minor realities in the here-and-now and, as such, has the potential to express anthropology's highest intention to both take seriously the existence of the other, and how the other, in the process, speaks to us. Methodologically, it is to understand that there is something about what is being said (by the other) that resonates with us and how this reveals there is something about us that is *already* other (Hage 2011: 8). What this means is that the possibility of finding other ways of being in the world goes beyond the imagination to the real (Hage 2011: 9). Hage concludes that

> western modernity's greatest 'achievement' has been to make us mono-realists, minimising our awareness of the multiplicities of realities in which we exist, always grounding our utopian thought in the past or the future, rather than in the present, where it has always been grounded.
>
> (Hage 2011: 12)

Taking seriously this argument, this chapter explores the existence of minor realities in the world of winegrowing. My research has examined why the winegrowers on the periphery of Geelong, a large post-industrial city in southeastern Australia, have been drawn to small-scale wine production when all economic analyses should warn them against it. In other words, the dominant reality for the industry of Australian wine is profit maximisation. Yet the presence of a dominant reality – and the admitted deployment of the term 'terroir' in neo-liberal marketing and branding strategies – must not detract from other minor realities at play in the world of Geelong winegrowers. The very fact that well-educated and otherwise successful individuals venture into small-scale wine production despite warnings against its profitability demonstrates that a far more complex picture is needed. In this chapter, I argue that what Geelong winegrowers are pursuing can, in part, be described as utopia, with the understanding that this is a real and present utopia that exists alongside dominant reality.

History tells us that there is an implied freedom for those writing about utopia. In the conclusion to this chapter, I grasp that freedom and explore whether a redefinition of the term 'terroir' as deep terroir might not offer us a new way to think about how we live in our environment. I do this by examining the indigenous notion of Country and the affective power invested within that notion.

The field: Geelong

The field site for my research is a one-hour drive south-west from Melbourne, the state capital of Victoria in south-eastern Australia.[1] Discussion of the contemporary wine industry in Geelong needs to take into account the region's history. The Wathaurong people inhabited the region for at least 20,000 years before the British hoisted the Union Jack there on a short visit in 1802. Settlers did not arrive until 1830 but when they did, the landscape changed forever. One of those early changes brought the construction of vineyards.

Geelong had a nineteenth-century wine industry that was virtually unequalled across Australia, but it was not to last. Referring to the arrival of the devastating grape vine parasite *Phylloxera vastatrix* into the port of Geelong in 1877, and the subsequent eradication of every grape vine in the district in the 1880s, W. S. Benwell (1978) described Geelong's destiny as the capital of a truly great vignoble, the Bordeaux of the Antipodes. He wondered if the fact that Geelong had once found, and then lost, something of permanent significance, had something to do with its current temper (Benwell 1978: 17). He observed how people from other places had regarded Geelong as an obstacle on their way to somewhere else, and how they have carefully guarded road plans of how to go past Geelong without actually encountering it (Benwell 1978: 14).

Phylloxera was not the only scourge to cast a shadow on Geelong. Rabbits arrived on the ship *Lightning* in 1858, initiating temperate Australia's greatest – and ongoing – environmental disaster. A series of difficulties since, the latest being a rapid deindustrialisation and a corresponding rise in unemployment, has made Geelong a source of ridicule in some quarters. I once heard the now-former editor of *The Lonely Planet*, Tony Wheeler, say that he would send his potential employees to Geelong and if they could write something interesting about it, he would give them a job. For decades, people from the state capital, Melbourne, have passed through Geelong on their way to the spectacular beaches of the Great Ocean Road. Others became acquainted with the district as they built their careers in the city of Geelong.

The 1970s saw a resurgence of interest in the wine. Across temperate Australia vineyards appeared in the landscape. Geelong was not overlooked. Yet while the casual observer might regard the growth of the wine industry in Geelong over the past forty years as substantial, wine production in Geelong makes up only small part of Australia's national wine industry. To provide some perspective, all of the wineries in Geelong combined crush less than 3,000 tonnes of grapes while the top 20 wine companies in Australia individually crush over 10,000 tonnes, the largest crushing a massive 290,000 tonnes. Geelong's 70 odd vineyards are thus small by industry standards and all are family-owned. Any expansion, however, did not appear to be linked to economic factors. The financial nature of the industry was laid bare when the Winemakers Federation of Australia (2016) reported that the proportion of all production that is unprofitable is estimated to have risen from 84% to 85% in 2015 (Winemakers Federation of Australia 2016). The business of wine production has been described by one business newspaper as Australia's worst industry (Treadgold 2011).

To gain some understanding of why people were drawn to small-scale wine production in Geelong despite the dire economic statistics indicated above, I asked winegrowers in and around Geelong what they thought was attractive about the wine industry. Some suggested that they simply liked wine, and when they had become financially successful in their chosen professions, they thought they should try to make some. One winegrower, when pressed, said that winegrowers like him had big egos. He said that because they had had successful careers in other professions, they thought that they could be economically successful as winegrowers too. Dire economic statistics added to the experience of 'a challenge'. Another winegrower, still working in a stressful job, said that she found relaxation in the routine of mindless tasks such as pruning and leaf-plucking. Another said that he planted a vineyard because he didn't want to become fat. One wanted to reunite his family employing them in different parts of his wine business. Another wanted his children to find out what it was like to do physical work. He had fond memories of being tired after working night shift in a tannery as a young man. The reasons given were as diverse as the people who offered them.

Outsiders, too, had their views. A horticulturalist, when asked why his clients engaged in small-scale wine production, said: 'two words: pure hedonism!' A winemaking consultant told me that he thought that his clients wanted to impose themselves on the world; that rather than find a successful wine production model (and he named a couple of wineries with such a model), most small-scale wine producers were interested in telling the world about themselves through their wine, at whatever cost. A contract winemaker I spoke to thought that having a vineyard and making wine was an easy way for wealthy people to satisfy their need to be creative.

The answers given above were interesting and not necessarily untrue. However, I always thought they failed to explain fully what was going on. Ellen Badone and Sharon Roseman point out, 'one of the perennial problems in ethnography has been precisely the difficulty of attaining clear insight into the motivations and inner experiences of Others, perhaps in part because motivations and experience are often contradictory or poorly understood by the ethnographic actors themselves' (2004: 2). The question has an added dimension for me because, as a winegrower myself, I had trouble explaining why I, too, was drawn to small-scale wine production.

One response from a winegrower interviewed in a newspaper article caught my attention and this was through his use of the word, 'epiphany'. When asked about the best part of winegrowing, he said, 'the highs are moments when I am working in the vineyard where I have an epiphanous connection. It might be stimulated by a falling leaf, a bird's call; it may be the beauty of a bursting bud or a beautifully formed Pinot Noir bunch. I have moments when that is overwhelming' (Port 2004: 12). Environmental epiphanies such as these have been described as 'experiences in which of the essential meaning of (one's) relationship to nature shifts in a meaningful manner' (Vining & Merrick 2012: 486). One study found that positive emotions such as awe and wonder, peacefulness, empowerment, gratitude, curiosity and excitement surrounded epiphanies and that the people interviewed described the nature of their epiphany as 'like giving birth, (but) in essence … giving birth to myself' (Vining & Merrick 2012: 489). Epiphany has been a driving force of many gardeners (Cooper 2006) and one that goes beyond language to symbols.[2] Cooper suggests that symbols provide a 'sense for' or an 'attunement to' what they symbolise and this notion is central to how something spiritual and possibly ineffable shows itself in sensible form, thus enabling us to gain a different sort of understanding. It is here that the ordinary is experienced as an epiphany (Cooper 2006: 130). 'Epiphany', as described above, forced me to re-consider the responses of my wine-growing informants. It allowed me to draw in an ethnography of their lives in a more complete way focused on not only their words but also their actions, especially as they related to place.

Ethnographic vignettes

With a vineyard with expansive and breathtaking views overlooking Port Phillip Bay, Peter was a self-made businessman with no agricultural background and failing health. Sixteen years previously, he had purchased 100 acres of highly sought-after land but insisted that the large amount of money paid was irrelevant because 'he needed this place'. It was a necessary part of his life now that he was no longer involved in his quantity surveying business in town, having passed it on to his children. The winery was impressive with its configuration of steel, glass and corrugated iron, nestled elegantly among the vines. Peter had hired an architect to design the many buildings that comprised his winery complex and noted how it was 'the integration of the buildings with the vineyards and doing everything properly' that was important for him. Despite dismissing any priority on money and profit for their own sake, there was no doubt that money and profit had enabled Peter to pursue another sort of ambition; one that spoke to his need for beauty, integration, and 'doing things well'.

Yet Peter's connection with his vineyard and its place was also evident in what he did. Going down to the water, sitting on a cliff, and looking out was part of a routine that gave him happiness: 'It's like I'm in heaven', he said. He followed up by adding: 'This place is not about making money. It's about sitting here enjoying the day…. I love the seasonality of the farm, not just the grapes but the other crops, too. That's what I like'.

At another farm on the other side of the Bellarine Peninsula, this sentiment of sitting in a place and connecting with it is echoed by another vineyard owner. David bought his 40-acre farm about thirty years ago while he was still practicing as a dentist in Melbourne. He and his wife moved permanently to the farm about 15 years ago before he retired and established a vineyard shortly after. Unlike Peter, he was much more involved in work with and maintenance of the vines and said,

> the longer you spend on land and are involved in changing it and managing it and looking after it, the stronger the attachment is … you can't enjoy money the way you can enjoy sitting here every morning and every evening and every day, on the property. The vineyard is part of that, but not just that…. We see neighbours now who have done things like plant olives…they've developed a similar passion and interest in the land.

After David retired from dentistry, he focused his full attention on the vineyard and – as other winegrowers did – committed himself to the early mornings, long hours, inclement weather, tedious tasks, and seasonal worries of looking after the vines. While he is undoubtedly concerned about crop yield, grape quality, and sales, these do not mutually exclude the sense of connection he has with the place and epiphanous moments that emerge through this connection.

These ethnographic vignettes describe what I now term the minor realities of small-scale wine production. As I outlined in my introduction, the minor realities of sitting, enjoying, feeling a connection with place and with other people occur alongside the dominant reality of wine production as an industry. In David's words: 'It's a three-dimensional thing for me. Bonding to the land, the industry itself, and the being with the people who are passionate about it'. It is these minor realities – fleeting though they may be – that are revealed by something I have called 'deep terroir' (Swinburn 2013).

Deep terroir and place

Terroir has long been used to explain various forms of agriculture,[3] but the modern emphasis on taste, place, and quality owes much to Paul Vidal de la Blache (1901) who was concerned with the relationship between humans and their environment. Vidal de la Blache's analysis of terroir implied that the environment determines the way of life, yet this is not unproblematic. While climate and water may influence the flavours of food, it is in the cultural domain that 'tastemakers' intervened and guided the relationship of the French people in particular, to taste and place (Trubek 2008: 19–20). At the level of experience, the idea of terroir moves consumers beyond simple issues of wine quality by providing them with a symbolic connection to a place and to the people who live there. This is because what they taste in the wine is, symbolically at least, the place itself. This can be a powerful motivating force for wine producers and consumers. One of my informants elaborated on this. He said,

> Because I've lost crops I've been forced to buy in grapes from other areas. But the people want to buy the wine from the grapes grown here. Even if they don't understand the concept of terroir, it comes through in their choices.

Yet the power of the idea has itself opened up various contestations around its use and deployment. From an historical perspective, the notion and associated practices have continually evolved (Demossier 2010: 205) and for mainly economic and socio-political reasons. Robert Ulin has demonstrated how, in the French region of Bordeaux, 'differences in soil and climate (have been) invoked rhetorically to conceal the historical construction of class privilege' (Ulin 1996: 8). And while terroir is a powerful idea, it is not an idea embraced by everyone. Some winemakers, especially but not exclusively in the 'new world', reject the concept altogether. These winemakers call on science to provide beneficial characteristics to their wine rather than letting nature take its course. The privileging of science over nature is particularly well suited to places that developed their wine industries after the advent of the industrial revolution (Charters 2008: 58), and the manipulation of wine by wine scientists is particularly well suited to an age where self-expression is considered an inalienable right (Kramer 2008: 229). There are 'old world' winemakers too, who see the privileging of terroir as a reminder of a peasant past better forgotten. As a result of these debates, some have concluded that 'the word terroir cannot simply be excised of its historical-cultural meaning in favour of a less value-laden alternative' (McIntyre 2011: 57).

The difficulty with the notion of terroir, however, lies not only in semantics and power, but also – and more crucially – in how terroir may reveal different ways of being in the world. Matt Kramer (2008) suggests that terroir is a foreign idea at odds with both science and commerce. It prospects for difference rather than seeking replication and it calls for a susceptibility to the natural world that is almost unfathomable today (Kramer 2008: 228). Where modern winemakers insert themselves between terroir and the wine, the traditional winemakers impart only the smallest of signatures on their wines. For the best, 'the self-effacement of these producers in their wines is very nearly Zen-like: their "signature" is an absence of signature' (Kramer 2008: 232). In short, 'understanding terroir requires a recalibration of the modern mind' (Kramer 2008: 225). To emphasise this aspect of terroir, I have previously argued for a formal distinction between a terroir as it is generally spoken about in the Australian context and a terroir as it is lived by, at least some, Australian winegrowers. Borrowing with respect a term coined by Arne Naess in 1973 (Naess 1992: 27) to refer to a different mentality of environmentalism known as 'deep ecology', I labelled the second form of 'terroir' a 'deep terroir' (Swinburn 2013) and, as the ethnographic vignettes above illustrated, is an aspect of winegrowing that prioritises connection and relationship to place.

For those who embody 'deep terroir', the concept of place is central. In essence, 'place' has come to mean 'space' imbued with meaning (Vanclay 2008: 3), yet it is also a notion that allows for the diversity and intensity of experiences of place. This focus on experience calls for 'lived-world' understandings of the environment rather than discussion of abstract and scientific terms of objectivity. As Edward Relph suggests 'place and sense of place did not lend themselves to scientific analysis for they are inextricably bound up with all the hopes, frustrations and confusions of life' (Relph 1980: Introduction). The understanding of the environment focusing on diversity and intensity of experience rather than abstract models came through in a number of discussions I had with my informants. One informant described himself as a custodian of the land and talked of the privilege it was to grow something that expressed the land's inherent quality. He described the connection he found from being part of the land, caring for it as you would a child. He said, 'there is a strong analogy between parenthood and being a custodian of the land. Both of them growing, both of them having seasons, both of them having implication for your conduct'.

Many who write on the relationship people have with their environments acknowledge an intellectual debt to Martin Heidegger. Ingold (2000: 153–173) notes the distinction between the process of building and the process of dwelling, where the former supposes that people inhabit the world to which meaning *has already been attached*, whereas the latter is constituted through the settings of practical activity. Dwelling allows for 'the development of specific dispositions and sensibilities that lead people to orient themselves in relation to their environment and to attend to its features in the particular ways that they do' (Ingold 2000: 153). A dwelling perspective highlights how people exist 'in the world' rather than confronting a world 'out there' (Ingold 2000: 173). For anthropologists, adopting a perspective of this kind means illuminating knowledge born of immediate experience by privileging the understandings that people derive from their lived, everyday involvement in the world.

'Dwelling … is *the basic character* of being' (Heidegger 2011: 254). For those who dwell, in the Heidegger sense, the task becomes, not to help themselves to the world, but to care for places, even through building or cultivation, without trying to subordinate them to human will (Hay 2002: 160). An in-depth quote from one of the Geelong winegrowers reveals this perspective of how one can build and cultivate – both activities that are part of a dominant reality of winegrowing – while, in the process, creating and finding meaning through place:

> A fortnight ago the vineyard was full of beautiful colored leaves, more than other years. Now they've all fallen off. I could start pruning. I love pruning. When I was a kid my father and I had a little business cleaning supermarkets. Little I.G.A.s. We'd walk in. It was always a mess. It was hard. We used to work like cut cats. And when we'd walk out, the place would be shining and it was very satisfying. That's how I feel about pruning. You start in the morning with a big mess and at the end of the day it's neat.… The one positive we reckon that's come out of the whole thing is the people you meet and the people you hang out with. The friends and the relationships.… That, and you're working in such a beautiful place. I loved the place, the birdlife is incredible, its peaceful, its undulating and I loved the seasons there. I couldn't live in the tropics. I need the seasons.

Through their work of building and cultivation, winegrowers of Geelong are able to dwell, and with this dwelling perspective, exist at least partly, in the minor reality of what I call a deep terroir. This aptly illustrates how

> the cult of 'technology' as a way of relating to the world that treats things only as objects of domination and consumption … is a mentality that can be overcome with a better insight into the true meaning of what it is 'to be' … and the rejection of reason's claim to be able to know the world exhaustively and put it entirely to human use.
>
> (Campbell 2005: 269)

Dieter Bognar (1985) identifies 'spirit of place' or *genius loci* as a special character of place. He says, 'people's capacity to relate intimately to their world is a poetic sensitivity which forms the foundation of ... *dwelling* ... an act by which people affirm their own existence' (Bognar 1985: 189).

It seems to me that some Geelong winegrowers have found something of substance, something that counts, in the places they live in. The grape vine is a reasonable metaphor here. The winegrowers of Geelong are, like the vines they plant, seeking to put down roots as people, since Neolithic times, have sought to put down roots.

Country

In a collection of essays focusing on place (Cameron 2003), different perspectives on place were explored. I would take seriously Cameron's overview that, 'whatever the merits of the various cases, it is now true that any discussion of sense of place in Australia must take an Aboriginal sense of place as a vital factor' (Cameron 2003: 5). If you look to the ground in my fieldsite, it is hard to ignore the past. There are stone knives, shell middens, ochre and grain grinding stones to act as a reminder of the people who lived there for thousands of years prior to European settlement. Until recently, not much was written about this in the area. One of the few earlier local histories of the Bellarine Peninsula, to the east of Geelong, reported that the last of the original inhabitants, Queen Eliza, died and was buried in Portarlington, less than 30 years after formal European settlement (Wynd 1988: 23). Later, Boyce (2012) detailed the nature of the invasion of the land that was to become the state of Victoria and the devastating impact it had on the people there. As a result, some have drawn into question whether it was possible to make wines of terroir in Australia because of its desecrated origins (Jefford 2010: 101; Scruton 2009: 82).

Australia's colonial past must be borne by all who have settled in this land, including the winegrowers of Geelong. Additionally, the colonial settlement of Australia has been characterised by environmental destruction on an unprecedented scale. Flores (1998), writing about the colonial American experience, and Gammage (2012) about the Australian one, have both said that what the settlers did not understand, or perhaps would not admit, was that the continent they took from the indigenous people was a human shaped one where tens of thousands of years of human interaction had shaped the ecology. In the 1930s, the historian W. K. Hancock identified among the settlers an 'impatience to possess' (Watson, D. 2014: 368). Elaborating on this theme of possession, Hage's recent book (2017) ties together the racism of dispossession and the possession of the environment through a term he calls 'generalised domestication', or the dominant mode of inhabiting and making ourselves viable in the world. In essence, generalised domestication is a mode of existence defined by its instrumentalisation. It is a mode of inhabiting the world based on dominating it. One's own interest is the primary organising principle, and what gets in the way is excluded or exterminated (Hage 2017: 95).

An acknowledgement of this is beginning to emerge. Hancock regretted the violence with which the bush had been destroyed, and he imagined a day when the wounds would heal and Australians would establish a true partnership with the land and find a rich permanence (Watson, D. 2014: 369). Don Watson (2014) calls for something resembling a philosophy to direct our future relationship with the land. Something more than science, something with an element of shared religion. He calls for Australians to cultivate something more profound, born of a more honest knowledge of the land, and he suggests that there are farmers who farm in a relationship with the land that does not demand submission from either party, built, as he says, more on knowledge than a hunger to possess. Farmers who find their meaning in efforts to understand and preserve rather than exploit and command (Watson, D. 2014: 372).

In many ways, winegrowers are a bad example of people who might have something to offer in relation to better ways to think about new ways of relating to the environment, or to use Hage's term, provide a 'counterhegemonic voice' (Hage 2017: 127–128). They are, for the most part, wealthy. Many of them do not rely on their vineyards to maintain their expensive lifestyles. I have seen them behave badly. But I have seen them – many who have both money and status to burn – stand for hours, days, and weeks in their vineyards pruning through long cold winters. They have allocated large swathes of their farms and begun to undo the damage done by 150 years or more of ill-adapted European agricultural systems undertaken by farmers. I have seen them find peace in their activities that they never found in their previous 'successful' careers. And I have seen them loudly acknowledge a pre-European history, which had long been a forbidden topic among farmers.

Conclusion

There is a certain freedom implied when asked to write about utopian vision. In this concluding section, I want take that freedom to speculate on how the notion of deep terroir and the idea of 'a spirit of place' might offer something worth fostering. Building on the words of one of my informants who suggests that, 'clinging to the "old world" to legitimise and give blind meaning to (winemaker's) lack of direction and vision are, surely, nearly at an end. The future is all about reflecting our respective places in a new world' (Glover 2015: 76), I want to reflect on our place in the world now.

The Port of Geelong not only delivered rabbits, *Phylloxera*, and endemic disease to the colony, it played a major part in one of the fastest land occupations in the history of empires (Boyce 2012: xiii). At one stage 'the Aborigines were largely dispossessed of a territory bigger than England in just five years' (Boyce 2012: 151). The historian, James Boyce (2012) documents what happened in these early years of settlement. He concludes his work by highlighting Guy Pearse's essay, which contemplates our future in relation to mining and climate change. In the essay, Pearse argues that it is our inability to imagine something different which is digging us deeper into danger as the immensity of the climate change hits home (Pearse 2009). Boyce argues that the 'quarry vision' we are blinded by today is similar to the inability of the government to control the squatter conquest of Victoria 180 years ago (Boyce 2012: 207) when settlers went on their rampage in search of wealth.

Flores (1998) offers an optimistic note when he suggests that despite the destruction, we are simply animals whose evolutionary trajectory has kept us intimately aware of local and regional landscapes until only the last few symbolic seconds of our species' life. He says that we are hardwired to experience the sort of landscape energy that undergirds place, and he refers to this landscape energy as a 'spirit of place' (Flores 1998: 31). 'Spirit', as he sees it, does not refer to the supernatural, 'but rather to essential and activating possibilities, to the inspiration that tangible phenomena – in this instance landscapes viewed either as real settings or as cultural texts – can impart to us humans' (Flores 1998: 11–12).

Earlier, I lamented that the French term terroir, had been compromised. I suggested that those who had a commitment to the term, in its original meaning, could use the term 'deep terroir', drawing on the work of the deep ecologists, to give the term its original gravitas. On reflection, I wonder if an acknowledgement of Country might not be a better model. I note the words here of one of my informants reflecting on the experience of his father in law when he returned to his childhood farm:

> He just came alive. He was home. The ruins of that house are still there and he just lit up when he saw them. He showed us where the old school house used to be. He said, 'you see those four gum trees, they were our goal posts.' And even though he, later on, developed this lovely irrigated property, the original farm was where his attachment was. That was his country.

I use the term 'Country' advisedly. I want to tentatively propose that wine-growers look to the term Country, not in its English meaning but in its Aboriginal one. The meaning of Country for indigenous people goes beyond the dictionary definition of the country to include 'all the values, places, resources, stories and cultural obligations associated with that area and its features. It describes the entirety of... ancestral domains' (Dodson 2016). As has been pointed out, for indigenous people: 'Country was not property. If anything, it owned' (Gammage 2012: 142).[4]

The anthropologist, Diane Bell, gives us some idea of what Country means to those who live it, even some non-indigenous people. Writing about her fieldwork among women of the Warlpiri at Warrabri in the Central Desert of Australia's Northern Territory, Bell recounts her first drive along the Stuart Highway north of Taylor Crossing to Warrabri. She agreed with those who had said it was the most barren stretch of country they had encountered (Bell 1988: 22).[5] However, with time, the landscape came alive for her:

(n)ow I can drive barely a mile without seeing something worthy of comment. In what was once open spinifex plains broken by the odd acacia stand, I now see highly differentiated foraging grounds, rich in small fruits and goanna; in burnt-out plains.... In the wide dry creek beds, I now find the wild potato runners, I recognise the potential water sources, the place where frogs may be hidden in the cool, damp sand. I scan the horizon for smoke; I see a red tinge in the rock and I look for ochres.

In the vast grandeur of the rolling sandhills I now recognise the body shape of certain ancestors, but in the finer details of clustering rocks, the overhanging wild figs and the patination on leaves, I have also learnt to see signs of 'intent towards man'. At one point on the northward-bound track to Warrabri, we would crane our necks and look for a particular tree – its name would be called by somebody and soft singing would accompany the telling of a story associated with the dreaming which that tree represented. At other points, we would drive quietly, so as not to disturb the dreamings who had passed through this area.

(Bell 1988: 22)

Perhaps calling for us to acknowledge an Aboriginal understanding of Country, and to try and learn from it, is not as unimaginable as it might first sound. Small-scale wine production in places like Geelong offers a glimpse of something new, for the people and the place, both perhaps, seeking redemption. I suggest that some winegrowers here have begun to embrace what they 'know in their bones' (Watson, P. 2014: 229). In many cases the relationship winegrowers have to the land can be seen as spiritual and, as a result, ineffable. These qualities lie at the root of an alternative meaning of terroir as deep terroir and perhaps of Country too. Small-scale wine producers – many of them – have searched for, and found, a home in this sensibility and in this utopia.

Notes

1 I spoke to winegrowers from places other than Geelong. Where appropriate, I have incorporated information gleaned from them.
2 Cooper points to Kant's definition of symbols as ideas that language alone can never render intelligible.
3 The concept of terroir has not always been limited to agricultural produce. An academic at a French business school drew attention a system of journal rankings that privileged those journals published in English, devaluing of what he called 'terroir journals' (Torrès 2006: 147).
4 An indigenous woman, Katherine Clarke, has suggested to me that winegrowers might be able to be the caretakers of Country but not gain a full indigenous understanding of it. I take her concerns seriously.
5 Gillen and Spencer had described that land as one of the most barren stretches of country the pair had encountered on their travels in 1901–1902. (Bell 1988: 40 footnote 7).

Acknowledgements

I would like to thank the editors of this volume and reviewers for their constructive comments to this work. I would also like to thank Gillian Tan for her comments on the final draft.

References

Badone, E. & Roseman, S. E. (2004). Approaches to the Anthropology of Pilgrimage and Tourism. In *Intersecting Journeys: The Anthropology of Pilgrimage and Tourism*, E. Badone & S. E. Roseman (eds), pp. 1–23. Urbana: University of Illinois Press.

Bell, D. (1988). *Daughters of the Dreaming*. Melbourne: McPhee Gribble.

Benwell, W. S. (1978). *Journey to Wine in Victoria*. Carlton: Pitman Publishing.

Bognar, B. (1985). A Phenomenological Approach to Architecture and its Teaching in a Design Studio. In *Dwelling, Place and the Environment: Towards a Phenomenology of Person and World*, D. Seamon & R. Mugerauer (eds), pp. 183–197. Dordrecht: Martinus Nijhoff Publishers.

Boyce, J. (2012). *1835: The Founding of Melbourne and the Conquest of Australia*. Melbourne: Black Inc.

Cameron, J. (2003). Introduction: Articulating Australian Senses of Place. In *Changing Places: Re-imagining Australia*, J. Cameron (ed.), pp. 1–13. Double Bay, Australia: Longueville Books.

Campbell, R. (2005). Heidegger. In *The Penguin Dictionary of Philosophy: The Language and Concepts of Philosophy Explained*, T. Mautner (ed.), pp. 269–270. London: Penguin Books.

Charters, S. (2008). *Wine and Society: The Social and Cultural Context of a Drink*. Amsterdam: Elsevier.

Cooper, D.E. (2006). *A Philosophy of Gardens*. Oxford: Oxford University Press.

Demossier, M. (2010). *Wine Drinking Culture in France: A National Myth or a Modern Passion?* Cardiff: University of Wales Press.

Dodson, M. (2016). Reconciliation Australia, Fact sheet: Welcome to and Acknowledgement of Country. Available online at www.australianstogether.org.au/stories/detain/welcome-to-country (accessed 09.02.19).

Flores, D. (1998). Spirit of Place and the Value of Nature in the American West. In *A Sense of the American West: An Anthology of Environmental History*, J. E. Sherow (ed.), pp. 31–38. Albuquerque, NM: University of New Mexico Press.

Gammage, B. (2012). *The Biggest Estate on Earth: How Aborigines Made Australia*. Sydney: Allen & Unwin.

Glover, M. (2015). Wine philosopher back on home soil. *Australian and New Zealand Grapegrower and Winemaker*, 619: 74–76.

Hage, G. (2011). Dwelling in the Reality of Utopian Thought. *TDSR*, 23(1): 7–13.

Hage, G. (2017). *Is Racism an Environmental Threat?* Cambridge: Polity.

Hay, P. (2002). *Main Currents in Western Environmental Thought*. Bloomington: Indiana University Press.

Heidegger, M. (2011). *Basic Writings: From Being and Time (1927) to The Task of Thinking* (1964). London: Routledge Classics.

Ingold, T. (2000). *The Perception of the Environment: Essays in Livelihood, Dwelling and Skill*. Oxon: Routledge.

Jefford, A. (2010). Mateship with Place: A Fine-Wine Future for Australia. *The World of Fine Wine*, 28: 96–105.

Kramer, M. (2008). The Notion of *Terroir*. In *Wine and Philosophy: A Symposium on Thinking and Drinking*, F. Allhoff (ed.), pp. 225–234. Malden, MA: Blackwell Publishing.

McIntyre, J. (2011). Resisting Ages-Old Fixity as a Factor in Wine Quality: Colonial wine tours and Australia's early wine industry. *Locale: The Australasian-Pacific Journal of Regional Food Studies*, 1: 42–64.

Naess, A. (1992). *Ecology, Community and Lifestyle: Outline of an Ecosophy* (translated and edited by D. Rothenberg). Cambridge: Cambridge University Press.

Pearse, G. (2009). Quarry Vision: Coal, Climate and the End of the Resources Boom. *Quarterly Essay*, 33: 1–122.

Port, J. (2004). Epicure: Don't give up your day job. *The Age Newspaper*, September 28: 10–11.

Relph, H. (1980). *Place and Placelessness*. London: Pion Limited.

Scruton, R. (2009). *I Drink Therefore I Am: A Philosopher's Guide to Wine*. London: Continuum.

Swinburn, R. (2013). The Things that Count: Rethinking Terroir, in Australia. In *Wine and Culture: Vineyard to Glass*, R. E. Black & R. C. Ulin (eds), pp 33–50. London: Bloomsbury.

Torrès, O. (2006). *The Wine Wars: The Mondavi Affair, Globalization and 'Terroir'*. New York: Palgrave Macmillan.

Treadgold, T. (2011). Wine a contender for worst industry. *The Western Australian Business News*, June 8. Available online at www.businessnews.com.au/article/Wine-a-contender-for-worst-industry (accessed 09. 02. 19).

Trubek, A. (2008). *The Taste of Place: A Cultural Journey into Terroir*. Berkeley: University of California Press.

Ulin, R. C. (1996). *Vintages and Traditions: An Ethnohistory of Southwest French Wine Cooperatives*. Washington, DC: Smithsonian Institution Press.

Vanclay, F. (2008). Place Matters. In *Making Sense of Place: Exploring Concepts and Expressions of Place Through Different Senses and Lenses*, F. Vanclay, M. Higgins & A. Blackshaw (eds), pp. 3–11. Canberra: National Museum of Australia Press.

Vining, J. & Merrick, M. (2012). Environmental Epiphanies: Theoretical Foundations and Practical Applications. In *The Oxford Handbook of Environmental and Conservation Psychology*, S. D. Clayton, (ed.), pp. 485–508. Oxford: Oxford University Press.

Watson, D. (2014). *The Bush: Travels in the Heart of Australia*. Melbourne: Hamish Hamilton.

Watson, P. (2014). *The Age of Nothing: How We Have Sought to Live Since the Death of God*. London: Weidenfeld and Nicholson.

Winemakers Federation of Australia (2016). *Vintage Report*. Winemakers Federation of Australia. Available online at www.wfa.org.au/assets/vintage-reports/Vintage-Report-2016-.pdf (accessed 09.02.19).

Wynd, I. (1988). *Balla-Wein: A History of the Shire of Bellarine*. Drysdale: The Shire of Bellarine.

14 Plain-sight utopia

Boutique winemakers, urbane vineyards and *terroir-torial* moorings

Peter J. Howland

Not in Utopia, – subterranean fields, –
Or some secreted island, Heaven knows where!
But in the very world, which is the world
Of all of us, - the place where in the end
We find our happiness, or not at all!
                (William Wordsworth, 1839)

Introduction

Utopia is everywhere and never. At its core utopianism is the desire for 'a better way of living or of being' (Levitas 2013: 42), a universal 'human propensity to long for and imagine a life otherwise' (Levitas 2007: 290 – also Bloch 1986). This is as apparent in the deceptively simple act of resistance that imagines 'a world turned upside down' (Scott 1985: 80), as it is in the insurmountable complexities of imagining whole new worlds as in the literature of H. G. Wells and others. 'Everything that reaches to a transformed existence is … utopian' (Levitas 2007: 290).

While arguably driven by socio-psychological experiences (from infancy onwards) of lack and longing (Bloch 1986; Levitas 1990, 2013), utopian desire remains eternally unfilled, particularly as ideal. This is primarily because to be human is to be flawed, is to never achieve, nor wholly exist in, perfection (Le Guin 2016; Levitas 2008). Furthermore, 'better ways' are frequently found to be 'lesser' when assessed against progressive pasts, presents or futures. The utopian impulse is therefore an attempt to rehabilitate past mistakes by striving for a better future while embroiled in a defective present: 'The only reason people want to be masters of the future is to change the past' (Milan Kundera quoted in Le Guin 2016 [1989]: 132).

Utopia is frequently depicted as an 'island' of betterment, of good (but literally 'not the best'), the aspired to and desired. Nevertheless, utopia is always 'close to the shore' (Miéville 2016: 13), linked – temporally and morally – to the here and now of the future. This is because utopia must first be imagined and planned in the present and as Jameson (1982) argues, much of our utopian thinking, bound by present and historical circumstances, reveals the limitations of our imaginations. Yet many utopias are already hidden in plain sight, often within the routine and habitual, within and despite our dystopian presents. Or as Le Guin notes: 'The nature of the utopia I am trying to describe is such that if it is to come, it must exist already' (2016 [1989]: 143). Consider, for example, the gifting and intimate care manifest in the everyday, banal, highly commodified provisioning of food, clothing and shelter to loved ones or the voluntary fund-raising, instrumental assistance and communal support of a wide variety of community-based institutions, ranging from sports clubs to ecological, animal welfare and social care services.

Indeed, whenever the seeds of potential utopian futures are planted in plain-sight it is incumbent on Utopianists to foreground such moments. Jameson does this when provocatively arguing that the US military has latent utopian potentialities in that it is the only 'extra-governmental' organisation with the institutional and practical resources to instigate and maintain radical utopian transformations. He therefore advocates that the entire USA citizenry be enlisted in an admittedly increasingly pacifist US military (2016). Jameson similarly noted the plain-sight utopian potentials of Walmart's 'just-in-time' production and distribution systems for strategically maintaining goods provisioning in any large-scale communist society (2009). Plain-sight utopias have also been noted by Althusser (1980) in his 'islands of communism' evident in the voluntarism of soccer clubs, trade unions and churches; in Hardt and Negri's (2009) patch-work of 'commonwealths' existent in contemporary capitalism, including natural resources, shared languages and various modes of social relationship caring; and in Wright's 'real utopias' of information sharing found in public libraries and Wikipedia, of economic egalitarianism and equal access evident in solidarity financing, worker-owned cooperatives, community land trusts, and in the politics of 'Randomocracy', such as is found in juries and which 'involves representation without election through randomly selected assemblies' (2013: 11). Even Marx and Engels, who 'scientifically' rejected all forms of 'social utopianism', nevertheless also expressed admiration of capitalism's 'immense development(s)' of commerce, navigation and 'communication by land' (2004 [1848]: 15) that would ultimately underpin the transition to advanced communism in which the 'free development of each is the condition for the free development of all' (Marx & Engels 2004 [1848]: 27). These scholars all highlight that utopia is frequently just a quick glance to the left.

Boutique, artisanal winemaking in New Zealand can be similarly framed as 'Utopiyin' and 'Utopiyang' (Le Guin 2016: 153) – a heterotopia (Foucault 1986) of plain-sight utopian ideals and practices that are mutually constitutive, harmonizing and contradictory. According to Le Guin, the Utopiyin is characterised by the feminine, nature, empathy, nurturance, creativity, passion, rhythm, process, serendipity, ephemerality – all evident in artisanal winemaking. I argue that Utopiyin winemaking is not only hidden in plain sight of, but is deeply implicated within, the contrariness of male-orientated, rationale, linear, competitive, proprietorial, goal and perfection fixated Utopiyang winemaking, which reproduces the productionist rationality, exacting middle-class hierarchies, and egotistic individuality of neo-liberal economics.

The wine industry in New Zealand is dominated by structural characteristics that reflect this Utopiyin–Utopiyang dialectic. First, the industry is dominated by the high-yield, profit-maximizing, industrial-scale production of Sauvignon Blanc. This accounts for 59.5% (22,085 ha) of producing hectares, 72% (285,862 tonnes – an average of 12.9 tonnes per hectare) of production, and 86% (217,890m litres) of exports – which means of course the production of all other wines in the remaining 40.5% (15,044 ha) is at considerably lower yields of 28% (110,138 tonnes – an average of 7.3 tonnes per hectare) (New Zealand Winegrowers 2017: 33, 37–38). Most Sauvignon Blanc is grown in Marlborough by industrial-scale producers (e.g. locally owned Villa Maria and Delegat) and transnational corporations (e.g. Pernod Ricard, Constellation and Fosters Group/Treasury Wine). This productionist praxis is further evidenced by unpackaged bulk wine, which in 2017 was 38% of total exports by volume (Deloitte 2017: 7).

Second, the industry is dominated – production-wise – by medium (annual sales of 200,000–4m litres) and large (i.e. over 4m litres annually) wineries. In 2017 the NZW (New Zealand Winegrowers) listed 77 medium and 18 large wineries, respectively 11.4% and 2.6% of registered[1] wineries, who potentially accounted for 70–80%[2] of total wine produced (Deloitte 2017; New Zealand Winegrowers 2017).

The third (first contrary) characteristic is the industry is dominated – numerically – by small wineries producing less 200,000 litres annually. In 2017 these represented 86% or 582 of registered wineries (New Zealand Winegrowers 2017: 34–35), with approximately 61% being less than 10 hectares and 37% less than 5 hectares. However, small wineries only account for 20–30% of total wine produced. Many are boutique, artisanal, labour intensive, family-run or owner-operated lifestyle wineries (Robinson & Harding 2015). Boutique vineyards typically have greater diversification of grape varietals, lower yields, produce higher quality, more expensive wines, incur higher running costs, and have recorded six years of financial loss in 12 years of the Deloitte's Benchmarking Survey, the latest being –3.1% before tax in 2017 (Deloitte 2017: 6, 11). By comparison, the largest wineries (NZ$20m plus) have never recorded a loss and their 2017 gross profit was 20.6% before tax (Deloitte 2017: 6).

It must be noted, however, that any Utopiyin – Utopiyang framing is mine alone.[3] Most artisanal winemakers I encounter aspire to both conjointly and regard Utopiyang winemaking as a necessary pre-condition of Utopiyin winemaking, with commercial success and high social status being 'objective' measures of their creative accomplishments. Nevertheless, most also regard the passionate, creative pursuit of fine wines as an ultimate goal. Obviously these two utopian goals are not necessarily or always contradictory. Nevertheless, many fine winemakers run foul of commercial success due to under-capitalisation and the vagaries of globalised markets, while conversely many commercially successful winemakers will never produce fine wines, even though their budget management and marketing initiatives are top-notch. Artisanal, boutique vineyards can be analysed as unlikely sites where the opposing

moralities of the Utopiyin and Utopiyang are locked in dialectic generation. This raises the question of whether this is a necessary, or even a
desirable, co-dependency. The answer perhaps lies in – has always lain in –
freely sharing a bottle of good wine with appreciative others.

Utopian wine and *terroir-toriality*

Utopia can only ever be becoming, imagining and experimentation. To be
utopian is to demonstratively embrace lack and longing, to accept reaching for,
but never fully grasping, the ideal and to constructively live in the consequent
tensions. It is to persistently daydream and manifestly improve as part of an
evolutionary and critical interrogation of the now, the past and the future.

This ethos resonates with vinophiles who appreciate that fine wine is
marked by nostalgia for a never-to-be-fully-realised future. By default, wines
simultaneously exist in the past (as vintage) and in an aspirational future of
yet-to-be-made. Moreover, they are only fleetingly enjoyed in the present. This
engenders an 'aesthetic of ephemerality' (Appadurai 1996: 84) evident across
a range of valued wine miscellany – the alchemies of vintages and cellaring;
the natural diversity of ever-changing seasons and ever-maturing vines; in
refinements to winemaking practices, technologies and tastes; and in differences between first and last mouthfuls. Since Dom Pierre Pérignon's 'golden
rules' of winemaking (circa 1718) such ephemeralities and diversities have
been increasingly sought out by winemakers and appreciative consumers
across the globe (Howland 2013).

Levitas cogently argues that 'critical utopianism' (2008: 24), as sociological
method (rather than goal), should be deployed to persistently interrogate past
and present conditions to generate the transformative moralities, practices
and institutions required for 'better ways of living and being' (Levitas 2008:
19). However, what constitutes 'better' is contestable and accordingly utopias
are necessarily multiple, dependent on one's particular social, political and
moral perspectives: 'One person's utopia is another's hell' (Levitas, 2008: 22).
This plurality resonates within the histories of fine wines, with considerable
disagreement over what constitutes a good, let alone the finest, wines, over
esteemed varietal characteristics and apposite winemaking techniques, and
how vintages compare across time (Johnson 2004 [1989]; Unwin 1996 [1991]).

As discussed, utopias – from Plato's self-sufficient *Magnesia* to Thomas
More's 'man-made' island of *Utopia* and Huxley's psychedelic *Island* of
Pala – are characteristically separated from, yet intrinsically connected to,
the *real* of the 'mainland'. Boutique, artisanal vineyards and wineries are
also clearly linked to, but distinct from, the metropolitan bustle and hustle
of market-based economics and associated sites of consumption, leisure,
urbanity and social distinction. As horticultural enterprises, boutique vineyards are routinely framed within contemporary tropes of the rural idyll,
which is aligned with the Utopiyin dynamics of nature, Mother earth,
rhythmic seasonality, and organic modes of creativity and spirituality. I have

argued that small-scale vineyards in New Zealand represent a 'metro-rural idyll' (Howland 2008: 77) in which romanticised ideals assigned to the vernacular 'rural idyll' (e.g. clean-green landscapes, cohesive rural sociality, etc) function as a moral reservoir that metropolitan wine tourists draw on to validate their middle-class consumption, reflexive individuality, elective sociality and status-conferring urbanity – another instance of the Utopiyin – Utopiyang dialectic.

These idyllic tropes are frequently inspired by contemporary quests for the 'agrarian utopia' (Trubek 2008: 35) – of which terroir and other origin, location-based claims are a significant part. Rural idyll and terroir-based tropes seek to essentialise, and thus authenticate, a wide range of agricultural commodities, pastoral practices and rural services by mooring these to the 'facts' of their emanation from, and embeddedness within, the grounded, immutable nature of localised production. Such forms of terroir-*toriality* are cast as authenticating truths that significantly determine wine tastes and quality (Paxson 2010; Trubek 2008; Weiss 2011). Within the worlds of fine wine, notions of terroir (especially as a tethering nexus of geographic location and associated soil and climate narratives) are accorded the objectivity of 'nature capital' (Howland 2019a; Taylor 2018). The more localised the *terroir-toriality*, the more natural, *origin*al, discrete and irreproducible a vineyard and its wines.

Terroir-toriality truths are thus aligned with the factual universality frequently assigned to 'human nature' (Levitas 1990) in utopian ideologies, and which, no matter how rendered, must be accounted for in any utopian dreamings and practice. Both terroir and human nature function as Badiouan (2007) truth claims that demand fidelity. Moreover, the essentializing ontologies of terroir and human nature act as 'solids' (Ritzer 2010), that is literal, seemingly fixed, bedrocks to which 'liquid' constructs such as wine ephemeralities, winemaking interventions and utopian dreamings may be securely moored.

Utopia is also a quest for, an experimentation in, moral and ethical truth claiming, albeit of truths that are more evidently shifting and just out of reach, and of truths that demand, and simultaneously decry, fidelity. In the moral and ethical economies, the utopian poetics, of fine wine, truth upon truth – human, nature, terroir, cultural, historical, aesthetic, value and worth – are tethered to each other, entangled and fused, only to be perpetually torn apart to be forever created anew, thus highlighting that all truths, all facts, are the evolving, often contradictory, meditations of their narrators. For example, the eighteenth to nineteenth century French distaste for the rusticity of terroir and the subsequent mid-nineteenth century shift to terroir*'s* adulation as a sacrosanct guarantee of quality within the *appellation d'origine contrôlée* (AOC) are well canvassed (Demossier 2011; Parker 2015). Indeed, utopia, terroir and fine wine are all gifts of truth that just keep on taking.

Notions and practices of terroir therefore manifest as historically specific moments of utopia or dystopia or of everything in-between and they are highly dependent on time, place and people. Forever at the mercy of capricious vintage evolutions, fine wines are always terminated and assigned to the atrophies of memory upon consumption. Thus, whenever framed in the utopian, fine wines are always grasped to be lost. To drink a fine wine is to experience utopia eluding, is to turn toward and goad the dystopian, is to experience truth descending into fiction. Mooring to the apparently grounded solidities and truths of *terroir-toriality* in contemporary winemaking is therefore yet another quest, this time for sure footholds amidst the constantly changing and destabilizing imbrications of the Utopiyin and the Utopiyang, of paradise found, paradise lost, paradise quested, in every bottle of fine wine.

All for one – Utopiyang wines

Le Guin (2016) argues the Utopiyang is rational, linear, systematic, mapped, and 'hot' in the Lévi-Straussian sense of being dominating, proprietorial, masculine, and fixated on social differentiation and hierarchy. The Utopiyang lets history in to provoke progressive change and through an overwhelming desire for perfection. However, perfection is ultimately static as it marks an end to striving for betterment and is, therefore, ultimately non-utopian. Utopiyang cultures are thus akin to machines, opposed to the organic. Many of these aspects are evident in the contemporary Utopiyang wine culture of New Zealand. As such, I canvas the agentic, reflexive individual celebrated in the 'cult of the winemaker'; the productionist, innovative, science-driven, instrumental rationality of New World winemaking; the orderly aesthetic central to the productionist picturesque; and the social distinctions and stratifications of metro-rurality.

Fine wine production in New Zealand only began to flourish in the 1970–1980s. Before then local wines were mostly poor and referred to as 'Château Fiji' (Stewart 2010: 194) to highlight their heavily sugared and fortified nature. Fine (mostly imported) wine consumption was restricted to enclaves of university-educated individuals and European migrants (Hadyn 1997; Stewart 2010). By the mid-1970s support for local table wines, bolstered by travelling Kiwis who had experienced European wine cultures, created a place for wine in the nation's liquor trade. In 1985 the industry celebrated the arrival of locally produced fine wine on the global stage when Cloudy Bay, a Marlborough-produced Sauvignon Blanc, 'sent a ripple through the international wine world', with one Australian critic describing it 'like hearing Glenn Gould playing the Goldberg variations' (Cooper 2002: 214).

The 1980s also coincided with the neo-liberal reforms of the 'New Zealand Experiment' (Kelsey 1995). Core government services and agencies were rolled-back and replaced by deregulated, free-market, corporatised and profit-orientated entities (Larner 1997). This neo-liberal turn promoted forms of governmentality in which individuals were structurally compelled to be, acclaimed or admonished as, the architects of their own destinies. Moreover, Utopiyang values of reflexive individualism, laissez-faire, market-based competition, and instrumental rationality (especially pro-duction and market-orientated, scientific, statistical, etc) were entrenched as cornerstone ethics.

These Utopiyang values and practices are found throughout the wine industry. Given the significant investments of economic and culture capital required, lifestyle and artisanal vineyards have mostly attracted profes-sional, educated, frequently urban, noticeably urbane (actual and aspiring), middle-class individuals – subjects with almost exemplary neo-liberal potentialities (Howland 2013; Overton & Murray 2012; Moran 2016). The middle-classes are socialised and operate within the 'reflexive habitus' (Sweetman 2003: 528) of liberal education and reflexivity-prompting occupations (e.g. advertising, policy analysts, self-employment, etc). More-over, they are drawn to fields where their *de facto* autonomy (Bauman 2000) is optimised. (e.g. educational and occupational advancement, life politics, identity projects, lifestyle consumption, etc – Howland 2008). It is not surprising therefore that winemaking in New Zealand is strongly associated with the 'cult of the winemaker' (Howland 2008: 77) in which individual, agentic and reflexive winemakers are foregrounded – although this is also due to the truncated history of fine winemaking and a lack of a codified terroir culture (Murray & Overton 2011).

Winemakers are regarded as conduits between the best of nature and humanity (especially scientific and aesthetic) and are charged with produ-cing fine wine through the deft deployment of personal creativity, knowledge of grapes, wines, vineyards (especially soil, climatic, seasonal and vintage-based) and winemaking techniques, and the innovative use of science and technology. Winemakers' personal palates and practices are considered to be key in the tastes and quality of resultant wines. For example, Shayne and Poppy Hammond, grape-growers and winemakers at Poppies Vineyard, Martinborough:

> Consider themselves caretakers of the land. *They selectively harvest* from carefully chosen vines around the area, *waiting for the perfect moments* in time to create expressive, delicate wines in small batches.
> (www.poppiesmartinborough.co.nz (accessed 06.10.18) – emphases mine)

Winemaking in New Zealand is frequently promoted as quintessentially New World and thus innovative, technological, science and research-driven, and bureaucratically rational. The latter attribute is evident in vineyard-based record-keeping (e.g. climatic, grape-growth, etc statistics are recorded annually), in the use of factual data (e.g. GIS – geographic information sys-tems), and the instrumentality of government policies on health and safety practices through to alcohol content assessments. For example, the Vinopt-mia, Gisborne, is enthusiastically acclaimed for:

The *deep thought* and *large-scale investment* behind the *state-of-the-art* winery and vineyards are immediately evident to all who visit this impressive estate.... With its *specifically designed tank space* to accommodate the harvested grapes, and its *temperatures-controlled oak oval barrels*, the winery is an architectural and engineering masterpiece.

(Douglas 2017: 104 – emphases mine)

Winemakers are charged with generating a heady mix of innovative, creative, rational and techno-scientific pioneership, along with a passionate commitment to urbane wine consumption – although they are also increasingly celebrated for their 'return' to more natural, less interventionist (more Utopiyin – see below) ways of winemaking. For example, Tony Bisch, a finalist in *Gourmet Traveller's* New Zealand Winemaker of the Year (2018), was celebrated as follows:

Bisch's *creative spirit* was unleashed in 2013, following a trip to South America where he experienced wine produced in egg-shaped tanks... with some *Kiwi ingenuity* and local know-how from NZ tanks, Tony built New Zealand's first concrete egg fermenters...

(www. gourmettravellerwine.com/new-zealand-winemaker-of-the-year-2018 (accessed 06.10.18) – emphases mine)

As implicitly sacred alchemists (Howland 2019b), local winemakers are celebrated for their middle-class distinction and urbane lifestyles. They are also noted for their business acumen (boutique vineyards/wineries of five to ten acres often require significant seven-figure investments) in profitably running what are family farms while also achieving 'work-life' balance. For example, Therese and Hans Herzog, Swiss emigrants who in 1994 established Hans Herzog Estate, Wairaru Valley, Marlborough, were recently praised for building a 'quintessentially Kiwi home'. Therese noted that the demands of their business meant their home had to be situated near to the winery:

Allowing easy transit and lunches together at home. But the space also had to be a sanctuary. 'It comes together now, full circle. The vineyard, the wine, the winery and then the living part.'

(www.stuff.co.nz/life-style/homed/houses/101572974/a-swiss-couples-quintessentially-kiwi-home (accessed 06.10.18))

Due to the public character of winemaking in New Zealand (cellar doors are typically open to visiting consumers – Mitchell et al. 2012), boutique vineyards, wineries and the homes of winemakers/vineyard owners have a performative element and are noted for the urbane aesthetics of their colonial and 'Euro-chic' or modern (Howland 2012: 113) architecture. For example, Mission Estate – the oldest, continuous winemaking enterprise in New Zealand (circa 1851) – 'provides a provides a notable early connection to ecclesiastical winemaking' (Kernohan 2014: 139) and is renowned for the elegant, colonial French architecture of La Grande Maison. Formerly a seminary for Marist priests, La Grande Maison is now noted for the luxury of its fine-dining restaurant, venue centre and wine sales area. Other wineries are celebrated for their modern, New World architecture. For example, the Peregrine Winery 'expresses both an aesthetic of modernity and also a clear analogical response to place ... the building is all about the anthropomorphic imagery of the Peregrine falcon hovering in the landscape of Central Otago' (Kernohan 2014: 145). This architecture, when considered alongside the high status accorded boutique vineyard owners and winemakers, and the significant economic investments and returns involved, are clearly conspicuous statements of social distinction, signalling a marked 'distance from necessity' (Bourdieu 2010 [1984]: 55) in what are Utopiyang, utilitarian and industrialised sites of agricultural-production.

Such vineyard, winery and home aesthetics, in part, reflect the acclaimed 'metro-rural' (Howland 2008: 77) idyll and urbanity discussed above. This is also evident in the newspaper story celebrating Therese and Hans Herzog's 'Kiwi' home:

> Two decades were devoted to the land, the vines and Hans Herzog wines, along with an award-winning restaurant and sophisticated bistro on the same site. Meanwhile the couple established idyllic gardens at the heart of the estate, 'anchoring' the buildings and drawing in the bird life Therese loves.
>
> (www.stuff.co.nz/life-style/homed/houses/101572974/a-swiss-couples-quintessentially-kiwi-home (accessed 06.10.18)).

Rural vineyards and wineries are typically presented as 'picture postcard perfect' (Martinborough wine tourist, female, aged 47) – or in productionist picturesque ways. The productionist ethos of order, efficiency, yield and profit maximization, is a central, vernacular feature of the European settler idyll and associated picturesque optics (Howland 2008). Today it finds currency in the pristine, hyper-cultivated, almost ornamental garden, aesthetics of vineyards, which are often precisely laid out and planted using GPS (global positioning systems). Wine producers and consumers alike celebrate the highly ordered, immaculate aesthetics of vineyards, together with the methodological and rational exploitations of nature that are central to Utopiyang New World winemaking.

Furthermore, the systematic and bureaucratic modalities of New World wine reflect a generalised ethos of rationality and objectivity that has been highly valued from modernity onwards (Gellner 1983; Larner 1997). New World wine is characterised by numerous 'objective' practices, measures and assessments, including precisely temperature-controlled fermentations, bureaucratic record-keeping, sugar, alcohol and volume measurements and quantitative assessment regimes such as Robert Parker's famous 100-point scale (McCoy 2005). Such practices underpin producers' aspirations to consistently reproduce taste and quality profiles across wine vintages. They also provide 'objective' product and quality assurances that function as Ritzerian 'solids' (Ritzer 2010) upon which the authenticity of a wine's tastes and quality can be impartially ascertained. This reflects the Utopiyang passion for scientific, social and other certitudes that can function as unequivocal facts and truths, and which can provide 'objective', and often singular, future trajectories. Such an ethos is wholly opposed to the foregrounding of process, and of constantly evolving and unfolding states of knowing and being, that characterises the Utopiyin.

Utopiyin – the love of wine, nature and others

Le Guin argues the Utopiyin is 'dark, wet, obscure, weak, yielding, passive, participatory, circular, cyclical, peaceful, nurturant, retreating, contracting, and cold' (2016 [1989]: 140). The Utopiyin is feminine, organic, processual, socio-centric and nurturant; dedicated to constant imaginings, serendipities and innovative pursuit of the better; attuned to the egalitarianisms of pre-Neolithic, rather than stratifications of post-Neolithic, societies.

Clearly many Utopiyin attributes are also components of Utopiyang winemaking – especially those focused on the agentic creativity, alchemy and passion of fine winemaking, which are widely considered integral characteristics of artisanal winemaking. Indeed, it can appear almost impossible to disentangle these contrasting utopian modalities and most Utopiyin winemakers (typically artisan, boutique, organic, biodynamic and natural) I encounter do not make such attempts. Instead they regard boutique winemaking as a holistic complex that routinely, and for the most part unproblematically, has competing, yet also mutually constitutive and supportive, components – art and science, creativity and commerce, personality and team-work. Moreover, they typically proclaim that the manner they adroitly and constructively attend to contradictory elements, in response to shifting commercial, natural or regulatory challenges, is a measure of their winemaker competencies, is largely determinative of their success in producing good quality wines and thus deserving of apposite economic rewards and social acclaim.

I argue most winemakers hegemonically believe the Utopiyang aspects of winemaking – especially the market-based demands of commodity production – are somehow naturalised and as such represent an apex of human endeavour. I first became aware of this when discussing what I thought was an exemplary artisanal winemaker with members of his local cohort. I explained that this winemaker said he would pour a vintage down the drain if he thought that it was 'not up to standard' and that he was enabled to do so, in part, because his wife earned substantial off-vineyard income. However, another winemaker shot back: 'But he's not even a real winemaker ... he doesn't have to get anything to market!' Although this encounter highlighted both the mutuality and boundaries of the Utopiyin and Utopiyang, the Utopiyang imperative to successfully produce commodities in the marketplace was nevertheless considered morally foundational and dominant.

With this caveat in mind I consider other Utopiyin elements of boutique winemaking in New Zealand and in particular their dedication to quality and associated contra-productionist practices; less interventionist, more hands-on, serendipitous, and collaborative winemaking; celebration of wine ephemerality and diversity as integral components of wine's *jouissance*; and their genuine ethos of hospitality and gifting.

Utopiyin winemakers are celebrated for creativity, innovations and artistry, and are often committed to yield minimizing, arguably contra-productionist, techniques to achieve desired quality and taste profiles. Such techniques include restricting the number of fruit-bearing canes, withholding irrigation, debudding, and discarding lesser quality fruit. Moreover, Utopiyin winemakers often delay wine releases through prolonged barrel contact (especially for reds) or through cellaring bottled wines before sale (Moran 2016). These anti-profit, anti-market capitalism initiatives are clearly Utopiyin and driven by winemakers' eternal quests for better quality wines.

Utopiyin winemakers also embrace modest (production quantity and income wise) enterprises characterised by less mechanised and scientific, more hands-on, sensory, labour intensive, natural and costly winemaking practices (Moran 2016; Skinner 2016). This is markedly Utopiyin and embraces the processual spontaneity, inconsistencies and inherent ephemeralities of wine production. This establishes the foundational and structural conditions whereby eternally striving for the better, not for the perfect (indeed, rejecting such a notion), is the default. This state of perpetual dynamism promotes constructive, enduring and context-acute states of critical (ecological and social) reflection and reflexivity – a never settling, intensely attentive to the unfolding now, always seeking to improve, ethos that is full-bodied Utopiyin. Utopiyin winemakers – boutique to natural – are integral in the movements toward slow, localised, biographised and de-fetishised food production in which the moralities of authenticity, origin, provenance, sustainability and transparency are highly valued (Feldmann & Hamm 2015; Wilk 2006).

Utopiyin winemakers also foreground non-individualistic mindsets that wholesomely acknowledge the many necessary collaborations of people, nature, climates and places in ways potentially more genuine than the cynical promotional deployment of such tropes by large-scale, commercially motivated, producers. For example:

> Cambridge Road Vineyard [Martinborough] is a *small family farmed estate* established in 1986 with the intention of making world class Pinot Noir and Syrah by focusing time and energy on perfecting and beautifying our land and *cultivating it according to natural biodynamic and eco-farming principles. We* believe in *minimal intervention winemaking, low yields, and healthy living wines. We* seek *purity of voice* in all our wines with a *respect for the taste of place.*
>
> (www.cambridgeroad.co.nz (accessed 10.10.18) – emphases mine)

Utopiyin winemakers also celebrate the ephemerality of wine – its ever-evolving, fleeting, ideally ever-improving, tastes and quality. Wine ephemerality has been highly valued since the seventeenth century invention of single vineyard, vintage[4] and bottled wines (Howland 2013). A clearly Utopiyin attribute – the 'pleasure of ephemerality' – is arguably 'at the heart of the disciplining of the modern consumer' as it invokes 'a tension between nostalgia for valued losses (real, imagined or anticipated) and fantasies of an idealised future that provokes consumers to "miss things that they have never lost" … [creating] much deeper wants than simple envy, imitation, or greed' (Appadurai 1996: 81–83). Although ephemerality is a triple-poisoned chalice in terms of the uncertainty that a wine will improve over time; consumption that effectively arrests any hope for, and future of, a potentially better wine to be procured through cellaring; and lastly the terminating, eternal loss of incumbent fine wines at the point of consumption.

Yet when viewed through a Utopiyin lens the utopian attributes of ephemerality – the constant desiring, yet never possessing, perfect wine – are sharply focused and amplified when situated alongside complementary attributes such as spontaneity and unpredictably of taste and quality, all of which are embraced as authentic expressions of vines, season and place. In this Utopiyin ferment wine ephemerality becomes genuine hope – an anticipatory laying down – of future pasts in pursuit of a better present. This ethos is exemplified in the citation announcing Dom Maxwell's, Greystone Wines, Waipara, New Zealand Winemaker of the Year (2018) award:

> I started with the romantic belief that the perfect wine existed, and it was my job to find the formula for producing it … but I've shifted the focus from trying to make the perfect wine to trying to best express site and season.
> (www.gourmettravellerwine.com/new-zealand-winemaker-of-the-year-2018 (accessed 10.10.18)).

Wine ephemerality and evolving vintages speak to a diversity of product, tastes, quality and consumption experiences. Product diversity is another hallmark of commodity/ market capitalism and particularly the discerning production and status-conferring consumption of fashionable, novel and/or innovative commodities such as clothing, cars and technology. Although the Bourdieuan consumption-social distinction nexus has been muddied by the rise of omnivoristic and democratised consumption, as Holt cogently reminds us (and Bourdieu would heartily concur) the 'inferred cultural aptitude of the consumer' (2010 [1984]: 5) remains paramount and unsurprisingly exclusive enclaves of elite consumption (e.g. VIP tastings, wine clubs, *Grand Cru* buyer lists, etc) – economic and aesthetic – still exist where connoisseurs and the wealthy robustly compete for wines and status (Beverland 2005; Demossier 2018).

However, wine diversity – especially among small-scale, artisanal winemakers and appreciative consumers – has a distinct Utopiyin hue that genuinely transcends the status-conferring, price-point maximizing, dictates of commodity fashion. First, the diversity inherent in wines from different seasons, vineyards, aging vines, winemaking techniques and the evolutions of vintage and cellaring are enthusiastically celebrated for the dynamic spontaneity and unpredictability this engenders. Wine-producing grapes are particularly sensitive to seasonal changes in climate, vine-age and winemaking, as wine is to variations in cellaring and consumption protocols. Indeed, boutique vineyards are often framed as heterogenic, highly localised and bio-graphised, monasteries of production and consumption (Howland 2019b) where distinct miracles and alchemies of winemaking occur, and which contrast with the cathedrals of consumption (e.g. shopping malls) that harbour standardised, homogenic commodities (Ritzer 2005).

This diversity – particularly evident in natural wines – is arguably so vibrant, extensive, kaleidoscopic and evolving that it implodes the foundations on which hierarchies of taste, quality and consumption status can be soundly based. This is especially apparent when recognising the subjectivity of wine tastes, which frequently goes beyond the 'niche consumption' cynicism of market optimization (Howland 2013). Some Masters of Wine (notably Tim Hanni – see www.timhanni.com (accessed 28.10.18)) argue that generic wine tastes and quality do not exist at all and all wine experiences are inherently individual and irreproducible. Moreover, the diversity, ephemerality and spontaneity of wine tastes are also manifestations of the unnameable excess of pleasure or *jouissance* (Zizek 1989) of wine tasting, evidenced in the fact that wine taste descriptors are mostly metaphoric or analogous (Lehrer 1975).

Lastly, for as long as wine has been a drink of privilege and status (Demossier 2004; Johnson 2004 [1989]), it has also been a modality of intense hospitality and gifting – indeed most wine, commercial and non-commercial, is freely shared with drinking companions. From ancient orgiastic Dionysian and Bacchanalian festivals, to contemporary champagne-fuelled birthday, Christmas and wedding celebrations, and the *in vino communitas* experienced by wine tourists (Howland 2008), wine has been a key lubricant of 'social jollification' (Horton quoted in Fuller 1996: 22). As an intoxicating alcohol, wine is obviously not unique in this regard. However, since the nineteenth century rise of connoisseurship, aesthetically appreciative wine consumption has ideally fostered convivial social interactions and concomitant conversations on wine aesthetics and other erudite matters, and by contrast actively discouraged drunkenness and lewd behaviour (Fuller 1996).

Gifting and hospitality are clearly Utopiyin practices based on reproducing empathetic, reciprocating social relationships (Derrida 2005; Mauss 2004 [1950]). Furthermore, wine-based Utopiyin gifting and hospitality routinely exists in a wide range of social situations, from the most banal consumption of table wines – arguably the majority of commodity wines are transformed into gifts as they cross household and restaurant thresholds – through to the most prestigious, socially exclusive consumption of Burgundian *Grand Crus*. Demossier argues that the 'trope of hospitality is deeply embedded in the Burgundian way of life' (2018: 71) and is an enduring element in Burgundy's terroir constructs. I have frequently been the beneficiary of winemaker hospitality and gifting, most notably receiving a spontaneous gift of a case of wine for my late wife's wake, alongside an additional case of 'special wines to drink as needed' in the aftermath of her death.

Conclusion

Highlighting existent utopias – no matter how partial, selective or fleeting – ideally disrupts dominating hegemonies and the 'taken-for-granted nature of the present' (Levitas 1990: 22). It also serves to identify pre-figurative utopian practices and promotes an education of desire and hope. Within this '*ontological mode*' (Levitas 2010: 544) of utopian dreaming the contemporary 'damaged self' can therefore experience, aspire to, and believe in a 'better otherwise self':

> Utopia creates a space in which the reader is addressed not just cognitively, but experientially, and enjoined to consider and feel what it would be like not just to live differently, but to want differently.
>
> (Levitas 2010: 542)

Moreover, many utopias – like fine wines – exist in plain-sight and given their inherently processual and consequent ephemeral nature, are everywhere and never. As such they are also predictably tethered to the narrative truths and seemingly grounded or natural solidities of human nature and terroir. Yet just as the value of any wine significantly exists in the palate of the imbiber, neither are all utopias equal and their value depends largely on the morality of those gazing from the mainland. This is not, however, to glibly assert that every cloud has a silver lining, but is a call to critically evaluate the morality and ethics of any utopian aspiration. In this I find accord with Le Guin who argues that the Utopiyang represents a 'power trip':

> A monotheocracy, declared by executive decree, and maintained by will-power; as its premise is progress, not process, it has no habitable present, and speaks only in the future tense. And in the end reason itself must reject it.
>
> (2016b [1989]: 176)

Likewise, I regard utopias that underpin or amplify the power and privilege of the dominant to the detriment of the subordinate to be traps in which the 'wishes of the weak are only those which the powerful wish them to have' (Levitas 2010: 544). In any stratified society you are therefore likely to find a dynamic, vested mix of contradictory, conflicting, complementary and/or mutually constitutive interests and consequently, of similarly hued utopias. Choosing which utopia to lobby for is not, however, a simple act of individual ethical choice, but rather should be guided by the betterment morality inherent in all utopia. Whereas the Utopiyin strives to achieve better for the many, ideally for the all, the Utopiyang strives for better for the few and by default, lesser (comparatively and absolutely) for the many. Accordingly, the Utopiyang is a lesser utopia compared to the Utopiyin as it is highly restrictive and selective in its betterment aspirations. Indeed, many would argue the Utopiyang is actually more dystopian than utopian, is restless delirium rather than vivid daydreaming. It is not surprising therefore that many Utopiyang, large-scale, bottom-line, wine manufacturing enterprises cynically invoke the passionate creativity of artisanal, boutique Utopiyin winemakers and the natural terroir-groundedness of their wines when promoting and marketing their brands – New Zealand Wine, the industry-wide representative organization, does this when promoting the local industry (Howland 2019b). Though by contrast, but also in accord, Utopiyin wine-makers often background, obscure or mute their own Utopiyang aspirations and imperatives (such as servicing debt, increasing profits, etc), leaving the impression that every winemaker is an artisan consumed by Utopian passion to eternally quest for ever better wines.

Nevertheless, in wine the Utopiyin lies firmly within the seemingly modest act of freely sharing a bottle with appreciative others and in doing so, repro-ducing the convivial, empathic and ongoing sociality of gifting communities. This unassuming, even banal, act reproduces the Utopiyin with every bottle opened. Moreover, it occurs persistently throughout the wine world – from the candid production and sharing of peasant or home-made wines through to the hospitality of commercial winemakers from Martinborough, New Zealand, to Burgundy, France, that frequently surpasses the cynicisms of financial spreadsheets and brand loyalties.

Wine has a deep and broad history in this regard, although so does the open, honest sharing of anything – from domestic care to the voluntarism of community services. And even though such gifting practices somewhat tragically provide a foundational (and free) platform necessary for the reproduction of Utopiyang capitalism (Hardt and Negri 2009), by adopt-ing a different, thoroughly more optimistic, optic the Utopiyin remains steadfastly in plain-sight.

Notes

1 Since 1975 all licensed commercial grape growers and winemakers in New Zealand have been statutorily required to register with NZW (formerly New Zealand Grape Growers Council and the Wine Institute of New Zealand), which acts as a lobby, promotional, research and good practice organization.
2 It is difficult to assess the production of the largest wineries, particularly as NZW do not publish production statistics by winery size. However, the 2017 Deloitte's Benchmarking Survey reported that 93% or 13,659,000 litres of its respondents' production was from companies in the top two brackets of NZ\$10–20m and NZ \$20m+ annual sales (13% and 80% respectively). These categories correspond with the majority of producers in the top two tiers of the NZW's categories (i.e. 200,000–4m and more than 4m litres annual production). Only 38,000 litres or 0.3% was produced by the smallest wineries in the NZ\$0–1.5m category (Deloitte 2017: 11). A note of caution, however: although Deloitte's 2017 respondents accounted for 56% by litres of wine produced in New Zealand, there were only 45 respondents in

total and most likely included one of the largest producers such as Constellation or Pernod Ricard.

3 My analysis is based on 20 plus years of anthropological/sociological and ethnographic study of wine production, consumption and tourism in New Zealand.

4 In 1660 *Haut-Brion*, named after the producing chateau in Bordeaux, was the vintage and vineyard-specific wine to be released (Johnson 2004 [1989]; Unwin 1996 [1991]).

Acknowledgements

Many thanks to the reviewers of this article for their constructive feedback and special thanks (once again) to my very erudite daughter, Corinna, for her typically insightful critiques and astute suggestions.

Bibliography

Althusser, L. (2017 [1980]). The Crisis of Marxism: An interview with Louis Althusser. Available online at www.versobooks.com/blogs/3312-the-crisis-of-marxism-an-interview-with-louis-althusser (accessed 01.07.18).

Appadurai, A. (1996). *Modernity At Large: Cultural Dimensions of Globalization.* Minneapolis: University of Minnesota Press.

Badiou, A. (2007). *Being and Event*. London: Bloomsbury.

Bauman, Z. (2000). *Liquid Modernity*. Cambridge: Polity.

Beverland, M. B. (2005). Crafting brand authenticity: The case of luxury wines. *Journal of Management Studies*, 42(5): 1003–1029.

Bloch, E. (1986). *The Principle of Hope*. Oxford: Blackwell.

Bourdieu, P. (2010 [1984]). *Distinction: A Social Critique of the Judgement of Taste.* London: Routledge & Kegan Paul.

Cooper, M. (2002). *Wine Atlas of New Zealand*. Auckland: Hodder Moa Beckett.

Deloitte (2017). *Vintage 2017 New Zealand Wine Industry Benchmarking Survey.* Auckland: Deloitte.

Demossier, M. (2004). Contemporary Lifestyles: the case of wine. In *Culinary Taste: Consumer Behaviour in the International Restaurant Sector*, D. Solan (ed.), pp. 93–108. Oxford: ButterworthHeinemann.

Demossier, M. (2011). Beyond terroir: territorial construction, hegemonic discourses and French wine culture. *Journal of the Royal Anthropological Institute*, 17(4): 685–705.

Demossier, M. (2018). *Burgundy: A Global Anthropology of Place and Taste*. Oxford: Berghahn Books.

Derrida, J. (2005). The Principle of Hospitality. *Parallax*, 11(1): 6–9.

Douglas, R. (2017). *100 Great New Zealand Wineries*. Auckland: Bateman Publishing.

Feldmann, C. & Hamm, U. (2015). Consumers' perceptions and preferences for local food: A review. *Food Quality and Preference*, 40: 152–164.

Foucault, M. (1986). Other spaces: The principles of heterotopia. *Lotus International*, 48: 9–17.

Fuller, R. (1996), *Religion and Wine: A Cultural History of Wine Drinking in the United States*. Knoxville: University of Tennessee Press.

Gellner, E. (1983). *Nations and Nationalism*. New York: Cornell University Press.

Hadyn, J. (1997). Our Love Affair with Wine. *New Zealand Geographic*, 35(July–Sept): 18–42.

Hardt, M. & Negri, A. (2009). *Commonwealth*. Cambridge, MA: Belknap-Harvard.

Holt, D. (1998). Does Cultural Capital Structure American Consumption? *Journal of Consumer Research*, 25(1): 1–26.

Howland, P. J. (2008). Martinborough's wine tourists and the metro-rural idyll. *Journal of New Zealand Studies*, 6–7: 77–100.

Howland, P. J. (2012). Euro-chic, benign cosmopolitanism and wine tourism in Martinborough, New Zealand. In *From Production to Consumption: Transformation of Rural Communities*, A. Boscoboinik & H. Horakova (eds), pp.113–130. Berlin: LIT Verlag.

Howland, P. J. (2013). Distinction by Proxy: the democratization of fine wine. *Journal of Sociology*, 49(2–3): 325–340.

Howland, P. J. (2019a). Enduring wine and the global middle-class. In *The Globalization of Wine*, D. Inglis & A. Almila (eds). London: Bloomsbury.

Howland, P.J. (2019b – forthcoming) Drinking the Divine: Fine wine and the socio-political in Aotearoa New Zealand. *Journal of Wine Research*.

Jameson, F. (1982). Progress versus utopia: or, can we imagine the future? *Science-Fiction Studies*, 27(9): 147–158.

Jameson, F. (2009). *Valences of the Dialectic*. New York: Verso Books.

Jameson, F. (2016). *An American Utopia: Dual Power and the Universal Army*. New York: Verso Books.

Johnson, H. (2004 [1989]). *Story of Wine*, London: Mitchell Beazley.

Kelsey, J. (1995). *The New Zealand Experiment. A World Model for Structural Adjustment*. Auckland: Auckland University Press.

Kernohan, D. (2014). Wine and Architecture – Structure and Elegance. In *Social, Cultural and Economic Impacts of Wine in New Zealand*, P. J. Howland (ed.), pp. 137–151. Abingdon: Routledge.

Larner, W. (1997). 'A means to an end': Neoliberalism and State Processes in New Zealand. *Studies in Political Economy*, 52(1): 7–38.

Le Guin, U. (2016a [1989]). A Non-Euclidean View of California as a Cold Place to Be. In *Utopia*, T. More, (1901 [1515]), pp. 128–152. New York: Verso.

Le Guin, U. (2016b). Utopiyin, Utopiyang. In *Utopia*, T. More, (1901 [1516]), pp. 153–155. New York: Verso.

Lehrer, A. (1975). Talking about wine. *Language*, 51(4): 901–923.

Levitas, R. (1990). Educated hope: Ernst Bloch on abstract and concrete utopia. *Utopian Studies*, 1(2): 13–26.

Levitas, R. (2007). Looking for the blue: The necessity of utopia. *Journal of Political Ideologies*, 12(3): 289–306.

Levitas, R. (2008). Being in Utopia. *Hedgehog Review*, 10(1): 19–30.

Levitas, R. (2010). Back to the Future: Wells, sociology, utopia and method. *The Sociological Review*, 58(4): 531–547.

Levitas, R. (2013). Some Varieties of Utopian Method. *Irish Journal of Sociology*, 21(2): 41–50.

Mauss, M. (2004 [1950]). *The Gift: The Form and Reason for Exchange in Archaic Societies*. London: Routledge.

Marx, K. & Engels, F. (2004 [1848]). *The Communist Manifesto*. London: Penguin.

McCoy, E. (2005). *The Emperor of Wine: The Rise of Robert M. Parker, Jr. and the Reign of American Taste*. New York: Ecco.

Miéville, C. (2016). Introduction. In *Utopia*, T. More, (1901 [1516]), pp. 11–30. New York: Verso.

Mitchell, R., Charters, S. & Albrecht, J. N. (2012). Cultural Systems and the Wine Tourism Product. *Annals of Tourism Research*, 39(1): 311–335.

Moran, W. (2016). *New Zealand Wine: The Land, the Vines, the People*. Auckland: Auckland University Press.

Murray, W.E. & Overton, J. (2011). Defining regions: The making of places in the New Zealand wine industry. *Australian Geographer*, 42(4): 419–433.

New Zealand Winegrowers (2017). *Annual Report 2017*. Auckland: New Zealand Winegrowers.

Overton, J. & Murray, W. E. (2012). Class in a Glass: Capital, Neoliberalism and Social Space in the Global Wine Industry. *Antipode*, 45(3): 702–718.

Parker, T. (2015). *Tasting French Terroir: The History of an Idea*. Berkeley: University of California Press.

Paxson, H. (2010). Locating Value in Artisan Cheese: Reverse-Engineering Terroir for New World Landscapes. *American Anthropologist*, 112(3): 442–455.

Ritzer, G. (2005). *Enchanting a Disenchanted World: Revolutionizing the Means of Consumption*. Thousand Oaks: Pine Forge Press.

Ritzer, G. (2010). *Globalization: A Basic Text*. Chichester: Wiley-Blackwell.

Robinson, J. & Harding, J. (eds.) (2015). Lifestyle Winery. In *The Oxford Companion to Wine*. Oxford: Oxford University Press. Available online at http://www.oxfor dreference.com

Scott, J. C. (1985). *Weapons of the Weak: Everyday Forms of Peasant Resistance*. New Haven: Yale University Press.

Stewart, K. (2010). *Chancers and Visionaries: A History of Wine in New Zealand*. Auckland: Godwit.

Skinner, W. (2016). Trust your senses: Growing wine and making place in McLaren Vale. In *Emotions, Senses, Spaces: Ethnographic Engagements and Intersections*, S. R. Hemer & A. Dundon (eds.): 175–191. doi:doi:10.20851/EMOTIONS-11

Sweetman, P. (2003). Twenty-first Century Dis-ease? Habitual Reflexivity or the Reflexive Habitus. *The Sociological Review*, 51(4): 528–549.

Taylor, A. (2018). How then could we live? Towards the pragmatic creation of sustainable ecological habitus in cities. PhD (unpub), Environmental Management. Massey University.

Trubek, A. (2008). *The Taste of Place: A Cultural Journey into Terroir*. Berkeley: University of California Press.

Unwin, T. (1996 [1991]). *Wine and the Vine: An Historical Geography of Viticulture and the Wine Trade*. London: Routledge.

Weiss, B. (2011). Making Pigs Local: Discerning the Sensory Character of Place. *Cultural Anthropology*, 26(3): 438–461.

Wilk, R. (ed.). (2006). *Fast Food/Slow Food: The Cultural Economy of the Global Food System*. Lanham: Rowman Altamira.

Wright, E. O. (2010). *Envisioning Real Utopias*. New York: Verso.

Wright, E. O. (2013). Transforming Capitalism Through Real Utopias. *American Sociological Review*, 78(1): 1–25.

Zizek, S. (1989). *The Sublime Object of Ideology*. London: Verso.

Index